Southern Biography Series

ZACHARY TAYLOR

GENERAL ZACHARY TAYLOR

BY WILLIAM G. BROWN, 1847

Reproduced by permission from an oil portrait in the Louisiana State Museum.

ZACHARY TAYLOR

BY

BRAINERD DYER

BARNES & NOBLE, Inc.
NEW YORK
PUBLISHERS & BOOKSELLERS SINCE 1873

Reprinted, 1967
by Barnes & Noble, Inc.
through special arrangement with
Louisiana State University Press

L. C. Catalog Card Number: 67-16626

Printed in the United States of America

To

Karin

PREFACE

Virginia, Kentucky, and Louisiana all rightfully claim Zachary Taylor. He was born on the red soil of the Old Dominion; he grew to manhood in Kentucky and entered the United States Army from that state; he engaged in planting activities in Mississippi and Louisiana and made his home in the latter state at the time of his election to the presidency. Taylor was a Southerner, but not a sectionalist. For forty years he served the entire nation in a military capacity and during his months in the White House he labored diligently to prevent the disruption of the Union. He belongs to no one state or section but to the nation.

In connection with the presidential campaign of 1848 numerous lives of Taylor appeared. These were little more than brief, uncritical summaries of his military career. Nearly fifty years later a somewhat more critical account of his life was published as a volume in the Great Commanders Series, but it, too, was concerned primarily with his military activities. Since the writer commenced work on the present biography two recent studies of Taylor have appeared. They have done much to gain for him his rightful place in the history of the country. It is hoped that the present volume will further illuminate the life story of this representative American who was so long neglected by historians and biographers.

The writer is indebted to librarians, archivists, and historians across the country who have taken an interest in his work and aided in its completion. The staffs of the Library of Congress, the National Archives, the Huntington Library, the Kentucky Historical Society, the Filson Club, the Historical Society of Pennsylvania, the Missouri Historical

Society, the New York Historical Society, the Wisconsin State Historical Society, the University of North Carolina Library, and the Library of the University of California at Los Angeles were especially helpful in making materials available for his use. Descendants of Taylor, Mrs. Alice S. Hardie and Mr. Trist Wood of New Orleans, generously permitted him to use valuable manuscripts and shared with him their knowledge of family lore.

The writer is indebted to his late colleague Professor John C. Parish for first calling to his attention the need for a study of Taylor's life. Thanks are also due to his colleagues Professors Joseph B. Lockey and Louis K. Koontz and to Dr. Fulmer Mood for reading and criticizing portions of the manuscript and to the editors of the Southern Biography Series who made many helpful criticisms. At every stage of his work the writer's wife, Karin Anderson Dyer, has given indispensable assistance and encouragement.

Brainerd Dyer

Los Angeles, California
July 9, 1946

CONTENTS

	Preface	vii
I	A Kentucky Pioneer	1
II	Beginning of a Career	13
III	Frontier Duty	38
IV	Interlude	57
V	The Black Hawk War	68
VI	Hide and Seek with the Seminoles	100
VII	The Army of Observation	128
VIII	The Army of Occupation	154
IX	The Capture of Monterrey	184
X	At Odds with the Administration	207
XI	The Battle of Buena Vista	226
XII	"My Unfortunate Plantation"	255
XIII	Presidential Election of 1848	265
XIV	The Spoils of Victory	302
XV	Peace—But Not At Any Price	336
XVI	A National Crisis	368
XVII	A Soldier in the White House	397
	Appendix	411
	Critical Essay on Authorities	420
	Index	435

ILLUSTRATIONS

General Zachary Taylor by William G. Brown, 1847 *Frontispiece*

Reproduced by permission from an oil portrait in the Louisiana State Museum.

facing page

Map of the Mississippi Valley Showing Forts and Towns Where Zachary Taylor Served 20

Map of the Seat of War in Florida 104

Reproduced from the original in the National Archives.

Map of the General Area of Military Campaigns . . 166

Reproduced from Edward D. Mansfield, *The Mexican War* (New York, 1849), p. 8.

Zachary Taylor 184

Reproduced by permission from an oil portrait in the Pennsylvania Academy of the Fine Arts.

Battleground of Buena Vista 230

Reproduced from W. S. Henry, *Campaign Sketches of the War with Mexico* (New York, 1847), p. 312.

John Jordan Crittenden 270

General Taylor's Residence at Baton Rouge When Elected President in 1848. Now the Grounds of the State Capitol 276

From an old number of *Harper's Magazine,* November, 1854. Courtesy Hill Memorial Library, Louisiana State University.

View of the Capitol at Washington, 1850 308

President Taylor, Vice-President Fillmore, and the Cabinet 316

Zachary Taylor as President of the United States . . 368

Reproduced from a lithograph by F. D'Avignon after a daguerreotype by Brady. Courtesy of the Library of Congress.

Henry Clay 384

An Early Picture of the White House 398

Chapter I

A KENTUCKY PIONEER

VICTORY for the Americans in their War for Independence was still several months away, but for Lieutenant Colonel Richard Taylor the war was over. He had entered the United States Army as a first lieutenant in the First Virginia Regiment of Continentals in September, 1775, had fought on both the Eastern and Western fronts, and now after five years and five months of active service he was returning home.[1] Home meant Hare Forest, near the Rapidan River in Orange County, Virginia; it meant a young war bride and a two-week-old son, named Hancock after an uncle who had been killed by Indians in Kentucky several years before.

Lieutenant Colonel Taylor was thirty-six, almost thirty-seven, years of age when he retired from the army in February, 1781. Sarah Dabney Strother, who had become his wife in August, 1779, was only twenty. She was a member of a cultured and respected Virginia family, the daughter of William and Sarah Bailey Strother of Orange County.[2] Few details of Sally Taylor's life and character have survived, but only a woman of courage, strength, and forti-

[1] John H. Gwathmey, *Historical Register of Virginians in the Revolution* (Richmond, 1938), 761; Autobiographical Fragment, in Taylor Papers (Division of Manuscripts, Library of Congress). Taylor's retirement was probably a result of the reorganization of the Continental Army which took place early in 1781 in accordance with the plan adopted by Congress some months before. W. C. Ford and others (eds.), *Journals of the Continental Congress* (Washington, 1904–1937), XVIII, 893–97.

[2] *Register of Kentucky State Historical Society* (Frankfort), XXV (1927), 300.

tude, a full match for her soldier husband, could have played the part in the strenuous pioneer life on the Kentucky frontier that she was destined to play.

Richard Taylor came of English forebears who settled in Virginia on the Mattapony River about 1640 when the population of that colony numbered some ten thousand persons and only a portion of the tidewater region had been occupied. The Taylors gained no unusual distinction or prominence in the colony, but in the eighteenth century they were one of the stable and respected families of the Piedmont section, connected by marriage with many other well-known Virginia families.[3] In 1716 James Taylor, Richard's grandfather, accompanied Governor Alexander Spotswood on his famous exploration over the Blue Ridge Mountains and into the Shenandoah Valley and thus became a member of the select Knights of the Golden Horseshoe. Shortly thereafter he acquired vast landholdings in the Piedmont forest on the Rapidan River. In 1721 his daughter, Frances, married Ambrose Madison and helped to establish the near-by Montpelier estate, later to be famous as the home of her illustrious grandson, President James Madison. Numerous other Taylors and Madisons settled in this Piedmont country and for many years the two families were closely associated in planting, in politics, and in religion.[4] That the Taylor stock was good stock is made apparent by the fact that from it came two Presidents.

Through the veins of Richard Taylor and his children coursed also the blood of the Lees of Virginia. His mother was Elizabeth Lee, granddaughter of Richard Lee whose

[3] Irving Brant, *James Madison, the Virginia Revolutionist* (Indianapolis, 1941), 24–27, 51–52; William H. Samson (ed.), *Letters of Zachary Taylor from the Battlefields of the Mexican War . . .* (Rochester, 1908), vii–viii. Hereafter cited as *Letters from the Battlefields.*

[4] Brant, *Madison,* 16, 24–27, 51–52; Leonidas Dodson, *Alexander Spotswood, Governor of Colonial Virginia, 1710–1722* (Philadelphia, 1932), 238–39; Ann Maury (ed.), *Memoirs of a Huguenot Family Translated and Compiled from the Original Autobiography of Rev. James Fontaine and Other Family Manuscripts . . .* (New York, n. d.), 282 ff.

descendants, Light-Horse Harry Lee and Robert E. Lee, have made the Lee name imperishable in the nation's history. Through Elizabeth Lee, Richard Taylor was also descended from Isaac Allerton and William Brewster, leaders of the Pilgrim Colony at Plymouth.[5] If blood tells, if heredity matters, Richard Taylor's children were clearly fortunate.

As Orange County had escaped the ravages of war the returning veteran was able to resume the operation of his plantation without delay. Even the invasion of Virginia by the British troops under General Cornwallis in the spring of 1781, and the final campaign of the war which ensued, did not reach into the northwestern portion of the state, and life at Hare Forest was not disturbed.[6] The months passed. Another son was born. He was named William Dabney Strother, for Sally Taylor's brother who had been killed in the battle of Guilford Courthouse early in 1781.[7]

Perhaps under any circumstances the Taylor family would have joined the stream of Virginians flowing into the Ohio Valley. But any doubt of this was removed late in 1783 when Lieutenant Colonel Taylor received from the state a war bonus of six thousand acres of western land.[8] The trans-Allegheny country was a region with which he already had some familiarity. During a portion of the war he had served under General Lachlan McIntosh, assigned by Washington to the command of strategic Fort Pitt.[9]

[5] *Letters from the Battlefields,* viii; *Lee of Virginia, 1642–1892, Biographical and Genealogical Sketches of the Descendants of Colonel Richard Lee with Brief Notices of the Related Families . . .* (Philadelphia, 1895), 529, 533.

[6] H. J. Eckenrode, *The Revolution in Virginia* (Boston and New York, 1916), 261–75; Louis Gottschalk, *Lafayette and the Close of the American Revolution* (Chicago, 1942).

[7] *Letters from the Battlefields,* viii.

[8] Gaius Marcus Brumbaugh (ed.), *Revolutionary War Records* (Washington, 1936), I, 117; Willard Rouse Jillson, *The Kentucky Land Grants* (Filson Club *Publications,* No. 33, Louisville, 1925), 125. Later Taylor received 2,166 additional acres. *Ibid.*

[9] Zachary Taylor to Lyman C. Draper, October 30, 1848, in *Register of*

Moreover, many years before, in 1769 when a young man of twenty-five, he had accompanied his brother Hancock Taylor and another Virginian, Abraham Haptonstall, on a trip down the Ohio and Mississippi rivers. In a small boat which they built or procured at Pittsburgh the pioneers moved down the Ohio, examining the country as they went. From the Ohio they passed into the Mississippi, explored one hundred miles up the river and then descended to the mouth of the Arkansas. About one hundred miles up the Arkansas, "a short distance above a small French settlement, the 'Post' so-called," they encamped and hunted until the spring of the following year. When they returned to the Mississippi, Richard Taylor separated from his companions. While they remained in the West through another year, he traveled east through the country of the Chickasaw, Choctaw, and Creek Indians in company with an Indian trader. From Georgia he turned north and passed through the Carolinas, eventually arriving home in Orange County, Virginia, after an absence of well over a year.[10]

When Taylor received his land warrant in September, 1783, it was too late in the year for a trip into the West, but the following year found him visiting Kentucky preparatory to moving his family there.[11] He doubtless selected at least a portion of his bounty land at this time and perhaps built the one-room log cabin which was the first Kentucky home of the Taylors. There is a story that Lieutenant Colonel Taylor had originally intended to take his family west with him in 1784, and that they had in fact actually started when it was decided that Mrs. Taylor should not make the long trip until after the birth of the child she

---

the Kentucky State Historical Society, XXXIII (1935), 70–77; Louise Phelps Kellogg, *Frontier Advance on the Upper Ohio, 1778–1779* (Madison, 1916), 25, 221.

[10] Zachary Taylor to Lyman C. Draper, October 30, 1848, *loc. cit.*

[11] *Ibid.*

was expecting in November. This story may have no other basis than the fact that Hare Forest had already been disposed of and Mrs. Taylor was living with a relative, Colonel Valentine Johnstone, near Barbourville in Orange County when her third son was born.[12]

On November 24, 1784, a third son was born to Sally Taylor—a son who half a century later, as President of the United States, was to bring renown to the entire Taylor family. To him was given the name Zachary, the name of his paternal grandfather and of his father's eldest brother.[13]

There is no record of the route followed by Colonel Taylor and his family as they traveled westward in the spring of 1785, but there were only two gateways to the trans-Allegheny West. Through one of these they must have passed. Possibly they followed Daniel Boone's old Wilderness Trail through rugged Cumberland Gap, entered Kentucky near the southeast corner of the present state and then by narrow, ill-made roads traversed the mountains and forests, forded countless streams, and finally reached the Ohio River. However, because they were destined for the little settlement that was growing up around the Falls of the Ohio it is more probable that they used the other gateway. This was, after all, the more popular route to Kentucky partly because it permitted the transportation of household goods and other heavy articles. If the Taylors took this second route they crossed the Blue Ridge Mountains into the valley of the Shenandoah, descended that river to the Potomac, and then turned west going up the Potomac Valley past Fort Cumberland and Fort Necessity, along the famous road traveled by George Washington and General Braddock thirty years before, over Laurel Hill, and on to Pittsburgh at the forks of the Ohio. From that point it was comparatively easy to float

[12] Willard Rouse Jillson, "Early Western Exploration," in *Register of the Kentucky State Historical Society,* XXXIII, 75.

[13] Autobiographical Fragment; *Letters from the Battlefields,* viii.

down the beautiful river six hundred miles to the Falls where the frontier settlement of Louisville was located. Though less strenuous this river journey was by no means devoid of peril. As they glided past forest-covered banks constant watch by day and night was necessary to ward off surprise attacks by the Indians who were ever ready to pounce upon the intruders. By this route the entire trip was about one thousand miles in length, but even when a party included women and children, and perhaps herds and flocks, it could be completed in two months' time unless unusual delays were encountered.

Richard Taylor established his Kentucky plantation, upon which he was to live for nearly forty-five years and upon which Zachary and the other children were to be brought up, about six miles northeast of Louisville on the Muddy Fork of Beargrass Creek which ran generally parallel to the Ohio about one-half mile south of that river. The creek, which emptied into the river at Louisville, was important to the town in its early years because it furnished a safe anchorage for river boats of all types.[14] Here, on the edge of the fertile, rolling Blue Grass section, Colonel Taylor slowly developed a plantation that in time offered the comforts, if not the luxuries, of the older plantations of the East.

In 1785 Kentucky was still part of Virginia. The territory northwest of the Ohio had recently been ceded to the central government which was then busy enacting legislation for the sale of lands and for the government of the territory—the important Land Ordinance of 1785 and the famous Northwest Ordinance of 1787. But Kentucky had not been ceded. Most of its land had already passed into private hands, and as far back as 1776, shortly after fearless pioneers had established Harrodsburg and Boonesboro, Virginia

[14] J. Stoddard Johnston, *Memorial History of Louisville from Its First Settlement to the Year 1896* (Chicago and New York, 1896), I, 64.

had created Kentucky County to meet the governmental needs of the frontiersman. During the Revolutionary War few homes were established west of the mountains, but with the definite establishment of peace in 1783 a rush of settlers to the western lands began. Revolutionary soldiers of Virginia, rewarded with western lands in lieu of gold, led the westward trek. Younger sons, landless under Virginia's system of primogeniture, and planters, fleeing the exhausted soil of the older region, joined in the migration. By 1785 Kentucky could boast a population of some twenty-five thousand. Only a few hundred, however, were settled in the vicinity of Louisville.[15] The great majority were located farther east in the heart of the Blue Grass section. Louisville was distinctly the outpost of civilization along the Ohio.

Although Kentucky was not the home of any Indian tribes, it was, and long had been, the great hunting and fishing preserve of the red men who lived north of the Ohio or south of the Cumberland and who were determined to protect it against the white intruders. There were no great Indian battles at the Falls, such as there were in southern Kentucky and Tennessee, but marauding bands of redskins frequently appeared and kept the lives of the frontiersmen in constant danger. Groups of savages crossed from the north side of the river where they held undisputed sway and after killing settlers and destroying or stealing their property fled across the Ohio to comparative safety. As late as March 10, 1795, a group of Jefferson County citizens raised a fund from which to pay rewards for every

[15] The Virginia legislature passed an act establishing the town, May 1, 1780, but two years earlier the first settlement had been made at the Falls by frontier families accompanying George Rogers Clark's expedition against the British. Johnston, *Memorial History*, I, 39–45; Anon., *Historical Sketches of Kentucky* . . . (Marysville, Ky., and Cincinnati, Ohio, 1848), 355; Robert M. McElroy, *Kentucky in the Nation's History* (New York, 1909), 147–48; Reuben T. Durrett, *The Centenary of Louisville* (Filson Club *Publications*, No. 8, Louisville, 1893).

Indian scalp taken in the vicinity of Louisville.[16] Year after year Kentucky militiamen joined in expeditions against the Indians of Ohio. Hundreds of them lost their lives in the disastrous efforts of Generals Josiah Harmar and Arthur St. Clair in 1790 and 1791 to curb the power of the northwest Indians. Others participated in the successful campaign of General Anthony Wayne which culminated in the victory at Fallen Timbers in 1794—a victory which gave southern Ohio and northern Kentucky a measure of relief from Indian attacks. It was another twenty years, however, before the tribes of Indiana were subdued and Kentucky freed from the task of fighting the savages.[17]

Zachary's father must have joined in many an expedition against the red men. He gained such a reputation as an Indian fighter that Governor Scott is reported to have said that "if he had to storm the gates of Hell, he should want Dick Taylor to lead the column!" [18] In these early years when the Taylors and their neighbors lived in constant fear of Indian attacks, Zachary himself was far too young to join in the warfare; but he was not too young to know the meaning of the nightly barricade and the Indian alarm, not too young to remember friends who had met death at the hands of the red men. The Indian was one of the inescapable facts of his boyhood.[19]

The new Taylor plantation, cut out of the forest on the far edge of civilization, gradually developed and as Zachary grew up he found himself a part of a moderately well-to-

16 *The Centenary of Kentucky* (Filson Club *Publications,* No. 7, Louisville, 1892), 77.

17 Johnston, *Memorial History,* I, 55–58; Anon., *Historical Sketches of Kentucky,* 355; *American State Papers* (Washington, 1832–1861), *Indian Affairs,* I, *passim.*

18 James A. Padgett, "The Letters of Colonel Richard Taylor and of Commodore Richard Taylor to James Madison, Together with a Sketch of Their Lives," in *Register of the Kentucky State Historical Society,* XXXVI (1938), 332. The Louisville *Weekly Courier,* May 1, 1847, tells the same story but substitutes Governor Grayson for Governor Scott.

19 Louisville *Weekly Courier,* May 1, 1847.

do planting family. Alongside the one-room cabin soon was built a substantial two-story house. Cabin and house still stand on slightly elevated ground on the north side of the Brownsboro Road about five miles out from Louisville. The tax lists for Jefferson County, in which Colonel Taylor's plantation was located, disclose that by 1797 he owned 1,650 acres of land in Jefferson County, 400 of which were first-rate land on the Beargrass watercourse. In other counties he owned some 10,000 acres,[20] not enough to place him among the great landowners of Kentucky, but sufficient with the frequent changes in his holdings to indicate that he joined in the land speculations of the frontier. But the 400 acres on the Beargrass, the home plantation, continued to be listed in his name as long as he lived.[21] The tax returns also indicate that Richard Taylor owned seven Negro slaves in 1790, nineteen in 1795, twenty-six in 1800, and thirty-seven in 1810. This was a sufficient number to place him among the larger slaveowners of his immediate neighborhood. Of forty-eight taxpayers listed on the Beargrass Creek in 1800 only four owned more slaves than Zachary's father. Eleven of his neighbors were listed as owning no slaves, eighteen as owning fewer than ten each, and the remaining fourteen as owning between ten and twenty-two each.[22] The Negro slave, like the Indian, was an inescapable fact of Zachary's boyhood years.

The Indians and the plantation did not take all of Colonel Taylor's time. The records show that he was one of the justices of the peace for Jefferson County appointed in 1785 by the governor of Virginia and that he continued to serve in that capacity, hearing and deciding legal controversies as to wills and property, for nearly ten years.[23] He

[20] Jefferson County Tax List for 1797, in the Kentucky State Historical Society.

[21] Jefferson County Tax Lists for 1799, 1800, 1808, 1810, 1827, 1828, *ibid.*

[22] Jefferson County Tax Lists for 1790, 1795, 1800, 1810, *ibid.*

[23] *Filson Club History Quarterly* (Louisville), VI (1932), 290; *Register of the Kentucky State Historical Society,* XXV, 55, and XXX (1932), 316.

also served for a period as collector of the port at Louisville by appointment of President Washington. In 1792, when after seven years of bitter disappointment and mounting discontent, Kentucky was finally admitted to the Union as a separate state, Taylor was a member of the convention that framed Kentucky's constitution and seven years later he aided in revising it. In addition he served one term in the Kentucky legislature just after the state was admitted to the Union and several terms twenty years later. A political office held by him that demanded little time, but which indicates that he had obtained a position of influence in the political life of the state, was that of presidential elector in the four elections 1812 to 1824. He supported his kinsman, James Madison, in 1812 and James Monroe in the next two elections. In 1824 he gave his support to his fellow Kentuckian, Henry Clay.[24] Although some of this political activity on the part of his father came after Zachary had left home to join the army, much of it was during his boyhood years and possibly served as an introduction for him to the field of politics and government even though its influence was small. It would be a rash biographer who would find in the political experience of the father the making of the future President.

The known details of Zachary's boyhood are exceedingly meager. With two older brothers, three younger brothers, and three younger sisters he surely did not want for playmates, even though there were no close neighbors. Two miles from the Taylor plantation was Locust Grove, the home of Major William Croghan and his wife, a sister of the famous Kentucky pioneer George Rogers Clark. During the latter years of his life Clark made his home with the Croghans and was doubtless a familiar hero to young Zachary. George Croghan, who as a young officer in the War of 1812 won renown for his gallant defense of Fort

[24] Padgett, "The Letters of Colonel Richard Taylor," *loc. cit.*, 332–33; Anon., *Historical Sketches of Kentucky*, 366.

Stephenson, was born at Locust Grove in 1791. He is frequently named as a playmate of Zachary Taylor during his boyhood years,[25] but a seven-year difference in their ages may well have prevented very close companionship. On somewhat more distant plantations, yet not too distant for occasional visits, lived numerous Taylor cousins with whom Zachary doubtless shared many frontier experiences.

Little is known concerning Taylor's education, but the shortcomings of his correspondence in later years arouse the strong suspicion that his formal schooling was not very extensive. For a brief period he received instruction from Elisha Ayer, an itinerant New England schoolmaster who set up a school at Louisville.[26] Some years later, early in the nineteenth century, he apparently studied with Kean O'Hara, a classical scholar who in subsequent years gained a significant place in Kentucky educational circles.[27] Available evidence does not indicate that Taylor's acquaintance with the schoolroom went beyond this. It is quite probable, however, that he benefited from additional instruction at home. His mother had been taught by tutors imported from Europe[28] and his father was a cultured gentleman whose education may have included study at William and Mary College.[29] Either could have instructed young Zachary in the three R's.

Some practical education must have resulted from association with the activities of the Ohio River. Down its waters floated not only Kentucky tobacco, hemp, and other crops on their way to New Orleans and the markets of the East, but also, as the years passed, the thousands of settlers for the farther West—Indiana, western Kentucky, Illinois,

[25] Louisville *Weekly Courier*, May 1, 1847.

[26] Joseph Reese Fry, *A Life of General Zachary Taylor* . . . (Philadelphia, 1847), 16; *Taylor and His Generals* . . . (Philadelphia, 1847), 13; Holman Hamilton, *Zachary Taylor, Soldier of the Republic* (Indianapolis, 1941), 28.

[27] Hamilton, *Zachary Taylor*, 28.

[28] *Ibid.*, 24.

[29] Padgett, "The Letters of Colonel Richard Taylor," *loc. cit.*, 330.

and Missouri. Because of the series of rapids, a mile and a half in length, known as the Falls of the Ohio, which necessitated a two-mile portage in dry seasons and the services of a skillful pilot at all times, Louisville became a busy river port.[30] How often did young Zachary visit it with his father? How often did he sit on the banks and watch the keelboats and flatboats silently making their way westward? Perhaps he was among the amazed spectators who at the turn of the century witnessed the ocean-going schooners arrive from Pittsburgh on their way to the West Indies or to Europe.[31] How much did he learn from the winter ice jams and spring floods? In addition to the Indian and the Negro slave, the great river was surely an influence upon young Zachary during his boyhood years in Kentucky.

Zachary apparently remained at home until the age of twenty-three when he joined the United States Army. The presumption is that he aided in the work of the plantation on which tobacco was probably the chief money crop. The routine manual labor was of course performed by the slaves, but a share in the supervision of the many phases of plantation life and work, and some of the special tasks, probably fell to him as he advanced in years. In later life he exhibited a real interest in plantations and a knowledge of their operation that must have resulted in part from the training received on his father's estate.

Brief and incomplete as it is, this is the story of Taylor's youth. In later life he made no speeches and wrote few letters or memoirs reminiscing about his early years. His acquaintances likewise recorded but little. Thus, we are left with the vague picture of a boy growing to manhood on the banks of the Ohio when the red savages were slowly being pushed back to make room for the white settlers and their black slaves, when Kentucky was achieving statehood and nourishing a democratic, nationalistic society.

[30] A. B. Hulbert, *The Ohio River: A Course of Empire* (New York, 1906), 267.

[31] *Ibid.*, 246–47.

Chapter II

BEGINNING OF A CAREER

IN April, 1808, when Europe was in the midst of twenty-two years of almost continuous war, when the United States was still excited by the bloody British attack on the frigate *Chesapeake* and by other humiliating events on the high seas, Congress approved the recommendation of President Jefferson and authorized the Secretary of War to treble the size of the United States Army. The army, which had consisted of one regiment of artillery, two regiments of infantry, and one corps of engineers, was to be increased by the addition of a regiment of light artillery, one of light dragoons, one of riflemen, and five of infantry. The army, which had consisted of three thousand men, was to be increased to nine thousand.[1] It was as part of this program of expansion that Zachary Taylor entered the army. He was one of the twenty-six Kentuckians recommended to the War Department by the Kentucky members of Congress a few days after the law was enacted,[2] and on May 3 he was appointed first lieutenant in the Seventh Regiment of United States Infantry.

In submitting the list of names to the War Department the Kentucky congressmen reported that they had endeavored as far as they could "to prefer the Sons of antient [*sic*] Settlers, who had distinguish'd themselves in the Defence of the Country or had suffered & withstood the In-

1 *American State Papers; Military Affairs,* I, 218, 227–28; *Niles' Weekly Register* (Philadelphia), XXXI (1826–1827), 109; *United States Statutes at Large* (Boston, 1845–1873), II, 481–83.

2 B. Thruston to the Adjutant General, April 16, 1808, in War Department Archives.

conveniences and Dangers of an early settlement therein." [3] This seems to indicate that Zachary's appointment was due in large measure to his father's past services to his country and his position and standing in the state. The appointment probably was due in part, however, to the influence of his father's cousin, James Taylor of Newport, Kentucky, who was in close touch with the administration, frequently recommended his relatives and other young men for commissions in the army,[4] and not many months before had given Zachary's brother, William Dabney Strother Taylor, a letter of introduction and commendation to the Secretary of State, James Madison.[5] If he did not recommend Zachary in advance of his appointment, he did so shortly afterwards when he wrote to Madison, now President-elect, "I think Z. Taylor will make a valuable Officer he is much Esteemed by all who are acquainted with him. He appears to possess a great deal of that frank bluntness and firmness which his father is so remarkable for." [6] Zachary's father may also have written to Madison in his behalf. He wrote requesting appointments or promotions for two other sons and it is quite probable that he did the same for Zachary.[7]

Zachary was the second of Colonel Richard Taylor's sons to receive appointment in the United States Army. A year before, February 27, 1807, William Dabney Strother Taylor, the son just older than Zachary, had been appointed second lieutenant of Artillerists. His military career proved to be of short duration, however, for on May 30, 1808, he died. A third son, Joseph Pannel Taylor, entered the army during the War of 1812.[8]

[3] *Ibid.*

[4] James A. Padgett, "The Letters of James Taylor to the Presidents of the United States," in *Register of the Kentucky State Historical Society*, XXXIV (1936), 103–30, 251–78, 318–46.

[5] *Ibid.*, 112–13.

[6] James Taylor to James Madison, February 26, 1809, *ibid.*, 252.

[7] Richard Taylor to *id.*, March 3, 1805, January 25, 1808, and July 23, 1816, *ibid.*, XXXVI, 337–38.

[8] Francis B. Heitman, *Historical Register and Dictionary of the United*

The army that Lieutenant Taylor joined was commanded by Brigadier General James Wilkinson, a veteran of the Revolutionary War who had retained his influence with the Jefferson administration in spite of his long-continued intrigues with the Spanish authorities at New Orleans. Except for a few junior officers, recently graduated from the newly established military academy at West Point, the officers of the army were without special training other than that which they gained in the practical school of experience. Few officers of merit remained in the service, for the all-too-frequent changes in the size of the army and the repeated reorganization of the service resulting from the vacillating policy of Congress had driven most able men into private life. The new officers appointed in 1808 were little better. Winfield Scott, who received his commission at this time, regarded most of his colleagues as either "coarse and ignorant" or "decayed gentlemen," as "imbeciles and ignoramuses." [9] Scott's characterization is extreme, but there is no denying that the new officers were political appointees and in most instances were without previous military experience.

As a first lieutenant Zachary Taylor received $30 a month and two rations per day. The daily ration consisted of one and one-fourth pounds of beef or three-fourths pound of pork, eighteen ounces of bread or flour, one gill of rum, brandy, or whiskey, salt, vinegar, soap, and candles. Officers who preferred were permitted to commute their rations at twenty cents per ration, but the enlisted men had no such option. When two years later Taylor was promoted to captain his pay became $40 a month and he was entitled to three rations instead of two.[10] Shortly after Tay-

States Army, from Its Organization, September 29, 1789, to March 2, 1903 (Washington, 1903), I, 949.

[9] Winfield Scott, *Memoirs* (New York, 1864), I, 31–36.

[10] *American State Papers: Military Affairs,* I, 225, 435; Raphael P. Thian (ed.), *Legislative History of the General Staff of the Army of the United States from 1775 to 1901* (Washington, 1901), 26, 333.

lor's appointment in 1808 the prescribed infantry officer's uniform was a knee-length, single-breasted blue coat with standing collar to the tip of the ear and with collar and cuffs trimmed according to rank; blue pantaloons, though officers of the general staff and field officers might wear white breeches; waist belts of white leather; a long chapeau or, when on duty, a leather cap. The red collars and cuffs and lace of earlier days were banned, but general officers might embroider their buttonholes. The rank and file also wore blue uniforms with leather caps.[11]

The Seventh Regiment to which Taylor was appointed existed on paper only, for it was one of the new regiments authorized by Congress in the preceding month. He remained in Kentucky, giving some attention to recruiting the regiment,[12] until the spring of 1809, when he led two companies down the river to New Orleans[13] where the government was hastily concentrating troops under General Wilkinson to defend the town and the vast Louisiana territory so recently purchased by Jefferson. This was a vulnerable and strategic point and the government feared that if war came Great Britain would lose no time in attacking it.[14]

Long before these raw troops were battling the British they were fighting mosquitoes, disease, and death. Their camp was poorly located in spite of instructions from the War Department to move to higher ground. Many were soon suffering from excessive fatigue resulting from the work of clearing and draining the campground and sleepless nights caused by the busy mosquitoes. Without wholesome food or proper medicines and with no shelter for the

[11] *American State Papers: Military Affairs,* I, 433–34.

[12] Zachary Taylor to the Secretary of War, November 24, 1808, in War Department Archives.

[13] James Taylor to Madison, February 26, 1809, in Padgett, "The Letters of James Taylor to the Presidents of the United States," *loc. cit.,* 252.

[14] *American State Papers: Military Affairs,* I, 272.

sick but tents, which neither protected them sufficiently from the heat of the sun nor kept them dry from the dews and rains, the troops were easy victims of disease. Chronic diarrhea, dysentery, scurvy, bilious and intermitting fevers, and other diseases decimated the ranks. During the ten months following May 1, 1809, there were 686 deaths, 108 desertions, and 58 discharges among the 2,000 troops concentrated at New Orleans.[15]

Among the victims of disease who escaped the death penalty was Zachary Taylor. The tradition is that he came down with yellow fever, though it may have been the more common but almost as serious dysentery. Whatever the disease, he returned to Kentucky to recuperate his strength.[16] By the end of November, 1809, he had presumably recovered, for at that time the War Department addressed him at Louisville and ordered him to report to the officer in command at Washington, Mississippi Territory,[17] where the main portion of his regiment was stationed.

When Lieutenant Taylor reached his post he found that numerous changes and shifts had left his regiment with no place for him and he was promptly ordered back to Louisville to await orders. How he spent the next year of his life is not entirely clear. No assignment to duty seems to have been made until July, 1811. Yet he was not forgotten by the War Department and clearly remained in favor with his superiors, for in November, 1810, he was promoted to the rank of captain.[18] Also during these months he was married to Margaret Mackall Smith, a native of Maryland and the daughter of Captain Walter Smith, a well-to-do planter who had died a few years before. The marriage license was

[15] *Ibid.*, 268–95.

[16] *Letters from the Battlefields*, xiii.

[17] Adjutant General to Lt. Zachariah Taylor, November 29, 1809, in War Department Archives.

[18] Autobiographical Fragment; Heitman, *Historical Register*, I, 949; Hamilton, *Zachary Taylor*, 36.

issued to Taylor and his bride-to-be on June 18, 1810, but no return seems to have been made by the clergyman performing the ceremony.[19] During the next thirty-five years Mrs. Taylor was usually with her soldier husband at frontier army posts. From time to time she was back in Louisville awaiting the arrival of another child, for all but one of their six children were born in or near that town. Their second child was born while Mrs. Taylor was with the Captain at Fort Knox, Indiana, in 1814, and received the name of Sarah Knox.[20]

It was in the early summer of 1811 that Captain Taylor was ordered to take command of Fort Knox, a frontier post on the Wabash just above Vincennes, the seat of the government of Indiana Territory.[21] From this time to the close of the war with Great Britain in 1815 he was actively engaged against the Indians of the Old Northwest. How or why Taylor was picked for this post is not clear, but his appointment seems to have been due to some manipulation or scheming. A few days after Taylor took up his new duties, William Henry Harrison, the governor of the territory and himself a military man, referred in a letter to "the very extraordinary manner by which Capt. T. became possessed of the command." Harrison stated, however, that Taylor deserved no share of the blame for he disapproved of the "whole proceeding." [22] Harrison may have been referring to the fact that the captain who had preceded Taylor in command at the fort had fled the territory after shooting and killing a subordinate officer,[23] but it seems more likely that the governor had in mind machinations

[19] Copy of the Marriage Records of Jefferson County, Kentucky, II, 693, in Kentucky State Historical Society; *Letters from the Battlefields,* ix.

[20] *Letters from the Battlefields,* x–xiii; Hamilton, *Zachary Taylor,* 57.

[21] Taylor to the Secretary of War, July 16, 1811, in War Department Archives.

[22] William H. Harrison to Captain D. Bissell, August 9, 1811, in Logan Esarey (ed.), *Messages and Letters of William Henry Harrison* (*Indiana Historical Collections,* Vols. VII and IX, Indianapolis, 1922), I, 551–52.

[23] *Id.* to the Secretary of War, June 25, 1811, *ibid.,* 524–26.

following this tragic event. Harrison had recommended Lieutenant Ambrose Whitlock for the post,[24] but other influences apparently resulted in the appointment of Taylor. Taylor was unknown to Harrison prior to this time, but the young officer quickly made a favorable impression upon him. Two weeks after Taylor assumed the command, Harrison wrote to the Secretary of War: "To all the qualities which are esteemed for an amiable man he appears to unite those which form a good officer. In the short time he has been a commander he has rendered the Garrison defensible—before his arrival it resembled anything but a place of defence." [25]

Well might Taylor give prompt attention to the task of making the garrison defensible, for when he took command at Fort Knox in July the populace and the authorities of the territory were thoroughly alarmed over the hostility of the red men under the leadership of Tecumseh and his brother the Prophet who for two years had been seeking to unite the Indians for a stand against the relentless advance of the whites. The administration in Washington had been counseling peace, but Harrison was now convinced that "unless some decisive and energetic measure is adopted to break up the combination formed by the Prophet we shall soon have every Indian tribe in this quarter united against us and you may depend on it that it will be attended with much trouble and expense and loss of blood to subdue them." [26]

During the few months that Taylor remained at Fort Knox, Harrison was preparing for the expedition up the Wabash Valley that culminated in the battle of Tippecanoe and the destruction of the Prophet's town. Taylor was to have had what he himself regarded as "a very handsome command" in that expedition, but shortly before it set

[24] *Ibid.*
[25] *Id.* to *id.*, August 6, 1811, *ibid.*, 548.
[26] *Id.* to *id.*, July 10, 1811, *ibid.*, 534.

forth he was ordered east to appear as a defense witness in the court-martial trial of Brigadier General James Wilkinson.[27] Consequently he did not participate in that famous engagement. By spring, however, he was back in Indiana Territory and was placed in command of Fort Harrison. This was a new outpost built by Governor Harrison about sixty-five miles above Vincennes during his campaign of the previous fall.[28] The battle of Tippecanoe had checked the growing power of Tecumseh and the Prophet, but Indian depredations and murders were continuing, the settlers were in constant fear of a general Indian war, and many were abandoning the territory for less exposed regions.[29]

In the middle of June war came—war not only with the Indians but with the British as well. Henry Clay and his fellow "War-Hawks," inflamed by the continued British interference with American commerce and by the support which the northwest Indians obtained in Canada, and spurred on by the hope of conquering that British colony and adding it to the United States, persuaded Congress to declare war on Great Britain on June 18. The attempted invasion of Canada by Brigadier General William Hull, governor of Michigan Territory, promptly following the outbreak of war ended in failure and the surrender of his entire force on August 16. By this date the British forces, aided by their Indian allies, had captured all of the American forts beyond the Wabash and the task of defending the frontier fell to Harrison and the troops under his command. They were soon face to face with the enemy.

A week before the surrender of Hull, Zachary Taylor

[27] Autobiographical Fragment; Taylor to Col. James Taylor, October 1, 1811, quoted in *American Clipper* (American Autograph Shop, Merion Station, Pennsylvania), September, 1937.

[28] Autobiographical Fragment; Esarey, *Messages and Letters of William Henry Harrison,* II, 49.

[29] William H. Harrison to the Secretary of War, May 13, 1812, in Esarey, *Messages and Letters of William Henry Harrison,* II, 48–49.

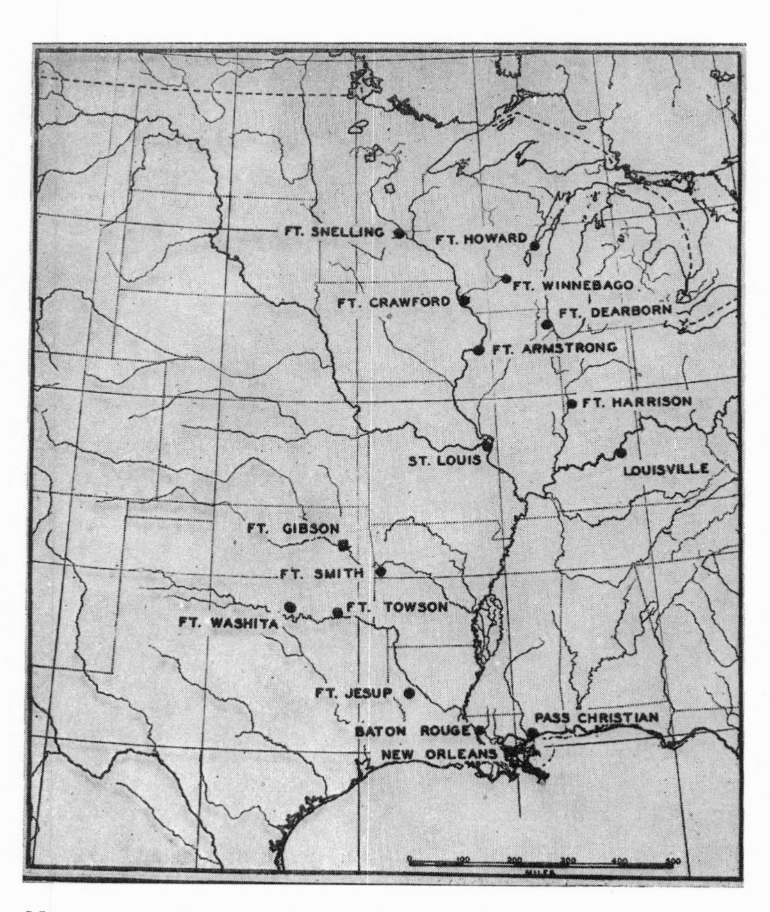

MAP OF THE MISSISSIPPI VALLEY SHOWING FORTS AND TOWNS WHERE ZACHARY TAYLOR SERVED

wrote from Fort Harrison to inform the governor that various friendly Indians had warned him that Tecumseh was gathering a force to strike an important blow against the whites and that "the full of this moon was the time fixed for his commencing hostilities." "They all agree," wrote the young captain, "that his present force is much larger than it was last fall and one of them says that he expects a large reinforcement" in time for the attack. "It is possible his first attempt will be against this post or Vincennes." [30]

The attack did not come quite so soon as Taylor expected, but it was not long delayed. One hour before midnight on September 4, Taylor was awakened by the firing of one of the sentinels. He hurried out to discover that the Indians had not only opened fire on the fort but had set fire to the lower blockhouse in which the provisions were stored. Taylor was still in a weakened condition from a severe attack of fever and many of his men were also partially or wholly incapacitated. The men were slow in executing Taylor's orders and as a result the fire spread rapidly and soon seemed out of control. In his own account, written a few days later, Taylor said:

As that block-house adjoined the barracks that make part of the fortifications most of the men immediately gave themselves up for lost, and I had the greatest difficulty in getting any of my orders executed and, sir, what from the raging of the fire, the yelling and howling of several hundred Indians, the cries of nine women and children (a part of soldiers' and a part of citizens' wives, who had taken shelter in the fort) and the desponding of so many of the men, which was worse than all, I can assure you that my feelings were very unpleasant and indeed there were not more than 10 or 15 men able to do a great deal, the others being either sick or convalescent and to add to our other misfortunes, two of the stoutest men in the fort, and that I had every confidence in, jumped the picket and left us. But

[30] Taylor to William H. Harrison, August 9, 1812, *ibid.*, 282.

my presence of mind did not for a moment forsake me. I saw, by throwing off part of the roof that joined the block-house that was on fire, and keeping the end perfectly wet, the whole row of buildings might be saved, and leave only an entrance of 18 or 20 feet for the Indians to enter after the house was consumed; and that a temporary breastwork might be erected to prevent their even entering there I convinced the men that this could be accomplished, and it appeared to inspire them with new life, and never did men act with more firmness and desperation.[31]

This plan of Taylor's worked well. Although the barracks caught fire several times during the night the exertions of the garrison prevented any serious damage. All through the hours of darkness "the Indians continued to pour in a heavy fire of ball and an innumerable quantity of arrows." About six o'clock in the morning the Indians withdrew beyond gun range. Hour after hour during the day the garrison labored unceasingly to fill up the gap in the fortifications resulting from the burning of the block-house. This they accomplished by pulling down the guard-house and erecting a strong row of pickets.[32]

It was with great difficulty that Taylor got word of the attack and the plight of the garrison to the officials at Vincennes. The Indians might strike again at any time and he would need every man at the fort. Moreover, he felt certain that the road and river would be carefully guarded by the red men and that messengers would have to find their way through the woods. Unfortunately there was no one at the fort who knew the woods well enough to undertake such an expedition. After five days had passed with no renewal of attack Taylor decided to send two men by the river route in the hope that they could get through. The men found that route thoroughly guarded by the

31 *Id.* to *id.*, September 10, 1812, *ibid.*, 124–28. The letter is also printed in *Niles' Weekly Register*, III (1812–1813), 90–91.

32 Taylor to William H. Harrison, September 10, 1812, in Esarey, *Messages and Letters of William Henry Harrison*, II, 124–28.

Indians and were obliged to return to the fort. Desperately anxious to get news of his situation to Harrison, Taylor decided to risk sending messengers through the woods.[33] Whether these men were successful the records do not reveal; nevertheless, news of the attack reached Vincennes, reached it in fact the day before Taylor's messengers headed into the woods. A small party of mounted men sent to Fort Harrison by the acting governor of the territory encountered the warring red men before they reached their destination and hastened back to Vincennes to report the perilous situation of the fort.[34] By September 12 the acting governor was apparently fully informed, for on that day he wrote of "the brave defense made by Captain Taylor at Ft. Harrison" as "one bright ray amid the gloom of incompetency which has been shown in so many places." [35]

The authorities in Washington were also well pleased with Taylor's gallant conduct and the President conferred upon him the brevet rank of major as of September 5.[36] This had been Taylor's one opportunity during nearly five years in the service to distinguish himself and he had not missed it. Taylor's report of the affair was published in *Niles' Register* and widely distributed through the country.[37] To the people of the Ohio Valley he was ever thereafter known as the man who as a young captain had led the garrison at Fort Harrison in repulsing the red men. Even in the late years of his life, when other victories were fresher in the public's mind, this early victory was regarded by many as the best and truest evidence of the stuff of which he was made.

On September 5, the very day that Taylor and his hand-

[33] *Ibid.;* Taylor to William H. Harrison, September 13, 1812, in *Niles' Weekly Register,* III (1812–1813), 91.

[34] John Gibson to *id.,* September 12, 1812, in Indiana Historical Society.

[35] *Id.* to Col. Hargrove, September 12, 1812, in Esarey, *Messages and Letters of William Henry Harrison,* II, 133.

[36] Secretary of War to Taylor, October 29, 1812, in War Department Archives.

[37] *Niles' Weekly Register,* III (1812–1813), 90–91.

ful of men were fighting for their lives at Fort Harrison, Governor Harrison, who was in the eastern part of the territory preparing an expedition to retake Detroit, called upon Governor Isaac Shelby of Kentucky for a force of volunteers to reinforce the defenses along the Wabash.[38] Harrison was as yet unaware of the attack on the fort, but he well knew the critical state of the frontier. Before the end of the month two thousand of Taylor's fellow Kentuckians, under the command of Major General Samuel Hopkins, a veteran of the Revolution, were at Vincennes ready to take up the burden of defending the Wabash Valley and the Illinois Territory.[39] By order of General Harrison, who on September 17 had been appointed to the supreme command of the northwestern army,[40] Hopkins was placed in command of all the armed forces in the Wabash Valley and the Illinois Territory.[41] Thus Zachary Taylor came under his command, and when, in the middle of October, General Hopkins led an expedition into the Illinois country Taylor accompanied him as an aide.[42]

There was little glory for Taylor or any other member of this expedition, for it ended in complete failure. According to the report which reached Governor Shelby and was by him communicated to General Harrison, Hopkins set out from Fort Harrison with about two thousand mounted men to operate against Peoria and the Kickapoo Towns on the Illinois River and

> marched first northwest a day or two and then nearly north, in all between five and six days, at or near 30 miles per day, when

38 William H. Harrison to Secretary of War Eustis, September 5, 1812, in Esarey, *Messages and Letters of William Henry Harrison,* II, 117–18; Isaac Shelby to Samuel Hopkins, September 8, 1812, *ibid.,* 120–21.

39 Isaac Shelby to William H. Harrison, September 26, 1812, *ibid.,* 153–54; Hopkins to *id.,* October 6, 1812, *ibid.,* 162–63.

40 Secretary of War to *id.,* September 17, 1812, *ibid.,* 136–37.

41 Acting Governor John Gibson to the Secretary of War, October 14, 1812, in Clarence E. Carter (ed.), *The Territorial Papers of the United States* (Washington, 1934–), VIII, 209.

42 Autobiographical Fragment; Taylor to Gen. J. Taylor, November 9, 1812, in *The Collector* (New York), XXII, No. 6 (April, 1909), 62.

their provisions were nearly exhausted, and their guides entirely bewildered and lost, not knowing which way to steer, the army discouraged and disheartened by their situation, all turned back and with much difficulty and distress, retraced their forward march, and got back to Fort Harrison, the Indians having fired the prairies in their rear, burnt all the grass, and their horses almost perished and themselves; at one time in the most imminent danger of being consumed by the flames . . . . thus has ended an enterprise on which the flower of Kentucky enlisted themselves, and are now returning home deeply mortified by the disappointment.[43]

Although he had failed to administer any blow to Indian activities in Illinois, General Hopkins was soon planning to take action against the Indians of the Wabash country. On November 11 he set out from Fort Harrison with about 1,250 officers and men on an expedition that lasted nearly three weeks. For eight days the main body of troops pushed north through the rain-soaked woods along the east bank of the Wabash while one battalion escorted up the river seven large keelboats loaded with provisions and military supplies. In the vicinity of Prophets Town, where Harrison had fought the battle of Tippecanoe two years before, they constructed works for the defense of their boats and supplies and proceeded to destroy the main Indian towns which had been evacuated by the red men. Buildings of every description were laid in ashes and the corn supplies were also burned. Although General Hopkins was unable to discover the main Indian camps he was well aware that they were not far distant, for one of his reconnoitering parties fell into an ambuscade from which eighteen casualties resulted. The pursuit of the enemy was handicapped by a severe snowstorm which set in almost as soon as the ambuscaded party returned to camp. As soon as the storm had subsided the army resumed its search but without success. Hopkins had intended to spend another week in

[43] Isaac Shelby to William H. Harrison, November 1, 1812, in Esarey, *Messages and Letters of William Henry Harrison,* II, 192.

operations against the Indians, but "the shoeless, shirtless state of the troops, now clad in the remnants of their summer dress; a river full of ice; the hills covered with snow," and the unanimous advice of his staff and field officers caused him to give orders for the return march to commence on the twenty-fifth.[44]

Zachary Taylor was a member of this expedition and was commended by General Hopkins for the "prompt and effectual support" given by him in every instance. To this commendation Hopkins added in his report, "the firm and almost unparalleled defense of Fort Harrison, by Captain Z. Taylor, has raised for him a fabric of character not to be effaced by my eulogy." [45]

At the close of this expedition Taylor was ordered to superintend the recruiting service in the territories of Indiana and Illinois and to muster and inspect their troops.[46] The details of this work which occupied him during the next few months are lost, but it transferred his headquarters from the wilderness of Fort Harrison to Fort Knox and the comparative comfort and security of Vincennes.

When summer came Taylor was again in the field. This time he was a member of Colonel William Russell's expedition against the Mississinewa towns on the Wabash some fifty or sixty miles above the scene of the previous fall's activities. This force of nearly six hundred men covered about five hundred miles during the four weeks they were out and, according to Colonel Russell, went to every place where they could expect to discover the enemy. But the Indian warriors were not encountered and the expedition had to content itself with destroying four or five native villages. The army marched in five distinct columns. In command of the center column was Major Taylor, who with the officers in charge of the other columns displayed "so much zeal for the success of the expedition" that they

44 Samuel Hopkins to Governor Shelby, November 27, 1812, *ibid.*, 231–34.
45 *Ibid.*, 234. 46 Autobiographical Fragment.

convinced Colonel Russell that "they would have done themselves credit had we encountered the enemy." [47]

In the spring of 1814, after nearly three years of active service in western Indiana, Taylor was ordered to St. Louis. On August 22, after several months of more or less routine activity, he was instructed by General Benjamin Howard who was in command of the troops in Missouri Territory to ascend the Mississippi River as far as the villages of the Sac Indians at the mouth of the Rock River, to destroy these villages and if possible the cornfields in their vicinity, and then to drop down to the mouth of the Des Moines River where on the Illinois shore he should construct a fort. Taylor's orders recognized that the low state of the river might make it impossible for his expedition to pass the rapids just above the mouth of the Des Moines River. If such proved to be the case he could not reach the Sac villages, but was to proceed with the construction of the new fort. The General fully expected that Taylor would encounter vigorous opposition from a large force of Indians, but he believed that with the artillery he would be able to defeat them.[48]

At noon on August 22, with a fair wind blowing, Major Taylor and his expedition of over four hundred men left Fort Independence at Cap au Gris for Rock River. Day after day for two weeks they bucked the current and slowly pushed northward. Not an Indian was encountered and nothing but a broken steering oar, a broken mast, an epidemic of measles, and one death marred the advance.[49]

[47] Colonel Russell to Governor Thomas Posey, July 25, 1813, in Esarey, *Messages and Letters of William Henry Harrison,* II, 497–98; *Niles' Weekly Register,* V (1813–1814), 9–10.

[48] Lt. I. Weaver, Acting Assistant Adjutant General, to Major Z. Taylor, August 22, 1814, quoted in full in Taylor's Autobiographical Fragment.

[49] Edgar B. Wesley, "James Callaway in the War of 1812," in *Missouri Historical Society Collections* (St. Louis), V (1927–1928), 74–77. In his report to General Howard dated September 6, 1814, and printed in *Niles' Weekly Register,* VII (1814–1815), Supplement, 137–38, Taylor states that he left Fort Independence "on the 2d ult." This seems to be a misprint for "22d ult."

Finally, on the evening of September 4, the expedition reached the mouth of Rock River. Quickly the quiet and calm were broken. Large numbers of Indians appeared on both banks of the river and canoes filled with the red warriors were soon crossing the river in both directions. The wind, which had been in Taylor's favor, began to shift about the time he reached Rock River and soon was blowing "a perfect hurricane." With some difficulty Taylor's party landed on a small island near the middle of the river and there spent the night—a night of wind and rain.[50]

Not a gun was fired by the Indians or by Taylor's men during the evening of their arrival nor during the ensuing night, but with the break of day the savages approached to within fifteen paces of one of the boats and opened fire. Taylor kept his men within the boats until it was perfectly light and then prepared to drive the Indians from the island. The red men did not wait to be driven; as soon as Taylor formed his troops the enemy waded through the shallow water to the next island just below. In his report, written the following day, Taylor said:

> Capt. [Samuel] Whitesides who was on the left, was able to give them a warm fire as they reached the island they had retreated to. They returned the fire for a few moments, when they retreated. In this affair we had two men badly wounded. When capt. Whitesides commenced the fire I ordered captain [Nelson] Rector to drop down with his boat to ground and to rake the island below with artillery, and to fire on every canoe he should discover passing from one shore to the other which should come within reach. In this situation he remained about one hour, and no indians making their appearance, he determined to drop down the island about sixty yards and destroy several canoes that were laying to shore.[51]

Captain Rector's men had just returned to their boats after destroying the canoes when Taylor discovered that

[50] Taylor to General Howard, September 6, 1814, in *Niles' Weekly Register,* VII (1814–1815), Supplement, 137–38.

[51] *Ibid.*

the Indians were not the only enemy confronting him. Suddenly the boats were subjected to fire from British artillery concealed on the east bank of the river. Neither General Howard nor Major Taylor had expected to encounter the British at Rock River. The Americans were fully aware of the presence of British troops along the upper Mississippi for, only a few weeks before, the newly established and weakly garrisoned American fort at the mouth of the Wisconsin River had been captured by them.[52] The American officers were not aware, however, that the Indians, who were informed of Taylor's expedition as soon as preparations for it commenced, had persuaded the British to send them aid. In response to earnest appeals from the Indians, the commanding officer at Fort McKay, as the British renamed the recently captured fort, had sent a detachment of thirty men under Lieutenant Duncan Graham with one three-pounder and two swivels. Furthermore, the British had also persuaded the Sioux to send warriors to join the Sacs in the battle against the Americans. Thus the force that Taylor encountered was much stronger than he had anticipated.[53]

General Howard's orders to Taylor had been based on the theory that his artillery would give him a clear advantage over the Indians. Now Taylor discovered that the well-placed artillery of the Indians' allies gave all the advantage to the other side. He quickly realized that the exposed position of his boats made resistance unwise and ordered them to drop down the river—but not before one of the boats, possibly the very one from which he was commanding, was hit and badly shattered.[54] In his own account he declared it was Lieutenant Hempstead's boat

[52] Kate L. Gregg, "The War of 1812 on the Missouri Frontier," in *Missouri Historical Review* (Columbia), XXXIII (1938–1939), 328.

[53] Thomas G. Anderson, "Anderson's Journal at Fort McKay, 1814," in *Wisconsin Historical Collections* (Madison), IX (1909 reprint), 213–20.

[54] Taylor to General Howard, September 6, 1814, in *Niles' Weekly Register*, VII (1814–1815), Supplement, 137–38.

and did not mention his own presence thereon, but John Shaw who accompanied the expedition to furnish supplies under contract insisted many years later that "the first cannon ball from the British battery passed through Taylor's boat." It may have been Hempstead's boat in the sense that he was in command of it, but, insisted Shaw, the boat hit was the *Commodore* on which Taylor himself was located.[55]

As soon as the British artillery opened fire, the Indians "raised the yell," reported Taylor, "and commenced firing on us in every direction, whether they were able to do us any damage or not, from each side of the river."

Capt. Rector, who was laying to the shore of the island, was attacked the instant the first gun was fired, by a very large party, and in a close and well contested contest, of about fifteen minutes, they drove them, after giving three rounds of grape from his three pounder. Capt. Whitesides, who was nearest to capt. Rector dropped down and anchored nigh him, and gave the enemy several fires with his swivel; but the wind was so hard down stream as to drift his anchor. Capt. Rector at that moment got his boat off, and we were then exposed to the fire of the indians for two miles, which we returned with interest from our small arms, and small pieces of artillery, whenever we could get them to bear.[56]

Taylor dropped down the river about three miles before a proper landing place was found. There the expedition halted while the wounded were cared for and the boats, damaged by the British artillery, were repaired. Soon the pursuing red men appeared, but when Taylor's troops prepared for action the Indians "returned in as great a hurry as they followed us."

After consultation with his officers who were of the opinion that the enemy outnumbered their own force at least

[55] Col. John Shaw, "Shaw's Narrative," in *Wisconsin Historical Collections,* II (1903 reprint), 220–22.

[56] Taylor to Howard, September 6, 1814, *loc. cit.*

three to one and that "it was not practicable to effect" the destruction of the Indian villages and corn, Major Taylor concluded that it would have been "madness" in him as well as a "direct violation" of his orders to have "risked the detachment without a prospect of success." He then determined to drop down to the Des Moines River and execute the principal object of the expedition, the erection of a fort to control the river route. High on the bank above the river, on the site of present-day Warsaw, Illinois, Taylor and his men rapidly constructed Fort Johnson. But this part of Taylor's expedition was doomed to failure also. When the fort was almost completed Taylor placed Captain James Callaway in command of the garrison and returned with the main body of troops to St. Louis. Three weeks later Taylor was shocked by the arrival in St. Louis of Callaway and the garrison. Provisions had not arrived as promised, Callaway declared, and consequently he had burned and evacuated Fort Johnson—the fort which Taylor and his men had labored so vigorously to build but a short time before.[57] Such action is difficult to explain. On September 25, shortly after taking command of the fort, Callaway wrote to his wife that he had provisions for ten days only and that Taylor had assured him that unless provisions reached the fort by the last of that month it would be evacuated.[58] Yet nearly a month later when the garrison arrived in St. Louis, Taylor insisted that provisions would have reached them in time and that there was no need for the evacuation.[59] Taylor knew what provisions were on hand when he left Fort Johnson for St. Louis and failure on his part to send supplies in time to hold the fort seems out of the question. If there was need for such a fort in August when the expedition started up the river to

[57] Wesley, "James Callaway in the War of 1812," *loc. cit.*, 71; Taylor to Howard, September 6, 1814, *loc. cit.;* Autobiographical Fragment; Gregg, "The War of 1812 on the Missouri Frontier," *loc. cit.*, 337.

[58] Wesley, "James Callaway in the War of 1812," *loc. cit.*, 71.

[59] Gregg, "The War of 1812 on the Missouri Frontier," *loc. cit.*, 337.

build it, surely after Taylor's experience with the British and the Indians at Rock River there was even greater need for it.

On the death of General Howard in September, Colonel William Russell of the Seventh Infantry hurried west from Vincennes to take command of the troops at St. Louis. Soon after his arrival he led an expedition two or three hundred miles up the Missouri River to protect a small settlement that was threatened by the Indians. Taylor, fresh from his Rock River trip, was a member of this new expedition.[60] Upon his return from this enterprise he was ordered to Vincennes to take command of the troops in that territory. There he remained, except for a brief furlough in Kentucky, until several months after the termination of hostilities.[61]

The armed forces of the United States had met with little success in their attempt to bring Great Britain to her knees. Their efforts to invade Canada had all been repulsed while the British had captured Washington, D. C., and forced the government to fly for safety. In the Northwest, to be sure, the early disasters had been somewhat redeemed. Following Commodore Oliver H. Perry's victories on Lake Erie, General Harrison moved his army across the lake and in October, 1813, defeated the British and their Indian allies at the Battle of the Thames in which the great Indian chief Tecumseh was killed. His death and the recapture of Detroit shortly thereafter gave the American forces the upper hand in the Northwest. The Indians of the Indiana, Illinois, Michigan, and Wisconsin region remained on the warpath until the close of the war, but the crisis in this section passed with the victories of the fall of 1813. The inconclusive nature of the war is clearly

[60] Thomas Posey to Secretary of War James Monroe, November 12, 1814, in Esarey, *Messages and Letters of William Henry Harrison,* II, 665; Autobiographical Fragment.

[61] Autobiographical Fragment; Alexander Stuart to the Secretary of War, December 3, 1814, in War Department Archives.

mirrored in the Treaty of Peace signed at Ghent, December 24, 1814. Silent as to the controversies that produced the war, the treaty provided for little more than the restoration of peace with the same status that existed on the eve of the conflict.

On January 2, 1815, just a week after peace had been concluded, but before that fact was known in Washington, the War Department informed Taylor that he had been promoted to the rank of major and assigned to the Twenty-sixth Infantry Regiment on the northeastern frontier.[62] This was indeed welcome news to the young officer, now thirty years of age, who had become dissatisfied with his slow progress up the military ladder. He had been brevetted major more than two years before for his heroic defense of Fort Harrison, but his lineal rank was still that of captain of the Seventh Infantry. He had witnessed the rapid promotion of others including his youthful Kentucky neighbor George Croghan who entered the army in 1812 as a captain and by early 1814 was a lieutenant colonel.[63] Always there was the case of the remarkable advancement of Winfield Scott who was commissioned a captain in 1808 at the same time Taylor's military career commenced and who by the close of 1814 was a brigadier general.[64] So dissatisfied was Taylor by the middle of 1814 that he talked of resigning and possibly went so far as to present his resignation to his commanding officer.[65] He seems to have enlisted the support of his congressman, for on October 21, Stephen Ormsby, an old Indian fighter from Taylor's home county who was serving in Congress, wrote to the Secretary of War, "Major Zachy. Taylor, the son of Colo. Richd. Taylor of Kentucky, who Gallantly defended Fort Harrison, complains, that he has been neglected & overlooked, while

[62] Adjutant General to Major Z. Taylor, January 2, 1815, in War Department Archives.

[63] Heitman, *Historical Register*, I, 339.

[64] *Ibid.*, 870.

[65] Alexander Stuart to the Secretary of War, December 3, 1814, *loc. cit.*

his junior officers have been promoted." The congressman characterized Taylor's "connections" as "numerous and respectable, as well as warm supporters of the Govt." and he recommended Taylor as a meritorious officer worthy of promotion.[66]

A few weeks later Alexander Stuart, who with Taylor had just returned from the expedition up the Missouri River with Colonel Russell, wrote to the War Department that Taylor was "a most valuable officer" with a "highly respectable" family who had had "the mortification to witness the promotion of several officers of inferior grade to majorities." [67]

Taylor himself apparently wrote to the department concerning his treatment and inquired whether it was due to complaints made by Colonel W. P. Anderson who for several months had been objecting to certain orders issued by Taylor which he claimed interfered with the recruiting service.[68] Taylor's letter is missing from the files but the answer from the Adjutant General acknowledged a letter of November 29 and continued:

No complaints have been made against you from any quarter which can affect your good reputation with the War Department. Col. Anderson has been directed by the Secretary of War, to march with his Regt. down the Mississippi & you are promoted to the 26th Regt. on the northern frontier. You will therefore repair to this place for further orders. I fear you have been under a mistake, relative to promotions—you have never been superceded [*sic*]. Brevoort & Baker were appointed to places which might have been filled by citizens or subalterns—those were original vacancies.[69]

[66] Stephen Ormsby to the Secretary of War, October 21, 1814, in War Department Archives; *Biographical Directory of the American Congress, 1774–1927* (Washington, 1928), 1372.

[67] Alexander Stuart to the Secretary of War, December 3, 1814, *loc. cit.*

[68] Col. W. P. Anderson to the Secretary of War, May 19, 1814, in War Department Archives; *id.* to *id.*, September 10, 1814, *ibid.*

[69] Adjutant General to Taylor, January 2, 1815, *ibid.*

Because Taylor's commission provided that his appointment as major was to date from May 15, 1814, it is frequently stated that he was promoted at that time. Actually, however, the appointment was not made until early 1815. In January he was informed of his promotion and his commission was formally issued under date of February 1.[70] Thus as the war closed Zachary Taylor's thoughts of resignation were swept away by a well-merited promotion. His satisfaction, however, was of short duration, for when in May the army was reduced to a peace footing he was selected for retention with the rank of captain. The army which had been increased to nine thousand men when Taylor was commissioned in 1808 had been augmented to over fifty thousand by the end of the war. With peace restored Congress promptly acted to reduce the army to ten thousand. The board of six generals appointed to aid in organizing the army in accordance with the act of Congress found its most difficult task to be the selection of the officers to be retained. Only 39 of the 216 field officers could be kept and all but 450 of the 2,055 regimental officers had to be dropped.[71] This difficult problem the board attempted to solve in part by retaining certain officers in ranks below those they had attained during the war. When Taylor, who was in Washington, learned that the board was preparing to recommend his retention with the rank of captain he joined Colonel Thomas D. Owings, also of Kentucky, in a letter of protest which President Madison had at hand as he reviewed the board's decisions. As Owings had entered the army only two years before, Madison saw no justification for his dissatisfaction. Taylor's case, however, he viewed in a different light and he wrote to A. J. Dallas, the acting Secretary of War, who was in charge of the entire reorganization, that unless there were

[70] Adjutant General to the author, July 22, 1941.

[71] *Niles' Weekly Register,* VIII (1815), 222–23; *American State Papers: Military Affairs,* I, 635.

flaws in Taylor's character that had not come to his knowledge he did not believe "that a continuance of him in his present rank would have warranted just complaint in others." President Madison reminded Secretary Dallas that Taylor had been a captain at the commencement of the war and was the first officer to be brevetted during that conflict. "The defence of Fort Harrison, that led to it," he wrote, "though on an obscure theater, has probably not been exceeded in brilliancy by any affair that has occurred. The circumstances of it put to the severest trial the military qualities of the commanding officer, and it appeared that the result was conspicuously favorable to him." This high praise the President followed with the frank admission that only the haste with which subsequent appointments were made prevented Taylor from attaining a higher rank.[72]

As it was the President's responsibility to make the final decisions in the reorganization he might well have insisted that Taylor be retained in the rank of major, but instead he clearly stated that he was not "pressing a revision of the selections, unless a change can be conveniently and satisfactorily made." A few days later, however, when informed that Colonel George Croghan had resigned, Madison wrote from Montpelier that this might open the way for a higher rank for Taylor.[73] Before this proposal reached Washington the board had completed its work and the new Army Register listing Taylor as captain had already been printed. Dallas declined to make the suggested adjustment.[74] Taylor, who had talked of resigning a few months before because he had not been promoted, had no intention of remaining in the army with his old rank of captain. He promptly resigned and returned to civil

[72] James Madison to A. J. Dallas, Acting Secretary of War, May 10, 1815, in George Mifflin Dallas, *Life and Writings of Alexander James Dallas* (Philadelphia, 1871), 412.

[73] *Id.* to *id.*, May 19, 1815, *ibid.*, 421–22.

[74] A. J. Dallas to James Madison, May 21, 1815, *ibid.*, 423.

life.[75] His brother, Joseph Pannel Taylor, who entered the army as a third lieutenant during the war and was commissioned first lieutenant in 1814, was among those honorably discharged when the army was reduced.[76] So Zachary and his brother, in spite of the fact that their cousin was in the White House, found themselves out of the service.

[75] Taylor to the Secretary of War, June 9, 1815. The letter is missing from the War Department files, but the substance of the letter is endorsed on the envelope which is available.

[76] Heitman, *Historical Register,* I, 947.

Chapter III

FRONTIER DUTY

SOMEWHERE in the Louisville area Zachary Taylor established his family in a "Cabin" and commenced growing corn and tobacco. His family at this time included in addition to Mrs. Taylor two daughters—Ann Mackall who was now four years old and Sarah Knox who was one. Near by lived his father and mother and several of his brothers and sisters, most of whom were younger than he and still at home on their father's plantation. After his years away from family and friends it must have been a pleasant change for Taylor to be again in their midst and to be engaged in agriculture, an occupation which had a strong attraction for him all through life. He had some longing for the Mississippi country but was happy to be in civilian life. "I can assure [you]," he wrote to his distant kinsman Major Taylor Berry in St. Louis, "I do not regreat [*sic*] the change of calling or the course I have pursued." [1]

Less than a month after Taylor had declared he had no regret over his decision to give up his military career he was given an opportunity to return to the army. In the spring of 1816 there were two vacancies in the rank of major in the infantry regiments, and one of these, that in the Third Regiment, was filled by the appointment of Taylor. At the same time Joseph P. Taylor was reinstated as a second lieutenant in the artillery.[2] There is no evidence

1 Taylor to Major Taylor Berry, April 25, 1816, in Missouri Historical Society.

2 *Niles' Weekly Register,* X (1816), 352.

that either sought the appointment, but it would be strange if it came entirely unsolicited. Once again James Taylor wrote to the President, shortly after the appointments were made, and spoke highly of Zachary and his brother.[3] Moreover, Joseph, who was dissatisfied with his appointment because it carried with it a reduction in rank, hastened to Washington while his father appealed to Madison in his behalf.[4] Joseph's efforts were in vain but he did not reject his commission.

What influences led Zachary to leave his family and friends and return to the army and its frontier life are not known. Certainly they were not financial, for the pay of a major in the United States Army at this time was $50 per month and his allowances. These latter included four rations per day at twenty cents per ration, forage for three horses at $8.00 per month for each horse, quarters of one room and one kitchen, one waiter who was allowed one ration, and transportation for five hundred pounds of baggage when ordered to distant posts.[5] Regardless of whether Taylor sought the appointment and regardless of the influences that guided him, he accepted the appointment and again took up the army life that was to be his for the next thirty-three years—until he resigned to accept the office of President of the United States.

In the summer of 1816 when Taylor resumed his military career Mrs. Taylor was expecting another child and was in no condition to travel. So, leaving his family in Louisville, Major Taylor headed for Detroit where Major General Alexander Macomb commanded the Fifth Military Department in which the Third Infantry were serving.[6] Still farther north he went, to Fort Mackinac on the

[3] James Taylor to James Madison, July 10, 1816, in *Register of the Kentucky State Historical Society,* XXXIV, 325.

[4] Richard Taylor to *id.,* July 23, 1816, *ibid.,* XXXVI, 338.

[5] *American State Papers: Military Affairs,* I, 800–802.

[6] Taylor to Major General Macomb, August 15, 1816, in War Department Archives.

straits between Lake Huron and Lake Michigan and then on to Fort Howard at the head of Green Bay where, after a stormy voyage, he arrived at the end of November as the winter ice was closing in.[7] Fort Howard had just been established. It was early August when Colonel John Miller arrived with an expedition five hundred strong from Fort Mackinac to construct a fort at Green Bay. About one mile above the mouth of the Fox River on the site where the old French fort had stood, the engineers laid out the new one. By the time Taylor arrived, the construction was well under way and quarters that would at least give shelter from the winter blasts were available.[8]

Fort Howard, which was to be Taylor's post for two years, was established as part of the design of the United States government to assert control over the Indians and fur trade of the Northwest. At the close of the War of 1812 the Indians were distinctly pro-British and anti-American in sentiment and for many years they continued to make annual trips to consult their "British Father" in Canada. As soon as peace was made, the United States reoccupied and strengthened the old forts at Mackinac and Chicago —forts that had been in British or Indian hands during most of the war. In 1816 new forts were established at Green Bay and at Prairie du Chien and three years later Fort Snelling was established near the Falls of St. Anthony on the upper Mississippi.[9] Before Colonel Miller left Mackinac to erect the fort at Green Bay he heard reports that the Indians who had just returned from a visit to Canada, especially the Winnebagos who lived at Stinking Lake some sixty miles up the Fox River, were preparing to op-

[7] *Wisconsin Historical Collections,* X (1909 reprint), 133–34.

[8] Colonel John Miller to Brigadier General D. Parker, August 22, 1816, in *Mississippi Valley Historical Review* (Cedar Rapids), XIII (1926–1927), 550–53; James W. Biddle, "Recollections of Green Bay in 1816–17," *Wisconsin Historical Collections,* I (1903 reprint), 51.

[9] *Wisconsin Historical Collections,* XX (1911), xii–xiii.

pose the building of the fort. Therefore he took with him as large a detachment of troops as could be spared from Mackinac and succeeded in discouraging the Indians from making any opposition.[10]

Fort Howard was located on the west bank of the river, a little nearer the mouth than the settlement known as Green Bay. The settlement consisted of some forty or fifty families and extended along both banks of the river for several miles above the fort. The settlers were mainly French-Canadian boatmen who had withdrawn from the employment of the fur companies and had taken Indian or half-breed wives. As the soil was fertile small grains and vegetables were easily produced.[11] The garrison and the inhabitants could also find a generous food supply in the fish, particularly the sturgeon, which abounded in these waters, and in the myriads of waterfowl that were attracted in the spring and fall by the wild rice that grew near the mouths of all the streams emptying into the Bay.[12]

When Zachary Taylor arrived at Fort Howard late in 1816, it was garrisoned by some three hundred men under the command of Lieutenant Colonel Talbot Chambers of the Rifle Regiment who was left in command when Colonel Miller returned to Mackinac soon after construction commenced. Under his supervision building operations proceeded throughout the winter. When spring came, Chambers and the companies of the Rifle Regiment were transferred to the new fort at Prairie du Chien and Major Taylor took command at Fort Howard. At the close of the year the garrison numbered 224 men, all from the Third In-

[10] Colonel John Miller to Brigadier General D. Parker, August 22, 1816, *loc. cit.*

[11] *Ibid.;* Biddle, "Recollections," *loc. cit.,* 52; *Wisconsin Historical Collections,* X, 136–38, XIX (1910), 436–39.

[12] Albert G. Ellis, "Fifty-Four Years' Recollections of Men and Events in Wisconsin," in *Wisconsin Historical Collections,* VII (1908 reprint), 265; *Wisconsin Historical Collections,* XIII (1895), 441–44.

fantry, and by late in 1818 the garrison had been reduced to 174.[13] So with a dozen officers, some two hundred men, and the French and half-breed population of the town, Taylor carried on for two years on the northern frontier.

What little evidence remains concerning Taylor's activities and life at Fort Howard does not reveal a very happy existence. In August, 1817, he was complaining that the command at Mackinac where the regimental headquarters were located had fallen to Captain Pierce and that he could not be expected to make his returns through a junior officer.[14] In October he was writing to his friend Thomas S. Jesup who had been appointed Lieutenant Colonel of the Third Infantry in the spring, but had not yet joined the regiment, that the regiment was "in the greatest confusion for want of a head." [15] Colonel Miller, the commanding officer of the regiment, had been absent on furlough for many months. Indeed, he was to remain absent until his resignation from the army in the following February. As he was the senior officer of the regiment with the troops, Taylor endeavored to have the regimental staff transferred from Mackinac to Fort Howard, but without success. He felt, therefore, that he had been deprived of the command of the regiment which was rightfully his. He also informed Jesup that Colonel John McNeil, who had until recently been in command at Mackinac, had used "vulgar and blackguard epithets" concerning him and that he had tried in vain to get the commandant of the department to appoint a court of inquiry. "I expect," he wrote, "to be compeled [*sic*] to appeal to higher authority." Finally he requested Jesup, who was in Washington, to see if he could arrange a transfer to a regiment assigned to the

[13] *American State Papers: Military Affairs,* I, 671, 788.

[14] Taylor to the Assistant Adjutant General, Detroit, August 14, 1817, in War Department Archives.

[15] *Id.* to Thomas S. Jesup, October 25, 1817, in Taylor Papers.

Southern Division, for he wished to go south as well as to "get clear" of his present department.[16]

So keenly did Taylor resent the conduct of McNeil that he contemplated making a personal affair of it and meeting him on the field of honor. But the distance that separated the two men and the passage of time held the controversy in check. By the spring of 1818 McNeil had left the Fifth Department and Taylor, acting on the advice of Jesup, decided to drop the matter at least for the time being.[17]

Winter cut off Fort Howard from water communication with the East before adequate food supplies had been received. In January, Taylor informed Major General Macomb, the commanding general of his department, "that unless considerable exertions are made to forward a supply of provisions early in the Spring, the Troops here must suffer very much—I have had an inventory taken of all on hand, and find a deficiency of six or eight thousand rations of meat, calculating to the 15th of May next, by which time a vessel may reach here from Detroit, should the Spring be favorable, and proper exertions made." [18] As an army ration at this time still consisted of eighteen ounces of bread or flour, one and a quarter pounds of beef or three-fourths pound of pork, and one gill of rum, brandy, or whiskey,[19] the shortage of meat was a serious one. The situation was made far worse a few weeks later when the spirituous liquor ran out and it was discovered that the traders in the community could supply but a small quantity and that little at such high prices that Taylor and the company commanders decided not to purchase it. All went well for a few weeks without the ration of whiskey; then Taylor discovered that Lieutenant Collin McLeod was much dissatisfied and "was carrying his dissatisfaction to such lengths

[16] *Ibid.; id.* to *id.*, no date, but approximately July, 1818, *ibid.*

[17] *Ibid.*

[18] Taylor to Major P. Willis, Assistant Adjutant General, January 17, 1818, in War Department Archives.

[19] *American State Papers: Military Affairs*, I, 781.

as was calculated to excite mutiny among the Troops if not put a stop to." Taylor did put a stop to it. McLeod was arrested and charges were filed against him. McLeod in turn joined Lieutenant Turbey F. Thomas, the regimental quartermaster, in preferring charges against Taylor for not ordering the purchase of such whiskey as was available in the community. "I hope the General will act on them," wrote Taylor, "I court investigation." [20] Taylor apparently won in this conflict of personalities, for by the end of the year both McLeod and Thomas had resigned from the army.[21]

Early in September Taylor returned to Louisville on furlough. Permission for this had arrived in June but he had postponed taking advantage of it until the difficulties with his officers had been fairly well adjusted.[22] At the expiration of his furlough Zachary did not return to the isolated post at Green Bay but remained for fifteen months in Louisville in charge of recruiting for the Third Regiment. No longer the crude frontier village that Taylor had known as a boy, this thriving town had seven or eight thousand inhabitants and boasted paved streets, a hospital, churches, banks, and a few manufacturing establishments. Steamers regularly plied between New Orleans and Louisville, but as the canal around the Falls had not yet been constructed they could not go on to Pittsburgh. Thus Louisville was still a transfer point for river traffic. After two years at such a distant outpost as Fort Howard, Taylor doubtless welcomed a tour of duty in his home town. His limited official correspondence of this period reveals that his chief problem was money. He frequently reported the inadequacy of the funds placed at his disposal and on one

[20] Taylor to Major P. Willis, February 24, 1818, in War Department Archives.

[21] Heitman, *Historical Register,* I, 676, 955.

[22] Taylor to Jesup, no date, but approximately July, 1818, in Taylor Papers.

occasion suggested that if the department lacked confidence in him he would be glad to rejoin his regiment and let someone else take charge of the recruiting service.[23] He also had some difficulty with intemperate young officers who were assigned to duty under him. He reported to the Adjutant General that their behavior lessened the respectability of the profession with the citizens and he urged that no officer be assigned to the recruiting service whose morals or deportment were questionable.[24]

The routine of the recruiting service was interrupted in the summer of 1819 when President James Monroe visited Kentucky and Taylor joined his party. A glimpse of the President's party in Frankfort, the state capital, is given in a letter of Mrs. John Brown, whose husband was one of Frankfort's most prominent citizens and a former United States senator. She wrote to her son, a student at Princeton at the time:

The President, *James Monroe* has arrived and departed. He was received with due public honors, as the papers will inform you. Yesterday morning he breakfasted with us, in company with General Jackson and that hero whose cool, determined and successful courage has never been rivalled in ancient or modern times, who so bravely defended Fort Harrison, Maj. Zachary Taylor. They spent the last evening at Mr. Bibb's, breakfasted this morning at the Governor's and are now on their way to Colonel Richard M. Johnson's where they will dine today, your father and uncle James Brown will accompany them. Your father presided at the public dinner, and has been much distinguished by the President.[25]

Another event that doubtless was of interest to Taylor during these months in Kentucky was the marriage of his

[23] *Id.* to the Adjutant General, October 27, December 10, 1818, January 18, May 7, July 14, 1819, in War Department Archives.

[24] *Id.* to *id.*, April 14, 1819, in War Department Archives.

[25] Mrs. John Brown to Orlando Brown, July 1, 1819, in Alice E. Trabue, *A Corner in Celebrities* (Louisville, 1922), 63.

sister Sarah Bailey Taylor to French S. Gray in September, 1819.[26]

From Taylor's point of view the most important event of 1819 was his promotion to the rank of lieutenant colonel on April 20 with assignment to the Fourth Infantry.[27] Even though the promotion carried with it only a slight increase in salary, from $50 to $60 per month with one additional ration allowance, it was nonetheless welcome. The knowledge that his services were recognized by his superior officers and the fact that he had taken another step up the military ladder gave him satisfaction.

Although no longer attached to the Third Infantry, Taylor remained for several months in charge of recruiting for his old regiment. Indeed it was the end of the year before his work in that service was completed and he was ready to join his new regiment.[28] By that time he had agreed to a transfer to the Eighth Infantry to accommodate Lieutenant Colonel George M. Brooke who was eager to return to his former regiment. Both regiments were on duty in the Florida and Alabama section in military departments commanded by Major General Edmund P. Gaines, and Taylor had no preference between them. His stay in Kentucky was further prolonged by the ice that clogged the river and prevented navigation until March. But with the coming of spring and the opening of navigation, Taylor headed down the river for New Orleans and the Eighth Infantry—for a country which he had come to know and to like ten years before.[29]

This time Taylor did not leave his family behind. When he went south he was accompanied by Mrs. Taylor and

[26] Copy of the Marriage Records of Jefferson County, Kentucky, II, 692, in Kentucky State Historical Society.

[27] Heitman, *Historical Register,* I, 949.

[28] Adjutant General to Taylor, September 1, November 12, 1819, in War Department Archives.

[29] Taylor to Brooke, June 18, 1819, *ibid.;* Brooke to the Adjutant General, August 23, 1819, *ibid.;* Taylor to Colonel James Johnson, January 23, 1820, in Kentucky Historical Society.

their four daughters—for to Ann and Knox had been added Octavia and Margaret. Indeed, when Taylor left Kentucky in the spring of 1820, it was with the thought of possibly making his permanent home somewhere in the lower Mississippi Valley.[30] His attitude toward portions of the country a few months after he had joined his new regiment he gave in a letter to Colonel Jesup, to whom he wrote:

> You request my opinion of the relative advantages of Louisiana, Alabama & Missouri, were I a man unencumbered with a family I would prefer the first as a political man, or planter, the sugar lands on the bank of the Mississippi in the vicinity of New Orleans, offer the gratest [*sic*] certainty of wealth to the cultivator of the soil, the only objection to them, is the capital that a man must posess [*sic*] to commence with, as a sugar planter, and the climate will prevent the country from being overrun with professional characters, which will be the case with Missouri. The products of the latter, which must be provisions, will never be in demand, unless there should be another thirty years war in Europe, which will hardly be the case in our time, unless another Bonapart should make his appearance on the stage. With Alabama I am not acquainted, but from what I have learnt, it offers every advantage to professional men they can wish, much greater I expect than Missouri, which alone has the advantage of the others of climate, which is a very considerable recommendation. But should you determine on abandoning the profession of arms, (which will hardly be the case [)], and turn your attention to politics & the bar, you cannot fail in either the above mentioned States, acquireing [*sic*] both fortune & distinction, the former much more rapidly in the two first.[31]

Taylor's plan of taking up his residence in the South was dealt a severe blow by the effect of the climate on the health of his family. As they descended the Mississippi, Taylor left his wife and daughters with Mrs. Taylor's sister

[30] Taylor to Jesup, April 20, 1820, in Taylor Papers.
[31] *Id.* to *id.*, December 15, 1820, *ibid.*

at Bayou Sara, just above Baton Rouge. During the summer they were all seriously ill. The two youngest girls died and at one time Zachary gave up all hope for the recovery of his wife. Fortunately his worst fears did not materialize, but Mrs. Taylor's delicate constitution was further weakened by this illness.[32] This experience, wrote Taylor in December, had almost deterred him from even thinking of settling in the Deep South and he added that when he "quit the army" it was more than likely that he would return to Kentucky.[33] When he "quit the army"—Taylor frequently talked of quitting the army and establishing himself as a planter. He did eventually acquire the plantation but he was never able to forsake the military life. In spite of its privations and hardships, it had a fascination for him and he remained with it.

Late in March, Taylor took command of about 460 men of the Eighth Regiment, mainly recent recruits lacking in discipline and organization, who were engaged in building the military road, or Jackson Road as it was called, which ran northeast from Madisonville on Lake Pontchartrain for some two hundred miles to Columbus. There it joined another road that led to Florence, Alabama, on the Tennessee River and on to Nashville. About 120 miles of the road had been completed and Taylor found the troops just on the edge of the territory of the Choctaw Nation through which the remainder of the road had to be built. Everything was in great confusion and work practically at a standstill. The troops, according to Taylor, were on half rations of bread and in a state of starvation. The surrounding country offered nothing except beef of the poorest quality. Moreover, the quartermaster was without funds and the credit of the government was nearly gone. Supplies had to come from New Orleans by way of the Pearl River and then nearly one hundred miles up the road they were

[32] *Id.* to *id.*, September 18, December 15, 1820, *ibid.*
[33] *Ibid.*

building. Taylor's first task was to get provisions for his men which he did as rapidly as possible.[34] He also found that because it was a busy time of year on the plantations the cost of hiring horses, oxen, and wagons to haul their provisions was exceedingly high. Moreover, the muddy condition of the road compelled the wagons to carry light loads, thus adding to the cost of transportation. So enormous did Taylor consider the expense of provisioning the army that he determined upon the utmost speed in finishing the road.[35] "With great exertions on the part of every officer, and after submitting to every privation that it was possible for men to undergo," to quote Taylor, he finished the road by the middle of June.[36] The estimated total cost of the completed project was $300,000, a large sum for road construction in that day. As it provided a route from New Orleans to Nashville some two hundred miles shorter than the old one through Natchez, it was, in spite of the cost, a worth-while enterprise.[37]

Upon the completion of the road, Taylor withdrew the troops to Bay St. Louis on the Gulf Coast of Mississippi which remained his headquarters for over a year. Here he was joined late in 1820 by Mrs. Taylor and the girls, all of them much improved in health now that the summer weather was past, but still feeling the effects of their illness. Here Taylor spent his time supervising the construction of quarters, drilling his troops, most of whom had spent all of their enlisted time on road work and were ignorant of drill regulations, and in the routine administrative duties of his regiment.[38] Little progress had been made in drill practice when two companies were ordered to Baton Rouge, Louisiana, to aid in the erection of barracks. This

[34] *Id.* to *id.*, April 20, 1820, *ibid.*

[35] *Ibid.*

[36] *Id.* to *id.*, September 18, 1820, *ibid.*

[37] William A. Love, "General Jackson's Military Road," in *Mississippi Historical Society Publications* (University), XI (1910), 409–10.

[38] *Ibid.;* Taylor to Jesup, December 15, 1820, in Taylor Papers.

interference with drill caused Taylor to complain that the government had such a passion for making roads and building barracks with army labor that the axe, pick, saw, and trowel had well-nigh supplanted the cannon, musket, and sword as the implements of the American soldier and that men who would make good overseers or Negro drivers were better qualified to serve as officers than were those who had received a first-rate military education.[39]

It was in the summer of 1821 while stationed at Bay St. Louis that Lieutenant Colonel Taylor was again faced, though only temporarily, with the choice of remaining in the service with reduced rank or of retiring to civil life. The hard times following the financial crisis of 1819 led Congress to look for ways of decreasing governmental expenses. One means determined upon was the reduction of the army. After much debate and long consideration, Congress, by act of March 2, 1821, decreed a reorganization and reduction of the army. One regiment of infantry, one of artillery, and one of riflemen were done away with. The Ordnance Department, as such, was abolished, and a few of its men and all of its work were assigned to the artillery. The act also provided for the elimination of one major general, two brigadier generals, and numerous subordinate officers.[40]

As in 1815, it was necessary to discharge many worthy officers and to reduce the rank of some who were retained. In the early stages of the work of the board of general officers charged with carrying out the act it was planned to include Taylor with the officers disbanded, but his longtime friend Brigadier General Thomas S. Jesup, who was on duty in Washington as Quartermaster General, got wind of the plan and intervened in his behalf.[41] When in May the General Order organizing the regiments and com-

[39] *Id.* to *id.*, September 18, 1820, *ibid.*
[40] *United States Statutes at Large*, III, 615–16.
[41] Taylor to Jesup, June 18, 1821, in Taylor Papers.

mands in accordance with the act of March 2 appeared, Taylor was assigned to be lieutenant colonel of the First Infantry with the provision, however, that if Brigadier General Henry Atkinson should choose to take a regiment of infantry instead of the office of Adjutant General various readjustments would be necessary and Taylor would become major of the Seventh Infantry.[42]

The discharges and reductions in rank, the innumerable shiftings in assignment involved in the consolidation of regiments, and the whole reorganization produced widespread dissatisfaction and charges of favoritism. One of the most dissatisfied officers was Zachary Taylor, who gave vent to his aroused feelings in two letters to General Jesup. As soon as the General Order reached him, Taylor wrote denouncing certain of the appointments as the greatest outrage on the rights and feelings of the junior officers of the army, with one exception, since the establishment of the nation. He requested Jesup to state unequivocally to the Secretary of War "that if I cannot be retained with my present rank, that it is my wish to be placed on the list of disbanded officers." [43] Three days later his blood was up to the boiling point and he wrote that he was not surprised at the course pursued in 1815 when "Mr. Madison a man perfectly callous, & unacquainted with the noble feelings of a soldier, was then at the head of the nation, [and] Mr. Dallas a lawyer grown grey in iniquity & chicanery, whose profession was to pervert right" was Secretary of War, "but that the late illegal, & outrageous acts of the present board, should be tolerated, or even countenanced while Mr. Monroe was the chief magistrate of the Nation, & Mr. Calhoun at the head of the War Dept. is to be lamented, by every independent man, who loves his country, & venerates its institutions." [44]

[42] *Niles' Weekly Register,* XX (1821), 196–201.
[43] Taylor to Jesup, June 15, 1821, in Taylor Papers.
[44] *Id.* to *id.,* June 18, 1821, *ibid.*

Taylor was especially bitter at the favoritism shown the artillery officers, many of whom he regarded as better qualified to superintend a garden or a cabinet workshop. Most of them, he said, managed to get their headquarters located at or near their permanent residences and gave so little time to the affairs of the army that their appointments were viewed by many citizens and officers as sinecures. In contrast, "ever since 1816, the time I was reinstated in the Army," he wrote, "I have been constantly on duty, & about four years of which time with the 3d. & 8th. Regts, the first at Greenbay, the latter in this country, during which time there was not a days duty done, by any other field officer in either of those Regts." [45]

Taylor believed both Congress and the executive were hostile to the army and was certain "that republicks are not congenial to the growth, or prosperity of military men." He assured Jesup that if his private affairs were not in some measure embarrassed he "would not remain in the army another moment on any terms," and that he thoroughly agreed that they ought to use "every honorable means" in their power to place themselves in a situation which would make it possible "to retire to civil life with dignity, when ever it is the will of the nation for us to do so, or when we cannot remain in service, with honor." [46]

It was more than a year before the storm aroused by this reorganization blew over and the army was able to settle down to work. In the end Taylor remained in the army with his rank of lieutenant colonel. Atkinson did choose to take command of a regiment, but certain resignations and the refusal of the Senate to confirm the appointment of Nathan Towson to be colonel of the Second Regiment of artillery—one of the appointments that so outraged Taylor—made it unnecessary to reduce Taylor to a majority.[47] From the First Infantry, to which he was assigned

[45] *Ibid.* [46] *Ibid.*

[47] *Niles' Weekly Register,* XXI (1821–1822), 9, XXII (1822), 406–23.

at the time of the reorganization, he was soon transferred to the Seventh and then on January 1, 1822, back to the First, which regiment he served as lieutenant colonel for ten years and as colonel for another ten years.[48]

The years 1822 and 1823 Taylor spent in Louisiana. During the former year he was in command of the troops engaged in building a new fort in the western part of the state, its name, "Cantonment Jesup," later "Fort Jesup," doubtless reflecting the friendship of Taylor for the Quartermaster General.[49] Cantonment Jesup, located just east of the Sabine River, which the recent treaty with Spain had named the boundary between the United States and Mexico, was on the edge of the Indian country and was designed, as were all the Western posts of this day, to control the Indians along the frontier and to give protection to the advancing settlements. War between the Cherokee and Osage tribes during the summer of 1821 had increased the need for protection along the frontier and had led General Gaines in July to order Colonel Matthew Arbuckle to hold the Seventh Infantry in readiness to occupy the Southwest frontier. This was the regiment that Taylor joined in August and he led a portion of the regiment up the Red River to Natchitoches while Arbuckle and the remainder ascended the Arkansas to Fort Smith.[50] Taylor spent the winter months at Fort Selden just above Natchitoches on the Red River.[51]

The selection of the site for the new post General Gaines reported to the Adjutant General in Washington in March, 1822, to whom he wrote:

[48] Heitman, *Historical Register,* I, 949.

[49] Fort Jesup Monthly Post Returns, May–November, 1822, in War Department Archives.

[50] Grant Foreman, *Indians and Pioneers: The Story of the American Southwest before 1830* (Norman, 1936), 113; E. P. Gaines to M. Arbuckle, July 14, 1821, in Headquarters, Western Department, Letter Book No. 97, War Department Archives.

[51] Taylor to the Adjutant General, January 6, 1822, in War Department Archives; J. Fair Hardin, "Four Forgotten Frontier Army Posts of Western Louisiana," in *Louisiana Historical Quarterly* (New Orleans), XVI (1933), 9.

After making due inquiry and examination of the country between this place and the Sabine River, through Lt. Col. Taylor, as well as by personal observation, I have selected a site for cantoning the troops in this quarter, which promises the advantages of health, combined with convenience of position for the protection of the settlements upon this frontier.

The site selected is about 25 miles south-southwest from this place, upon the ridge which divides the waters of the Sabine from those of the Red River, and near the road leading from Natchitoches to the principal settlements in Texas; and not more than 18 miles upon a direct line from the Sabine River; having a constant running spring of good water (a thing seldom to be found in this country) with a dry, airy ridge, and sufficient space of public land with excellent timber, for every purpose of building and fuel for an army of twenty thousand men.[52]

General Gaines soon left the Red River for Fort Smith, Arkansas, and Louisville, Kentucky. Before his departure he issued the following special order placing Taylor in charge of the new post.

Lt. Col. Taylor, with the troops under his command, will, as soon as practicable occupy the position at Shields' Spring, 25 miles S.S.W. from this place; where he will canton the troops in huts of a temporary kind, sufficient for their health and comfort during the ensuing summer. The huts will be built by the troops; and to facilitate their completion, tools, waggons, and teams, planks and nails will be furnished by the quartermaster department. . . .

Lt. Col. Taylor is charged with the defense of the southwestern Frontier of Louisiana; and will contribute as far as the means under his control will enable him to afford protection to the inhabitants of the interior as well as those of the frontier.[53]

Late in 1822, after a year on the edge of civilization, Taylor left Fort Jesup to become the commanding officer

[52] General E. P. Gaines to Adjutant General James Gadsen, March 31, 1822, in J. Fair Hardin, "Four Forgotten Frontier Army Posts of Western Louisiana," *loc. cit.*, 14.

[53] Headquarters, Western Department, Special Orders No. 19, March 28, 1822, *ibid.*, 15.

of the post at Baton Rouge where three companies of the First Infantry were located. He had been assigned to this regiment at the beginning of the year but continued to serve with the Seventh until November. At Baton Rouge in the midst of the Louisiana plantation country Taylor had an opportunity to examine, as he had long desired, the agricultural advantages of the lower Mississippi, and actually to begin his experiences as a Louisiana planter. Early in 1823 he purchased a small plantation in West Feliciana Parish, about forty miles north of Baton Rouge. At the close of his first year's planting he found that his profits fell considerably short of his expectations. In reporting his experience to General Jesup he wrote in January, 1824:

I worked last year on as good land as any in the Country, 18 prime hands & made only 40 bales of cotton which is worth at present about 60 dollars pr bale, deducting the wages of an overseer, & other expenses, the net proceeds will not exceed $1,500 if it will amount to that sum, considerably less than $100 pr hand— The crop of last year however may not be considered a fair experiment, owing to the rot, & a violent hurricane we had in Septr. the planters all agree that it was the most unfavourable season they have experienced in this country for a number of years; add to which, a part of my negroes only was acclimated, & I had a very worthless overseer.[54]

Taylor was not discouraged. His prospects for the second year he regarded as "more flattering," and he looked forward to a much better profit, provided the weather were more favorable. He had gathered together twenty-two hands, all but one of whom had been in the country for a year, and he had obtained from Kentucky "a first rate young man as a manager, who will have as much done as I wish my hands to do, & will have every thing as well attended to as if I was personally present." [55]

[54] Taylor to Jesup, January 20, 1824, in Taylor Papers.
[55] *Ibid.*

Early in 1824, just when Taylor and his family were happily located at Baton Rouge and he was making plans for his second year's effort in cotton culture, he was surprised and disappointed to be ordered to Louisville to superintend the recruiting service.[56] Pleasant as a tour of duty in Louisville might be, Taylor was eager to carry out his plans of establishing himself as a Louisiana planter. Moreover, the cost of removing himself and his family to Kentucky was not a welcome prospect. As he wrote to Jesup at the beginning of the year: "The state of the currency in Ky. & the course pursued by the legislature of that State for several years past, in relation to contracts, has embarrassed me beyond measure & it is now with the greatest prudence & economy I can keep my head above water." [57]

In the early spring of 1824 Taylor left Baton Rouge for Kentucky. In 1827 and 1828 he was to return for another year's duty in Louisiana, and in 1831 he was to make a brief visit, but not till the close of 1840 was he again to serve for any length of time in the lower Mississippi country and to have opportunity to attend to his planting interests.

[56] Adjutant General to Taylor, March 17, 1824, in War Department Archives; Taylor to Jesup, January 20, 1824, in Taylor Papers.

[57] Taylor to Jesup, January 20, 1824.

Chapter IV

INTERLUDE

WHEN in the spring of 1824 Zachary Taylor was ordered to superintend the recruiting service for the Western Department the growing number of desertions from the army had created a serious problem and had greatly increased the need for recruits.[1] During the three years from October 1, 1822, to September 30, 1825, there were some 2,500 desertions. As the army numbered only about 8,000, this amounted to a desertion of 10 per cent of the troops each year. In addition, of course, there were the regular discharges taking place at the expiration of the term of enlistment, and it was necessary to recruit men to fill these places. For two years, until early 1826, Taylor was engaged in this work. Louisville was his headquarters, but under his superintendence also were rendezvous located at St. Louis, Natchez, and Cincinnati, with some of the work of the latter station carried on at Newport just across the Ohio.[2] His duties at the two most distant places were apparently handled by correspondence but he frequently visited Newport and Cincinnati.

Once again, as when on recruiting duty in 1819, Taylor seems to have been concerned with the behavior of his subordinate officers for, when requested by the Adjutant General to give his views on the recruiting service,[3] one point that he made was that "none but officers of experi-

[1] *American State Papers: Military Affairs,* II, 701–702, III, 194–99.

[2] *Ibid.,* III, 116; the Adjutant General to Taylor, April 9, 1824, February 21, 1826, in War Department Archives.

[3] The Adjutant General to Taylor, August 3, November 23, 1825, *ibid.*

ence, industry, inteligence [*sic*], & the most exemplary morals should be selected for the recruiting service, & who would conciliate the good feelings of the citizens among whom they were located, instead of geting [*sic*] into difficulties with the civil authorities." [4]

Shortly after he was relieved from recruiting duty in the spring of 1826, Taylor was detailed as a member of a general court-martial at Cincinnati for the trial of Major Samuel Babcock of the Engineers Corps.[5] In the fall of the year he was ordered to Washington to serve on a board of officers to report on the organization of the militia, to state "the defects, if any, of the existing organization," and to recommend "such remedies as in its judgment will render our militia as skilful and effective as it is brave and patriotic." [6] During November, Taylor sat in Washington with this board of eight officers including Major General Winfield Scott, the president of the board, the Adjutants General of Massachusetts and North Carolina, and Major General T. Cadwalader of the Pennsylvania Militia.

The officers had before them not only the various plans for the organization and instruction of the militia which had from time to time been submitted to Congress by committees or by the War Department, but also numerous communications from state officials and other distinguished citizens in reply to a circular request for information and suggestions which had been sent out by the Secretary of War several months before.[7] After studying these documents and weighing their own experience, the board concluded that the primary defect of the existing system was that by including all males eighteen to forty-five years of age the militia was so large a group that satisfactory disci-

[4] Taylor to the Adjutant General, December 31, 1825, *ibid.*

[5] Order No. 25, April 8, 1826, in Order Book No. 3, Headquarters, Western Department, *ibid.;* Taylor to the Adjutant General, May 10, 1826, *ibid.*

[6] Report of the Board to Secretary of War Barbour, November 28, 1826, in *American State Papers: Military Affairs,* III, 388.

[7] *Ibid.*, 388, 393–94.

pline and equipment were impossible. They recommended, therefore, a minimum age of twenty-one and the establishment in each state of as many brigades as it had representatives in Congress; each brigade to consist of approximately 2,000 men and the total force to aggregate 400,000. On the maxim that "good officers make good soldiers" they further recommended that instruction camps for officers only be created by each state, that the War Department furnish instructors for such camps, and that every militia officer be required to attend a ten-day encampment each year.[8]

This report was submitted to Congress with the annual report of the Secretary of War for 1826 but that body took no action. Five years later Secretary of War Lewis Cass called Congress' attention to the plan embodied in this report and expressed the conviction that it was the only one which offered any real prospect of improvement or efficiency.[9] Again Congress failed to act.

In 1826 Washington was no longer the mudhole it had been when the national government was established there at the beginning of the century, but it still bore more resemblance to a quiet country town than to a bustling metropolis. The Capitol, commenced many years before and partially destroyed during the British occupation of Washington in 1814, had just been finished. The great dome and the present wings, of course, were not added until much later, but the original design was completed. The rebuilding of the White House, burned during the war, had also been accomplished. The area between the Capitol and the executive mansion was partially built up, but Washington was still known as the city of magnificent distances.[10]

[8] *Ibid.*, 388–92.

[9] *Niles' Weekly Register*, XXXI (1826–1827), 265; XLI (1831–1832), 318.

[10] Ben Perley Poore, *Perley's Reminiscences of Sixty Years in the National Metropolis* (Philadelphia, 1886), I, 44–45.

Taylor's weeks in the national capital in 1826 gave him an opportunity to observe the Federal government at work and doubtless to meet public officials. The Virginia dynasty, to be sure, was no longer in the White House, but James Barbour, the Secretary of War, was a prominent citizen of Taylor's native county and a neighbor of many of his Virginia relatives. Henry Clay, the leading citizen of Kentucky, was Secretary of State. Congress was not in session when Taylor arrived in the capital, but unless he hastened back to Kentucky immediately upon the completion of the board's work he was on hand early in December when Congress met and when President John Quincy Adams' second annual message was read. Certainly Taylor welcomed the chance to visit with Quartermaster General Jesup and Mrs. Jesup, who before her marriage was Ann Croghan, daughter of Major William Croghan, neighboring planter to Colonel Richard Taylor for some thirty-five years. Zachary had no better friends in these days, and his frequent letters to Jesup reveal more of his personality than any other source. The closing sentences of his letter written immediately upon his return to Louisville are typical of his letters to Jesup and clearly reveal their friendly relation. "Mrs. Taylor joins me in wishing to be remembered to Mrs. Jesup in the warmest terms," he wrote. "Kiss your dear children for me, & accept our sincere wishes for for [*sic*] the health happiness & prosperity of you & yours through life." [11]

A picture of Colonel Taylor's winter journey by stagecoach and steamer from the national capital to Louisville is also found in this letter.

> By traveling the whole of two nights & the greater part of the third I reached Wheeling on thursday morning about 7 Oclock which made me three days & five hours from Washington, during which time I was not more than two hours in bed—

[11] Taylor to Thomas S. Jesup, January 29, 1827, in Taylor Papers.

And was fortunate in meeting with a small Steam Boat which set out on the evening of the same day for this place, but owing to the low state of the river, we were seven days in getting down, we could not run of nights, & was [*sic*] frequently aground, which delaid [*sic*] us considerably, besides which, we had to break the ice the whole of the last days run, the river being frozen entirely over; Since which all communication by water has been entirely stoped [*sic*] above & blow [*sic*] the falls, there has been commencing the day after Christmas thirty days of the coldest weather experienced in this country for the last thirty years, or perhaps since the first settlement of the State.[12]

Other glimpses of Taylor's personality in the middle of the 1820's, about the time that he was celebrating his fortieth birthday, are found in letters to Dr. Thomas Lawson who was stationed at Fort Jesup when Taylor was in command there and for some years thereafter. In October, 1824, Taylor chided him for not finding himself a Louisiana wife [13] and eighteen months later, after Lawson had been transferred to Fortress Monroe in Virginia, Taylor urged him to follow the good example recently set by General Henry Atkinson, a man of age, prudence, rank, and experience who had just married "a fine blooming lady of 22 years." In joking vein he continued:

There is now a bill before Congress authorizing . . . the President to occupy a position at . . . [the] mouth of the Columbia or Oregon river, should I be so unfortunate as to be one among the number selected for that purpose, & you should remain in your present blessed state of singleness, I shall certainly urge your being also one of the party. You had therefore, unless you have a wish to be sent into exile, better loose [*sic*] no time in persuading some kind harted [*sic*] fair one, to take pity on you so far as to take you under her especial care & protection during the balance of your life.[14]

[12] *Ibid.*

[13] Taylor to Dr. Thomas Lawson, October 12, 1824, in New York Historical Society.

[14] *Id.* to *id.*, February 17, 1826, *ibid.*

After expressing his regret that Dr. Lawson had not traveled east by way of Louisville and given Mrs. Taylor and himself the pleasure of seeing him, Taylor wrote of his own family and reported the addition of two members since returning to Kentucky—Mary Elizabeth, to be known as Betty, who was born in April, 1824, and Richard, his only son, born in January, 1826. "Ann & Knox is [*sic*] at a boarding school," he wrote, "the latter as wild & sprightly as ever & frequently inquires after you. Mrs Taylor is rather in bad health, she desires to be remembered to you in the warmest terms. Write me occasionally of your movements, as you have no friend more sincerely interested in your wellfare [*sic*] than myself. Wishing you health, happiness & prosperity & remain sincerely your Friend Z. Taylor." [15]

This long letter to Dr. Lawson also included Taylor's views on the system of compensation for army officers—a subject which naturally was of great interest to him. The existing system provided not only for a monthly salary and allowances for subsistence, forage, servants, and transportation of baggage, but also "extra" pay for various "extra" services, especially in connection with assignment to administrative duties in Washington. Thus, though the salary of all officers of a given rank was the same, the actual sums received would vary by hundreds of dollars.[16] "You are correct in supposing me formerly in favour of a fixed sum to the officers of the army, instead of the present mode of compensating them," Taylor informed Lawson, and "[I] have seen nothing since to alter, but everything to confirm the correctness of my opinions on that head." He had written to a member of Congress, he said, urging him to bring forward the salary bill again, and pointing out "at considerable length, its advantages over the present mode."

[15] *Ibid.*

[16] *American State Papers: Military Affairs,* III, 500–504, lists the amounts received by each officer in the years 1823, 1824, and 1825.

He had included in his letter two of Lawson's arguments in support of this view, "the equalizing the pay of the officers of the same grade, & to put a stop to the disgraceful & degrading practice, which was daily resorted to in our army, to increase the pay of a portion of the officers by signing false certificates," and had referred "to the pay accounts of the officers generally of the army for the last five years, to prove the correctness" of this position. His letter, he added, had had no effect and he did not expect it to because "the opinions of an humble individual unknown to the chief magistrate of the nation, to every member of the cabinet, & to the members of congress save two or three, would weigh but as a feather in opposition to those" of the Major General of the army, the Quartermaster General, the Paymaster General, the Commissary General, and the Surgeon General, "all of whom are on the spot, & who by uniting could put down, or carry any measure they might feel themselves interested in." The salary bill, Taylor was certain, did interest them, for "it would prevent their drawing considerable sums of money on sweeping certificates & for extra services, which the framers of the law never contemplated." The signing of false certificates, Taylor believed, was not confined to the officers of highest rank. "I do not exaggerate," he wrote in concluding his discussion of this subject, "when I say that one fourth of the officers of our army would be cashiered, if arraigned before an honest, & inteligent [*sic*] tribunal on the charge of signing false certificates . . . nineteen out of twenty of the courts that would be organized to try an officer on charges of that kind, would in all probability have a majority of its members who were guilty of the same act, consequently they would not pass sentence on another for acts they are in the habit of committing themselves." [17]

While in Kentucky during the 1820's Zachary Taylor

[17] Taylor to Dr. Thomas Lawson, February 17, 1826, in New York Historical Society.

watched with keen interest the bitter struggle between the state legislature and the court of appeals growing out of the chaotic banking and currency situation in the state. After peace had been made with Great Britain in 1815 hundreds of thousands of Americans turned to the West and Kentucky enjoyed an era of boom prosperity and speculative mania. To meet the currency needs of the speculators the Kentucky legislature chartered two score banks which promptly let loose a flood of paper money. Soon the bubble burst; the banks were forced to close their doors; and thousands of Kentuckians found themselves deeply in debt as a result of their rash and heavy borrowing. When the legislature passed numerous relief laws the court of appeals set aside the more extreme legislation as in conflict with the Constitution. An aroused legislature, responsive to public opinion, endeavored to supplant the court with a new and more co-operative tribunal. For a brief period it succeeded, but in the end the more sober and conservative elements of the population triumphed and in 1826 the old court was re-established.[18] Taylor, like other persons of property, believed that no country could be prosperous "without an able & independent judiciary, & a sound currency" and he was pleased at the failure of the efforts of the legislature to subject the court to its will. In his judgment, however, the struggle had driven several thousand of the most respectable citizens out of Kentucky and had done the state irreparable injury.[19]

Taylor's personal economic interests were so hard hit by the depressed and disturbed conditions in Kentucky that his days of "castle building" passed and he gave up even "the most distant hope of acquireing [*sic*] a moderate share of wealth." [20] Many years later General Winfield Scott recorded in his *Memoirs* that he had been in Louisville in

[18] Thomas D. Clark, *A History of Kentucky* (New York, 1937), 198–210.

[19] Taylor to Jesup, January 29, 1827, in Taylor Papers.

[20] *Id.* to *id.*, portion of letter without date, but approximately 1822, in Taylor Papers.

command of the Western Department of the army during a portion of this period and that Zachary Taylor endorsed and eventually became responsible for the heavy obligation of a friend. Taylor refused to take any relief from the stay laws or to pay in the paper currency, and "although a dear lover of money, persistently paid his endorsement in specie." Scott remembered not only Taylor's arrival in Louisville "with the heavy bags which finally freed him from debt," but also that "the parting with the cash agonized him not a little, but soon he recovered, and the next morning felt happy in his double-proof integrity." [21]

The full extent of his losses in Kentucky during this period Zachary Taylor reported in 1830 to his cousin, who was handling certain legal matters concerning his property. Taylor wrote that since the commencement of the period of economic distress he had "lost by failures & securityship twenty thousand dollars" which had in a "great measure blighted" his hopes "as to the acquirement of anything like fortune." "This I will not suffer to prey on my spirits," he continued, "or to operate on my exertions to make myself easy in my old age." [22] These financial reverses did, however, cause Taylor to give up "all hopes" of establishing himself "comfortably in Kentucky" and led him to take even greater interest in Louisiana and his planting operations there.[23]

Such correspondence of Zachary Taylor as has survived does not reveal any great interest on his part in matters of general government or international affairs. This is not surprising, for long residence at isolated frontier posts is hardly calculated to arouse interest in public affairs. Yet there are occasional paragraphs in his letters that indicate Taylor was thoroughly alive to national and international

[21] Winfield Scott, *Memoirs*, II, 390–91.

[22] Taylor to William Taylor, April 12, 1830, in Kentucky Historical Society.

[23] *Ibid.*

problems. In the summer of 1821 he commented to Jesup upon the activities of the Holy Alliance in Europe and concluded: ". . . I should not be at all surprised if you & myself lives [*sic*] to see, this nation brought into collision with them, & that we will have to contend at no distant period on our own soil with them, for our very existence, but if we are united, & have men of talents, virtue, & integrity, at the head of the nation, we have nothing to fear, but a change of men, & measure, before that time must take place." [24]

When in December, 1823, the President's annual message, including what came to be known as the Monroe Doctrine, was published, Taylor again revealed interest and understanding. He thoroughly approved Monroe's stand on Latin-American affairs and was confident that the American people would go to any lengths in preventing the European powers from interfering in the affairs of Latin America. He also approved the President's policy of noninterference in the Greek war for independence. On this point he wrote:

> We all no doubt feel interested for the success of the Greeks, but at the same time, I do not believe that it would be policy for us to interfere in the convulsions of that country; the crowned heads of Europe, might complain of our interfering in the affairs of Greece, with the same propriety that we would in their intermedling [*sic*] with those of South America or Mexico—Father [*sic*] than humanity is concerned, & the wish we have to see every Nation free, I believe it to be very immaterial, as regards the interest to this country, whether the Crescent, or Cross prevails; This subject however appears to swallow up every other, in some parts of our Country even the presidential question, appears to be merged in the cause of the Greeks.[25]

Early in 1827 Taylor's tour of duty in Louisville came to a close. As soon as the river was navigable, he took passage

[24] Taylor to Jesup, June 18, 1821, in Taylor Papers.
[25] *Id.* to *id.*, January 20, 1824, *ibid.*

for Baton Rouge to resume command of the four companies of the First Infantry stationed there. He remained on the lower Mississippi, sometimes at Baton Rouge and sometimes at New Orleans, until the summer of 1828 when a considerable shuffling of the troops took place and he found himself and the troops under his command transferred to Fort Snelling nearly two thousand miles up the Mississippi.[26]

[26] *Id.* to *id.*, January 29, 1827, *ibid.*; *id.* to the Adjutant General, March 9, 1827, in War Department Archives; *American State Papers: Military Affairs*, III, 626.

Chapter V

THE BLACK HAWK WAR

IN 1828 when Zachary Taylor was transferred to the upper Mississippi the country above the northern boundary of Missouri was still the home of the red man. The white settlers were rapidly taking over northwestern Illinois and exploiting the lead mines there and across the border in what is today southern Wisconsin, but elsewhere in the region of present-day Iowa, Wisconsin, and Minnesota there were no white men except the few at the army posts and Indian agencies. The most important tribes of this country were the Ioways in the southern part of the state that bears their name; the Sacs and Foxes on the Iowa bank of the Mississippi and up the Rock River Valley of Illinois; the Sioux who occupied western Iowa, southern Minnesota, and much of South Dakota; the Chippewas along the southern and western shores of Lake Superior; the Menominees in the Green Bay country of eastern Wisconsin; and the Winnebagos in the southern portion of that state.

Within this region the United States Army maintained several forts: Fort Snelling far up the Mississippi, Fort Crawford at the mouth of the Wisconsin, Fort Armstrong on an island where the Rock River empties into the Mississippi, Fort Winnebago recently established at the portage between the Fox and Wisconsin rivers, and Fort Howard on Green Bay. The latter fort fell within the Eastern Department of the army but the others were in the Western Department commanded during most of this period by

Major General Gaines. Under Gaines, with headquarters at Jefferson Barracks, St. Louis, was the commander of the northern portion, or right wing, of the Western Department. When Taylor went to the Northwest this position was filled by Brigadier General Henry Leavenworth and shortly thereafter by Brigadier General Henry Atkinson. During the summer of 1827 the army had been engaged in war with the Winnebagos, but when Taylor arrived in the following year the Indians and whites were again at peace.

Taylor's period of service in this northwest section stretched over nine years—to the late summer of 1837. The first year he was stationed at Fort Snelling, at the junction of the St. Peters and Mississippi rivers, seven miles below the Falls of St. Anthony. It was the farthest outpost of American authority in that direction and though steamboats began ascending the river to that point in 1823 their visits were still irregular and the fort had very little communication with the South and East. The well-constructed stone buildings of Fort Snelling were large and numerous and afforded unusually convenient and comfortable quarters for so distant a post. Indeed, in the opinion of General Gaines, the fort was constructed with more thought for the comfort of the troops in peace than for security against the attack of an enemy.[1]

The reports of the General Commanding the Army show Taylor in command at Fort Snelling as late as December, 1831, but he was not present after July, 1829, when he was ordered to Fort Crawford,[2] three hundred miles down the river at Prairie du Chien a little above the mouth of the Wisconsin River. Fort Crawford was much less isolated than Fort Snelling and life there was more varied. Troops, officers on tours of inspection, Indian agents, missionaries,

[1] Report of Inspection for half year ending December 31, 1827, in *American State Papers: Military Affairs,* IV, 122–23.

[2] *American State Papers: Military Affairs,* IV, 9, 159, 592, 724; Taylor to Thomas S. Jesup, December 15, 1829, in Taylor Papers.

and occasional visitors on their way to or from Forts Winnebago, Howard, and Snelling passed through Prairie du Chien and frequently stopped for at least a day. Moreover, small though the settlement of Prairie du Chien was, it was an important station of the American Fur Company and the location of an important Indian agency of the United States government. The persons connected with these two enterprises gave some variety to the population and life.[3]

When Taylor was transferred to Fort Crawford in the summer of 1829 work was just getting under way on the construction of new buildings on higher ground a mile from the old site. The old buildings, erected in 1816 almost at the river's edge on low ground separated somewhat from the mainland by a slough or bayou, had become decayed by the frequent overflowing of the river which sometimes brought water to a depth of four feet in the barracks.[4] The site of the new buildings had been selected and a large quantity of stone had been hauled to it before Taylor's arrival. Soon thereafter actual construction commenced. After several months of work on the new fort Taylor became convinced that it had been unwisely located. He came to this conviction in part because of the difficulty of getting wood and water to it, but also because of its proximity to the growing settlement where, according to Taylor, at least every other house was a whiskeyshop. "Owing to which circumstance, & the drunken materials the rank, & file of our Army are now composed of," he complained, he had had more trouble with the soldiers than he had ever before experienced in double or treble the time. If the fort had been located on the opposite bank of the Mississippi on Indian lands, the garrison could have "kept clear of whiskey sellers, & other huxters," and obtained an adequate fuel

[3] John H. Fonda, "Early Wisconsin," in *Wisconsin Historical Collections,* V (1907 reprint), 237–39.

[4] *American State Papers: Military Affairs,* IV, 123–25.

supply at a saving to the Quartermaster's Department of two thousand dollars a year. The only objection to that site, in his opinion, "would have been the trouble of making a road up a bluff some 2 or 3 hundred feet high, which I am confident could have been done in less than 12 months, by the labour of one half the men who will be lying in the guard house here to sober." So disgusted was he with the soldiers that he concluded that, all things considered, "it would be cheaper for the govt. to erect such buildings as we are putting up by contract, than with drunken soldiers, & in fact all permanent works." [5]

A Wisconsin pioneer who served as a corporal with Taylor's troops and was entrusted with responsible duties in connection with the expeditions after stone and timber for the fort remembered many years later a difficulty of another nature that Colonel Taylor had with one soldier at this time. As he recalled the episode:

> On one occasion when all the soldiers were mustered for "dress parade," Taylor came sauntering in from his quarters, and running his eye along the front rank, observed a large, stout German recruit, out of line. The German was a raw recruit anxious to do his duty, but did not understand the English language. So when the order was given "dress," the soldier remained as before. Col. Taylor remarked this, and thinking it a willful neglect on the soldier's part, walked up to him and after one or two trials, got hold of his ears and shook the fellow severely. This treatment was called "wooling," a favorite mode of punishment with Taylor, but the German not knowing how to appreciate it, nor why it was inflicted on him, had no sooner got his head free than drawing back he struck Taylor a blow that felled him to the ground like a dog. This was mutiny and the officers and guard would have cut him down, if Taylor had not rose up and said, "let that man alone, he will make a good soldier." [6]

[5] Taylor to Jesup, December 15, 1829, in Taylor Papers.
[6] Fonda, "Early Wisconsin," *loc. cit.*, 240–41.

Through the spring and early summer of 1830 Taylor continued to be busy with the construction of the new fort as well as with Indian problems growing out of an attack upon a party of Fox Indians by a group of Sioux and Menominees and the killing of several influential chiefs of the Fox Nation.[7] Fortunately Taylor's warning to the Indians to bury the tomahawk was heeded and it was not necessary to use armed force as contemplated. Late in the summer Taylor left Fort Crawford on furlough and did not return to the upper Mississippi for over a year and a half.

Taylor's activities during his eighteen months' absence from the Northwest are in some respects a mystery. The few Taylor letters for this period that have survived throw little light on his activities. How he spent his furlough is not entirely clear, but it seems probable that a part of it was spent in Kentucky and perhaps another part in Louisiana. On the whole it could not have been too happy a time. He was much depressed by the numerous deaths in his family during the preceding year.[8] The loss of his brother George and of both his mother and father affected him deeply. Always before when he had returned to the Beargrass Creek plantation his parents had been there to welcome him, but this time they were both missing. The Revolutionary soldier and Kentucky frontiersman had died in January, 1829, in his eighty-fifth year. The death of his courageous pioneer wife occurred in the following December. The old plantation was surely a dreary and comfortless place to visit in 1830. Nor could Taylor find much pleasure in the state of his business affairs. Neither in Kentucky nor in Louisiana had they prospered as he had hoped they might. His plantation in the latter state had been "most miserably managed" and he had lost many of his slaves

[7] Taylor to Major General Gaines, May 14, 1830, in War Department Archives.

[8] *Id.* to Jesup, December 15, 1829.

through sickness.[9] Even his army status created a spirit of discontent. Since 1812 the laws of the nation had authorized the president to confer brevet commissions upon officers who served ten years in any one grade. Presidents Madison, Monroe, and Adams regularly exercised this authority, but in 1829, just as Taylor completed his tenth year as Lieutenant Colonel, the Jackson administration abandoned the policy and withheld from Taylor the brevet which he felt was justly due him. At the same time Jackson did not hesitate to confer brevet commissions for meritorious ccnduct and even to confer brevets on brevets. Taylor keenly resented the change in policy and the discrimination involved. He particularly resented Jackson's action in conferring a brevet commission of brigadier general upon Colonel Charles Gratiot for meritorious service. He had held the rank of colonel for less than a year and during that period had been doing desk duty in Washington. Taylor believed that Gratiot's service was no more meritorious than that of most officers and that by singling him out for a brevet award President Jackson had "passed a direct censure on a large majority of the officers of the army."

While on furlough Taylor freely expressed himself on this subject in lengthy letters to two United States Senators, Josiah S. Johnston of Louisiana and George Poindexter of Mississippi.[10] He stated his complaint frankly and pointed

[9] *Ibid.*

[10] The letter to Poindexter, in the Taylor Papers in the Library of Congress, is dated Louisville, December 26, 1829, while the one to Johnston, in the Historical Society of Pennsylvania, is dated December 24, 1831. The letters are practically identical and it seems that one if not both are misdated. The date 1829 is clearly erroneous for the letter to Poindexter, as Taylor was not in Louisville in December, 1829, and Poindexter, who is addressed as "U. S. Senator, Washington City," did not become senator until October, 1830. In both letters Taylor states, "I was promoted to a Lieut Colonelcy the 20th of Apl. 1819 & have served constantly in that grade ever since . . . which is near twelve years. . . ." This statement would seem to make the correct date for both letters December, 1830, near the close of Taylor's furlough when it is highly probable that he was in

out that much of the difficulty relative to brevet commissions grew out of an act of 1818 which provided that officers on duty and having command according to their brevet rank should receive the pay and emoluments of that rank. This provision, he believed, had resulted in a system of favoritism and intrigue and in injury to officers having only lineal rank. "No institution can be either respectable, or prosperous when such things are tolerated," he wrote; "let us all be placed on an equality, & let the scramble for honors of that description be for services rendered on the frontiers or in face of an enemy, & not in the drawing rooms at Washington." He suggested, therefore, that when all officers entitled to brevets for ten years' service in one grade had received them Congress should repeal all laws on the subject of brevet rank, "letting us all down to our proper linear rank," and that in the future brevet commissions should be conferred only for gallant actions during war and should be purely honorary, carrying no right to higher command or increased pay. No change in the laws was made at this time, however, and for many years brevet rank with its many opportunities for favoritism and injustice continued to be an almost constant source of discontent in the army.

Early in 1831 when his furlough expired Colonel Taylor was ordered by General Gaines to Baton Rouge as a member of a general court-martial to convene on March 10 for the trial of Brevet Major John Mountfort of the Second Artillery and of such soldiers as were held on capital charges in several southwestern posts.[11] Upon the adjournment of the court Taylor apparently went north. On July 4 he wrote from Louisville that he was leaving for the upper Mississippi where there was serious trouble,[12] but a week

Louisville. He was in Louisville in December, 1831, but at that time he should have written "near thirteen years" instead of twelve.

11 Order No. 2, January 16, 1831, in Order Book No. 17, Headquarters, Western Department, in War Department Archives.

12 Taylor to Jesup, July 4, 1831, in Jesup Papers (Division of Manuscripts, Library of Congress).

later General Gaines in a special order instructed him to "repair to the state of Louisiana, where he will report to Colonel Clinch, and be assigned by him, to duty in that state, until otherwise directed." [13] This order was doubtless issued in response to Taylor's own request, for his constant preference was for a southern post and at this time, when he had just lost the services of the "fine young man from Kentucky" who had managed his plantation since 1823, he was especially anxious to be in the South.[14] This same preference for a southern station led him to seek a temporary exchange with Lieutenant Colonel David E. Twiggs of the Fourth Infantry, but the Washington authorities not only disapproved his request but ordered him back to the Northwest after he had served but a few months as commander of the garrison at New Orleans.[15]

That the officials of the War Department were not entirely clear as to Taylor's status during this period is evident from the following letter of the Adjutant General to Major General Jesup in 1833:

> In answer to your inquiry of yesterday's date, respecting the circumstances of Col. Taylor['s] presence, on duty at New Orleans, and Baton Rouge in the Spring and summer of 1831, I have to state, that it appears, that subsequent to the adjournment of the Court of which he was President, and which convened at Baton Rouge about the 10th of March 1831, Col. Taylor was assigned to the command of the Garrison at New Orleans, in virtue of "orders" emanating from Major General Gaines—it seems that Col. Taylor had been on furlough prior to the 10th of March, 1831.[16]

When in October, 1831, Taylor was ordered to join his regiment at Fort Snelling, he felt that some censure was involved, but the department informed him that none was

[13] Special Order No. 45, July 11, 1831, in Order Book No. 19, Headquarters, Western Department, in War Department Archives.

[14] Taylor to Jesup, December 4, 1832, in Taylor Papers.

[15] *Id.* to the Adjutant General, September 23, 1831; Adjutant General to Taylor, October 5 and 19, 1831; in War Department Archives.

[16] Adjutant General to Major General T. S. Jesup, June 14, 1833, *ibid.*

intended.[17] He was in no hurry to reach his new post. He traveled north by way of Louisville, and there he remained, with the permission of the War Department, until the opening of spring navigation.[18] Thus he did not reach his regiment until nearly six months after he received the original order to join it.

Taylor arrived in the Northwest just in time to take a prominent part in the Black Hawk War famous in history and legend. Black Hawk, or Makataimeshekiakiak, as he was known to his own people, was the aged but restless and ambitious leader of the faction of the Sac Indians known as the British Band because of their long and close relations with the British. They had fought on the British side during the War of 1812 and still made frequent visits to their British Father at Malden. As far back as 1804 the United States had concluded a treaty with the Sac and Fox Indians by which the red men ceded the region east of the Mississippi and between the Wisconsin and Illinois rivers with the proviso that they should continue to enjoy the right to live and hunt upon it as long as it remained a portion of the public domain. Within this area was the chief seat of the Sac power—a town of some five hundred Indian families located on the north or west bank of the Rock River about three miles above its mouth. Here was their burial ground and round about were their cornfields.[19]

In the mid-1820's settlers moved into these northern Illinois counties and slowly but steadily encroached on the Indian towns and cornfields. Black Hawk began to insist that this land had not been ceded to the United States. By the spring of 1831 the situation had become so bad that Black Hawk threatened to drive the squatters out by force unless they departed of their own accord. The frightened

[17] *Id.* to Taylor, October 5, November 19, 1831, *ibid.*

[18] Taylor to the Adjutant General, December 19, 1831, *ibid.;* Adjutant General to Taylor, January 13, 1832, *ibid.*

[19] R. G. Thwaites, "The Story of the Black Hawk War," in *Wisconsin Historical Collections,* XII (1892), 218–22.

settlers, though clearly without rights, appealed for protection to the governor of the state and to General Gaines. Late in June a force of 1,600 mounted volunteers and ten companies of regulars moved on Black Hawk's town. Confronted by this powerful force Black Hawk and his British Band withdrew in the darkness of the night to the west bank of the Mississippi where they joined the other members of their tribe who months before had yielded to the pressure of the whites and removed to the Iowa shore. A few days later the proud red man agreed to relinquish all claim to land east of the river and never to return to the east bank.[20]

With the arrival of spring in 1832 Black Hawk felt the urge to return to his Rock River home and in April with about five hundred warriors, mostly Sacs, their squaws, children, and baggage, crossed the Mississippi below Rock River and proceeded up the east bank of that stream. He had no immediately hostile intentions, but his plans apparently called for war in the fall after his people had raised a crop and gathered a food supply.[21] The settlers were determined that the Indians should not remain and again appealed for troops. Among those who joined in the campaign and for three months tracked the elusive red men through the wilds was Zachary Taylor. A few days after the war closed Taylor wrote an account of it and of his part in it to Dr. Lawson who was asked to keep in mind while reading it that "I was writing to not only an old soldier, but to an old friend, who I knew would pardon everything like egotism if too much indulged in, as well as bad writing, & spelling to both of which I plead guilty." This interesting letter, with more errors in punctuation than in writing or spelling and with surprisingly little egotism, describes the campaign so well that Taylor's part in the

[20] *Ibid.*, 225–26; George A. McCall, *Letters from the Frontiers* (Philadelphia, 1868), 228–32; Report of the Secretary of War, 1832, in *House Executive Documents,* 22 Cong., 2 Sess., No. 2, pp. 29–30.

[21] Thwaites, "The Story of the Black Hawk War," *loc. cit.*, 230–31.

Black Hawk War is presented chiefly in his own words.[22]

A few days before setting out from Louisville for his new station at Fort Snelling, so wrote Taylor to Lawson, he received word from General Atkinson "that he was on the point of leaving Jefferson Barracks" for the north to settle some difficulties which had arisen among the Indians, "as well as to suppress some hostile movements of the Sac's, & Foxes against the whites" and that he wished Taylor to join him as soon as practicable. Early in May, Taylor caught up with Atkinson at Rock Island where he "found the Genl. preparing to pursue the hostile Indians who had . . . ascended Rock River & located themselves on it, about one hundred miles above its mouth, & about thirty above Dixons ferry on that river, the only crossing place from the interior, to Galena, & the mineral district of country around it, & the only house above its mouth, but without committing depredations of any kind." A few days later, after 1,600 Illinois militia under Brigadier General Samuel Whiteside had joined his force, Atkinson commenced a forward movement. "We set out in pursuit of the enemy," Taylor wrote, "with the six companies of the 6th & four of the first Infy. amounting to about three hundred & twenty rank & file in addition to the militia, the latter moving by land on horseback & the regulars on foot up rock river & carrying with the greatest difficulty & exertion it was possible to make use of in boats up that river, the ordnance stores, & about twenty, or twenty five days rations for the whole army."

After nine days of slow progress up the river the regulars reached Dixon's Ferry to discover that the faster-moving, mounted militia had arrived several days before and that a detachment of them under Major Isaiah Stillman had eagerly pushed forward and attacked the Indians, "but on the Indians joining battle with them & killing one white

[22] Taylor to Dr. Thomas Lawson, August 12, 1832, in New York Historical Society.

man, they became panic struck, & fled in the most shameful manner that every [ever] troops were known to do, in this, or any other country, there were some seven or eight killed in the pursuit, & it is probable, had it not been just at night when the attack was made on the Indians, that a very large proportion of the whites would have been killed, the cover of the night enabled them to get off." The regulars promptly moved up to the place where the Indians had been encamped but discovered that they had withdrawn "to the almost impenetrable marshes & swamps on the head waters of the Rock river" from which safe refuge small parties soon "commenced an indiscriminate massacre of men, women & children" along the frontiers of Illinois and of Michigan Territory.

General Atkinson sent Taylor in command of the militia to protect the upper settlements on the Illinois and Fox rivers, while he took steps to reorganize and strengthen his forces and to gather the necessary supplies for the more extended campaign that now seemed inevitable. Before Taylor's troops reached the settlements, the Indians struck, murdering three entire families, except for two young women who were carried off as prisoners. "You have no idea, nor can I describe the panic & distress produced by this, & other murders," Taylor informed Lawson. "The people on that frontier immediately fell back for twenty, or thirty miles leving [*sic*] everything even their clothing, behind them, & in that situation were crowded together in such places of defence as could be hastily constructed; the panic was not confined to women, & children, but prevailed among a large portion of the men of that part of the state, who fancied they saw an Indian in every bush, or behind every tree or stump, whenever they were out of sight of a Fort."

It was late June before Atkinson was ready to take the offensive. The regulars had been increased to "about four hundred & fifty bayonets" by the arrival of two additional companies of the Sixth Infantry from the cantonment at Leavenworth and two companies of the Fifth from Fort Winnebago. The thirty-day term of service of the militia had expired and these undisciplined troops, who had caused Atkinson and Taylor unending trouble, had been replaced by another force of three thousand Illinois volunteers commanded by Brigadier Generals Alexander Posey, Milton K. Alexander, and James D. Henry. Several hundred militia from Michigan Territory, led by Colonel Henry Dodge, were also on hand. The final phase of the war—the fruitless search for the savages in the swampy region of Lake Koshkonong, the march across present-day Wisconsin, and the victorious encounters at Wisconsin Heights and the Bad Axe—Taylor briefly related. "After I may say a forced march of near thirty days, during which we suffered every privation & hardship common to our profession (owing to the impossibility of procuring transportation even for a full supply of provisions, in wading daily swamps & marshes & passing over a number of hills that in Europe would be termed mountains which before had never been passed by a white man even a trader, much less an army) we succeeded on the morning of the second inst. in overtaking them [the Indians] on the bank of the Mississippi while in the act of crossing & preparing to cross about forty miles above this place [Fort Crawford] & completely defeated them, killing I presume about one hundred, & making fifty or sixty prisoners, besides destroying a large portion of their baggage, & killing, & capturing a number of their horses with a loss on our part of some twenty seven killed, & wounded; since which a number of prisoners has been picked up, mostly women & children in attempting to recross the Mississippi to the west side."

Taylor's account to Dr. Lawson needs little addition to complete the story of the war. He might well have enlarged upon the difficulties and hardships of the regulars as they ascended the Rock River at the outset of the campaign, wading in the rain-swollen, turbulent stream and pushing their keelboats and Mackinaw boats against the rapid current. In picturing the panic that ensued when Black Hawk raised the tomahawk and scalping knife against the settlers along the northern Illinois border he could well have related that within a few weeks scores of persons, perhaps as many as two hundred, met death at the hands of these warriors. Also the terrible plight of the Indians during the last days of July as the troops relentlessly pursued them west across southern Wisconsin might have been included. The troops found not only abundant evidence that the Indians were eating herbs and bark and the flesh of their worn-out ponies in a vain effort to maintain their strength, but found also a trail strewn with the corpses of starved red men for whom the pursuit had become too hot. The final defeat of Black Hawk's band, the battle of Bad Axe, was even more complete and decisive than Taylor claimed. Few of the hunted red men survived. Those who were not slain by the bullets of the troops were drowned in their efforts to cross the river or were set upon and killed by their Sioux enemies as they reached the western bank. Pandemonium reigned as the conquering whites drove their weary enemy before them. In one other respect Taylor's story of the campaign is not adequate. In the pursuit of Black Hawk across Wisconsin and in the final victory at the mouth of the Bad Axe the volunteer forces were in the hottest of the fighting and won a large share of the credit for victory. They alone had driven the enemy from the field at Wisconsin Heights. Taylor was fully justified in characterizing the defeat of Stillman's force as a shameful affair, but he ought also to have recognized the zeal and the courage with which other volunteers tracked Black Hawk to his doom. Outnumbering the regulars three to one, they contributed in large measure to the success of the campaign.[23]

[23] Major General Alexander Macomb to Secretary of War Lewis Cass, November, 1832, in *American State Papers: Military Affairs,* V, 29–31;

At the close of the year as Taylor looked back upon the war he felt that certain errors had been made in its conduct. It was his opinion that the high state of excitement among the Indians as the year opened, a condition which must have been known to Major General Alexander Macomb, the general in command of the army, as well as to General Atkinson, should have led to a strengthening of the garrison at Fort Armstrong the moment the Mississippi was clear of ice. Had this been done "there would have been no indian war." In spite of this error, he believed the war might have been prevented, or at least greatly shortened, if Atkinson had not permitted the Indians to ascend the Rock River with their fleet of canoes laden with supplies of all kinds. How General Atkinson could have prevented this he does not, however, make clear. Finally, it was Taylor's judgment that if the General had had more confidence in his troops Black Hawk could have been cornered and defeated high up on the Rock River or between it and the Wisconsin some ten or fifteen days sooner than his downfall actually came.[24]

Black Hawk himself was not among those killed or captured at the battle of Bad Axe. He, with a few of his followers, escaped into the interior of Wisconsin. Within a few days, however, he gave himself up to, or was captured by, the Winnebagos and by them was taken to Prairie du Chien and turned over to General Joseph M. Street, the Indian Agent at that station, and Colonel Taylor, in command at Fort Crawford. After a winter as prisoner at Jefferson Barracks the captive chief was taken to the East where he promised President Jackson that if allowed to return to his people he would live in peace, a promise which he

---

Thwaites, "The Story of the Black Hawk War," *loc. cit.*, 234–35, 241–42, 251–61; Cyrenus Cole, *I am a Man. The Indian Black Hawk* (Iowa City, 1938), *passim;* Frank E. Stevens, *The Black Hawk War* (Chicago, 1903), *passim;* Charles Bracken, "Further Strictures on Ford's Black Hawk War," in *Wisconsin Historical Collections,* II (1903 reprint), 410–14.

[24] Taylor to Jesup, December 4, 1832, in Taylor Papers.

faithfully kept for the few remaining years of his life.[25]

Just as the Black Hawk War was coming to a close in the summer of 1832 another pestilence reached the upper Mississippi. This was the Asiatic cholera, a scourge that was to be no less destructive than the warfare spread by the hard-pressed red men. Cholera appeared in New York in the spring, perhaps as early as April, certainly no later than June.[26] It was carried west in July by infected boats on which General Winfield Scott and nearly a thousand troops hastened by way of the Great Lakes to join in the campaign against Black Hawk. Soon after leaving Buffalo the troops were stricken. Leaving the dead and dying at various points en route, Scott continued on his way. On July 11, eight days after sailing from Buffalo, he finally arrived at Fort Dearborn, Chicago, with only two hundred men. Many of these were already victims of the unseen enemy and by the nineteenth, fifty-nine had died and fifty were still sick.[27]

Late in July when the cholera had almost disappeared at Fort Dearborn, General Scott headed west for the battle front and was followed a few weeks later by the troops. Suddenly on August 26 the disease appeared at Fort Armstrong where Scott, after a brief visit to Fort Crawford, had made his headquarters and where the negotiations with the defeated Indians were under way. In five days nearly one hundred and fifty persons were attacked and twenty-six died. The panic at the fort became so great that on the night of the thirtieth, seventeen enlisted men stole a boat and deserted. A few days later they surrendered themselves at Jefferson Barracks and reported that they had fled only from the cholera. Five members of a small detachment that escorted some of the Indian prisoners to St. Louis during

25 Cole, *I am a Man*, 230–33, 236–37, 245–49; General Robert Anderson, "Reminiscences of the Black Hawk War," in *Wisconsin Historical Collections*, X (1909 reprint), 171–72; *Wisconsin Historical Collections*, VIII (1908 reprint), 316 n.

26 J. S. Chambers, *The Conquest of Cholera* (New York, 1938), 45–46.

27 *Ibid.*, 86–97; "The Cholera Epidemic of 1873," in *House Executive Documents*, 43 Cong., 2 Sess., No. 95, pp. 569–73.

the first days of September were buried on the passage down the river. By the ninth of the month, after taking the lives of four officers and fifty-two enlisted men, the scourge had run its course at Fort Armstrong.[28]

Fortunately Colonel Taylor and his family were not at Fort Armstrong during these weeks. At the close of the war he took up his duties as commanding officer at Fort Crawford, the headquarters of the First Infantry, a post to which he was then entitled, for he had become the colonel of that regiment following the death of Colonel Willoughby Morgan on the eve of the war.[29] From Fort Armstrong the cholera spread west and south, but not north. Consequently Prairie du Chien and the garrison at Fort Crawford escaped that pestilence during the dreadful summer of 1832.

The following year, the cholera, in much milder form, did reach Fort Crawford. Early in 1833 it appeared at New Orleans and from that city was carried northward by the river boats to St. Louis and Prairie du Chien.[30] At St. Louis it caused widespread suffering but Prairie du Chien apparently escaped lightly. Because of its presence, however, Taylor had to abandon an expedition into northern Wisconsin to preserve peace between the Sioux and Chippewas. The risk to the men and the danger of spreading the disease into new areas caused Taylor to keep his troops at the fort.[31]

For five years following the close of the Black Hawk War Taylor was on active duty on the upper Mississippi with his headquarters at Fort Crawford. Although the new fort was not completed until late in 1834, it was sufficiently advanced by the end of 1832 for the entire garrison to move to the

[28] *Ibid.*, 574–79.

[29] *American State Papers: Military Affairs*, V, 138, 147; Taylor to the Adjutant General, August 23, 1832, in War Department Archives.

[30] "The Cholera Epidemic of 1873," *loc. cit.*, 588–89.

[31] Brigadier General Henry Atkinson to Taylor, May 30, June 9 and 10, July 7, 1833; *id.* to the Adjutant General, July 15, 1833, in War Department Archives.

new quarters. This fort was a large and imposing work. The main buildings were constructed of stone and were arranged to enclose a large rectangular parade ground. On the east and west sides were the barracks—two 175-foot structures, separated by a sally port, forming each side. The north and south ends were each formed by one long building—nearly 250 feet long—used for officers' quarters and for storerooms. All of these buildings consisted of an elevated basement and one story. Their gable roofs projected inside the fort and formed the roof of a paved porch, ten feet wide, facing the parade ground. Outside the fort proper were the hospital and the commandant's home—the former to the south and the latter to the north.[32]

Fort Crawford was distinctly a frontier post but life there was fairly comfortable and pleasant. When the first census of Wisconsin Territory was taken in July, 1836, there were thirteen women, twenty-three children, and seventeen slaves present at Fort Crawford to add to the joys and comforts of life. Moreover, some six hundred other civilians were residents of Crawford County in which the fort was located and many of these shared in the social and recreational activities of the post.[33] Travelers in the Northwest frequently tarried a few days at Fort Crawford and invariably enjoyed the friendly hospitality of Colonel Taylor and the other officers. The commandant not only invited them to his table, but at least on occasion served them old wine from his cellar.[34] Some visitors remained for a longer period. When Reverend Alfred Brunson arrived in Prairie du Chien in 1835 to establish a Methodist mission he and his family lived at the fort until their house was completed and

[32] Bruce E. Mahan, *Old Fort Crawford and the Frontier* (Iowa City, 1926), 138–39.

[33] *Wisconsin Historical Collections*, XIII (1895), 254.

[34] C. F. Hoffman, *A Winter in the West* (London, 1835), II, 7–8; Charles A. Murray, *Travels in North America* (London, 1841), 110; Caleb Atwater, *Remarks Made on a Tour to Prairie du Chien; Thence to Washington City in 1829* (Columbus, 1831), 178.

they received many courtesies from the commanding colonel and his officers.[35]

Occasional dances furnished recreation or entertainment, but more important were the theatricals presented by the soldiers of the garrison. A large barrack room was fitted up as a theater with scenery painted by the soldiers and lights ingeniously placed on bayonets. The seats, arranged to rise like the pit of a theater, separated the audience into three divisions: the officers and their families constituted one, the soldiers another, and Indians and Negro servants the third.[36] One visitor to the fort who attended a presentation of two English comedies, "Who Wants A Guinea," by George Colman, Jr., and Henry Fielding's "Don Quixote in England," was surprised at the skill and judgment with which the soldiers played.[37] Another traveler, who witnessed the presentation of Colman's comedy, "The Poor Gentleman," thought that with few exceptions the actors had neither sense nor feeling and that "Miss Emily was personated in a most astounding manner; such a monster in petticoats, and stick in feeling, probably never was exhibited before." Nevertheless he recognized the importance of diverting the common soldiers from "low debauchery" by turning their attention to "intellectual exhibitions of this kind." [38]

The intellectual interests of the officers and their families were also served by a library, or reading room, which they maintained at their own expense. Works of history, science, and military subjects were available and from time to time newspapers arrived from the eastern cities.[39] Educational facilities for the children at the fort were provided in a post school, under the direction of the commandant, but taught

35 Ella C. Brunson, "Alfred Brunson, Pioneer of Wisconsin Methodism," in *Wisconsin Magazine of History* (Menasha), II (1918–1919), 137.

36 Hoffman, *A Winter in the West,* II, 3.

37 *Ibid.,* 2–4.

38 George W. Featherstonhaugh, *A Canoe Voyage up the Minnay Sotor* (London, 1847), I, 213.

39 Atwater, *Remarks Made on a Tour to Prairie du Chien,* 179.

by the chaplain or some other person engaged for the task.[40] During the years that Colonel Taylor was stationed at Fort Crawford the post school usually included among its pupils one or more of his children.

The monotony of routine military life at the fort was relieved for many of the officers by hunting expeditions, for the surrounding country abounded in grouse, ducks, elk, bear, and wolves. There is no clear evidence that Taylor joined any of these parties but some of the game reached his table and afforded a welcome change from the usual fare.[41]

As Colonel of the First Infantry, Taylor had to perform the manifold routine functions of a regimental commander. Monthly reports covering all companies of the regiment, some of which were at Fort Snelling while others were at Fort Armstrong, had to be sent to Washington. The entire regiment, particularly the new recruits who arrived from time to time to fill the thinning ranks, required drilling and disciplining. The many desertions and numerous discharges on surgeon's certificate of disability Taylor attributed to the many whiskey establishments "occupied by individuals of the most dissolute habits, and character, whose object and business is to debauch the soldiers." [42] Occasionally he was concerned with court-martial proceedings involving officers of his command or with such cases as that of a private who, apparently without provocation, fired his loaded musket at his captain while he stood happily by in conversation with a fellow officer.[43]

The whole subject of the general welfare of his troops and the condition of the fort under his immediate command required his attention. The many aspects of this

[40] Mahan, *Old Fort Crawford,* 244.

[41] Hoffman, *A Winter in the West,* II, 7–8; Murray, *Travels in North America,* 111–30.

[42] Taylor to Brigadier General Henry Atkinson, July 5, 1836, in War Department Archives.

[43] *Ibid.*

responsibility and the way in which it was met by Taylor is indicated in an inspection report of October, 1836. The inspecting officer reported the messrooms clean and neat and the rations properly cooked and served. The arms and equipment, the bunks and clothing were found in proper condition. The regimental and company books were correctly kept. The health of the post was good, but the inspecting officer considered the hospital poorly arranged. The sutlers sold goods to the soldiers at reasonable prices and gave general satisfaction. The drill of the troops was reported good but not up to what it had been some years before and the near-by liquor shops, open at all hours, were recognized as making the task of maintaining discipline a difficult one. The provisions and military supplies were found to be abundant and neatly and properly stored; the powder and ammunition were in good order in as fine a magazine and gunhouse as was to be found in the country. The administration of the post was reported to be correct in every particular.[44]

Soon after the war against Black Hawk and his warriors, Taylor was faced with the difficult problem of white trespassers upon Indian lands on the Iowa shore of the Mississippi—trespassers whom he later characterized as "worse to manage than the Seminoles or even the Mexicans." [45] This was the revival of a problem that had confronted him a few years before. In the summer of 1830 when an attack by the Menominee Indians forced the Foxes to abandon temporarily their lead mines in the region of present-day Dubuque, miners from the Illinois side rushed over to prospect in this new field. But they were trespassing on Indian land and could not be allowed to remain. To Taylor and the Indian Agent fell the task of ousting these

[44] Mahan, *Old Fort Crawford,* 211–13.

[45] Lucius H. Langworthy, "Dubuque: Its History, Mines, Indian Legends, Etc.," in *Iowa Journal of History and Politics* (Iowa City), VIII (1910), 366–422.

hardy pioneers. When Taylor appeared in person and warned them to depart within a week, they boldly insisted that they were in possession and intended to remain. "We shall see to that my boys," replied Taylor. They apparently realized that he was not to be fooled with, for when troops, sent by him, arrived a few days later they found only three remaining trespassers to arrest.[46]

These mines were included in territory that the Sacs and Foxes were required to cede at the close of the Black Hawk War, but the Indians were to remain in full possession until June, 1833. The frontiersmen could not wait, however. Once again they rushed to stake out their claims. Within a few weeks 150 miners and their families crossed the river to the Dubuque mines. Once again Taylor had to help the Indian Agent expel the trespassers, many of them veterans of the Black Hawk War. For six months during the winter and spring of 1833, this problem demanded his attention. This time he did not go in person but sent troops under Lieutenant E. F. Covington. When his harsh measures proved ineffective he was replaced by Lieutenants John J. Abercrombie and Jefferson Davis whose diplomacy succeeded where threats of force had failed.[47] Taylor believed squatters on Indian lands were a definite menace to the peace of the frontier and advocated their prompt ejection. He suggested to the Washington officials that the officers in command of frontier posts be given general instructions to proceed against such trespassers without awaiting further orders in each individual case. They should be authorized to "burn and destroy the establishments of all squatters together with every other description of property, and to

[46] Jacob Van der Zee, "Early History of Lead Mining in the Iowa Country," *ibid.*, XIII (1915), 40–44.

[47] *Ibid.*, 47–51; Oliver P. Shiras, "The Mines of Spain," in *Annals of Iowa* (Des Moines), 3d Series, V (1901–1903), 329–30; "Correspondence on the Subject of the Emigration of Indians," in *Senate Documents,* 23 Cong., 1 Sess., No. 512, III, 223, 558–60, 633, IV, 2, 70, 110, 457.

remove them, and all other whites who may attempt to trespass, encroach or enter upon the Indian Territory without being legally authorized to do so." [48]

The demonstration of power made by the whites in the Black Hawk War kept the northwest Indians fairly well subdued. Consequently Taylor was not greatly bothered by Indian attacks or even threats thereof. As late as February, 1837, he declared the Indians were still decidedly pacific toward the whites and could only be driven to assume a hostile attitude by the most unjust oppression or outrageous treatment. Intertribal conflicts, however, were rather frequent and occasionally were so serious as to threaten a general Indian war from which the whites would surely suffer. In the adjustment of these conflicts Taylor frequently played a part. One such instance was in May, 1835, when the marauding Sacs and Foxes were summoned to Fort Crawford and persuaded to sign a treaty of friendship with the Winnebagos and Menominees who but a short time before had been subjected to bloody massacre.[49]

In general, however, Taylor considered the policy of trying to enforce peace among the Indians as "truly an unfortunate one" because it was "at variance with their habits and inclinations" and "contrary to their very natures." Particularly unfortunate did he regard the course usually pursued by the government of bringing the Indians together under the auspices of government agents who

> induce or prevail on them to enter into the most solemn treaties, as far as forms are concerned, to live in peace and friendship with each other, and among other reasons to induce them to enter into such engagements, state to them, that their great father the President of the U. S. was not only determined that they should bury the hatchet and warclub forever, but that he would take part against the first agressors or whoever should

[48] Taylor to the Adjutant General, February 20, 1837, in Archives of Department of the Interior, Office of Indian Affairs.

[49] Mahan, *Old Fort Crawford*, 206.

first violate any of the stipulations in said treaties, and would punish them in the most prompt and exemplary manner.[50]

The failure of the government to carry out such threats or promises when treaty after treaty had been violated, "some of them before the ink comparatively speaking, was hardly dry," had rendered the agents and all others who had official relations with them "contemptible in their eyes so far as truth is concerned" and must "destroy the effects in their minds, as to the power, justice and energies of the nation, which under other circumstances they could be impressed with." [51]

Taylor and his troops also had to give some attention to the construction of a military road from Fort Crawford to Fort Winnebago at the Portage, while other troops built the section from that point to Fort Howard at Green Bay. This road had been planned as early as 1830, but little was done on it before the spring of 1835. At that time three companies from Fort Crawford spent several months constructing the western end of the road.

The section built under Taylor's general supervision was 110 miles in length and involved cutting down several steep hills and constructing a number of small bridges and causeways as well as seven substantial bridges over running streams. The result, as Taylor reported at the conclusion of the work, was that "the heavyest loaded waggon could pass the whole distance with the greatest of facility." Crude though this road was it provided a route between Forts Howard and Crawford that was one third shorter than the ancient Fox-Wisconsin waterway.[52] The following year, 1836, Taylor was appointed one of the commissioners to lay out a new military road along the frontiers of Missouri and Arkansas, but in consideration of "circumstances" stated

[50] Taylor to the Adjutant General, February 20, 1837, in Archives of Department of the Interior, Office of Indian Affairs.

[51] *Ibid.*

[52] Mahan, *Old Fort Crawford,* 208–10; Adjutant General to Taylor, April 15, 1835, in War Department Archives; Taylor to Quartermaster General Thomas S. Jesup, June 5, 1835, and August 14, 1835, in State Historical Society of Wisconsin.

by him in a letter now missing from the files he was relieved from that duty.[53]

In the summer of 1834, in accordance with a recent law of Congress, Joseph M. Street, the Indian Agent at Prairie du Chien, was transferred to Rock Island, and all the affairs of the Agency at the former place were put in the hands of the commandant of Fort Crawford. Thus to Taylor's regular military duties were added those of Indian Agent for the Winnebagos and for a portion of the Sioux.[54] His letter of instructions authorized him to employ an interpreter; to nominate persons competent to act as teachers, mechanics, farmers, and laborers as called for by treaty; reminded him that he was to fix the time and place for the payment of the annuities; and directed him to be present in person when the payments were made. The letter stated further that:

For the payments that may be required in fulfillment of treaty stipulations, an account will be presented to the Qr. Master, receipted by the parties and certified by yourself. To this account will be attached a requisition, signed by you, calling for the payment, which he will always make, so far as the funds in his hands, applicable to the particular object of expenditure, will permit. If a payment be made erronously, he will be credited with the amount, which will be charged to the person issuing the requisitions. You will make quarterly returns of the requisitions drawn by you, exhibiting the date, object, amount, and the names of the payees. It will be well for you also, to keep a record, explanatory of the reasons for every expenditure, not of an ordinary character, that you may be able to secure yourself, if any payments upon these requisitions are suspended here as erroneous. You will communicate with this office and this Department, through the Superintendent at St. Louis.[55]

[53] Adjutant General to Taylor, July 16 and September 9, 1836, in War Department Archives.

[54] Elbert Herring, Commissioner of Indian Affairs, to Taylor, July 22, 1834, in Archives of Department of the Interior, Office of Indian Affairs.

[55] *Ibid.*

By a treaty made with the Winnebago tribe in September, 1832, the government undertook to establish and maintain for twenty-seven years a school for such Winnebago children as should be "voluntarily sent to it." The school was to be located near Fort Crawford and was to offer instruction in reading, writing, arithmetic, gardening, agriculture, carding, spinning, weaving, sewing, "and such other branches of useful knowledge as the President of the United States may prescribe." [56] This school was a favorite project of Agent Street who was deeply disappointed when he was required to transfer authority over it to Colonel Taylor.[57] The latter's instructions from Washington were to assume the general superintendence of the school and of the erection of the buildings for which Street had already contracted and to "digest, in concert with the teachers, who have been selected, a system of instruction and discipline, to be submitted for the approval of the Department." [58]

The work of Indian Agent was performed by Taylor for two years with as much grace as possible, but he was never really happy about it. Imposed as it was on top of his regular duties and without additional pay, it was burdensome. Moreover, it was not a traditional part of an army officer's work and was regarded as hardly an appropriate assignment. The failure of the officials in Washington to take notice of his occasional suggestions for improvement in Indian relations and their inefficient attention to the forwarding of funds to meet treaty obligations thoroughly aroused him. When in the summer of 1836 he received a circular request for a mass of information about the Indians of his Agency he could no longer restrain himself. A long letter, every

[56] Charles J. Kappler (ed.), *Indian Affairs: Laws and Treaties* (Washington, 1904–1929), II, 346.

[57] Ida M. Street, "A Chapter of Indian History," in *Annals of Iowa,* 3d Series, III (1897–1899), 601–23; and "A Second Chapter of Indian History," *ibid.,* VI (1903–1905), 364–75.

[58] Herring to Taylor, July 22, 1834, *loc. cit.*

paragraph of which bore clear evidence of his thorough dissatisfaction with the whole business, was sent off to the Commissioner of Indian Affairs in Washington. Attention to some of the provisions of the circular, he wrote, would interfere with his military duties; therefore he would not comply with them even should he lay himself "liable for not doing so to be reported to the President of the United States." [59] He then added:

> Under ordinary circumstances I should consider it somewhat singular that the duties of Indian Agent at this place where they are more arduous and complicated owing to so many treaty stipulations than at any other point on the Upper Mississippi or it's [*sic*] tributaries, should have been assigned to a Commanding Officer of a Regiment, who should be ready at any moment to take the field at the head of the Regiment the command of which he had been entrusted with, without being embarrassed with the adjusting and settlement of accounts unconnected with his proper profession, when too there was an Indian Agent removed from here when the duties were assigned to me, to Rock Island only a short distance, and where an Indian Agent was much less necessary as regarded the duties to be performed than at this place, also an Agent located at Fort Snelling whose duties bore no comparison as to the amount of those which ought to be attended to and performed here.[60]

A few months later Taylor escaped from further service as Indian Agent. On December 1 he commenced a five months' residence at Jefferson Barracks as commander of the right wing of the Western Department while General Atkinson was on furlough.[61] When he returned to Fort Crawford in the following May he found that the pleas of Agent Street to be stationed at Prairie du Chien instead of at Rock Island had at last been successful and that the

[59] Taylor to Commissioner C. A. Harris, September 4, 1836, in Archives of Department of the Interior, Office of Indian Affairs.

[60] *Ibid.*

[61] Taylor to the Adjutant General, December 1, 1836, and May 8, 1837, in War Department Archives.

commandant of Fort Crawford was freed from these burdensome duties.[62]

While at Jefferson Barracks, Taylor joined with Colonel Enos Cutler of the Fourth Infantry in making application for an exchange of regiments. The headquarters of the Fourth were at Baton Rouge and Taylor would have welcomed the opportunity to return there, in part because of his planting interests, and in part because the colder northern climate had not benefited Mrs. Taylor's health. But the department declined to agree to the proposal.[63] About the same time Taylor was granted a six months' leave of absence which he had requested in order that he might visit his children who had long been away at school in Philadelphia and Kentucky and attend to his private affairs in Louisiana and Mississippi.[64] It had been his desire that the leave should begin as soon as General Atkinson resumed command at St. Louis, but apprehension on the part of the governor of Wisconsin Territory that Indian troubles were imminent caused Taylor to postpone his leave and to return to Fort Crawford to be ready to contribute his "mite in restoring peace in that quarter." [65] No serious trouble developed, but before Taylor was able to avail himself of the leave of absence granted, his services were required in a distant corner of the nation where the Indians were giving the army a most difficult time.

The children at school in Philadelphia and Kentucky must have been the two younger ones—Betty who reached her thirteenth birthday in April, 1837, and Dick, two years her junior. The two older girls had long before abandoned the schoolroom and had become wives of young army officers. Among the small company at Fort Snelling during the year Taylor was stationed there was Dr. Robert Crooke

[62] Mahan, *Old Fort Crawford,* 214.

[63] Taylor to the Adjutant General, April 4, 1837, and the Adjutant General to Taylor, April 24, 1837, in War Department Archives.

[64] Taylor to the Adjutant General, March 19, 1837, *ibid.*

[65] *Ibid.; id.* to *id.,* May 8, 1837, *ibid.*

Wood, a young assistant surgeon from New England. He apparently found time from his duties to pay attention to the Colonel's eldest daughter, Ann, a seventeen-year-old Kentucky belle, and was successful in winning her hand. In September of the next year, 1829, just after Taylor had been transferred to Fort Crawford, life at that post was enlivened by the wedding of the young surgeon and Ann Taylor. During the next six years two sons were born to them at Fort Snelling and two daughters at Fort Crawford to which post Dr. Wood was transferred.[66] The second son, Robert Crooke Wood, Jr., became the favorite of his grandparents, at some stage was taken into their home, and was brought up by them.[67]

Colonel and Mrs. Taylor's second daughter, the sprightly Knox, was also captured by an army officer. The story of her marriage to Jefferson Davis, a handsome lieutenant in her father's regiment, in the face of parental opposition, has been told time and again with little variation except as to the extent of Colonel Taylor's opposition and the reason therefor. The family tradition, recorded many years later by a granddaughter of Colonel Taylor, is that he opposed the marriage on two grounds—one, that he was "slightly prejudiced against Lt. Davis on account of a trifling incident in military life," and the other, that he did not want his daughter to endure the hardships of a soldier's wife of which he was well aware.[68] It was the latter of these reasons that Taylor gave to Major Stephen W. Kearny. To that officer's pleas in behalf of Davis, Taylor blurted out: "I will be damned if another daughter of mine shall marry into the Army. I know enough of the family life of officers. I scarcely

[66] *General Zachary Taylor, The Louisiana President of the United States* (A publication of the Louisiana State Museum, August 5, 1937), 45–48.

[67] *Ibid.*, 48; Statement of Mr. Trist Wood, son of Robert Crooke Wood, Jr., to the author, July 13, 1939.

[68] Memorandum on Zachary Taylor's Ancestry, prepared by Mrs. W. R. Stauffer, in Hardie Collection.

know my own children, or they me." [69] There is no evidence that Taylor offered any opposition to the marriage of either of his other daughters to army men and it is not likely that this was the controlling factor in Knox's case. More important was the incident in military life, an incident that may not have been so "trifling," for the haughty and sensitive Lieutenant, it is said, was ready to challenge the Colonel to a duel but was dissuaded therefrom by the friend he approached to act as his second.[70] The details of this incident are not known, but some clues to its nature are found in a brief reference to it by Davis many years later, long after he and Taylor had been reconciled. At that time he declared that "a mean fellow misrepresented" him to the Colonel. "The Col. believed him," Davis continued, "and assailed me harshly, imputing to me motives the reverse of those by which I was actuated." [71] Davis became so angry and poured out his story to his friends with so much feeling that some of them who were not acquainted with Taylor were influenced to a lifelong dislike of him.[72]

Taylor's opposition to the marriage was so decided that Knox was not permitted to receive Jefferson Davis at the Taylor home; but she found occasion to see him at the home of her close friend Mary Street, the daughter of the Indian Agent, who was facing a similar problem,[73] and elsewhere with the aid of Mrs. Samuel McRee, wife of another officer of the regiment.[74]

Knox was only fifteen years of age when Colonel Taylor and his family removed to Fort Crawford in the summer of

[69] Robert McElroy, *Jefferson Davis, the Unreal and the Real* (New York, 1937), I, 32.

[70] *Ibid.*, 23.

[71] Jefferson Davis to L. B. Northrup, April 25, 1879, in Dunbar Rowland (ed.), *Jefferson Davis, Constitutionalist* . . . (Jackson, 1923), VIII, 383.

[72] *Ibid.;* Northrup to Davis, April 17, 1879, *ibid.*, 378–80.

[73] George Wilson, "George Wilson: First Territorial Adjutant of the Militia of Iowa," in *Annals of Iowa*, 3d Series, IV (1899–1901), 565–66.

[74] McElroy, *Jefferson Davis*, I, 23.

1829. Just when Davis began to give his attention to her is not known, but it was most likely three years later, after the Taylors returned from their eighteen months' sojourn in Kentucky and Louisiana. It was the next spring, 1833, when Knox was celebrating her nineteenth birthday that Lieutenant Davis was transferred to the newly formed mounted regiment of dragoons and ordered away from the Northwest and the girl of his choice. Colonel and Mrs. Taylor doubtless breathed a sigh of relief when the unwelcome suitor departed, but in this case it was not "out of sight, out of mind." The determination of Davis and Miss Taylor to be married remained unshaken. Two years later with the reluctant consent, if not approval, of her parents, Knox traveled to Kentucky and was married at the home of her Aunt Elizabeth, Zachary's sister, on June 17, 1835.[75] Before she left Fort Crawford she had her mother's aid in the preparation of her trousseau and after arriving in Kentucky she received a "liberal supply of money" from her father. Further evidence that the wedding was at least acquiesced in by her family is found in the presence of her sister Ann; her brother-in-law, Dr. Wood; and her father's eldest brother, Hancock Taylor, whose oath was accepted as proof of her lawful age.[76]

Colonel and Mrs. Taylor were never again to see their daughter. Immediately following the wedding Jefferson Davis took his bride to Mississippi to establish their plantation home. Only a few weeks after their arrival both were seized with the dread malarial fever. After a severe struggle Davis threw off the disease and recovered, but his hard-won wife was unequal to the fight and died on September 15 at

[75] Memorandum on Zachary Taylor's Ancestry, *loc. cit.;* Autobiography of Jefferson Davis, in Rowland (ed.), *Jefferson Davis, Constitutionalist,* I, xx.

[76] Memorandum on Zachary Taylor's Ancestry, *loc. cit.;* statement to the author by Mr. Trist Wood, July 13, 1939; McElroy, *Jefferson Davis,* I, 34; Marriage Records of Jefferson County, Kentucky (copy in Kentucky State Historical Society), II, 692. One of the fullest and most accurate accounts of this affair is Walter L. Fleming, "Jefferson Davis' First Marriage," in *Mississippi Historical Society Publications* (University), XII (1912), 21–36.

the home of Davis' sister, Locust Grove plantation, just across the line in Louisiana.[77]

[77] McElroy, *Jefferson Davis*, I, 38; *General Zachary Taylor, the Louisiana President of the United States*, 49, 57.

Chapter VI

HIDE AND SEEK WITH THE SEMINOLES

COLONEL TAYLOR abandoned all thoughts of a furlough when he received General Order No. 50, dated July 31, 1837, ordering him to prepare his regiment for service in Florida and to take up the line of march in time to arrive at Tampa Bay between the tenth and fifteenth of October.[1] For eighteen months the Seminole Indians of Florida had been on the warpath and the army had pursued them through marsh and swamp in vain efforts to bring them to battle. Now it was determined to place an effective force of four thousand regulars in the field for the autumn campaign and the First Infantry, veterans of the Black Hawk War, were ordered to the battle.

Early in the eighteenth century refugees from several southeastern tribes and a number of fugitive slaves began to gather in northern Florida in the country of the Apalachicola and Suwannee rivers. In time they became known as the Seminole Indians, a name which means "separatist" or "runaway" Indians.[2] For many years these Indians and their slaves, held in a form of benevolent bondage, cultivated the soil, raised cattle, and lived in peace in this Spanish territory. Occasionally they were raided by Georgians in search of runaway slaves.[3] By the early nineteenth century, however, this refuge for fugitives had become such

1 *Niles' Weekly Register,* LII (1837), 373.

2 Frederick W. Hodge, *Handbook of American Indians North of Mexico* (Washington, 1912), II, 500.

3 Grant Foreman, *Indian Removal, The Emigration of the Five Civilized Tribes of Indians* (Norman, 1932), 315.

a nuisance that the United States government began to use armed force against it, and with Andrew Jackson in command fought what is known as the first Seminole War. Shortly thereafter the Spanish government was persuaded to sell Florida, and the Seminole country became a part of the United States.

Soon after the United States acquired Florida, the Seminole chiefs were induced to sign a treaty ceding all their cultivated lands in northern Florida and agreeing to remove to the region below Tampa Bay. An exception was made in the case of six of the principal chiefs who were allowed, "in consideration of their friendly disposition, and past services to the United States," to remain in the northern district.[4] When the natives discovered the poor quality of most of the land of southern Florida many of them refused to abandon their old homes and remained there as white settlers moved in. The usual border conflicts, intensified by escaping slaves and expeditions to recover the fugitives, ensued, but stopped short of open war.[5]

In 1832, as part of its general policy of removing the Indians to the country beyond the Mississippi, the government prevailed upon the Seminoles to sign another treaty, the Treaty of Payne's Landing, agreeing to send seven of their "Confidential Chiefs" to examine the territory assigned to the Creeks west of the Mississippi River and promising, "should they be satisfied with the character of that country, and the favorable disposition of the Creeks to reunite with the Seminoles as one people," to relinquish all claim to territory in Florida and within three years to emigrate to the country assigned to the Creeks.[6] At the close of their tour of inspection the confidential chiefs stipulated in a supplemental agreement that they were satisfied and that "their nation shall commence the removal to their new

[4] Kappler (ed.), *Indian Affairs: Laws and Treaties,* II, 203–206.
[5] Foreman, *Indian Removal,* 318–19.
[6] Kappler (ed.), *Indian Affairs: Laws and Treaties,* II, 344–45.

home, as soon as the Government will make arrangements for their emigration, satisfactory to the Seminole nation." [7] The government soon discovered that the Treaty of Payne's Landing was not entirely clear as to who was to be satisfied. Many of the Seminoles, loath to depart from Florida, insisted that the nation, not the confidential chiefs, had to be satisfied. The United States officials, on the other hand, claimed that as the chiefs were satisfied the conditions of the treaty had been met and the migration must commence. No less an authority than Grant Foreman considers the Indian interpretation "obviously" the correct one and he declares the government guilty of sharp practice and duplicity in persuading the chiefs to sign the second agreement.[8] Much as one may sympathize with the Indians in their desire to remain in their eastern home, it is difficult to find their interpretation more obvious than that of the government. However, there does seem to have been sharp practice in the negotiation of both agreements. The chiefs who signed the Treaty of Payne's Landing did not represent all the Indians of Florida, though the treaty was to affect all. Moreover, there is reason to believe that the interpreter at the negotiations, who was paid by the United States, deceived the Indians as to the true meaning of the treaty and that the second agreement was signed by the chiefs only after much persuasion and many threats. The efforts of the United States to carry out the terms of these treaties and to remove the Seminoles from Florida brought on the war in which Zachary Taylor became involved late in 1837.[9]

When Taylor arrived in Florida the war had been on for nearly two years. It began at the end of December, 1835. The Indians, warned that troops would be sent for them

[7] *Ibid.*, 394–95.

[8] Foreman, *Indian Removal*, 321.

[9] On the causes of the Seminole War see *American State Papers: Military Affairs*, VI, 58–61; E. A. Hitchcock to Secretary of War John Bell, January 11, 1841, in E. A. Hitchcock Papers (Division of Manuscripts, Library of Congress).

unless they assembled at Tampa Bay ready to take ship for New Orleans on January 8, 1836, decided that the time had come to act. Led by Osceola, a bold and daring young warrior, a subordinate chief of the Mikasukies, who had risen to leadership through his energy and talents, the Indians chose war rather than deportation. On December 28, a lieutenant in the United States Army and a government Indian agent were attacked and killed just outside Fort King, about one hundred miles north of Tampa Bay, in the heart of the Indian country. Near by, in his home, the fort sutler and his two clerks were also killed. On the same day a party of eight officers and one hundred and two noncommissioned officers and men en route from Tampa Bay to Fort King were ambushed by the Indians—all but three were killed.[10] These attacks inaugurated a seven years' war in which most of the officers and men of the army were to see service; a war marked by long marches through morasses, swamps, wilderness, and "pathless tracts of spongy pine barren" in search of the elusive Indians; a war that was to cost hundreds of lives and millions of dollars.

On the first news of the Seminole outbreak General Edmund P. Gaines, in whose department Florida fell, rushed to the territory with additional troops. After a fruitless march in search of the enemy he surrendered command to General Winfield Scott who had been sent from Washington and departed to appear before a court of inquiry into the failure of his campaign.[11] Scott marched the army up and down the country, was equally unsuccessful in locating the enemy, and soon departed to face a similar inquiry into his military operations.[12] During the summer and fall of 1836, Governor R. K. Call of Florida Territory was in charge of the military operations. His efforts were no more successful than those of his predecessors and the first year

[10] Foreman, *Indian Removal,* 326–27; *American State Papers: Military Affairs,* VI, 561–65.

[11] *American State Papers: Military Affairs,* VI, 817–18, 1043; VII, 365–447.

[12] *Ibid.,* VII, 125–68.

of the war came to an end with nothing accomplished.[13]

In December, Major General Thomas S. Jesup, on leave from his duties as Quartermaster General, arrived to try his luck at the game of hide and seek. By March, 1837, some of the Seminole chiefs, apparently a bit weary of the conflict, sought a conference with Jesup and agreed to emigrate. Within a few weeks so many Indians had presented themselves at Tampa Bay that Jesup reported the war was over. But early in June, while the Indians were still waiting at Tampa for transportation to their new home, they were suddenly surrounded by a party of their own warriors indisposed to surrender in this fashion to the whites, and were carried off to the interior.[14] As the summer heat had already set in, a new campaign was impossible for some months. Jesup had to content himself with planning for the autumn. For a successful campaign against the Seminoles, he reported to the Secretary of War, he needed no less than 6,000 men; some 1,700 to garrison the numerous forts, 750 to escort and protect supply trains, and 3,750 to take the field.[15] The government was most anxious to bring this long-drawn-out affair to a successful conclusion and co-operated thoroughly in meeting Jesup's request for troops.[16] The western forts were stripped of their garrisons and every available regular was ordered to Florida. In addition some four thousand volunteers were mustered into service.[17]

As the fall campaign opened, Jesup, with nearly nine thousand men under his command, felt that he had "a sufficient force for every purpose, either in the field or coming on." [18] He took immediate command of operations in the eastern part of the peninsula, establishing his headquarters at Fort Mellon on Lake Monroe, nearly 150 miles south of St. Augustine. Colonel Taylor, who was now on hand with the First Infantry, was placed in command of all

[13] *Ibid.*, VI, 992–1002; VII, 807.
[14] *Ibid.*, VII, 587, 794 ff.
[15] *Ibid.*, 872–74.
[16] *Ibid.*, 811–12.
[17] *Ibid.*, 582, 588, 596.
[18] *Ibid.*, 889.

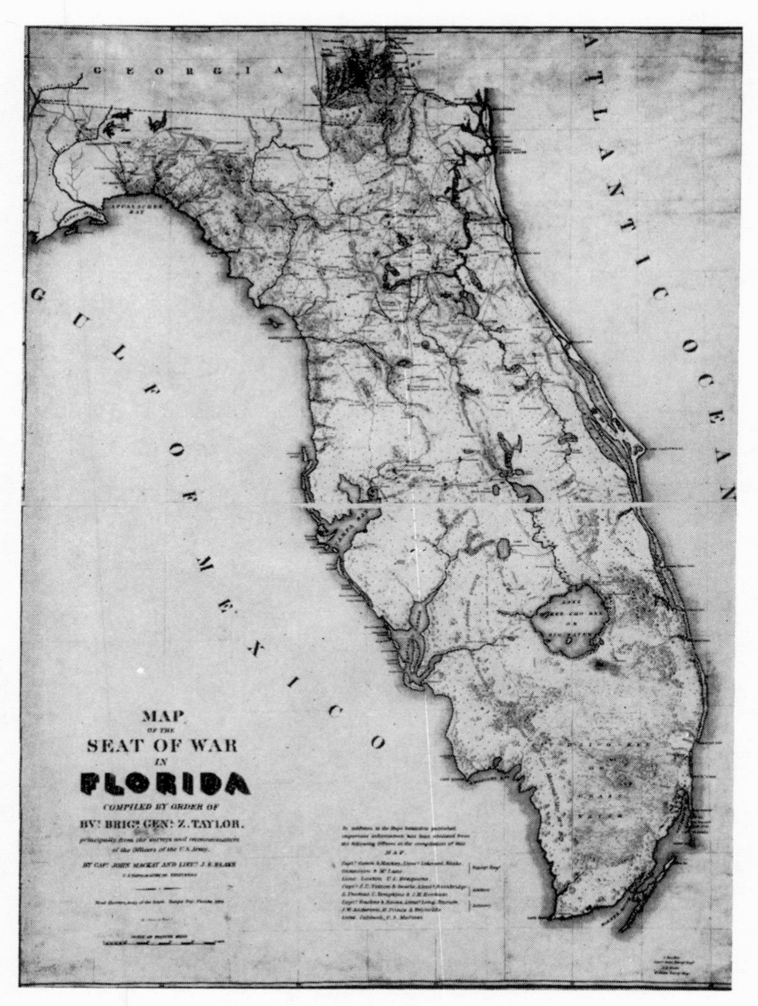

MAP OF THE SEAT OF WAR IN FLORIDA

Reproduced from the original in the National Archives.

operations southeast of Tampa Bay.[19] During late November and early December, Taylor was busy organizing his troops which included several regiments of regulars; volunteers from Florida, Louisiana, and Missouri; and a group of Delaware and Shawnee Indians. The Missouri volunteers were raised as mounted troops, but two thirds of their horses were lost in a storm en route from New Orleans and it was necessary for those without mounts to fight as infantry or not at all. Most of them chose the latter alternative. Taylor sent a portion of his forces under Colonel P. F. Smith down the coast to scour the country east of Charlotte Harbor. With the remainder of his troops he prepared to move inland almost directly east from Tampa Bay in search of the enemy.[20] Because of a shortage of transportation, Taylor adopted the plan of throwing forward his supplies and sent an advance force to construct a depot and a bridge at Pease Creek some fifty miles to the east. When this depot, named Fort Fraser, was completed and well stocked with provisions Taylor and his whole force moved forward from Tampa Bay.[21] After a brief stop at Pease Creek, Taylor, confident of his ability to defeat the enemy if only he could be found, pushed farther east to the western end of Kissimmee Lake and there established another depot, or post, to which the name Fort Gardiner was given.[22] With the aid of his Shawnee and Delaware allies he was soon in conference with Oulatoochee and Jumper, two of the leading men of the Seminoles. The former was the brother and heir of Micconopy, the head of the nation; Jumper was the principal counselor. They declared their readiness to emigrate and left the conference to gather their people for that purpose.[23]

[19] *Niles' National Register,* LV (1838–1839), 29–31.

[20] Taylor to Thomas S. Jesup, November 20, 23, and 26, 1837, in War Department Archives.

[21] *Ibid.*

[22] Fort Gardiner was frequently spelled "Gardner," but as it was named in memory of Captain George Washington Gardiner who lost his life at Dade's massacre the correct spelling is with an "i." Taylor also named Fort Fraser and Fort Basinger after officers killed at Dade's massacre.

[23] Taylor to Jesup, December 7, 1837, in War Department Archives.

Taylor had hopes that other of the chiefs would also agree to a peaceable migration, but in this he was to be disappointed.

On December 19, while still encamped on the Kissimmee, Taylor received word from General Jesup that the efforts to bring the war to a close by negotiation had failed—that although the Indians were in a wretched state they were determined to die in the country the Great Spirit had given them. He was instructed to proceed with the least possible delay against any portion of the enemy within striking distance.[24] Taylor immediately started part of his force down the Kissimmee River and on the next morning followed with the balance of his command which consisted of one company of the Fourth Artillery, 35 in number; the First Infantry, 197 strong; the Fourth and Sixth regiments of Infantry, containing 274 and 221 men respectively; 180 Missouri Volunteers; another group of Missourians known as Morgan's Spies, 47 in number; 30 "pioneers"; 13 "pontoniers"; and 70 Delaware Indians; a total force, exclusive of officers, of just over 1,000. A portion of his Shawnee allies had been detached for other service and the remainder refused to accompany him, some under the pretext that they were sick, others because they were without moccasins.[25]

With this force Taylor marched rapidly down the west side of the river. Late in the evening of the first day's march he came upon the Indian chief Jumper with a part of his band, sixty-three in all, who gave themselves up in accordance with the agreement made some two weeks before. The next morning the captives were escorted on toward Tampa Bay, while Taylor continued his march aided by three friendly Seminoles whom he sent ahead to spy out the position of the enemy. After a night march at the head of the mounted Missouri Volunteers, Taylor came upon a camp

[24] *Id.* to the Adjutant General, January 4, 1838, in *American State Papers: Military Affairs,* VII, 986.
[25] *Ibid.*

that Alligator, another of the Indian chiefs, had abandoned a few days before, but where twenty-two Indians, mainly women and children, were waiting to give themselves up. From these he learned that about twenty-five miles distant on the east side of the Kissimmee were Alligator and all the war spirits of the Seminoles including Sam Jones (Arpincki) and 175 members of the Mikasuki band. The next morning on the banks of the Kissimmee, Taylor established a temporary depot, later named Fort Basinger, where he left all of his heavy baggage, including the artillery, eighty-five sick and disabled infantry, the pioneers, the pontoniers, most of the Delaware Indians, who refused to go farther because their feet and legs were badly cut by the saw palmetto, and one company of able-bodied infantry. With his force reduced to eight hundred Taylor plunged on through cypress swamps, open prairies, and dense hammocks. As he pushed rapidly ahead he came upon hastily abandoned encampments with fires still burning, fresh beef lying on the ground, and hundreds of cattle grazing near by. On two occasions he captured young Indian warriors who were apparently spies. At another point four warriors were seized and impressed into service as guides. Twice the trail became so hot that Taylor disposed his troops for battle, only to have no enemy appear. Finally, on the morning of December 25, he came upon the enemy "occupying one of the strongest and most difficult places to approach and enter in Florida." [26]

The Indians had taken up their position on a cypress-covered hammock which could be reached only by wading knee deep through the mud and water of a swamp three fourths of a mile wide and covered with a thick growth of saw grass five feet high. The swamp was totally impassable for mounted troops and nearly so for those on foot.[27] At the

[26] *Ibid.;* Taylor to Jesup, December 26, 1837, in *Niles National Register,* LIII (1837–1838), 337.

[27] *Id.* to the Adjutant General, January 4, 1838, in *American State Papers: Military Affairs,* VII, 987; *Niles' National Register,* LIII (1837–1838), 323.

edge of the swamp all the men were dismounted and the horses and baggage left under a suitable guard. With the Missouri Volunteers and Morgan's Spies in the first line, instructed to fall back in the rear of the regular troops if they were too hard pressed, Taylor's army entered the swamp and plunged on toward the enemy. When they reached the edge of the hammock they were met with a heavy fire from the Indians. For a short time the Volunteers stood their ground and returned the fire, but when their commander, Colonel Richard Gentry fell, mortally wounded, they broke, and, instead of falling back in rear of the regulars, fled across the swamp to their baggage and horses. "Nor could they be again brought into action as a body," wrote Taylor in his report, "although efforts were made repeatedly by my staff to induce them to do so." [28]

As the Volunteers fell back the troops of the Fourth and Sixth Infantries moved into the front line and in the face of a withering fire from the Indians continued to advance. The brunt of the fight was borne by five companies of the Sixth Infantry. Their commander, Lieutenant Colonel A. R. Thompson, and his adjutant were killed; and all the other officers but one, "as well as most of the non-commissioned officers, including the sergeant major and four of the orderly sergeants," were killed or wounded. In one of these companies only four men escaped untouched. "I am not sufficiently master of words," declared Taylor in his final report on the battle, "to express my admiration of the gallantry and steadiness of the officers and soldiers of the 6th regiment of infantry." After nearly three hours of severe fighting the Seminoles were driven back to the shores of the great lake, Okeechobee, which was in the rear of their position and along which their encampment extended for more than a mile. The hard-pressed Indians "gave one fire and retreated, being pursued by the 1st, 4th, and 6th, and some of the volunteers, who had joined them, until near

[28] Taylor to the Adjutant General, January 4, 1838, *loc. cit.*

night, and until these troops were nearly exhausted, and the enemy driven in all directions." [29]

As soon as the Indians were completely routed Colonel Taylor turned to caring for the wounded. To facilitate their removal from the hammock which had been the main battlefield to his encampment across the swamp he directed his brother, Captain Joseph P. Taylor, who was with the troops as commissary of subsistence, to construct a "small foot-way" across the swamp. With great exertion on the part of every available man this was completed shortly after dark "when all the dead and wounded were carried over in litters made for that purpose, with one exception, a private of the 4th infantry, who was killed and could not be found." At this point in his official report, written a week after the battle, Taylor observed:

> And here, I trust, I may be permitted to say that I experienced one of the most trying scenes of my life; and he who could have looked on it with indifference his nerves must have been very differently organized from my own. Besides the killed [twenty-six], among whom were some of my personal friends, there lay one hundred and twelve wounded officers and soldiers, who had accompanied me 145 miles, most of the way through an unexplored wilderness, without guides, who had so gallantly beat the enemy, under my orders, in his strongest position, and who had to be conveyed back, through swamps and hammocks, from whence we set out, without any apparent means of doing so.[30]

The day after the battle Taylor and his troops remained at their encampment on the edge of the swamp, occupied in caring for the wounded, "in the sad offices of interring the dead," and in collecting nearly a hundred horses, many of them saddled, and about three hundred cattle which the Indians had left behind. That night "in a cabbage-tree hammock, in the center of a large prairie," by the light of burning pine knots, Taylor wrote his first report of the

[29] *Ibid.*

[30] *Ibid.*

battle "on a very dirty sheet of paper, which is the only one in camp." "The victory was dearly purchased," he wrote, "but I flatter myself that the result will be equivalent to the sacrifice made." [31] The following morning, with the wounded on litters constructed of poles and dry hides found in great abundance at the Indian encampment fastened to the backs of the "weak and faltering horses," Taylor led his little army on the return march. When they reached Fort Gardiner, the post on the Kissimmee from which they had set out on December 19, the Fourth and Sixth Infantries and all of the wounded were sent forward while Taylor and the First Infantry remained to make preparations for taking the field again as soon as horses and supplies were available.[32]

Because of the large number of casualties the battle of Okeechobee was at first regarded by the public as "one of the most disastrous battles" of the war,[33] but it was characterized by General Jesup in his final report on operations in Florida during his command as "one of the best fought battles known in our history." [34] It was in reality one of the very few occasions when the Seminoles were relentlessly pursued, no matter where the trail led, and forced to battle with the whites. Their policy had been to fly to the interior wilderness on the appearance of an army, knowing full well that when summer came the heat would fight their battles for them and drive the army from the country. But Taylor had tracked them to the shores of Lake Okeechobee, in the very heart of their wild retreat, and fought them on a battleground of their own choosing. The Seminole losses in the battle were probably somewhat under those of Taylor's force, the known dead totaling fourteen, but the power of the whites was demonstrated and hundreds of Indians surrendered to Taylor during the next few months. By the

[31] Taylor to Jesup, December 26, 1837, in *Niles' National Register,* LIII (1837–1838), 337.

[32] *Id.* to the Adjutant General, January 4, 1838, *loc. cit.*

[33] *Niles' National Register,* LIII (1837–1838), 305.

[34] *Ibid.,* LV (1838–1839), 29.

middle of 1838 he had secured 484 Indians and Negroes.[35] Much as they regretted the loss of gallant officers and men, the President and the commanding general of the army were pleased with the battle. In a general order conveying the thanks of the President for the discipline and bravery exhibited, Major General Macomb declared: "The gallantry and steadiness displayed in the attack, are highly creditable to the corps engaged; and the conduct of Colonel Taylor, in pursuing the enemy and bringing him to action, is deserving of high commendation." [36]

The battle of Lake Okeechobee won for Taylor not only the thanks of the President and the commendation of the commanding general, but also a brevet commission as brigadier general.[37] This reward came to him as somewhat of a surprise. There had been some mention of the possibility in the press, but Taylor's official report that the Missouri Volunteers had fled from the battle and could not be brought back to it had aroused such a storm of protest and criticism in Missouri and in Congress that he believed no such commission would be given him. He admitted to his friend Colonel Davenport that it would be flattering to be noticed in that way, but said "if it is withheld in consequence of my report I feel gratified that it is done as I consider there is now more true courage evinced in telling the truth than in winning a battle." [38]

On February 14, 1838, Senator Thomas H. Benton of Missouri introduced a resolution calling for Taylor's official reports of the battle, because he believed the volunteers from his state had been mistreated. He criticized Taylor for placing his constituents in the first line where they would receive the full power of the Seminole fire. That was the place, not for the citizen soldiers, but for the regular professional troops. That error on the part of Taylor could

[35] *Ibid.* [36] *Ibid.*, LIII (1837–1838), 401.

[37] Heitman, *Historical Register*, I, 949.

[38] Taylor to Col. William Davenport, March 20, 1838, in Historical Society of Pennsylvania.

have been overlooked, said Benton, had he not censured the volunteers when they should have been applauded.[39] A week later, when submitting the documents, Secretary of War Joel R. Poinsett defended both Taylor and the volunteers. The one place Taylor could use the volunteers, he maintained, was as skirmishers to draw the enemy's fire. They were not sufficiently steady or disciplined to serve as the main body to storm the enemy stronghold nor as the reserve, which must consist of picked troops who could if necessary save the battle. On the other hand, it was no disparagement of their character or their efforts to state that they broke and retired in disorder under the murderous fire of the enemy. They had done all that could be expected of them.[40]

Secretary Poinsett's letter with its commendation of the volunteers pleased and satisfied Benton, but in Missouri criticism of Taylor was not so easily overcome. It remained a source of irritation to Taylor for years to come. When in the spring of 1839 the Missouri legislature formulated charges against him he asked for a court of inquiry.[41] A few months later, having received no reply to this request, he repeated it and finally in October was informed by the Secretary of War that the necessary officers could not be spared from their duties in Florida to participate in such an inquiry and that, moreover, there was no need for one. His reputation with the government, with the army, and with his fellow citizens generally was secure, Secretary Poinsett informed him, without vindication by a court of inquiry. The report made by the War Department to the United States Senate, wrote Poinsett "was deemed amply sufficient by that body, and declared to be perfectly satisfactory by the Senators from Missouri." [42]

[39] *Congressional Globe,* 25 Cong., 2 Sess., 182–83. [40] *Ibid.,* 193.

[41] Major General Alexander Macomb to the Secretary of War, May 6, 1839, in War Department Archives (letter missing from file).

[42] Taylor to Secretary J. R. Poinsett, August 1, 1839, and Poinsett to Taylor, October 8, 1839, in War Department Archives.

As late as July, 1841, the Missouri criticism rankled so deeply that when referring to it in a letter to Major E. A. Hitchcock, Taylor characterized it as a transaction without parallel, "as regards iniquity, since the organization of our gov't.," and continued:

> In my report so much complained of, I certainly done [*sic*] the volunteers ample justice; I had no motive in misrepresenting them, not being an aspirant for office of any kind; nor after the most mature reflection would I now, or at any subsequent period, change my report so as to make it more favorable to them. . . . I could not have said more in their favor without an utter disregard to the truth; I stated things simply as they occurred, solely with the view to showing the gov't. & people the difference between instructed and uninstructed troops.[43]

For several months following the battle of Okeechobee, as long as the climate permitted, Taylor continued to direct troop movements in search of the Indians in southern Florida. One expedition was sent down the Kissimmee and around the eastern shore of the lake[44] while another was sent into the Everglade country southwest of the lake.[45] A few Indians were taken here and there and finally in April, 1838, Alligator and his whole band of 360 surrendered to Taylor.[46] No further battles were fought. The red men had learned that no matter how strong their position they could not oppose the overwhelming numbers of the whites and that it was folly to stand and fight when they could always find safety in flight.

Early in the spring of 1838, General Jesup, who had been urging upon the government the abandonment of the plan for the immediate removal of the Seminoles, was instructed to turn over the command of operations in Florida to Brig-

[43] Taylor to Major E. A. Hitchcock, July 28, 1841, in Taylor Papers.

[44] *Id.* to Captain J. Monroe, January 28, 1838, in New York Historical Society.

[45] *Id.* to Colonel William Davenport, March 20, 1838, in Historical Society of Pennsylvania.

[46] Foreman, *Indian Removal*, 362.

adier General Zachary Taylor.[47] Jesup's proposal that the government content itself for the time being with establishing the Indians upon a reservation in southern Florida was disapproved by the Secretary of War who reminded him that the Treaty of Payne's Landing was the law of the land and must be enforced. The Seminoles must be removed. The war must go on.[48]

By the time Taylor took command, over two thousand Seminoles had been captured or had surrendered themselves and had been sent to their new home west of the Mississippi.[49] At the outset of hostilities the number of Seminoles had been variously estimated at from three thousand to five thousand.[50] Thus there remained to face Taylor an undetermined number, but certainly fewer than the three thousand maximum estimate. Shortly after taking command Taylor considered the war "pretty much at an end" so far as it related to the main group of the Seminoles. Only a small portion of that tribe remained in Florida and they were not "disposed to harass the settlements or carry on the war in any other way," he informed the department. But there were four or five hundred warriors, and their families, consisting of Mikasukies, Tallahassees, and refugee Creeks who were dispersed in small parties over a country four hundred miles in length and two hundred in breadth, from near St. Marks to Florida Point and from the "Atlantic to the Gulf." [51] In truth the war was far from over. These small parties dispersed over all of Florida, suddenly appearing to attack a settlement or a detachment of troops and as suddenly disappearing into the swampy wilderness, caused

47 General Order No. 7, April 10, 1838, in *Niles' National Register,* LIV (1838), 97.

48 Major General Thomas S. Jesup to Secretary J. R. Poinsett, February 11, 1838, and Poinsett to Jesup, March 1, in *Niles' National Register,* LIV (1838), 51–52.

49 Jesup to Secretary Poinsett, July 6, 1838, in *Niles' National Register,* LV (1838–1839), 29–31.

50 *American State Papers: Military Affairs,* VII, 997.

51 Taylor to the Adjutant General, June 16, 1838, in War Department Archives.

Taylor two years of ceaseless trouble. Then he turned the job over to others who carried on for two years more before the war was in a measure ended.

During the summer of 1838 Taylor's attention was concentrated mainly on the northern part of Florida where the Indians were causing consternation among the settlers by their renewed attacks.[52] One group, possibly fugitive Creeks, made their murderous assault and fled to the Okefanokee swamp on the Georgia border near the head of the St. Mary's River. All summer long troops searched in vain for these wily red men. Other Indians attacked west of the Suwannee River in the region known as Middle Florida. As the commanding general, Taylor was almost constantly in the saddle moving from post to post, disposing his troops to give the best possible protection to the settlements, and ever seeking an opportunity to bring the enemy to battle.[53]

Early in the fall Taylor made the long trek from Fort Brooke at Tampa Bay to the Apalachicola River country west of Tallahassee to aid the Indian Agent there in dispatching a large group of red men for the West. The entire band of Apalachicola Indians, numbering three hundred, and a party of thirty-four Creeks, had agreed to emigrate, but there was always the possibility that they would have a change of heart before their actual departure. Taylor decided to be on hand to meet any emergency that might arise.[54] When the appointed time for their departure came the Indians refused to embark until they were paid for their lands according to the previous agreement. At General Taylor's direction the Agent, Daniel Boyd, procured the necessary specie, though with some difficulty, and made the payment. It was also Taylor's suggestion that it would be unsafe

[52] *Niles' National Register,* LIV (1838), 386.

[53] Taylor to the Adjutant General, July 13, September 21, October 21, 1838; the Adjutant General to Taylor, August 17; Secretary of War to Taylor, August 20; in War Department Archives.

[54] Taylor to the Adjutant General, August 4 and September 21, 1838, *ibid.*

to send so large a number of Indians on board one steamer which led the Agent to charter two schooners for the trip.[55] Without further incident the embarkation of these Indians took place and Taylor returned to East Florida to prepare for the winter campaign. The acting governor of Florida Territory, who had been fearful that great difficulty would be encountered in removing the Apalachicolas, was present at their embarkation and subsequently wrote to the Secretary of War that the success of the undertaking was due to the exertions of the Agent and to the presence of an efficient force under the immediate command of General Taylor.[56]

From time to time Taylor offered suggestions to the War Department concerning the best means of prosecuting the war. He believed that it was essential to protect the actual settlers and to encourage others to migrate to Florida. Therefore he opposed calling the militia of the territory into service. At least in the more thinly settled areas he thought it essential that the men remain to protect their immediate families. Because those who had lived in Florida for some time were more familiar with the country and better acclimated, Secretary Poinsett was inclined to favor the use of Florida militia rather than that from neighboring states, but he agreed with Taylor that the militia should be drawn from such parts of the territory as were not in danger from the Indians and that in the other sections the settlers should be on hand to defend their own firesides.[57]

Another of General Taylor's proposals received the approval of the Secretary of War, but aroused much opposition in other quarters. This was the proposal that bloodhounds be procured from Cuba to track and discover the Indians.[58] "The cold blooded and inhuman murders lately perpetrated

[55] Daniel Boyd to the Commissioner of Indian Affairs, October 28, 1838, in Archives of Department of the Interior, Office of Indian Affairs.

[56] John P. Duvall to J. R. Poinsett, November 6, 1838, *ibid.*

[57] Taylor to the Adjutant General, August 4, 1838; Secretary Poinsett to Taylor, October 20, 1838; in War Department Archives.

[58] Taylor to the Adjutant General, June 6 and July 28, 1838, *ibid.* (letters missing).

upon helpless women and children by these ruthless savages," wrote Secretary Poinsett in approving this proposal, "render it expedient that every possible means should be resorted to in order to protect the people of Florida and to enable the United States forces to follow and capture or destroy the savage and unrelenting foe." General Taylor was therefore authorized to obtain as many dogs as he deemed necessary, "it being expressly understood, that they are to be employed to track and discover the Indians not to worry or destroy them." [59] In spite of this authorization, Taylor took no steps to carry into effect his own recommendation. The territorial officials, however, sent an agent to Cuba who obtained a pack of thirty-three dogs. Some of these were made available to Taylor who experimented with them early in 1840 with little success. The dogs evidenced no interest in following the Indian trails.[60] As soon as it became public that dogs were being used in the Florida war objection was registered in Congress and numerous petitions from irate citizens were introduced. Most of the congressmen were satisfied when Secretary Poinsett reported that General Taylor had not ordered the dogs, but some continued their objections as long as there was a possibility that the animals would be used. For four or five months memorials against the use of the bloodhounds continued to be presented by senators from several of the northern states.[61] The matter caused less excitement in the House of Representatives where it was handled with a touch of humor. John Quincy Adams presented a resolution calling upon the Secretary of War to report not only as to the number of dogs imported and the cost thereof, but also "the natural, political, and martial history of bloodhounds,

[59] Adjutant General to Taylor, August 31, 1838, *ibid.*

[60] Secretary Poinsett to *id.*, January 26, 1840, *ibid.*; *Niles' National Register*, LVIII (1840), 137; Taylor to the Adjutant General, January 30, 1840, in War Department Archives.

[61] *Congressional Globe*, 26 Cong., 1 Sess., 183, 198, 201, 203, 223, 226, 228, 233, 255, 321, 390, 430.

showing the peculiar fitness of that class of warriors to be associates of the gallant army of the United States . . . and whether he deems it expedient to extend to the said bloodhounds and their posterity the benefits of the pension laws." [62]

When Taylor opened his winter campaign in mid-November, 1838, his primary object was to scour the country north and west of Tampa Bay and to drive the Indians from the vicinity of the settlements—to drive them south of a line of forts which he proceeded to construct across the peninsula from the Bay in a northeasterly direction to New Smyrna on the Atlantic Coast.[63] Week after week the troops sought to accomplish this object. While one body of troops under Colonel Alexander Cummings and Major de Lafayette Wilcox opened roads and built forts across the peninsula, other columns under Colonel David E. Twiggs, Colonel William Davenport, and Lieutenant Colonel John Greene, and many smaller parties, searched every hammock and swamp between St. Augustine and Tallahassee and south to the line of forts. Regardless of privation, fatigue, and danger General Taylor and his eager troops followed every clue and pursued the elusive natives through countless miles of wilderness. In spite of efforts which Taylor regarded as "amounting to recklessness" and as "unparalleled in the annals of Indian Warfare" little was accomplished. It was always the same old story. No matter how fast the army moved they were too slow to catch the fleet-footed red men. They could drive the Indians from hammock to hammock or from one swamp to another, but they could not capture them or bring them to battle. It was, as Taylor stated, "a complete game of hide and seek." [64]

The apparent hopelessness of driving the Indians out of

[62] *Ibid.*, 252.

[63] Taylor to the Adjutant General, November 17, 1838, in War Department Archives.

[64] *Id.* to *id.*, November 17, 1838, January 1, January 5, and March 8, 1839, *ibid.*

the northern part of the territory led General Taylor early in January, 1839, to recommend to the Secretary of War that the entire region north of the Withlacoochee River—the region in which settlers had located—be laid off into districts twenty miles square, and that a post garrisoned by an officer and twenty men be established in the center of each district. It was his opinion that this would "at once give complete security to the exposed inhabitants of Florida and enable all to return to their homes." He would still have sufficient troops to occupy eight or ten stations around the peninsula and these "in conjunction with four or five armed vessels of light-draught kept constantly off the coast" could prevent all intercourse with the Indians "who in two years or less time would be compelled to emigrate or be destroyed." [65]

Approval of this plan reached Taylor about the middle of the following month and he proceeded with all possible dispatch to carry it out.[66] It was well under way by the beginning of April when General Alexander Macomb, the commanding general of the army, arrived in Florida to try his skill at negotiating a treaty with the Seminoles whereby they would agree to end hostilities on condition that they be allowed to occupy the southern portion of the peninsula. Congress had appropriated $5,000 to defray the cost of negotiations with the Seminoles and the administration was ready to make peace, or at least a truce, with the wily foe. General Jesup's suggestion, rejected the year before, was to be given a trial.[67]

After six weeks during which Taylor naturally cooperated with the commanding general to the fullest, Ma-

[65] *Id.* to *id.*, January 5, 1839, *ibid.*

[66] *Id.* to *id.*, July 20, 1839, *ibid.* In his summary of the campaign that began in the fall of 1838 General Taylor pointed out that his troops had built or rebuilt fifty-three forts, constructed nearly four thousand feet of bridges and causeways and opened almost one thousand miles of new roads in addition to old ones repaired.

[67] *Ibid.*; *Niles' National Register,* LVI (1839), 130, 249, LVII (1839–1840), 178.

comb succeeded in reaching an agreement with the Indians. They were to retire within sixty days to the country below Pease Creek and hostilities were to cease. No promises were given that they could remain permanently in Florida and nothing was said of the necessity for future emigration.[68] Immediately following the conclusion of negotiations Macomb issued a general order announcing the termination of hostilities and issued instructions to Taylor to discharge the militia under his command and to send north a portion of his regular troops.[69] Secretary Poinsett promptly instructed Taylor to adopt vigorous measures to protect the Indians in the quiet possession of the territory set apart for their residence and to prevent intrusion by any white person without written authority or license.[70] A verbal treaty of peace had been made. The war presumably was over.

Macomb's "treaty" found little favor with the Florida settlers who were convinced that there could be no peace until the Indians were exterminated or removed from the peninsula. The agreement was bitterly denounced in the territorial press and in public meetings held at Tallahassee, the territorial capital, as disgraceful, insulting, and dangerous. Resolutions "most earnestly and solemnly" protesting the agreement were adopted and sent to the President and to the Secretary of War.[71] In Taylor's judgment, this attitude was due in part to the fact that for political and pecuniary reasons, but primarily the latter, a portion of the people of Florida would not permit the war to terminate "as long as an Indian remains in the country, & Congress will make the necessary appropriations for carrying it on." [72]

Events quickly proved that the treaty did not mean peace.

[68] Macomb to Secretary Poinsett, May 22, 1839, in *Niles' National Register,* LVI (1839), 249.

[69] *Id.* to Taylor, May 19, 1839, in War Department Archives.

[70] J. R. Poinsett to *id.,* June 4, 1839, *ibid.*

[71] *Niles' National Register,* LVI (1839), 241, 265, 321.

[72] Taylor to Jesup, without date, but endorsed "Recd. 7th Oct. '39," in Taylor Papers.

On June 17 Taylor reported to Washington that the Indians had committed murders north of the military road from Tampa to Fort King.[73] About the middle of the following month the Floridians were horrified by an attack upon the plantation of Green Cheares only ten miles from Tallahassee. After firing into the house and killing Mrs. Cheares who was busily sewing, the savages set fire to the dwelling and burned to death the two youngest children of the family. A few days later other murders were committed in this middle Florida section.[74] Civilians were not the only victims of the murderous attacks. On July 23 a detachment of troops, establishing under the terms of Macomb's agreement a trading post for the Indians on the Caloosahatchee River east of Charlotte Harbor, were attacked while encamped for the night and some thirteen of the party of twenty-eight were killed.[75] Clearly the war was not over.

Taylor had grown exceedingly weary of the contest against the savages whom one officer described as "scattered wolves endowed with human intelligence & ingenuity and that too of no mean order." [76] The business of fighting an enemy that would not fight was exasperating. "Could the enemy be brought to battle even in his own strong-holds, the war would soon be closed; no matter at what sacrifice of life on the part of officers and soldiers," Taylor wrote late in July. If nature has made the Indian "fleeter of foot than the white-man," he continued, "and given him a country where no tracks are left when he flies—and if we have not overtaken him 'tis our misfortune not our fault." [77] As early as May 1, when General Macomb was in Florida, Taylor had asked to be relieved from duty in that section. Three

[73] *Id.* to the Adjutant General, June 17, 1839, in War Department Archives (letter missing).

[74] *Niles' National Register,* LVI (1839), 373.

[75] *Ibid.,* 369.

[76] E. A. Hitchcock to John Bell, January 11, 1841, in E. A. Hitchcock Papers.

[77] Taylor to the Adjutant General, July 20, 1839, in War Department Archives.

months later, having received no reply to this communication, he expressed his willingness to remain for the coming fall and winter campaign but renewed his request to be relieved from command. He had frequently pointed out to the department that so few company officers were on duty in Florida that the conduct of the war was severely handicapped. In March he had protested that the Second Infantry was "nearly paralyzed for want of officers." [78] This shortage of officers Taylor now made the basis for his request to be relieved of command. "Our troops might as well be disbanded," he wrote, "if officers cannot be had to command them. This I speak in sober earnestness." [79] An additional reason for a change of commanders was, as Taylor pointed out, "the evident hostility" existing toward the regular army and particularly toward himself among a portion of the people of the territory. This hostility, he said, "has been brought about by some of the Militia field officers, in conjunction with other people, because this species of soldiery has not been called, and kept in service, so as to partake of the public expenditures." [80] Taylor, never enthusiastic about volunteers or militia, had repeatedly objected to calling such troops into service in Florida and had always seized the first opportunity to send them home. Without question this policy, coupled with the fact that the regular troops were not successful in protecting the exposed settlements from attack, did arouse dissatisfaction among the militia and their friends.

Secretary Poinsett, in declining to accede to Taylor's request, pointed out that neither the hostility to the regular army nor the shortage of officers would be remedied by a change of the commanding officer. "At present it appears to me," Poinsett continued, "that your experience fits you better than any other officer in the service, to conduct it to

[78] *Id.* to *id.*, March 19, 1839, *ibid.*
[79] *Id.* to Secretary of War J. R. Poinsett, August 1, 1839, *ibid.*
[80] *Ibid.*

a successful issue; and it gives me great satisfaction to assure you, after a careful perusal of your despatches, and examination of your acts, that the department reposes entire confidence in your zeal, ability and perseverance, and that it is satisfied with what you have done, and willing to rely on your conduct and exertions to carry on the future operations of the War in Florida." [81]

Disappointed that his request to be relieved had been denied, but much pleased by the Secretary's unexpected and complete support, General Taylor began to plan for another campaign. He was soon in receipt of instructions to concentrate on driving the marauding Indians out of the region of the settlements. The Indians were to be driven south of a line extending from the mouth of the Withlacoochee River on the Gulf to Pilatka on the St. John's River southwest of St. Augustine.[82] This line would be nearly one hundred miles north of the line from Tampa Bay to New Smyrna established by Taylor's troops the year before.

Just as Taylor was ready to commence his fall campaign he became ill with the fever which for some months had been making ravages among the officers and soldiers on duty in Florida. He was confined to his bed for nearly two weeks and was unable to render any service or pay even a friendly visit to the many who were dying around him. Large doses of calomel and a diet consisting entirely of hot drinks finally subdued the disease but left the General very much debilitated. At the time of his illness, Taylor was fortunately at Fort Brooke at Tampa Bay, the Florida headquarters of the army. Here he had the care not only of his son-in-law, Surgeon Wood, who was on duty with the troops in Florida, but also of Mrs. Taylor who was living at the fort.[83]

Early in December, though still weak from the fever,

[81] Poinsett to Taylor, October 8, 1839, in War Department Archives.
[82] General Macomb to *id.*, October 17, 1839, *ibid.*
[83] Taylor to Joseph P. Taylor, January 11, 1840, in Taylor Papers.

Taylor took to the saddle and for three months rode the wilderness trails between Tallahassee and St. Augustine in search of the Indian foe. By the end of January he believed they had found "every camp of the enemy, no matter how small, or how carefully hidden from view," in the region from St. Marks east to the Suwannee River, "and their tenants driven in advance of the troops until forced, for the most part, to cross the Suwannee River, a barrier which, if properly guarded, will prevent their return to Middle Florida." [84] Sending Colonel Davenport west to scour the swamps of the Apalachicola, Taylor rode east to St. Augustine inspecting posts en route. The country southwest of that town was thoroughly examined and several companies of dragoons and artillery were strategically posted to protect the inhabitants residing east of the St. John's River. Once again Taylor turned west and, returning by a slightly more southern route to Middle Florida, joined in a final effort to discover any red men who might threaten the settlements of that section.[85]

This campaign was less arduous than those of the two preceding winters. Few of the enemy were encountered and there was little actual combat. But that it was a successful campaign is clear from the absence of Indian attacks upon the settlements. Several small detachments of troops in eastern Florida suffered attack, but the settlers in both Middle and East Florida were able to proceed with their planting with greater safety than at any time since the commencement of hostilities.

As the end of the season for active operations in the field approached, Taylor renewed his request to be relieved of the command of the army in Florida and to end his services in that territory. Anxious to avoid delay and to get away by the first of May, Taylor sent his request in duplicate and

[84] *Id.* to the Adjutant General, January 30, 1840, in War Department Archives.

[85] *Id.* to *id.*, February 16, 1840, *ibid.*

asked that answers be sent to him at both Tallahassee and Gareys Ferry.[86] This time Secretary Poinsett acceded to his request, and Taylor, pleased with the prospect of visiting Dick who was away at school, and of attending to his planting and other personal affairs, prepared to leave for New Orleans.[87] Under date of April 21, Brigadier General W. K. Armistead was ordered to assume command of the army in Florida,[88] but neither the General nor the order had reached Taylor by May 1, the date agreed to by Poinsett for his relief. Impatiently Taylor waited for a successor or instructions. Finally on May 11, still without instructions, he transferred the command to Colonel David E. Twiggs of the Second Dragoons and left the swamps and heat of Florida for New Orleans and Louisville.[89]

As General Taylor closed his two and a half years of service in Florida he suggested to the Secretary of War that the best means of prosecuting the war further was the establishment of a line of posts almost directly across the peninsula from Waccassassee Bay, near Cedar Key, to the Atlantic Coast, some thirty or forty miles below St. Augustine. From these posts the Indians should be constantly harassed as far as possible to the south. If, in addition, the entire coast of the peninsula from St. Marks on the Gulf around to St. Augustine on the Atlantic were blockaded and no vessels allowed to trade with the Indians the war would soon be terminated. He suggested further that the citizens should be persuaded "to rely more upon their own resources to repel a few marauding Indians from their neighbourhoods, and not so much upon the general Government and the Army. The idea of putting a guard at every mans [*sic*] door throughout most of the country and to furnish escorts when

86 *Id.* to *id.*, February 26, 1840, *ibid.*

87 *Id.* to Joseph P. Taylor, January 11, 1840, in Taylor Papers; *id.* to the Adjutant General, May 11, 1840, in War Department Archives.

88 *Niles' National Register*, LVIII (1840), 145.

89 Taylor to Secretary Poinsett, May 11, 1840, in War Department Archives.

they travel is out of the question and should not be thought of."[90]

"Old Rough and Ready," as Taylor was now frequently called,[91] was commander of the forces in Florida for two full years—a longer period than that served by any other of the numerous commanding officers in the Seminole War. But whether he contributed more to the winning of that war is not easy to determine. Probably he did not. The severest fighting took place before he assumed command. Likewise, the greatest progress in removing the Indians, if progress be measured in numbers removed, was made under his predecessors. The direct results of Taylor's two years of war against the Seminoles were disappointingly small, but the persistence with which he harassed them and drove them from one hiding place to another made their life miserable and contributed to their final decision to abandon Florida. In some respects the task he faced was more difficult than that of his predecessors. The Indians, fewer in number, traveled in smaller parties, and more effectively concealed themselves from their pursuers. Moreover, the Indians who remained in Florida when Taylor took command were those most determined to live and die in the land of their fathers.

Taylor's effect on the Seminole War was, perhaps, less than the war's effect upon him. The battle of Lake Okeechobee gave him the chance to demonstrate anew his courage and his determination to carry a campaign through, no matter what obstacles might confront him. His leadership in that battle won for him a brevet commission as brigadier

[90] "Memorandum for the Secretary of War," enclosed in *id.* to *id.*, May 11, 1840, *ibid.*

[91] *General Taylor and His Staff* (Philadelphia, 1848), 81. "Sergeant Harris" is here given as authority for the statement that the sobriquet "Rough and Ready" had its origin in the Seminole campaigns and was introduced into the Mexican War by soldiers who had served under Taylor in Florida. It doubtless refers to his plain, almost rough dress and his readiness to share the hardships of his men and to lead them forward in the face of obstacles that would have turned back a less vigorous and determined officer.

general and elevated him to a position among the first half-dozen officers of the army. This rank and the experience gained and the administrative ability exhibited as the commanding officer of several thousand troops during his two years at the head of the Florida war made possible his selection as commander of the troops sent to the Mexican border which in turn placed him before the public and eventually in the White House.

Chapter VII

THE ARMY OF OBSERVATION

FOR six months following his return from Florida, General Taylor enjoyed a well-earned leave. He arrived at New Orleans with his family on May 21 and with little delay proceeded up the river to Louisville to visit his brother Hancock, his sisters, and other relatives whom he had not seen since he departed in the spring of 1832 for the Black Hawk War. This was to be his last visit with Hancock and with his sisters, Emily and Elizabeth. Hancock and Emily died the next year and Elizabeth in the spring of 1845 as Zachary was preparing to lead troops into Texas. Of Zachary's eight brothers and sisters only Joseph and Sarah lived to share his later triumphs.

Taylor's property holdings in Kentucky were not extensive at this time and did not require much attention from him. In addition to stock in the Bank of Louisville and the Northern Bank of Kentucky, he owned three large storehouses on Wall Street and a lot on Market Street in Louisville. These interests of Taylor were cared for during his long absences by Captain J. S. Allison, the husband of his sister Emily.[1]

Early in the summer General and Mrs. Taylor interrupted their Louisville visit to travel east to Washington, Philadelphia, and New York. In the capital, Taylor reported to the War Department on the Florida war. At Philadelphia he and Mrs. Taylor were joined by their youngest daughter, Betty, who had been attending a boarding school

[1] Copy of Testamentary Paper drawn by Zachary Taylor, November 20, 1837, in Hardie Collection.

in the Quaker City and who now accompanied them as they traveled on to New York City, Niagara Falls, and west to Louisville.[2]

Although Zachary Taylor's own formal education had been very limited he was always deeply interested in the education of his children and grandchildren. He made every effort to give his own children the best educational opportunities and when grandchildren arrived he urged the importance of education for them. "The rearing up our children & establishing them in life so that they can sustain themselves," he wrote to his son-in-law, Dr. Wood, "is in my opinion the most important of our duties." [3] "There is nothing more important to insure a young man a high standing either in the army or navy than literary attainments," he wrote on another occasion, "& a taste for study if he has books etc. will be a source of amusement as well as occupation which will prevent" time from hanging heavy on his hands and keep him "from resorting to certain means to kill time which so frequently results in the destruction of so many young men in both arms of the public service." [4] Taylor's fullest expression of parental duty in the training and education of children is found in another letter to Dr. Wood, to whom he wrote:

> We should do the best for our children in our power; instilling into their minds at an early age the necessity of good principles as regards honesty & truth, as well as good morals, encourage them in the propriety of employment of some kind or other, & to give them a taste for reading, after which they must take their chances, & we must try & be satisfied let matters as regards them eventuate as they may. If they turn out well it will be a source of the greatest possible gratification to their parents, should they do badly, the reverse will be the case in like proportion. Let us do our duty to them & others, to the best of our ability & bear up against what may afterward occur even

[2] Hamilton, *Zachary Taylor,* 142.
[3] Taylor to Wood, May 30, 1847, in *Letters from the Battlefields,* 102.
[4] *Id.* to *id.,* October 5, 1847, *ibid.,* 138.

if unfavorable, at least with propriety & resignation in the best way we can. . . . It is perhaps as well if not better not to make to [*sic*] favorable calculations in favor of our children in early life for should they fail to meet or come up to them the disappointment will be felt with double the effect it would be under different circumstances.[5]

Taylor had no desire to return to duty in Florida, which he regarded a "miserable country . . . where an officer who has any regard for honesty, truth or humanity, has but little to gain, & everything to lose." [6] Therefore, as the expiration of his leave approached, he requested to be assigned to duty anywhere except Florida, but preferably in Louisiana, at Baton Rouge or the barracks near New Orleans.[7] His wishes were honored by the War Department and early in November he was ordered to assume command of all forces in the vicinity of New Orleans and Baton Rouge and to establish his headquarters at either of those towns.[8] Taylor hastened to comply with his orders and on the twentieth of the month arrived in Baton Rouge where for the next six months his headquarters were located.[9] The duties at this station were very light. Taylor found time, as he had hoped, to attend to his private affairs and even to take some interest in politics. He urged upon President-elect Harrison the appointment of John Bell of Tennessee to his Cabinet as Secretary of War, and when that was done he recommended to Bell that he call to Washington Major Ethan Allen Hitchcock, whom Taylor had known since 1820 when Hitchcock, a young lieutenant, served as his regimental adjutant at Bay St. Louis.[10] Major Hitchcock, Taylor urged,

[5] *Id.* to *id.*, September 3, 1846, in Huntington Library; also printed with slight differences in *Letters from the Battlefields*, 52–53.

[6] *Id.* to Major E. A. Hitchcock, May 19, 1841, in Taylor Papers.

[7] *Id.* to Major General Thomas S. Jesup, November 4, 1840, *ibid.*

[8] *Id.* to the Adjutant General, December 6, 1840, in War Department Archives; J. Fair Hardin, "Four Forgotten Frontier Army Posts," *loc. cit.*, 139.

[9] Taylor to the Adjutant General, December 6, 1840, in War Department Archives.

[10] Grant Foreman (ed.), *A Traveler in Indian Territory, The Journal of Ethan Allen Hitchcock* (Cedar Rapids, 1930), 221.

would be of invaluable assistance in the "herculean undertaking" of reforming and resuscitating the military establishment of the country "by restoring its discipline, economy, energy & harmony." [11] This was also done. The appointment, however, may not have been influenced by Taylor for Hitchcock was already well known to Bell and indeed was distantly connected with him by marriage.[12] Hitchcock remained on duty in Washington until the dissolution of Harrison's Cabinet and for some months thereafter. Thus for a period Taylor had another friend near the military heads.

The death of President Harrison only a month after his inauguration and the resignation shortly thereafter of the entire Cabinet except Webster, who remained to complete important negotiations with Great Britain, was viewed by Taylor as a great misfortune for the nation. To Hitchcock he wrote that no one could regret these changes more truly and sincerely than he for

> I do not believe a purer, more talented & independent body of men could have been brought togather [*sic*] or selected for the Stations they filled, or who had more at heart the interest & wellfare [*sic*] of the country, & who in point of disinterestedness & every other qualification I do not ever expect to see replaced during my time as I look upon the Whig party as broken up & in the scramble which is to follow for place, the direction of our national affairs is as likely or more so to fall into the hands of such men as Benton, Linn, Allen, Walker [13] & as any others, but I will not despair of the republic let what come that may.[14]

On his arrival at Baton Rouge, Taylor found his personal affairs "in a much worse state" than he had anticipated.

[11] Taylor to Hitchcock, May 19, 1841, in Taylor Papers.

[12] W. A. Croffut (ed.), *Fifty Years in Camp and Field. Diary of Major General Ethan Allen Hitchcock, U. S. A.* (New York, 1909), 120, 128, 130 ff. Hereafter cited as Hitchcock, *Fifty Years in Camp and Field.*

[13] Taylor doubtless refers to the Democratic senators, Thomas Hart Benton and Lewis F. Linn of Missouri, Robert J. Walker of Mississippi, and William Allen of Ohio.

[14] Taylor to Hitchcock, November 3, 1841, in Taylor Papers.

Several years before he had given security for some of his friends who had since died insolvent, leaving him responsible for liabilities to the amount of several thousand dollars. He had paid some of these obligations and was making every effort to meet the remainder when in May, 1841, he was ordered to Fort Gibson in the Indian Territory to take command of the Second Military Department.[15] Although Taylor regarded the assignment to this important post as a mark of confidence in him, he was disappointed by it because he had hoped to remain at Baton Rouge for another year. He was anxious not only to pay off the $4,000 still due these creditors, but also to put his affairs in such a condition that he might soon retire and "make room for younger & better soldiers." He was beginning to feel some of the infirmities of age and more than ever was thinking of retirement. "I do not wish to continue a day longer than I am qualified for the active duties of the field," was his attitude. "The army is now paralyzed by too many broken down officers . . . who must be gotten clear of in some way or other, before it can be restored to a proper state of health & efficiency." [16] Moreover, Taylor believed that when such officers as Generals John E. Wool, Hugh Brady, and Henry Atkinson were stationed year after year in the closest proximity to their homes, in some instances establishing their headquarters in their own residences, he who had spent nearly a decade at the most remote and out-of-the-way posts in the country, far from where he could give the slightest attention to his private concerns, might have been permitted to remain at Baton Rouge for more than six months.[17]

Taylor was not the only person disgruntled by his new assignment. The friends of General Matthew Arbuckle, whom Taylor succeeded in command of the Second Depart-

[15] *Id.* to *id.*, July 28, 1841, *ibid.;* the Adjutant General to Taylor, May 1, 1841, in War Department Archives.

[16] Taylor to Hitchcock, May 19 and July 28, 1841, in Taylor Papers.

[17] *Id.* to *id.*, November 3, 1841, *ibid.*

ment, felt that Arbuckle was disgraced by the transfer from the command of a department to the command of a post at Baton Rouge where there was not a single company of troops and no duties to perform. Arbuckle's friend, Senator A. H. Sevier of Arkansas, offered a resolution calling upon the President to explain the causes of the transfer and in speaking in behalf of its adoption declared that Arbuckle was being sent into exile at Baton Rouge. After a brief but warm debate the resolution was laid on the table.[18] Taylor regarded Sevier's object as purely political. He believed the senator had no real interest in "the old gentleman," Arbuckle, but merely desired to harass and annoy the new Secretary of War.[19] This may have been Sevier's object, but General Arbuckle had been at Fort Gibson most of the time for nearly seventeen years and had many friends in Arkansas who doubtless were displeased by his removal.

As soon as General Taylor could secure passage, which was on June 2, he reluctantly embarked with his family for Fort Gibson some eight hundred miles up the Mississippi and Arkansas rivers. Because of the low stage of water in the Arkansas they reached Little Rock only after considerable delay and great difficulty. There they "found the river so low that steam boats of the smallest class could ascend no higher," so Taylor "hired land transportation" and proceeded nearly two hundred miles to Fort Smith. Leaving his family at that post, he continued on another sixty miles to Fort Gibson where he found and relieved General Arbuckle. Because of the lack of comfortable officers' quarters at Fort Gibson, Arbuckle had shortly before secured permission to transfer his headquarters to Fort Smith. Taylor decided to act on this authority and returned to Fort Smith where his headquarters were located for the next three years.[20]

[18] *Congressional Globe,* 27 Cong., 1 Sess., 14, 29, 43.
[19] Taylor to Hitchcock, July 28, 1841, in Taylor Papers.
[20] *Ibid.*

General Taylor, who frankly declared that he was "a decided advocate for the most rigid economy in the management of all our political and public concerns," was shocked by what he regarded as the useless expenditure of labor and money at Fort Smith which though started many years before was still far from complete. Not only was the fort located too close to the river and the adjacent marshy lands, but it was being constructed on such a grand scale that he declared if finished it would "serve as a lasting monument of the folly of those who planned, as well as him who had the same executed." The immense stone blockhouses, the large bastions, and the thick fifteen-foot stone wall which was to enclose the entire area he regarded as quite unnecessary at a point where there was no danger of Indian attack. "The plan of the establishment is highly objectionable," he wrote, "& if carried out will cost three times as much, or even more than that there was any necessity for." [21]

Shortly after General Taylor assumed his new duties, an officer who immediately won the confidence of the General joined his staff. This officer was Captain William Wallace Smith Bliss who served Taylor as adjutant to the end of his military career and as private secretary during his year and a half in the White House. Captain Bliss was a well-educated and widely read man. Many a spare hour or long evening at Fort Smith he spent in translating German articles on philosophy which he forwarded to his friend, Major Ethan Allen Hitchcock who, though well educated and a constant reader, apparently did not read German. For years the correspondence of these two scholarly officers was devoted to philosophical and literary discussions.[22] Bliss not only won the confidence of the General, but won his way into the hearts of the Taylor family, among whom he was

[21] Taylor to Hitchcock, November 3, 1841, in Taylor Papers.

[22] Bliss to *id.*, July 11, 1840, September 14, 1841, July 29, 1842, and April 30, 1843, in Hitchcock Papers.

known as "Perfect Bliss." In particular did he capture the heart of Betty Taylor, seventeen years of age when he joined General Taylor's staff. Seven years later Betty became Mrs. Bliss and the third of Old Rough and Ready's daughters to marry an army officer.

Soon after establishing his headquarters at Fort Smith, Taylor received official notification of the death of Major General Alexander Macomb who had been the commanding general of the army for thirteen years. On July 27 the garrison paid the departed general "the last sad honors . . . by firing a six pounder during every half hour from the rising to the setting of the sun." The vacancy caused by Macomb's death was filled, as Taylor expected it would be, by the promotion of Winfield Scott who for thirteen years had been chafing over the fact that Macomb rather than he had been made commanding general in 1828. "Old Fuss and Feathers," as Scott was called, continued at the head of the army through the remainder of Taylor's life and for many years thereafter.[23] Although Taylor had long known Scott the two men had never been closely associated for any length of time and had not developed any close friendship. Taylor's relations with Scott as commanding general were formal and without moment until the outbreak of the Mexican War when they became severely strained by professional and political rivalry.

As commander of the Second Military Department, General Taylor's chief concern was again with the unending problem—the Indian. Forts Gibson and Smith were both in Indian Territory near the new homes of the Cherokees, the Creeks, and Taylor's old Florida enemies, the Seminoles. Fort Gibson was regarded by Taylor as one of the most important posts on the whole Indian frontier. A respectable garrison there, he believed, would do much to preserve peace among the most formidable tribes of the border as

[23] Taylor to *id.*, July 28, 1841, in Taylor Papers; Charles W. Elliott, *Winfield Scott: the Soldier and the Man* (New York, 1937), 399–400, 741–42.

well as to prevent any general attack against the whites.[24] One hundred and forty miles south of Fort Gibson was Fort Towson, close to the Chickasaws and Choctaws. It was located on the Red River, the southern boundary of the United States, and guarded both the western and the southern frontiers. One of Taylor's first tasks was to establish a new fort higher up the Red River to protect the emigrant Chickasaws and Choctaws from the wild tribes of the prairies and from Texas raiding parties in pursuit of marauding Indians. For years there had been consideration of the need for such a new fort, but not till 1841 were any definite steps taken. In the spring of that year Captain Benjamin D. Moore examined the country between the Blue and Washita rivers and recommended a site near the mouth of the latter.[25] Having received instructions to make a definite selection of a site and to proceed to establish a fort,[26] Taylor left Fort Smith late in September for the Washita River. He examined the country on both sides for some twenty miles above the mouth and chose the site recommended by Captain Moore in the spring. It was on the east side of the river about one and a half miles from the stream and nearly twenty miles up the river from its junction with the Red.[27]

Actual building operations commenced the next spring and continued for more than a year. Before the new fort, named "Fort Washita" by Taylor,[28] was completed it narrowly escaped abandonment. In spite of its strategic location, giving the army contact with events in a widespread country, the War Department informed Taylor in March,

24 Taylor to Hitchcock, November 3, 1841, in Taylor Papers.

25 H. P. Beers, *Western Military Frontier, 1815–1846* (Philadelphia, 1935), 161.

26 Adjutant General to Taylor, August 11, 1841, in War Department Archives.

27 Taylor to the Adjutant General, October 14, 1841, *ibid.* (letter missing); Grant Foreman, *Advancing the Frontier, 1830–1860* (Norman, 1933), 100.

28 Taylor to the Adjutant General, May 31, 1842, in War Department Archives; Foreman, *Advancing the Frontier,* 100.

1843, that the general-in-chief was inclined to abandon the new fort.[29] Prompt and vigorous protests from Taylor, who expressed his belief that no post on the frontier exerted a more salutary influence, convinced the department of the value of the fort and the order to suspend work was revoked.[30] Fort Washita, one hundred miles up the Red River from Fort Towson, was a definite advance of the frontier and by curtailing the predatory raids across that river by the Indians and the Texans, contributed in large measure to the preservation of peace in that quarter.[31]

Taylor was also concerned with the abandonment of the partially constructed Fort Wayne situated on the eastern edge of the Indian Territory about eighty miles north of Fort Smith. Soon after assuming command of the Second Department, Taylor recommended that the site of the post be changed because it was occupying some of the best of the Cherokee lands and interfering with some of the most improved farms among the half-breeds. The Cherokees, he wrote, were very much opposed to its selection as well as to its continued occupancy. Within fifteen or twenty miles another site, with all the advantages and none of the disadvantages of this one, could be found.[32] At the close of the year, he was authorized to abandon Fort Wayne in the spring and to establish another post wherever he might decide.[33] Shortly thereafter Major Hitchcock visited the Indian Territory as the special agent of the War Department and reinforced Taylor's recommendation that Fort Wayne be abandoned but suggested that the new fort be established much farther north where it could control the Osages, "the

[29] Adjutant General to Taylor, March 9, 1843, in War Department Archives.

[30] Taylor to the Adjutant General, March 29, 1843, *ibid.;* Adjutant General to Taylor, May 12, 1843, *ibid.*

[31] Rex Wallace Strickland, "History of Fannin County, 1836–1843," in *Louisiana Historical Quarterly,* XXXIV (1930), 54.

[32] Taylor to Hitchcock, November 3, 1841, in Taylor Papers; Adjutant General to Taylor, September 11, 1841, in War Department Archives.

[33] *Id.* to *id.,* December 1, 1841, *ibid.*

greatest thieves near the frontier." [34] These suggestions found favor with the department and Taylor was soon busy removing troops and equipment from Fort Wayne and establishing a new post, Fort Scott, to the north on the military road to Fort Leavenworth.[35]

The white settlers and traders in the vicinity of Fort Wayne were thoroughly displeased by the abandonment of that post, for they had been profiting by the sale of liquor and other supplies to the garrison. With the aid of the Governor and the legislature, they portrayed the defenseless state of their frontier and petitioned the President to re-establish the fort. The slightest disturbance among the Cherokees, their nearest Indian neighbors, was the occasion for renewed appeals that they be given protection against the bloodthirsty savages who had been set down at their very door.[36] These appeals and the concurrent demands of the Texas authorities that the United States be more vigilant in preventing Indian raids into Texas territory resulted in heavy reinforcements being sent to Taylor late in March. The Sixth Infantry and five companies of dragoons were ordered from Jefferson Barracks and Fort Leavenworth to Fort Towson, increasing the force at Taylor's disposal from less than seven hundred to two thousand.[37] In spite of these reinforcements the citizens of Arkansas continued their demands for protection. Taylor was fully aware of the true motives back of these petitions and opposed them in outspoken fashion. In December, 1842, he urged the Secretary of War to disregard these representations of the dangerous state of affairs on the frontier "unless confirmed by the reports of the officer commanding on the frontier, and responsible for its safety." He declared these represen-

[34] Hitchcock to Secretary of War J. C. Spencer, January 9, 1842, in Foreman (ed.), *A Traveler in Indian Territory*, 245–48.

[35] *Ibid.*, 221; Foreman, *Advancing the Frontier*, 78–80; Taylor to the Adjutant General, May 15, 1842, in War Department Archives.

[36] Foreman, *Advancing the Frontier*, 81–82.

[37] Secretary of War J. C. Spencer to Taylor, March 26, 1842, in War Department Archives.

tations rested upon the false assumptions that the tribes on that border retained their warlike habits and that they would combine in an attack upon the settlements, and then continued:

> By far the strongest tribes on this frontier are the Cherokees, Choctaws, and Creeks; without the consent or cooperation of one or all of them, no hostile combination against the states can possibly be formed in this quarter. Now, anyone who has visited these people in their new homes, knows that they have completely laid aside their warlike habits, and are assiduously cultivating the arts of peace. For more than a hundred miles, the state of Arkansas has for neighbors the Choctaws, whose boast it is, that they have never killed a white man; for the remainder of its frontier, it has the Cherokees, who are quite too intelligent, whatever may be their internal quarrels, to meditate a war against the whites. The Creeks, who lie farther back from the frontier, are not at all behind the other two tribes in their disinclination to war. The improbability, I might almost say, impossibility, of any one of these tribes taking arms against us, is only exceeded by that of a hostile combination among them, the declared apprehension of which is really too preposterous to merit notice.[38]

In spite of this clear-cut statement by Taylor, the War Department did not entirely ignore the petitions and protests from Arkansas. When three months later Taylor received instructions relating to anticipated troubles among the Cherokees, he replied that his previous report had been made with the "view of sparing the Department the needless anxiety often caused by the representations of ignorant or interested persons" but that it had apparently failed of its object. Again he asserted that no intelligent citizen of Arkansas honestly entertained apprehensions of trouble among or with the Cherokees. "The War Department may rest assured," he wrote, "that such fears are seldom or never expressed here; and if they reach Washington, it is with a

[38] Taylor to the Adjutant General, December 23, 1842, *ibid.*

view to some ulterior and private object—in this case, very evidently, the reoccupation of Fort Wayne, and consequent expenditures of public money in that quarter." After a vigorous denial of any need for the re-establishment of that fort, Taylor recommended that all "citizens of Arkansas" expressing fears of probable Cherokee excitements be referred to "the Commanding General of this Department, who is responsible for the security of the frontier, and who will not fail, on proper applications, and probable grounds of danger, to take the most efficient measures to preserve the peace." This policy, he declared, would not only save the War Department much trouble, but would also satisfy the applicants if they were really sincere.[39]

General Taylor's steadfast opposition to these frontier demands and his advocacy of rigid economy in all public concerns helped win the admiration of his adjutant. At the outset, Captain Bliss was hoping his stay in that distant country would be short,[40] but in time he came to feel that association with Taylor was full recompense for isolation. To Hitchcock he wrote:

> We have the usual annual excitement about Cherokee affairs —Petitions for the re-establishment of Fort Wayne &c &c. The Gen'l's reports are not at all in accordance with the wishes of the miserable population on the frontier who cannot live, but on public expenditures. He neither wishes more troops, nor more forts, nor more money spent, and tells the dept. plainly that it will be soon enough for them to be alarmed, when *he* reports danger. I consider it one of the most fortunate circumstances of my life to have been brought in near official relation with so single-hearted a man.[41]

The peacetime relations between the Indians and the United States government were in the hands of the Indian

[39] *Id.* to *id.*, March 28, 1843, *ibid.*
[40] Bliss to E. A. Hitchcock, July 29, 1842, in Hitchcock Papers.
[41] *Id.* to *id.*, April 30, 1843, *ibid.*

agents. The military were present to help maintain peace and to restore it if unfortunately it should be broken. Taylor fully realized this and was careful to make such communications with the Indians as he found necessary through the agents in order not to deprive them of their proper importance and influence with the tribes. Yet, as commander of the Second Military Department, and with his long experience in Indian affairs, Taylor naturally took an interest in all phases of Indian relations. During his years at Fort Smith he attended two Indian councils. The first of these, called by General Roley McIntosh, the chief of the Creek Nation, met at the Deep Fork council ground near Fort Gibson, in May, 1842, and was attended by over two thousand Indians representing sixteen tribes. Its purpose was to redress all grievances among the tribes, to smoke the pipe of peace, and to enhance the influence of the Creek Nation.[42] General Taylor, Colonel James Logan, the Creek agent, and Captain William Armstrong, the Acting Superintendent of Indian Affairs in the Southwest, addressed the council as the invited representatives of the United States. Taylor advised the Indians of the necessity of keeping peace among themselves and of refraining from any interference in the contest between Texas and Mexico. He also urged them to cooperate in the return of white prisoners held by prairie tribes. This appeal brought some results, for a few weeks later a party of Kickapoo Indians surrendered at Fort Gibson a ten- or eleven-year-old white boy whom they claimed to have bought from the Comanches for $400, and shortly thereafter another youth who had also been purchased from the Comanches was brought in. These boys had been captured in Indian raids on Texas at such an early age that when they arrived at Fort Gibson the only language they spoke was that of their captors. Their ransom was paid by

[42] James Logan to the Commissioner of Indian Affairs, May 30, 1842, in Archives of Department of the Interior, Office of Indian Affairs; Foreman, *Advancing the Frontier*, 205.

order of General Taylor and in time they were returned to their homes.[43] Taylor remained at the council two days and found only the most friendly feelings exhibited toward the United States. "All seemed animated with a desire to cultivate peaceable relations with our government and with each other," he reported.[44]

In June of the following year Taylor was present at an even larger Indian council held on the council ground of the Cherokee Nation at Tahlequah. The official delegates, representing eighteen tribes, numbered only two hundred and eleven, but there were some three or four thousand persons in daily attendance.[45] John Ross, chief of the Cherokees and Roley McIntosh of the Creeks addressed the council and both emphasized "their lingering love for their former homes, respect for their ancestry, a cautiously-expressed sense of the injustice done them by their removal, a reluctant resignation to their fate, and a desire to cultivate the arts of peace and to provide for their offspring." [46] General Taylor was impressed by the pacific nature of the council and reported to Washington that its results would be beneficial for both the red man and the whites.[47]

Taylor's sympathetic understanding of the Indian's plight is seen in his handling of the question of trespassing on Cherokee lands by Alligator and his Seminole followers. When the matter was first called to his attention by the Cherokee agent, he informed the Seminoles that unless they removed to their own lands by the first of May

[43] James Logan to Commissioner of Indian Affairs, May 30, 1842, *loc. cit.;* Taylor to the Adjutant General, May 31, 1842, in War Department Archives; Foreman, *Advancing the Frontier,* 202–204; Grant Foreman, *Pioneer Days in the Early Southwest* (Cleveland, 1926), 284–85.

[44] Taylor to the Adjutant General, May 31, 1842.

[45] Foreman, *Advancing the Frontier,* 205–206; P. M. Butler, Cherokee Agent, to the Commissioner of Indian Affairs, June 21, 1843, in Archives of Department of the Interior, Office of Indian Affairs.

[46] Foreman, *Advancing the Frontier,* 210.

[47] Taylor to the Adjutant General, June 14, 1843, quoted *ibid.,* 206.

he would be compelled to use military force against them.[48] At the same time he planned the use of a force strong enough to overawe the Indians and prevent bloodshed. When he discovered, however, that the Seminoles had planted crops, he gave them permission, with the consent of the Cherokees, to remain until their harvest was completed.[49] When autumn arrived the Cherokee agent, whose co-operation Taylor desired, was absent and action was deferred until his return. "His absence, however, was so long protracted," reported Taylor, "that it became an obvious dictate of humanity to postpone the removal altogether until the spring, rather than drive women and children from comfortable huts, and expose them to the vigor of an inclement season."[50] Shortly after Taylor reached this decision, he learned that the Cherokees were opposed to the forcible removal of Alligator's party and he informed the department that he would take no steps in that direction "until a formal, official application shall be made through the Agent, by the constituted authorities of the Cherokee nation."[51] Taylor's course and views in relation to the removal of the Seminoles won the complete approval of the Secretary of War who characterized them as "judicious and humane."[52] A few years later, the presence of the Seminoles having become increasingly objectionable to the Cherokees, they were with much difficulty induced to remove to their own land.[53]

At all times it was General Taylor's hope to preserve peace among the Indians and between the two races by following a policy of honesty and impartiality. He was fully disposed to co-operate with the Indian chiefs in maintaining law and order and was always ready, when called upon by the agent,

[48] *Id.* to *id.*, March 27, 1842, in War Department Archives.

[49] *Id.* to *id.*, May 15, 1842, *ibid.* [50] *Id.* to *id.*, December 23, 1842, *ibid.*

[51] *Ibid.*

[52] Adjutant General to Taylor, January 17, 1843, in War Department Archives.

[53] Grant Foreman, *The Five Civilized Tribes* (Norman, 1934), 228–35.

to send troops in pursuit of Indians charged with murder. He was also ready to aid in breaking up suspected plots or conspiracies against the laws and order of the Indian nations and to prevent unlawful councils or assemblages. He realized that Indian troubles all too frequently resulted from the activities of unscrupulous whites and regretted that he had no authority to act against such persons within the limits of the state of Arkansas. However, he could and did resist the demands of the troublemakers for action against the Indians when he believed they were motivated by selfish interests.[54]

Throughout the years that Taylor was in command in the Southwest the relations of the United States and Texas were a significant factor in all military policies in that section. When he took command of the Second Military Department in 1841 it included Louisiana as well as Arkansas and the Indian Territory. Consequently the entire border between the United States and Texas came under his supervision. The next year Louisiana was placed in the limits of the reorganized First Department, but a large portion of the borders still fell within his jurisdiction. In the spring of 1844, when border troubles were becoming critical, Taylor was transferred to the command of the First Department and his headquarters were established at Fort Jesup, the American fort nearest the occupied portion of Texas. Thereafter he was even more concerned with the relations of the United States and her southern neighbor.

When Taylor took command in the Southwest the independence of Texas had been recognized by the United States and by some of the important nations of Europe, but Mexico had taken no such action and from time to time she made renewed efforts to re-establish her authority over Texas. These efforts always created a flurry of excitement

[54] Taylor to the Adjutant General, February 14, 1844, and enclosures, in War Department Archives.

along the southern border of the United States. The annexation of Texas to the United States, which many persons in both countries had championed from the beginning of the Texas revolution, had thus far been defeated by partisan and sectional politics in the United States. The issue was by no means a dead one, however, and the measures and negotiations looking toward annexation frequently involved the troops on the border.

The border relations of the two nations were generally friendly, but occasionally some incident caused friction and made trouble for Taylor. Indians who crossed the border and committed depredations were the chief cause of trouble, although at times the actions of civil or military officials resulted in controversy. On one occasion a party of armed Texans in search of illegal traders were apprehended near the border by some of Taylor's forces and were arrested and disarmed. The Texas government, protesting that the arrest had taken place on Texan soil, denounced the whole proceeding as an outrageous invasion of her territory and insisted that adequate apologies and reparations be made.[55] At another time troops from Fort Towson crossed the Red River into Texas and seized supplies which had been destined for that post but were held by a Texas revenue official. Again Texas vigorously protested.[56] Both of these incidents required investigation by Taylor.

But the border problem that most affected Taylor was that of raids across the line by Indian bands. As early as September, 1841, Taylor was instructed to adopt whatever measures he deemed "necessary and proper, for restraining the United States Indians from entering the territory of Texas for any purpose," [57] and shortly thereafter five com-

[55] William R. Manning (ed.), *Diplomatic Correspondence of the United States. Inter-American Affairs* (Washington, 1932–1939), XII, 314–16, 332–38.

[56] *Ibid.*

[57] Adjutant General to Taylor, September 29, 1841, in War Department Archives.

panies of the Second Regiment of Dragoons were sent to Forts Jesup and Towson to help in this task.[58] In the following spring when Texas was faced by invasion from Mexico, the Texas chargé d'affaires in Washington made a passionate appeal to the United States to send sufficient troops to the border to restrain the Indians so that Texans could leave their homes and join in defending their country against the Mexicans with confidence that "the Tomahawk, and scalping knive [*sic*], will not be raised by the savage foe against the helpless women and children left behind." [59] This may have been a mere excuse to get a powerful enough force on the border to influence the Mexican invaders, but Washington, called upon at the same time by Governor Archibald Yell of Arkansas for better protection for the people of his state, hastened to increase General Taylor's forces and to instruct him to exercise the "utmost vigilance" to prevent any Indians from raiding into Texas.[60] Soon after receiving these instructions, Taylor traversed the border from the newly established Fort Washita to Fort Jesup, some three hundred miles, and back to Fort Towson. He found the frontier perfectly quiet and reported "no excitement seems to exist in relation to any invasion by Mexico, or of that power, by Texas." [61] Part of this journey was made on the Texas side of the border, giving Taylor an opportunity to confer with Memucan Hunt, the inspector general of Texas, and to gather firsthand information about conditions south of the border.[62] "The Texan population along the line is orderly and well disposed towards the United States," he informed Washington, "indeed, most of the people look anxiously to the annexation of Texas, as their only hope of permanent prosperity." [63]

[58] Beers, *The Western Military Frontier, 1815–1846,* 160.

[59] James Reily to Secretary Webster, March 28, 1842, in Manning, *Diplomatic Correspondence,* XII, 230–31.

[60] Secretary J. C. Spencer to Taylor, March 26, 1843 (2 separate instructions of the same date), in War Department Archives.

[61] Taylor to the Adjutant General, May 31, 1842, *ibid.*

[62] *Id.* to *id.,* July 5, 1842, *ibid.*

[63] *Ibid.*

President John Tyler was a warm advocate of the annexation of Texas, but as long as Daniel Webster remained his Secretary of State no action to this end could be taken. When Abel P. Upshur took over the State Department and sought to open treaty negotiations with Texas, he found President Sam Houston insistent that the United States furnish protection against attack from Mexico during the negotiations. Houston well knew how aroused Mexico would be by a treaty of annexation and he demanded that troops be sent to the border and ships to the Gulf Coast of Texas. A promise of such protection given by the United States chargé d'affaires in Texas [64] was disavowed by Washington,[65] but Tyler promised protection as soon as the treaty was signed. Texas consented to negotiate on this basis and on April 12, 1844, a treaty was agreed to.[66] In keeping with Tyler's promise to the Texans, prompt measures were taken to furnish protection. Naval vessels were concentrated in the Gulf waters [67] and General Taylor was ordered to Fort Jesup to command a *"corps of observation"* with instructions to hold his troops "in readiness for service at any moment." [68] He was further instructed to take prompt measures to open communications with the President of Texas "in order to inform him of your present position and force and to learn and to transmit to this office (all confidentially) whether any, and what external dangers may threaten that government or its people." Should such dangers appear imminent he was to march his forces to the Sabine River "but not proceed beyond the frontier without further instructions." [69] The transfer of General Taylor from the

[64] William S. Murphy to Anson Jones, February 14, 1844, in Manning, *Diplomatic Correspondence*, XII, 327–29.

[65] *Id.* to *id.*, April 12, 1844, *ibid.*, 346–47.

[66] Oliver P. Chitwood, *John Tyler, Champion of The Old South* (New York, 1939), 350.

[67] Message of President Tyler to the Senate, May 15, 1844, in J. D. Richardson (ed.), *Messages and Papers of the Presidents* (Washington, 1897–1905), IV, 316–18.

[68] Adjutant General to Taylor, April 23 and 27, 1844, in War Department Archives.

[69] *Ibid.*

Second Military Department to command the troops on the border at this critical moment is evidence of the high regard in which he was held by the officials in Washington. With great confidence in Taylor's "judgment and discretion" and "full reliance" in his "prudence," the Secretary of War in consultation with General Scott, the commanding general of the army, selected him to take charge of the most important military operations undertaken in many years.

On June 17, the very day that Taylor arrived at Fort Jesup, he dispatched Captain Lloyd J. Beall of the Second Regiment of Dragoons to President Houston with word that he was on the border with one thousand effective men. Taylor instructed Beall not only to bring back any communication from Houston but also to keep a full and accurate journal of his trip noting particularly distances, rivers and other obstacles to troop movements, and supplies of water, corn, and cattle. The character of the inhabitants and their attitude toward annexation should also be observed. The General was expecting immediate orders to occupy Texas with his troops and wisely seized this opportunity to obtain a reconnaissance report.[70] The movement of troops into Texas did not come, however, for another year. The United States Senate, more interested in the politics of presidential elections than in annexation of territory, rejected the treaty and ended any immediate call for the protection of Texas. President Tyler, however, was not to be denied Texas so easily and promptly submitted the treaty and documents to the House of Representatives whom he urged to find some other means, presumably joint resolution, of acquiring Texas.[71] Meanwhile the concentration of troops on the border was maintained.

The force under Taylor's immediate command was com-

[70] Taylor to the Adjutant General, June 18, 1844, enclosing copies of Taylor to President Houston, June 17, 1844, and to Captain L. J. Beall, June 17, 1844 (2 letters), all in War Department Archives.

[71] Richardson, *Messages and Papers of the Presidents,* IV, 323–27.

posed of the Second Regiment of Dragoons and the Third and Fourth Infantry Regiments. The dragoons had long been garrisoned at Fort Jesup and continued to occupy the available barracks. The infantry were encamped to the east on high ground between the fort and the Red River. Ulysses S. Grant, then a young second lieutenant with the Fourth Infantry, recalled many years later that the camp was well located and was entitled to its name "Camp Salubrity." [72] In command of the Third Infantry was Taylor's friend, Hitchcock. He was now lieutenant colonel and in the absence of the aged and infirm colonel of the regiment was its commanding officer.[73]

The year of watchful waiting on the border was in general a quiet one. Grant retained very agreeable recollections of his stay at Camp Salubrity, of social enjoyments among the officers, and pleasant relations with the planters on the Red River.[74] Hitchcock had taken with him to Fort Jesup nearly a thousand volumes of philosophy, literature, and music and he found his chief enjoyment in them. Day after day his diary, almost silent on military matters, records reading in the works of Spinoza, Plato, Aristotle, Gabriel Rossetti, Walter Scott, and numerous other men.[75]

On July 1, shortly after assuming the command of the Army of Observation, Taylor suffered a severe attack of bilious fever and five days later was reported by Captain Bliss as being in a dangerous condition. Fortunately the disease was then at its worst, and the next day the General began to make slight gains.[76] Before many days he was able to leave his bed and resume his duties, but the weakening effects of the attack were felt for several months.[77] Indeed,

[72] Ulysses S. Grant, *Personal Memoirs* (New York, 1885–1886), I, 53.

[73] Hitchcock, *Fifty Years in Camp and Field,* 185–90.

[74] Grant, *Memoirs,* I, 56.

[75] Hitchcock, *Fifty Years in Camp and Field,* 188, 190.

[76] Captain W. W. S. Bliss to the Adjutant General, July 5, 1844, in War Department Archives.

[77] Taylor to Joseph P. Taylor, January 29, 1845, in Taylor Papers.

Taylor's health was beginning to show the effects of his nearly forty years' service on the frontier, and henceforth he was incapacitated by illness more frequently than he had ever been in the past. His illness at this time gave serious concern to the War Department which felt that "it would be difficult to replace him in his present important command" and expressed the hope that it would not be necessary to do so.[78]

Except for two brief visits to his plantation and New Orleans, one just after Christmas and the other in May,[79] Taylor spent the year from June, 1844, to June, 1845, at Fort Jesup with little of importance to mark it. Early in October, however, there was some excitement when he received "confidential" instructions to hold his troops in readiness to march on short notice to such points on the border or in Texas as the United States chargé d'affaires in Texas might designate "in order to restrain any hostile incursion on the part of the border Indians, as required by the provisions of existing treaties." [80] Taylor knew there was no danger from the Indians and considered the order "a mere pretext for our troops to cross the Sabine" into Texas,[81] but the army was made ready for the march. No call for troops came, however, and soon the camp returned to watchful waiting. Taylor's view of the purpose of this order was shared by Colonel Hitchcock who regarded the instructions as "extraordinary" and "infamous." [82] It may be that Taylor and Hitchcock were correct in their interpretation, for President Tyler was leaving no method untried in his eagerness to accomplish annexation. Yet the tone of the instructions to the chargé d'affaires, Andrew J. Donelson, and the fact that he made no attempt to use this authority raise considerable

[78] Adjutant General to Bliss, July 20, 1844, in War Department Archives.

[79] Taylor to Joseph P. Taylor, January 29, 1845, in Taylor Papers; Bliss to E. A. Hitchcock, May 18, 1845, in Hitchcock Papers.

[80] Adjutant General to Taylor, September 17, 1844, in War Department Archives.

[81] Taylor to Joseph P. Taylor, January 29, 1845, in Taylor Papers.

[82] Hitchcock, *Fifty Years in Camp and Field,* 187.

doubt that any such embroilment was contemplated.[83] Taylor's own explanation of the failure of the order to result as expected was based on the erroneous belief that the objectionable instructions were issued to Donelson's predecessor, Tilghman A. Howard, who died at his post. "Before his place could be supplied," wrote Taylor to his brother, "the time had so nearly arrived for the anual [*sic*] meeting of Congress it was I presume deemed safest by those in power to take no further steps in the matter, but to refer it to the national legislature." [84] In truth, however, the instructions were issued to Donelson just as he was leaving for Texas.

When Congress met in December, 1844, Tyler again urged annexation by joint resolution. After warm debate through many weeks, the House and the Senate reached agreement and on March 1 sent to the President a resolution providing for the annexation of Texas as soon as the government and people of Texas agreed to the terms. Tyler promptly put his signature to the resolution and three days later retired from office, satisfied that annexation was assured.

Once again there was prospect of action and Taylor had to give up all thought of a long leave to which he had been looking forward, partly to attend Dick's graduation at Yale and partly to give much-needed attention to his plantation.[85] Mexican forces were gathering on the Rio Grande, ready to invade Texas. Persuaded by the British, Mexico was ready to recognize the independence of Texas, but only on condition that she agree never to seek annexation to her northern neighbor. If annexation were attempted, reconquest of Texas, even at the expense of war against the United States, would be undertaken. Once again the United States prepared to protect Texas. On May 23, James Buchanan,

[83] For the instructions to Donelson see Manning, *Diplomatic Correspondence,* XII, 80.

[84] Taylor to Joseph P. Taylor, January 29, 1845, in Taylor Papers.

[85] *Ibid.;* the Adjutant General to Taylor, May 6 and 24, 1845, in War Department Archives.

Secretary of State in the newly established Polk administration, responded to the appeals of the Texas government with the assurance that as soon as Texas accepted the terms of the joint resolution of annexation, President Polk would "conceive it to be both his right and his duty to employ the army in defending that State against the attacks of any foreign power." In order that this might be done promptly and efficiently "three thousand men shall immediately be placed upon the border, prepared to enter Texas and to act without a moment's delay." [86] Five days later General Taylor was ordered to put his forces "into a position where they may most promptly and efficiently act in defense of Texas." [87]

Texas was still uneasy. Rumor placed seven thousand troops on the Rio Grande. What if Mexico attacked while Texas was still considering the terms of annexation? Would the United States stand idly by or drive the invaders out? Buchanan hastened to assure the Texas officials that President Polk preferred that Texas herself should drive any intruders from her soil before the convention had accepted the terms of annexation, but that, if after the Congress of Texas had acted favorably on annexation a Mexican invasion should prevent the convention from assembling or should disturb it in its work, he would "feel himself bound at once to repel such an invasion." [88] The same day that Buchanan sent this promise to Texas, General Taylor was instructed to advance without delay "to the mouth of the Sabine, or to such other point on the Gulf of Mexico, or its navigable waters, as in your judgment may be most convenient for an embarkation at the proper time for the western frontier of Texas." [89] These instructions reached Taylor

[86] James Buchanan to A. J. Donelson, May 23, 1845, in *Senate Documents*, 29 Cong., 1 Sess., No. 1, p. 41.

[87] Secretary Marcy to Taylor, May 28, 1845, in *House Executive Documents*, 29 Cong., 1 Sess., No. 196, pp. 68–69.

[88] Buchanan to Donelson, June 15, 1845, in *Senate Documents*, 29 Cong., 1 Sess., No. 1, pp. 42–44.

[89] Acting Secretary of War Bancroft to Taylor, June 15, 1845, *ibid.*, 69–70.

at Fort Jesup on June 29 and preparations were immediately commenced for the forward movement. On July 3, the Fourth Infantry started for New Orleans and was followed four days later by the Third. Meanwhile the dragoons prepared their horses and wagon train for the long march overland to San Antonio. On July 9, the General bade farewell to Mrs. Taylor and Betty and left Fort Jesup for New Orleans.

Taylor was instructed not to occupy a position in Texas until he was informed that that state had accepted annexation or until he received directions from Donelson. Two days before leaving Fort Jesup, Taylor received word from Donelson that all branches of the Texas government had consented to annexation and that the convention called for July 4 would certainly approve also. Donelson added that the invasion of Texas by Mexico was so probable that an immediate removal of Taylor's troops to the western frontier of Texas would be justified. With this assurance, Taylor determined not to tarry in New Orleans but to concentrate his troops as rapidly as possible at Corpus Christi at the mouth of the Nueces River, a point recommended by Donelson not only because it was the most western point occupied by Texas, but also because it was convenient for supplies and was "as healthy as Pensacola." [90] The Army of Observation was about to become the Army of Occupation.

[90] Taylor to the Adjutant General, July 8, 1845, and enclosure from Donelson, June 28, in War Department Archives.

Chapter VIII

THE ARMY OF OCCUPATION

AT three o'clock on the morning of July 23 the steamer *Alabama,* with General Taylor, his staff, and eight companies of the Third Infantry aboard, left her moorings at the barracks below New Orleans, headed down the great river and, after crossing the bar at the southwest pass about noon, turned west for the coast of Texas. The remaining troops followed in sailing vessels convoyed by the sloop of war *St. Mary's.*[1] Two days of uneventful steaming brought Taylor to the islands off Corpus Christi Bay—part of the long chain of low-lying islands which extends for two hundred miles along the southern coast of Texas and behind which the shallow waters are navigable only by boats of the lightest draught. High wind, a rough sea, and the absence of lighters made landing difficult and dangerous, but it was eventually accomplished and a temporary camp established on St. Joseph's Island. The next morning the whole camp breakfasted on fish and oysters.[2]

In spite of shallow water which kept army transports many miles from the mainland and made exceedingly difficult the movement of large numbers of men and tons of

[1] W. W. S. Bliss to Commander John L. Saunders, July 23, 1845, in John L. Saunders Papers (Division of Manuscripts, Library of Congress); Taylor to the Adjutant General, August 15, 1845, in *House Executive Documents,* 29 Cong., 1 Sess., No. 196, pp. 86–87; Hitchcock, *Fifty Years in Camp and Field,* 193; William S. Henry, *Campaign Sketches of the War with Mexico* (New York, 1847), 12–13.

[2] Taylor to the Adjutant General, July 28, 1845, in *House Executive Documents,* 29 Cong., 1 Sess., No. 196, p. 84; Hitchcock, *Fifty Years in Camp and Field,* 193–94.

supplies, it was essential that Taylor's Army of Occupation be encamped on the mainland where it could move rapidly against an invading foe. After careful examination of Corpus Christi and Aransas bays, Taylor selected a site at the head of the former and just west of the mouth of the Nueces River.[3] To this site he promptly moved the troops from St. Joseph's Island and began an encampment that was to last for seven months. In transferring the troops from the island Taylor learned by bitter experience that it did not pay to be optimistic about the depth of the water. In spite of warnings that the water was too shallow he determined to take two companies aboard the lighter *Undine* and proceed between the islands and the mainland down Aransas Bay into Corpus Christi Bay. Lieutenant Colonel Hitchcock, who shared the experience, recorded in his diary:

> . . . we finally got off before noon, and ran aground about 5 miles down the bay. There we stayed all day and all night; but we at last landed some men and provisions on a raft. Another night passed. It was still found impossible to cross the flats and General Taylor directed the quartermaster to hire all the fishing boats that had gathered around us from curiosity and transfer the men and cargo to them. He was quite beside himself with anxiety, fatigue, and passion. I undertook to tell him that the troops could be very comfortable on St. Joseph's Island till a high southwest wind should give us high water on the flats; but he would not listen to me and was exceedingly impatient to have the companies off. We finally were got on board of seven small boats and left the steamer about 11 A.M. yesterday and landed here [Corpus Christi] at sun-down.[4]

In the face of such difficulties it was exceedingly slow work getting troops and supplies ashore at Corpus Christi, but by the middle of August most of the infantry that Taylor had brought from Fort Jesup were on hand and the

[3] Taylor to the Adjutant General, August 15, 1845, in *House Executive Documents,* 29 Cong., 1 Sess., No. 196, p. 86.

[4] Hitchcock, *Fifty Years in Camp and Field,* 194.

dragoons who were marching by way of San Antonio were not many days distant. During September reinforcements were sent to Taylor and by early fall he had nearly four thousand men, half of the United States Army, encamped on the beach at Corpus Christi. With him were one regiment of dragoons, five regiments of infantry, and sixteen companies of artillery.[5] Their tents stretched for more than a mile along the beach and reached "from the water's edge back some five hundred yards to the chaparral." [6]

During the late summer and early fall the army found life at Corpus Christi fairly pleasant. Many of the men enjoyed the excellent bathing so easily accessible. The region abounded in deer, geese, cranes, turkeys, and the long-eared hare, and the officers spent many an hour hunting.[7] The weather was pleasant. The sun was hot, but the fresh sea breeze was cooling. Lieutenant George Gordon Meade, who later won fame as the victorious general at Gettysburg, reported the climate to be "delicious" and the region as "delightful" and "healthy" as any spot in the world.[8] Not many weeks passed, however, before the weather became disagreeable and the health and happiness of the army suffered. Meade no longer found the weather "delicious." On October 21 he wrote to his wife, "Though I should not call the climate bad, I by no means call it good," and five weeks later he reported that the incessant rains and the cutting cold gales which swept across the open beach made the Corpus Christi winter climate "the most disagreeable and trying" he had ever experienced.[9]

[5] Taylor to the Adjutant General, August 26 and October 15, 1845, in *House Executive Documents,* 29 Cong., 1 Sess., No. 196, pp. 89, 96; Report of the Adjutant General, November 26, 1845, in *Senate Executive Documents,* 29 Cong., 1 Sess., No. 1, pp. 220 ff.

[6] McCall, *Letters from the Frontiers,* 429.

[7] *Ibid.,* 435; Henry, *Campaign Sketches,* 40–44; Grant, *Memoirs,* I, 75–76; E. Kirby Smith, *To Mexico with Scott: Letters of Captain E. Kirby Smith to His Wife* (Cambridge, 1917), 19–22.

[8] George Meade, *The Life and Letters of George Gordon Meade* (New York, 1913), I, 25, 27.

[9] *Ibid.,* 33, 37.

Thin and leaky tents furnished little protection against drenching rains or the freezing temperatures that formed ice on the near-by river. For days at a time, if not for weeks, the men and their possessions were thoroughly soaked.[10] Bad water, a scarcity of fuel which limited fires to those used for cooking, and improper attention to the sanitation and policing of the camp were additional factors in the increasing amount of sickness among the troops.[11] Hundreds of men were incapacitated by diarrhea and dysentery. The month of November, when more than 11 per cent of the officers and over 14 per cent of the enlisted men were on the sick list, found the health of Taylor's army at its worst. It remained poor during the next two months and only with the return of better weather in February was marked improvement evident.[12]

Taylor shared the inconveniences and discomforts of his men but his own health remained good. Indeed, in early January he wrote to his daughter Betty that it had never been better.[13] Because of his own readiness to put up with such discomforts and his disinclination to waste public funds it is probable that Taylor did not make as adequate provision for the health of his army as he should have. He could have done nothing about the brackish water, but he might have obtained a more adequate fuel supply and, had he ascertained in advance the nature of the winter weather at Corpus Christi, he might have made provision for more satisfactory shelter. In October the Secretary of War, William L. Marcy, inquired of Taylor whether it would be advisable to put the troops in huts for the winter;

10 "The Army in Texas," in *Southern Quarterly Review* (New Orleans), April, 1846, p. 448; John Porter Hatch to Eliza Hatch, November 22, 1845, in Hatch Papers (Division of Manuscripts, Library of Congress); Smith, *To Mexico with Scott*, 20.

11 Louis C. Duncan, "A Medical History of General Zachary Taylor's Army of Occupation in Texas and Mexico, 1845–1847," in *The Military Surgeon* (Washington), XLVIII (1921), 80.

12 *Ibid.*, 78–80.

13 *The Autograph* (New York), I, No. 4 (March–April, 1912), 71–72.

and the General replied that tents had been "extensively used for camps of position in Florida, and will, I cannot doubt, form a sufficient protection here." [14] He did attempt to get lumber for tent floors, but it arrived too late to be of much value.[15] Moreover, there is no evidence that Taylor was aware of the necessity for adequate sanitation or that he took any steps to ensure the health of his camp in this regard.

When Taylor's army arrived Corpus Christi was a small town of about one hundred inhabitants, but fast on the heels of the troops came merchants, professional men, and speculators of all sorts who rapidly swelled the population to many times one hundred. Lawyers, doctors, barbers, hairdressers, and photographers were soon on hand. By the first of the new year a newspaper had been established and a theater opened.[16] Liquor vendors, gamblers, and other undesirable elements flocked to Corpus Christi, creating conditions that were thoroughly bad. Taylor had no authority to exercise jurisdiction over the town and was powerless to cope with the situation.[17]

The months at Corpus Christi were not months of complete idleness for Taylor and the troops. The officers of the Engineers Corps were engaged in surveys of the coast both above and below the camp and of the country between the Nueces and the Rio Grande.[18] Doubtless if Taylor had carried on more of this work he would have had better information concerning transportation problems when he started his advance to Matamoros. All of the troops spent some time in the practice of field maneuvers which the

[14] Marcy to Taylor, October 16, 1845, in *House Executive Documents*, 29 Cong., 1 Sess., No. 196, pp. 76–77; Taylor to the Adjutant General, November 7, 1845, *ibid.*, 97.

[15] John Porter Hatch to Eliza Hatch, November 22, 1845, in Hatch Papers; "The Army in Texas," *loc. cit.*, 448 ff.

[16] Lota M. Spell, "The Anglo-Saxon Press in Mexico, 1846–1848," in *American Historical Review* (New York), XXXVIII (1932–1933), 20–21.

[17] "The Army in Texas," *loc. cit.*, 449; Hitchcock, *Fifty Years in Camp and Field*, 203, 206.

[18] Meade, *George Gordon Meade*, I, 26–48.

concentration of so large a force made possible. In the middle of October, Taylor reported to Washington that "the utmost activity prevails in the instruction of the brigades and regiments." [19] It is doubtful, however, that much progress was actually made in this work, for Hitchcock believed that he was "the only field officer on the ground who could change a single position of the troops according to any but a militia mode." [20] It was his opinion that General Taylor knew "nothing of army movements" and that neither he nor Colonel William Whistler could form the troops into line. Brigadier General William J. Worth and Colonel David E. Twiggs were little better.[21]

While the army was encamped at Corpus Christi, General Taylor was faced with a controversy over questions of rank growing out of the fact that some of the officers held brevet commissions as well as lineal commissions. For instance, Worth who was colonel of the Eighth Infantry, but who had been brevetted brigadier general for distinguished service in Florida, insisted that he outranked Colonel Twiggs of the Second Dragoons even though he had been commissioned colonel two years later than Twiggs. This question as to the legal effect of brevets had been a source of controversy and much ill will in the army for at least thirty years. It was the cause of lifelong hostility between Scott and Gaines and it nearly drove the former from the army in 1828 when the government refused to recognize his claim to command the army by virtue of his brevet rank.[22]

This question arose soon after the army was established at Corpus Christi. Taylor decided adversely to the brevets, but submitted the matter to Washington. The answer came from General Scott in the form of a circular of information

[19] Taylor to the Adjutant General, October 15, 1845, in *House Executive Documents,* 29 Cong., 1 Sess., No. 196, p. 96.

[20] Hitchcock, *Fifty Years in Camp and Field,* 198–99.

[21] *Ibid.,* 198, 215.

[22] James B. Fry, *The History and Legal Effect of Brevets in the Armies of Great Britain and the United States from their Origin in 1692 to the Present Time* (New York, 1877), *passim.*

giving precedence to brevet rank. This was displeasing to the army and a memorial to Congress, asking for a clarification of this whole question, was drafted by Lieutenant Colonel Hitchcock and signed by more than 150 of the officers at Corpus Christi. Senator Thomas H. Benton brought the memorial to the attention of President Polk, urging him to act on the matter and to decide in favor of lineal rank. This Polk did in an order of March 12, 1846. Thus Taylor's original position of the previous fall was upheld.[23]

Before this order was issued, however, the controversy in Taylor's army reached a climax. When, early in 1846, the General planned a review of his troops he unwisely appointed Colonel Twiggs to command—in spite of Scott's circular in support of brevet rank. Brigadier General Worth refused to accept this situation. Taylor, unwilling to compel obedience to his order, and fully aware that open conflict threatened, called off the review. Weeks later when the presidential order upholding Taylor arrived, the impetuous Worth promptly tendered his resignation and hastened to Washington to present his grievance there.[24]

The army had been sent to Texas to protect that state from the Mexicans, but during the months it was encamped at Corpus Christi there was little prospect of armed conflict. In August, before Taylor had his camp well established, when he had few infantry, no artillery and no dragoons on hand, there was a report that Mexico had declared war on the United States.[25] Taylor was not much disturbed by this report, but prepared to hold his position "to the last extremity." [26] The government and people of the United States, however, became greatly alarmed for Taylor's safety and hurried support to him. General Gaines, in New Or-

[23] *Ibid.*, 162–80; Hitchcock, *Fifty Years in Camp and Field,* 204–206; Milo Milton Quaife (ed.), *The Diary of James K. Polk During his Presidency, 1845 to 1849* (Chicago, 1910), I, 284–85. Hereafter cited as Polk, *Diary.*

[24] Fry, *History and Legal Effects of Brevets,* 181–88; Meade, *George Gordon Meade,* I, 87–88.

[25] Bliss to Captain John L. Saunders, August 14, 1845, in Saunders Papers.

[26] Bliss to Hitchcock, August 14, 1845, in Hitchcock Papers.

leans, without awaiting instructions, sent to Taylor's rescue two regiments of Louisiana volunteers.[27] Secretary Marcy authorized Taylor to call for troops from the governors of six southwestern states.[28] It soon became apparent that no declaration of war had been made and that no Mexican army was ready to challenge Taylor's force. Except for this early flurry of excitement there was nothing to threaten the peace of Taylor's camp during the fall and winter of 1845.

Before leaving Fort Jesup, and for some weeks thereafter, Taylor was opposed to the annexation of Texas and did not hesitate to denounce it.[29] This fact caused rumors among the officers that he would be relieved of the command at an early date.[30] Soon after reaching Corpus Christi, however, his views apparently underwent a change. He began to talk frequently with Lieutenant Colonel Hitchcock of moving his troops to the Rio Grande and he impressed that officer as having "lost all respect for Mexican rights" and as "willing to be an instrument of Mr. Polk for pushing our boundary as far west as possible." [31] Not only did he talk to Hitchcock in this vein, but he also proposed to the Washington authorities that his force was now strong enough to occupy Point Isabel and Laredo, both on the Rio Grande. Corpus Christi, he said, is too far from the border "to impress the government of Mexico with our readiness to vindicate, by force of arms, if necessary, our title to the country as far as the Rio Grande," and it had been occupied only because his original force was too weak to justify a more advanced position.[32] When, however, Taylor learned that

27 General E. P. Gaines to Adjutant General Jones, August 17 and 31, 1845, in *Senate Documents,* 29 Cong., 1 Sess., No. 378, pp. 23, 26.

28 Marcy to Taylor, August 23, 1845, in *House Executive Documents,* 29 Cong., 1 Sess., No. 196, pp. 72–73.

29 Hitchcock, *Fifty Years in Camp and Field,* 200.

30 Meade, *George Gordon Meade,* I, 26.

31 Hitchcock, *Fifty Years in Camp and Field,* 202–203.

32 Taylor to the Adjutant General, October 4, 1845, in *House Executive Documents,* 29 Cong., 1 Sess., No. 196, pp. 93–95.

the Mexican government had expressed a willingness to discuss the Texas question with an American envoy, he concluded that it would be well for the army to remain at Corpus Christi while the negotiations were in progress.[33] This was in accord with the views of Secretary Marcy, so all thought of moving to the Rio Grande was abandoned for the time being.[34]

While Taylor and his Army of Occupation maintained their position at Corpus Christi, President Polk eagerly sought a peaceful adjustment of all controversies between the two nations. The Texas boundary and unpaid claims of Americans for damages in the civil strife that had been almost continuous in Mexico since the establishment of independence were the chief points in issue. To settle these points and to purchase California, which Polk was eager if not determined to acquire, John Slidell was sent to Mexico as envoy extraordinary and minister plenipotentiary. Mexico had severed diplomatic relations promptly upon the adoption by Congress of the joint resolution for the annexation of Texas, but Polk had quietly and patiently worked for their re-establishment and by the fall of 1845 he believed that Mexico was ready and willing to receive Slidell. However, he was mistaken. The Mexican government, influenced by an anti-American public opinion that would tolerate no government inclined to make concessions to the United States and possibly hopeful of aid from Great Britain with whom the United States was bitterly contesting the Oregon boundary question, refused to receive Slidell.[35]

It was January 12, 1846, when news of this rebuff reached Polk. The next day Taylor was ordered to advance and occupy positions on or near the east bank of the Rio Grande. "It is not designed, in our present relations with Mexico," wrote Secretary Marcy, "that you should treat her as an

[33] *Id.* to *id.*, November 7, 1845, *ibid.*, 97.

[34] *Ibid.*, Marcy to Taylor, October 16, 1845, *ibid.*, 76–77.

[35] The correspondence of the Slidell mission may be found in *House Executive Documents*, 30 Cong., 1 Sess., No. 60, pp. 12–78.

enemy; but, should she assume that character, by a declaration of war, or any open act of hostility towards us, you will not act merely on the defensive, if your relative means enable you to do otherwise." [36] On the same day Commodore David Conner, whose United States fleet had been withdrawn from the vicinity of Vera Cruz when Slidell was dispatched to Mexico, was ordered to return to those waters. He already had instructions to seize Tampico and Vera Cruz if war came and Commodore John D. Sloat had similar orders to seize the ports of California.[37]

The new instructions to General Taylor made war almost inevitable. Perhaps it would have come anyway, for the Mexican authorities were by no means in a conciliatory frame of mind, and had early declared that the occupation of any part of Texas by American troops would constitute an invasion of Mexico and a cause for war. Yet, as long as Taylor remained at Corpus Christi, Mexico took no steps to attack his troops and there remained a chance for peace. Taylor's advance beyond the Nueces, however, was seized upon by the Mexican government as an additional reason for not renewing diplomatic relations with the United States, thus making impossible an amicable settlement of controversies. Whatever chance there was of peace vanished as Taylor and his troops marched south to take up their position face to face with the Mexican army at Matamoros.[38]

Taylor received Marcy's orders early in February, just as the wet and cold of winter were giving way to beautiful, dry, spring weather and he promptly began preparations for the advance. As there was no immediate threat from the Mexicans and as his instructions were to move "as soon as it can be conveniently done with reference to the season

[36] Marcy to Taylor, January 13, 1846, in *House Executive Documents*, 29 Cong., 1 Sess., No. 196, pp. 77–78.

[37] George Bancroft to Commodore John D. Sloat, June 24, 1845, in *House Executive Documents*, 30 Cong., 1 Sess., No. 60, p. 231; Bancroft to Commodore David Conner, July 11, 1845, *ibid.*, 232–33.

[38] E. I. McCormac, *James K. Polk, A Political Biography* (Berkeley, 1922), 414.

and the routes by which your movement must be made," Taylor acted without undue haste. Although historians since have been inclined to criticize him for taking five weeks to make preparations which might have been made during the winter, his superiors at the time found no cause for complaint. Some of the civilians at Corpus Christi who saw in the army's departure the ruin of their own economic fortunes made "the most gigantic efforts to frighten" Taylor from going by warning him of the tremendous Mexican force ready to oppose him.[39] Taylor, however, was not easily frightened and bluntly told the civilians that "if there were fifty thousand Mexicans he would try his best to get there." [40]

By March 8 preparations had been completed and the advance column composed of the cavalry and Major Samuel Ringgold's light artillery took up the line of march. Three days later the last of the troops, including Taylor and his headquarters, started for the Rio Grande 180 miles to the south. Most of the supplies were shipped by water to the mouth of the river, but 307 wagons, one quarter of them pulled by oxen and the remainder by mules and horses, accompanied the troops. After four days of marching through pleasant country abounding in wild horses and hogs, deer, antelope, and wild flowers, the army came upon a sixty-five-mile stretch of hot, sandy territory with almost no vegetation. The wind and sun burned their faces and Taylor, like many of his men and officers, suffered from raw lips and a badly burned nose. Water was very scarce and some of the men nearly died of thirst.[41] One of the worst

[39] Meade, *George Gordon Meade,* I, 50; Taylor to the Adjutant General, February 16, 1846, in *House Executive Documents,* 29 Cong., 1 Sess., No. 196, p. 102.

[40] Meade, *George Gordon Meade,* I, 50.

[41] Madison Mills, Diary of Surgeon Madison Mills, March 11, 1846–November 6, 1847, copy in Filson Club, Louisville, 1–3; Henry, *Campaign Sketches,* 52–58; Samuel G. French, *Two Wars: An Autobiography of Gen. Samuel G. French* (Nashville, 1901), 42–43; Smith, *To Mexico with Scott,* 22–28.

days was March 18. Of this day Dr. Madison Mills, one of the medical officers with Taylor's forces, wrote in his diary:

> Very hot day. Great scarcity of water. Ponds all brackish and some of them so strongly impregnated that salt crystalizes on their margins. Men suffer greatly for want of water. Lt. Bragg fortunately discovered a pond of fresh water near the summit of an eminence in the prairie but for which I believe some of our men would have died of thirst. Some of the men had fallen out and were 3 miles behind the column, others could scarcely keep on. Waited two hours till all had come up and refreshed themselves, then moved on 3 miles and encamped. . . . The sand was hot and very deep. Not a green thing to be seen—very dusty.[42]

After four days of marching, this desertlike country was left behind and the army again traversed a vast garden of delightfully fragrant wild flowers. They also came upon wild cattle and added to their ration fresh beef—"fat, sweet and juicy, but coarse and tough." [43]

Although there were constant rumors of a great Mexican force in his front, Taylor encountered no sign of opposition until the afternoon of March 19. He had just reached the Arroyo Colorado which he described as a salt river or lagoon, "nearly one hundred yards broad, and so deep as barely to be fordable." On the western bank of that river Taylor discovered Mexican cavalry, variously estimated at from 30 to 150 in number. While Mexican buglers sounded up and down the river to give the impression of a large force, the commanding officer informed Taylor that an attempt to cross the river would be considered an act of hostility and would be resisted by force. Taylor, undismayed, proceeded to cut down the bank so that his wagons could reach the river's edge and to make plans for crossing in the morning. Early on the twentieth Taylor disposed his forces to cross under fire if necessary and informed the Mexicans that if any of them showed themselves after the passage was com-

[42] Mills, Diary, 2.

[43] *Ibid.*, 3.

menced they would face the fire of his artillery which was in place with matches lighted. The size of the American force and the obvious determination of their commander convinced the Mexicans of the folly of opposition and as soon as Taylor's men entered the river the enemy disappeared into the chaparral.[44] The crossing was accomplished without the firing of a shot. A reconnaissance of cavalry soon discovered the Mexicans retreating toward Matamoros, but no attempt was made to pursue them for Taylor's instructions had been not to treat Mexico as an enemy unless she assumed that character by a declaration of war or by an open act of hostility.[45]

Taylor continued his advance toward the Rio Grande with his troops constantly prepared to resist attack, but no other Mexican force was encountered. When the army reached a point eighteen miles from Matamoros and ten miles from Point Isabel, at the mouth of the river, Taylor left the infantry under command of General Worth and continued with the cavalry to the latter town which he had selected for his base of supplies and to which supply ships had been ordered before he left Corpus Christi. Taylor arrived to find a portion of the town in flames, apparently fired by the port captain on the approach of Taylor's troops and the transports which arrived in the harbor two or three hours in advance of Taylor. The fire was soon put out and Taylor proceeded with his plans to organize a supply base and to provide for its protection.[46] When this work was well under way he rejoined his main force. A short time before noon on March 28 Taylor made camp on the left bank of the Rio Grande opposite Matamoros while the curious

[44] Taylor to the Adjutant General, March 21, 1846, in *House Executive Documents,* 29 Cong., 1 Sess., No. 196, pp. 107–109; Mills, Diary, 3; Henry, *Campaign Sketches,* 59–60; Grant, *Memoirs,* I, 88–89; Smith, *To Mexico with Scott,* 29–31.

[45] Taylor to the Adjutant General, March 21, 1846, *loc. cit.;* Marcy to Taylor, January 13, 1846, in *House Executive Documents,* 29 Cong., 1 Sess., No. 196, pp. 77–78.

[46] Taylor to the Adjutant General, March 25, 1846, *ibid.,* 111.

MAP OF THE GENERAL AREA OF MILITARY CAMPAIGNS

Reproduced from Edward D. Mansfield, The Mexican War *(New York, 1849), p. 8.*

populace of that town watched from their housetops.[47] "All remark upon the perfect *sang froid,*" noted Colonel Hitchcock a few days later, "with which General T. sat down and continued here under the guns of Matamoros." [48]

In spite of Taylor's prompt assurance to General Francisco Mejía, who commanded the Mexican troops at Matamoros, that the advance of the American army to the Rio Grande was not an act of aggression or hostility, the Mexican General insisted on regarding it as such.[49] He promptly threw up batteries opposite the United States camp and placed guns to rake it. Taylor, with equal promptness, began the construction of defensive works and soon completed emplacements for four eighteen-pound cannon which were made to bear directly upon the public square of the Mexican town. The construction of a bastioned field fort for a garrison of five hundred men was also commenced, and in spite of several days of very heavy rain that flooded the whole camp it was rapidly pushed toward completion. Late in April when attack seemed imminent Taylor spent hours at a time in personal superintendence of the work.[50]

During the first days after the arrival of American troops the citizens of Matamoros showed much interest in the activities across the river. Evenings they lined the west bank to listen to the army bands play "Yankee Doodle," "The Star-Spangled Banner," "Hail Columbia," and sweet opera airs for the *señoritas,* and in return to serenade the Americans with Spanish melodies.[51] In spite of this friendly curiosity on the part of the citizens, the moment Taylor's troops made their camp on the Rio Grande they were viewed with hostility by the Mexican authorities and each passing day in-

[47] *Id.* to *id.*, March 29, 1846, *ibid.*, 112–13; Mills, Diary, 5; McCall, *Letters from the Frontiers,* 438.

[48] Hitchcock, *Fifty Years in Camp and Field,* 220.

[49] Taylor to the Adjutant General, April 6, 1846, and enclosure, in *House Executive Documents,* 29 Cong., 1 Sess., No. 196, pp. 113–17.

[50] *Ibid.;* Mills, Diary, 7, 10; McCall, *Letters from the Frontiers,* 441–43; Henry, *Campaign Sketches,* 64 ff.; Smith, *To Mexico with Scott,* 35–36.

[51] French, *Two Wars,* 45; Henry, *Campaign Sketches,* 67–68.

creased the tension and the probability of armed conflict. The second night in camp the army slept on its arms, ready for instant action, because a large body of Mexican cavalry was reported across the river.[52] A few days later Colonel Trueman Cross, chief quartermaster officer with the army, was robbed and killed about four miles from camp, though his exact fate was not known for nearly ten days.[53] Shortly thereafter two members of a party searching for the missing Colonel were killed when attacked by an ambuscade of forty Mexicans.[54] On April 12 General Pedro de Ampudia, who had just arrived with large reinforcements and had superseded Mejía in command, ordered Taylor to withdraw his force within twenty-four hours and to fall back beyond the Nueces. Taylor not only refused to withdraw but countered with an order blockading the mouth of the Rio Grande and stopping all supplies for Matamoros—an order which he regarded as justified by Ampudia's insistence that a state of war existed. He believed that this blockade would compel the Mexicans either to withdraw their army from Matamoros, where it could not be subsisted, or to assume the offensive north of the river.[55] On the night of April 14 Taylor fully expected an attack and the army slept fully clothed, ready for immediate action. But no attack was made, for even as Ampudia moved troops and vehicles through the darkness with the full intention of taking the offensive with the rising of the sun, he received word that he had been superseded in command and that all operations were to be suspended until his successor arrived.[56]

52 Hitchcock, *Fifty Years in Camp and Field,* 218; Rhoda van Bibber Tanner Doubleday (ed.), *Journals of . . . Philip Norbourne Barbour and his Wife . . .* (New York, 1936), 21.

53 Taylor to the Adjutant General, April 23, 1846, in *House Executive Documents,* 29 Cong., 1 Sess., No. 197, pp. 1–3.

54 *Ibid.*

55 Taylor to the Adjutant General, April 15, 1846, *ibid.,* No. 196, p. 118; *id.* to *id.,* April 23, 1846, *ibid.,* No. 197, p. 2.

56 Mills, Diary, 9; Albert C. Ramsey (ed), *The Other Side: or Notes for the History of the War Between Mexico and the United States* (New York, Ca. 1849), 39–40.

On April 25 a party of sixty-three dragoons encountered a large enemy force about thirty miles above the camp and all were killed or captured.[57] Taylor regarded this attack as the commencement of hostilities, as indeed it was intended by the new Mexican commander, General Mariano Arista.[58] Without delay Taylor called upon the Governors of Texas and Louisiana for four regiments of volunteers each and urged that they be "ordered into service with the utmost despatch and for the longest period authorized by law." [59] At the same time he urged the administration to seek Congressional authorization for the raising of twelve-month volunteers. Taylor was eager to prosecute the war with energy and to carry it into the enemy's country as soon as the troops from Louisiana and Texas arrived.[60]

Taylor was not alone in viewing this disastrous attack on his dragoons as the commencement of hostilities. "To arms!" cried the New Orleans *Daily Delta,* "to arms! in maintenance of our national honor! in support of our undoubted rights! in revenge for our slaughtered countrymen—to arms!" [61] When news of the attack reached President Polk he hastened to ask Congress to declare that war existed by the act of Mexico whose troops had "invaded our territory, and shed the blood of our fellow-citizens on our own soil." [62] Even before Taylor's report reached Washington, Polk and all but one member of his Cabinet had agreed to ask Congress for a declaration of war against Mexico because of the "aggravated wrongs done to our citizens in their persons

[57] Taylor to the Adjutant General, April 26, 1846, and May 3, 1846, Captain T. B. Thornton to Bliss, April 27, 1846, Report of Captain W. T. Hardee, April 26, 1846, in *House Executive Documents,* 29 Cong., 2 Sess., No. 119, pp. 17–21.

[58] Ramsey, *The Other Side,* 42.

[59] Taylor to the Adjutant General, April 26 and May 3, 1846, *loc. cit.; id.* to Governor Isaac Johnson, April 26, 1846, in New Orleans *Daily Delta,* May 3, 1846.

[60] *Id.* to the Adjutant General, April 26, 1846, *loc. cit.*

[61] May 3, 1846.

[62] Polk, *Diary,* I, 386–90; Polk's War Message to Congress, May 11, 1846, in *House Executive Documents,* 29 Cong., 1 Sess., No. 196, pp. 1–6.

and property." [63] The attack on the dragoons made the Cabinet unanimous, hastened the President's war message, and removed any doubt that Congress would act as requested. A few congressmen vigorously opposed a declaration of war, but with little debate or delay the two branches, by overwhelming majorities, voted that war existed, appropriated money for its prosecution, and authorized the raising of troops.[64]

War had not waited for the President or Congress to act. Almost at the very time Polk was discussing with his Cabinet the question of a declaration of war General Taylor and his army were locked in battle with the main Mexican force under General Arista. On the last day of April Taylor learned that the Mexicans were crossing the river in force below Matamoros with the design of attacking his communications and his supply depot at Point Isabel.[65] Although Taylor had reported two weeks before that Point Isabel was "well supplied with artillery, and in a good condition to resist attack," [66] he now made haste to protect it. Leaving the Seventh Infantry under Major Jacob Brown and two companies of artillery to hold the fort which he believed was now sufficiently advanced to withstand assault, Taylor marched with the main force under his immediate command for Point Isabel twenty-six miles away. The army left camp at three o'clock on the afternoon of May 1, marched till after midnight, halted and slept on their arms without fire or supper. They resumed the march at daybreak and reached Point Isabel just after noon without discovering any signs of the enemy whose crossing had been retarded by the lack of boats.[67] The forced march

[63] Polk, *Diary,* I, 384–85.

[64] *Congressional Globe,* 29 Cong., 1 Sess., 782–817.

[65] Mills, Diary, 14; Taylor to the Adjutant General, May 3, 1846, in *House Executive Documents,* 29 Cong., 2 Sess., No. 119, p. 18.

[66] *Id.* to *id.,* April 15, 1846, in *House Executive Documents,* 29 Cong., 1 Sess., No. 196, p. 118.

[67] *Id.* to *id.,* May 3, 1846, *loc. cit.;* Mills, Diary, 14–15; Doubleday (ed.),

called forth loud complaint against Old Rough and Ready. "He is becoming very unpopular," recorded Surgeon Mills. "The march yesterday afternoon and last night was the most harrassing I ever saw or performed and quite unnecessarily so. Both officers and men speak boldly and say it is an outrage." [68]

With most of the American troops at Point Isabel, General Arista believed that he had a golden opportunity to destroy the American fort and garrison opposite Matamoros before Taylor could intervene. Almost at once the Mexican General turned upon the fort not only the fire of the batteries south of the river but also that of a powerful attacking force on the north bank. When at daybreak on the morning of the third the sound of heavy gunfire came from the direction of Matamoros, Taylor's first impulse was to march his forces back to camp, and he so ordered. Before a start was made, however, he decided against this step [69] and instead sent Captain Samuel H. Walker and a party of Texas rangers to communicate with Major Brown at the fort. Walker returned on the morning of May 5 to report that he had successfully reached the fort, that all was well, and that there was no immediate need for relief. Thus reassured that the hastily constructed fort could withstand the assault of the Mexicans, Taylor remained at Point Isabel, strengthening the defenses of that depot and awaiting ordnance supplies and recruits expected from New Orleans.[70]

Two days later, leaving the newly arrived recruits to strengthen the garrison at Point Isabel, Taylor, ready to test his strength against the Mexicans, ordered his army to

---

Journals of . . . Philip Norbourne Barbour . . . and his Wife . . ., 50–51; Ramsey, *The Other Side*, 43.

[68] Mills, Diary, 15.

[69] *Ibid.;* Smith, *To Mexico with Scott*, 44.

[70] Taylor to the Adjutant General, May 5, 1846, Major Brown to Bliss, May 4, 1846, in *House Executive Documents*, 29 Cong., 2 Sess., No. 119, pp. 21–23.

begin the return march. "It is known that the enemy has recently occupied the route in force," his order read, "if still in position, the general will give him battle." [71] In the same spirit Taylor informed Washington, "If the enemy oppose my march, in whatever force, I shall fight him." [72] When, a few weeks later, Taylor's correspondence was made public by the War Department, the vigorous and determined simplicity of this sentence caught the public fancy and it took its place along with such famous military statements as Prescott's "Don't fire until you see the white of their eyes" and Commodore Perry's "We have met the enemy and they are ours." At the time all credit for the vigor of Taylor's dispatches was given to him, but later when he became a political figure it was frequently asserted that Captain Bliss, his adjutant general, was responsible for any merit the dispatches had. The marked contrast between the clear, crisp statements of Taylor's military correspondence and the long and confused sentences in his private letters supports the view that the literary adjutant had an important part in the writing of Old Rough and Ready's dispatches. Meade, who on the whole thought well of Taylor, and claimed Bliss as a good friend, was sure that the latter wrote all of the General's military correspondence.[73] Hitchcock, who was very close to both Taylor and Bliss, was of the same opinion.[74] Another officer with Taylor's army, George A. McCall, who at the beginning of the war was a captain in the Fourth Infantry, recorded evidence to the contrary. Several months after the above famous dispatch was written McCall had opportunity for frequent visits with Bliss who admitted occasionally polishing Taylor's reports but insisted that they were always in the General's own language and that the famous dispatch sent from

[71] Order No. 58, May 7, 1846, in *House Executive Documents,* 29 Cong., 1 Sess., No. 207, p. 2.

[72] Taylor to the Adjutant General, May 7, 1846, *ibid.*

[73] Meade, *George Gordon Meade,* I, 131.

[74] Hitchcock, *Fifty Years in Camp and Field,* 367.

Point Isabel on the instant of marching to the relief of the besieged fort had been copied "verbatim from the old Chief's handwriting." [75] Taylor's private correspondence reveals that he was capable of many a well-turned phrase and that his chief difficulty resulted from interminable sentences. Bliss's "polishing" probably involved the reconstruction of sentences and was far more extensive than he admitted.

Late in the afternoon of May 7 the army, nearly 2,300 strong, accompanied by two hundred supply wagons, marched out on the road to Matamoros determined to fight the enemy in "whatever force" he might appear. They marched seven miles, camped till morning, and then marched on. About noon, when the advanced cavalry had reached the water hole of Palo Alto, the Mexican troops were discovered. Three fourths of a mile away, across the open prairie, the enemy line was plainly visible. Some six thousand troops blocked Taylor's advance. He ordered a halt to rest and refresh his men and to form his line of battle. About two o'clock all was in readiness and the march was resumed. The American army had not advanced far before the Mexican artillery opened fire. Taylor promptly deployed into line and brought his own artillery into action. The first battle of the war was under way. Except for a lull or suspension of an hour or so while volumes of smoke from the burning prairies nearly concealed the armies from each other, the battle lasted till darkness fell.[76]

The battle of Palo Alto was primarily an artillery duel. The American forces were outnumbered nearly three to one, but the superiority of their artillery gave them a distinct advantage which in the end brought victory. The balls from the antiquated Mexican cannon fell short of the American line and rolled forward so slowly that the soldiers

[75] McCall, *Letters from the Frontiers*, 466–67.

[76] Taylor to the Adjutant General, May 16, 1846, in *House Executive Documents*, 29 Cong., 1 Sess., No. 209, pp. 2–4.

could usually avoid them by a sidestep at the proper moment. Meanwhile the American artillery, which included Major Samuel Ringgold's battery on the right, Captain James Duncan's battery on the left, and two heavy eighteen-pounders in the center, poured a destructive fire of grape, cannister, and shrapnel into the charging enemy, which "mowed them down in great numbers," cut openings "through their ranks from one side to the other," [77] and threw them into the "utmost confusion." [78] In his first brief report of the engagement Taylor declared that his artillery was the arm chiefly engaged and that "to the excellent manner in which it was manoeuvred and served is our success mainly due." [79] The havoc and horrid wounds made by the artillery were seen by Surgeon Mills the next morning as he traversed the field of battle. "I saw heads and limbs severed from their bodies and trunks strewed about in awful confusion. Many a body I saw that had been cut in twain by our 18 pdrs and such ghastly spectacles I hope never to behold again." [80] Not only Americans, but Mexicans as well recognized the superiority of the American artillery and noted the "horrid ravages" made by it in the ranks of the Mexican army.[81]

The infantry, however, were not mere observers. At several points they entered the battle against the oncharging enemy. Their chief action came when a large force of Mexican cavalry attempted to turn Taylor's right flank, seize Ringgold's battery which had been severely punishing them from the outset of the battle, and attack Taylor's wagon train stationed to the rear. Taylor promptly sent the Fifth Infantry to check this flanking movement. When five hundred of the cavalry charged, the infantry immediately

77 Mills, Diary, 17.

78 Lieutenant John Porter Hatch to his sister, May 19, 1846, in Hatch Papers.

79 Taylor to the Adjutant General, May 9, 1846, in *House Executive Documents*, 29 Cong., 1 Sess., No. 207, p. 3.

80 Mills, Diary, 18.

81 Ramsey, *The Other Side*, 48.

formed square and poured into the horsemen a fire which emptied about thirty saddles. The infantry soon had the support of two pieces of Ringgold's battery which had moved to new positions and the Mexican cavalry were turned back in utter confusion. Later in the afternoon, after the cessation of hostilities imposed by the heavy smoke screen had terminated, the Eighth Infantry joined Duncan's battery in driving back the Mexican right wing. But once again it was the artillery that was most effective. The fire of Duncan's guns, wrote a lieutenant in the Third Infantry, "was really terrible in its effect entirely breaking their [the Mexicans'] ranks and throwing them into the utmost confusion." [82]

After nearly five hours the Mexicans were driven from their position and Taylor's army bivouacked on the ground the enemy had occupied at the start of the battle. The American losses were nine killed, forty-five wounded including Major Samuel Ringgold whose wounds proved mortal, and two missing. The Mexican losses, estimated in part from the number actually counted upon the field, Taylor placed at not less than two hundred killed and four hundred wounded.[83]

The ninth of May dawned amidst the piteous and heart-rending groans of the wounded Mexicans who had been left on the field. As soon as a light fog which hung over the prairie lifted, the enemy was seen retreating into the chaparral through which the road to Matamoros ran. Before Taylor could resume the attack the Mexicans had disappeared. In spite of the advice of the majority of the officers whom he called in consultation—advice to entrench and await reinforcements—General Taylor decided to pursue the enemy.[84] He advanced his army to the edge of the chaparral and there halted for several hours while the

[82] John Porter Hatch to his sister, May 19, 1846, *loc. cit.*

[83] Taylor to the Adjutant General, May 16, 1846, *loc. cit.*

[84] Doubleday (ed.), *Journals of . . . Philip Norbourne Barbour . . . and his Wife . . .*, 57.

wounded were sent to Point Isabel, the supply train was entrenched, and a thorough reconnaissance was made.[85]

The Mexican army was discovered occupying a strong position athwart the road at a point where it passed through a slight ravine and where dense chaparral and undergrowth obstructed passage on either side. In this terrain the American artillery could not be used to full effectiveness and any attempt to drive the Mexicans from their ground would involve the infantry to a much greater degree than on the previous day. Taylor did not hesitate. "If the enemy oppose my march, in whatever force, I shall fight him," was still his determination and he promptly ordered his men to advance. A small detachment of infantry under Lieutenant Stephen D. Dobbins was sent forward to draw the fire of the Mexicans and disclose the position of their guns. The main force followed close upon them and when the Mexicans opened fire, killing one man and wounding three others of the advance party, Taylor deployed his infantry to the right and left of the road while Ringgold's battery, now under Lieutenant Randolph Ridgely, moved forward and opened fire upon the enemy's guns.

The infantry, broken into small parties by the thick, thorny, and almost impenetrable chaparral, was soon engaged with the Mexican infantry. At the same time they were under fire from the well-placed Mexican artillery which the American batteries could not silence. Realizing that the enemy's guns must be silenced if victory were to be won, Taylor ordered Captain Charles A. May and his dragoons to charge the Mexican batteries and drive the cannoneers from their posts. With reckless courage May and his squadron dashed across the ravine and charged upon seven of the enemy's guns and gun crews, turned and charged again, drove off a few remaining gunners, captured

[85] Taylor to the Adjutant General, May 17, 1846, in *House Executive Documents*, 29 Cong., 1 Sess., No. 209, pp. 6–9; Mills, Diary, 18; John Porter Hatch to his sister, May 19, 1846.

General Diaz de la Vega, and returned to the American lines. Ten men and eighteen horses killed, and ten men and an equal number of mounts wounded was the price of this charge. The dragoons were not able to retain possession of the Mexican batteries, but Taylor soon followed this cavalry attack with an infantry charge that seized and held these guns.

Victory had not yet been won, but the tide of battle had been turned. For two hours the conflict raged. In many areas there was desperate hand-to-hand fighting—bayonet to bayonet and sword to sword. "The enemy . . . fought like devils," declared Captain E. Kirby Smith. But the Americans fought with equal desperation. Infantry, dragoons, and artillery were almost constantly engaged. Late in the afternoon the stanch defense of the Mexican army collapsed. In utter confusion, leaving behind them their wounded, great quantities of munitions, much baggage, and several hundred pack mules, the entire Mexican force fled to the Rio Grande some seven miles distant with the Americans in hot pursuit. Many of the Mexicans escaped across the river in boats, others swam the stream, but many met death in their vain attempts to put the river between them and their pursuers. Thus with the close of day, the battle of Resaca de la Palma,[86] so called from the near-by point where Taylor wrote his report, ended in complete triumph for Old Rough and Ready and his gallant little army. The superior fighting quality of the American troops and the inspiring leadership of their officers, which contrasted sharply with the strange conduct of General Arista, had won the day. While the Mexican General remained in his tent until almost the close of the battle, writing reports, it is said, General Taylor with reckless disregard of his personal safety moved about the field of battle seeing with his own

[86] Captain E. Kirby Smith stated that the name came from the pond or lagoon which was the watering place of the Palma family. *To Mexico with Scott,* 56.

eyes, ordering with his own lips, and encouraging by his own example.

The strong position selected by the Mexicans for their second stand made the casualties in the American army far heavier than at Palo Alto. A week after the battle Taylor reported three officers and thirty-six men killed and eighty-three wounded. The loss of the Mexicans was far greater. Nearly two hundred Mexican dead were buried by the Americans on the day after the battle. Many more lost their lives in the Rio Grande and in addition some 150 officers and soldiers were captured by Taylor's forces.[87]

Although more costly than his first victory Taylor's triumph at Resaca de la Palma was also more decisive. The enemy was driven south of the river and all threat to Taylor's camp, his supply depot, or his communications was ended. Had the government supplied Taylor with the pontoon bridge which he had requested months before but which no bureau chief in Washington could find funds for, he could have crossed the river and taken possession of Matamoros on the next day. Even without this equipment he could have crossed in a day or two by bringing up the river the scows and flats of the Quartermaster's Department at Point Isabel; but Taylor saw no need for haste. Speed was not a characteristic of his plans or actions and he was content to wait secure in the knowledge that he could take the town at his pleasure.[88]

When the news of Taylor's decisive triumph over the enemy reached the United States the American people hailed him as a military genius. They had been led by the

87 This account of the battle of Resaca de la Palma is based upon the following materials: the official reports of Taylor and his subordinates in *House Executive Documents,* 29 Cong., 1 Sess., No. 209; Taylor to Betty Taylor, May 13, 1846, in *The Autograph,* I, No. 5 (May–June, 1912), 100–101; Mills, Diary, 18; John Porter Hatch to his sister, May 19, 1846; Doubleday (ed.), *Journals of . . . Philip Norbourne Barbour . . . and his Wife . . . ,* 57–60; Smith, *To Mexico with Scott,* 49–53; Ramsey, *The Other Side,* 51–56; Meade, *George Gordon Meade,* I, 80–83.

88 Meade, *George Gordon Meade,* I, 98; Justin H. Smith, *The War With Mexico* (New York, 1919), I, 469.

papers to believe that his little army was in grave danger and they were prepared to hear of its annihilation. Instead came news of victory—overwhelming victory—and Old Rough and Ready became the hero of the people. Historians may point out that Taylor issued few orders while the battle raged and exhibited no great skill as a tactician, but the people were not concerned with tactics. They were content that he had led his men to victory. Nor were they concerned with the criticism that his own shortcomings, his lack of foresight, his poor judgment, his failure to protect properly his base of supplies, and his selection of a position for his troops that left his line of communication exposed to the enemy, were largely responsible for the dangers he faced.[89] They knew he had defeated the enemy who threatened him. They knew he was a fighting leader. They knew he was their hero.

Congress shared the people's admiration and enthusiastically adopted resolutions tendering their thanks "to Major General Zachary Taylor, . . . his officers and men, for the fortitude, skill, enterprise, and courage, which have distinguished the recent brilliant operations on the Rio Grande," and authorizing the President to present to Taylor in the name of the Republic, "as a tribute to his good conduct, valor, and generosity, to the vanquished," a properly designed and inscribed gold medal.[90] The legislature of Rhode Island and a great public gathering at Raleigh, North Carolina, adopted similar resolutions of praise and thanks, while the legislature of Louisiana appropriated $500 for the purchase of a sword to be presented to the victorious general.[91]

After a hurried trip to Point Isabel to arrange with Commodore David Conner for joint naval and military action

[89] James E. Saunders to President Polk, May 5, 1846, in Polk Papers (Division of Manuscripts, Library of Congress); William L. Marcy, "Diary," *American Historical Review*, XXIV (1918–1919), 462.

[90] *Congressional Globe*, 29 Cong., 1 Sess., 1064, 1080, 1108.

[91] *Journal of the Senate of the United States*, 29 Cong., 1 Sess., 321, 425.

on the river and a day's incapacity due to "considerable fever" which confined him to his tent, Taylor commenced preparations to cross the Rio Grande a respectable distance above Matamoros.[92] On May 17, when these preparations were nearing completion, General Arista, now well aware of the caliber of the enemy he had aroused, proposed an armistice which Taylor promptly declined. He countered with an offer to permit the Mexican troops, including the sick and wounded, to be withdrawn from Matamoros provided all the public property in that town were delivered up. When the Mexican General demurred that many of the wounded could not be removed, Taylor replied that he "never made war on the sick, wounded, or woman [*sic*] or children," but that he was determined to cross the river the next day, and "if the town made any resistance would destroy it." [93] The following morning the American troops made the crossing without opposition and soon discovered that Arista and his forces had abandoned the town and were retreating toward Monterrey. Taylor was far too weak to pursue the retreating enemy in force through a hostile country. So, except for the harassing activities of the American cavalry, the Mexican army escaped in peace.[94]

Old Rough and Ready was scrupulously careful to protect the citizens and private property of the town that had fallen into his hands. Colonel Twiggs was placed in command of the city with a small guard to preserve order. The army was not quartered in the town but was encamped on its outskirts, and only a limited number of men were allowed to go in at a time. There was no looting and no prize of any kind for officers or men except government-owned tobacco which Taylor seized and distributed among his troops.[95]

[92] Taylor to the Adjutant General, May 12, 1846, in *House Executive Documents,* 29 Cong., 1 Sess., No. 207, p. 5; *id.* to Dr. R. C. Wood, May 19, 1846, in *Letters from the Battlefields,* 3.

[93] *Ibid.;* Taylor to the Adjutant General, May 18, 1946, in *House Executive Documents,* 29 Cong., 1 Sess., No. 119, p. 26.

[94] *Id.* to *id.,* May 18, 21, and 24, 1846, *ibid.,* 26–29.

[95] Meade, *George Gordon Meade,* I, 86; Fry, *Taylor,* 172.

The American troops were much disappointed in Matamoros, which they found far less attractive than it had appeared at a distance. Moreover, the better class of citizens had fled from the town and those who remained impressed Lieutenant Meade as "the most miserable-looking beings" he ever saw; instead of "black-eyed senoras" he found "nothing but old hags, worse looking than Indians." [96] Taylor himself preferred his tent to the city and pitched it under a small tree about half a mile distant.

While Taylor was driving the Mexicans south of the river and taking Matamoros, the administration in Washington was concerned with the question of the proper commander for the American forces. Taylor had been selected to command the troops that had been sent to Texas to protect that state rather than to make war on Mexico. But war had come. If offensive operations against Mexico were to be undertaken, who should conduct them? The logical person seemed to be Major General Winfield Scott—the egotistical, political-minded veteran, "Old Fuss and Feathers,"—who since 1841 had been the commanding general of the United States Army. On May 13, the very day that Congress declared war, President Polk placed Scott in command of the army in the field.[97] Although the President did not instruct Scott to proceed at once to the border to assume command, it was apparently his intention that he should do so, for when he learned that Scott expected to remain in Washington through the summer raising troops and organizing supplies and to proceed to the Rio Grande only about the first of September, he became disgusted and threatened to supersede him.[98] Scott was soon engaged in a controversy with the Secretary of War, William L. Marcy, in the course of which he was thoroughly indiscreet and exhibited what Polk regarded as hostility toward his administration. These indiscretions further convinced Polk

[96] Meade, *George Gordon Meade*, I, 86.
[97] Polk, *Diary*, I, 396. [98] *Ibid.*, 407–408.

that Scott was not the man to command the army in Mexico.[99] But he hesitated, for he had no one to put in Scott's place, no one with a reputation that could justify placing him in the position that everyone expected Scott to fill. On May 23, as the controversy between Scott and Marcy raged, the President informed his Cabinet that if he could find any other qualified officer he should be assigned to the command in the place of Scott. That evening news of Taylor's victories at Palo Alto and Resaca de la Palma reached Washington and Polk's problem was solved.[100] Not only had Taylor proved his ability, but he had become a military hero of the first magnitude. Scott was promptly removed from the command of the army against Mexico. Taylor was nominated to be major general by brevet for "gallant conduct and distinguished services in the successive victories over superior Mexican forces," [101] and a few days later he was informed that the President intended to continue him in command and to commit to him the conduct of the ensuing campaign.[102] When in June Congress authorized the appointment of an additional major general the administration promptly selected Taylor for the place. At last he was at the top of the ladder. At the time there was no higher grade in the army and he outranked all his fellow officers except Winfield Scott, who also held the rank of major general and who was his superior by virtue of seniority and his position as commanding general of the United States Army.

Taylor received the news that he was to conduct the campaign against Mexico with little enthusiasm. For weeks he had been expressing the hope that General Scott was on his

[99] *Ibid.*, 413–15; Scott to Marcy, May 21, 1846, in *Senate Executive Documents*, 29 Cong., 1 Sess., No. 378, pp. 4–7; Marcy to Scott, May 25, 1846, *ibid.*, 7–9.

[100] Polk, *Diary*, I, 421.

[101] Polk to Taylor, May 30, 1846, in *House Executive Documents*, 29 Cong., 1 Sess., No. 119, pp. 12–13.

[102] Marcy to *id.*, June 8, 1846, *ibid.*, 48–50.

way to assume the command that was properly his.[103] He was anxious for quiet and an opportunity to attend to his private affairs. Two days after taking Matamoros he wrote to his son-in-law, "I heartily wish the war was at an end." [104] A month later he said, "I want nothing more than to see this campaign finished & the war brought to a speedy and honorable close." [105] When, at the end of June, he received word that Scott was not coming and that he was to conduct the operations against Mexico, he declared that he neither wished nor expected the assignment and would have avoided it if he had been consulted. But in true soldierly fashion, with loyalty to his country, he determined to carry on with zeal and energy and to the best of his ability.[106]

[103] Taylor to Dr. R. C. Wood, June 3, 12, and 21, in *Letters from the Battlefields*, 7, 10, 15.

[104] *Id.* to *id.*, May 19, 1846, *ibid.*, 4.

[105] *Id.* to *id.*, June 21, 1846, in the Huntington Library.

[106] *Id.* to *id.*, June 30, 1846, in *Letters from the Battlefields*, 20.

Chapter IX

THE CAPTURE OF MONTERREY

AT the outbreak of the war with Mexico, Zachary Taylor was in his sixty-first year. He was of medium height, heavy set, short legged, and undistinguished in appearance. A Texas volunteer, seeing him for the first time, "found him a plain old farmer-looking man—no particular indications of smartness or intellect." [1] To another volunteer he appeared to be "an ordinary looking old man" with "a keen eye and a large nose." [2] A second lieutenant in an Illinois regiment wrote home: "Taylor is short and very heavy, with pronounced face lines and gray hair, wears an old oil cloth cap, a dusty green coat, a frightful pair of trousers and on horseback looks like a toad." [3] Brigadier General Gideon J. Pillow, who became one of Taylor's severest critics, described him to his wife after a first visit at the General's headquarters as "a frank and manly old gentleman about the size of myself except that he is quite fat, not so fat as your Brother William, but more so than your father." [4]

Taylor's ordinary appearance was due in part to plain, or even careless, dress. He seldom wore his uniform or even anything to indicate that he was an officer.[5] He was usually

[1] James K. Holland, "Diary of a Texan Volunteer in the Mexican War," in *Southwestern Historical Quarterly* (Austin), XXX (1926–1927), 19.

[2] J. L. Williams, Jr., to his father, August 21, 1846, in Division of Manuscripts, Library of Congress.

[3] Otto B. Engelmann, "The Second Illinois in the Mexican War," in *Journal of the Illinois State Historical Society* (Springfield), XXVI (1933–1934), 438.

[4] Gideon J. Pillow to his wife, August 16, 1846, in Historical Society of Pennsylvania.

[5] Grant, *Memoirs,* I, 100–101; George C. Furber, *Twelve Months Vol-*

ZACHARY TAYLOR

Reproduced by permission from an oil portrait in the Pennsylvania Academy of the Fine Arts.

to be found in attakapas pantaloons and a linen roundabout, though in colder weather he donned an old brown coat which became almost as famous as the man. Consequently even his own soldiers, if they had not previously seen him, sometimes mistook him for a private citizen. On one occasion, dressed in much this fashion and mounted on a large and gentle mule, he visited the Illinois Volunteers and was almost ignored by the soldiers who thought the smartly dressed orderly who accompanied him was the general. One of the few times Taylor ever appeared in full uniform was early in the war when he went to Point Isabel to confer with Commodore Conner. As the Commodore had a reputation for perfection in dress, Taylor decided to put on his uniform for the conference. Conner, however, knowing of Taylor's dislike for uniforms, dressed as simply as possible. When they met, each was astonished by the appearance of the other, and Taylor was more than ever committed to his simple, careless attire.[6]

When in the summer of 1846 Congress authorized the preparation of a medal for presentation to General Taylor, no portrait or other likeness of him was available.[7] Not until an artist visited Taylor's camp and painted his portrait could the work be done. Early in 1847 Jesse Atwood of Philadelphia journeyed to Mexico and made two portraits of Taylor, one in full uniform, the other as "Rough and Ready" in his usual costume.[8] Shortly thereafter another artist, a Mr. Brown of Richmond, visited Taylor's camp and also made a portrait. The likenesses painted by Atwood, Taylor thought were "tolerable"; the one by Brown he was

---

unteer: or Journal of a Private . . . in the Campaign in Mexico (Cincinnati, 1849), 329.

[6] *Taylor and his Generals . . .* (Philadelphia, 1847), 75–77; J. F. H. Claiborne, *Life and Correspondence of John A. Quitman* (New York, 1860), I, 288.

[7] William L. Marcy to Taylor, October 5, 1846, in *House Executive Documents*, 29 Cong., 2 Sess., No. 119, pp. 113–14.

[8] *General Zachary Taylor's Letter to Jesse Atwood.* (A broadside in the Huntington Library, advertising Atwood's portraits.)

told by persons "who understand or are judges of such matters" was "a much better painting." [9] Prior to the work of these artists newspapers had been publishing poorly drawn sketches that were labeled "Zachary Taylor," but which bore little resemblance to the General. They did not portray correctly his finely shaped head, his high forehead, and his keen eye. Indeed, they made him appear not only ordinary but almost ugly and repulsive. The Atwood and Brown portraits gave the American people their first opportunity to see a reasonable likeness of the old General.[10]

Taylor's dislike for show or parade was also evident in the simple headquarters which he maintained, in his unguarded tent which he persistently refused to abandon for more elaborate quarters, and in his democratic manners and relations with his army. No one felt ill at ease, jealous, or inferior in his presence. A wounded sergeant, home from the battle of Monterrey, described him as approachable at all hours: "He will sit and talk with the commonest soldier in the most affable manner . . . enter minutely into the private affairs of the soldiers under his command, give them his advice when asked, as it frequently is, and when that is over, read to them from the newspapers the anecdotes of the army, which have made their way into print in the northern cities, at which he would laugh as heartily as any of them." [11] Taylor's troops came to have a warm affection for him. When, early in 1847, a large number of them were separated from his command and ordered to join Scott's expedition many an eye was wet with tears as the order was read, and the troops departed with "much the same feelings a child has when parting forever from a father." [12]

When the conduct of the offensive campaign against

[9] Taylor to R. C. Wood, July 13, 1847, in *Letters from the Battlefields*, 113.

[10] *General Zachary Taylor's Letter to Jesse Atwood.*

[11] *General Taylor and His Staff* (Philadelphia, 1848), 80.

[12] John Blount Robinson, *Reminiscences of a Campaign in Mexico* (Nashville, 1849), 200; Henry, *Campaign Sketches*, 298–99.

Mexico was committed to General Taylor in June, he was informed that the President was determined that the war be prosecuted with vigor and that "a peace . . . be conquered in the shortest space of time practicable." He was left to his own discretion and judgment so far as specific measures were concerned, but was informed that it would be "desirable" to capture and hold Monterrey and that it was "presumed" he would hold both banks of the Rio Grande "to a considerable distance from its mouth, and secure uninterrupted use of that river for the transportation of supplies." "I hope," wrote Secretary Marcy, "you will be able to take and hold in possession all places on it as high up as Laredo." Beyond the capture of Monterrey no plans had been made. Whether Taylor should confine his operations to the northern provinces of Mexico or should penetrate into the interior and push southward with a view to striking at Mexico City had not been determined. His opinions on this point were sought by the department.[13]

Instructions to operate against Monterrey met Taylor's full approval, for that town, situated some 250 miles southwest of Matamoros in the valley of the San Juan River, was the next logical objective. Founded early in the seventeenth century, it was now a town of some fifteen thousand inhabitants, spacious plazas, and a magnificent cathedral. It was the capital of the state of Nuevo León and the most important city of northern Mexico. Strategically located at the eastern end of an important mountain pass, it controlled the best route from the plains of the Gulf Coast to the highlands of the interior. As long as it remained in Mexican hands it blocked any American advance upon the Valley of Mexico from the north. If Monterrey were captured by Taylor, the long route south to the heart of the nation would be open.

Late in the war Taylor claimed that the plan of campaign

[13] William L. Marcy to Taylor, June 8, 1846, in *House Executive Documents*, 29 Cong., 2 Sess., No. 119, pp. 48–50.

had not been approved by him.[14] Although this claim was true for the campaign as a whole, Taylor had advised moving against Monterrey immediately following his occupation of Matamoros and was already making his plans to that end before instructions came from Washington.[15] He did not believe, however, that communications could be kept open very far south of Monterrey, and he replied to the department's request for his views that it was his opinion "operations from this frontier should not look to the city of Mexico, but should be confined to cutting off the northern provinces." [16]

The most direct route from Matamoros to Monterrey was overland through a vast expanse of arid land which could furnish scant food and water for an invading army and would necessitate great numbers of pack mules for the transportation of supplies. An alternate route was up the shallow waters of the Rio Grande to its southern tributary, the San Juan River, and thence south through the valley of the San Juan to Monterrey. Taylor preferred this river route, but as no steamers were available at Matamoros, where indeed only one had ever been seen, he had to await their arrival from distant American ports before any advance could be made. As week after week passed without the arrival of a single transport, Taylor became impatient and bitterly critical of the Quartermaster's Department. Without question the Quartermaster General showed little foresight as to Taylor's transportation needs. The moment Taylor was ordered to the Rio Grande the probable need for transports on that river should have been seen and steps taken to provide them. But nothing was done. Even after the General's request for boats was made, orders were issued in routine fashion and no sense of urgency characterized

[14] Taylor to James Buchanan, August 29, 1847, in *Letters from the Battle-fields*, 176.

[15] *Id.* to the Adjutant General, May 21, and June 3, 1846, in *House Executive Documents*, 29 Cong., 2 Sess., No. 119, pp. 28, 33.

[16] *Id.* to *id.*, July 2, 1846, *ibid.*, 54–57.

the Quartermaster General's work. At the same time, it must be admitted that Taylor also showed no foresight in this regard. He made no request for river boats until after he had occupied Matamoros and then his request was only for one. Ten days later, however, he realized that one boat would be inadequate, and to hurry matters he dispatched Captain John Sanders of the Engineers Corps to New Orleans to aid the quartermaster officer at that point to secure four boats. Sanders was further instructed that if he could not get the boats at New Orleans, he should ascend the Mississippi and the Ohio as far as necessary.[17] Even four boats could not meet his needs, and the request for so few indicates not only Taylor's usual close and strict economy in all public expenditures, but also a failure to comprehend the magnitude of the transportation problem that he faced. In time the efforts of Captain Sanders and of the Quartermaster's Department bore fruit. By the middle of July, eight small boats were in operation on the river, and a week later the number had been increased to twelve. About September 1, three or four additional boats, obtained by Sanders in far-off Pittsburgh, arrived and completed the transport system for Taylor's army.[18]

For many months Taylor had felt that his greatest want was "a strong and efficient corps of quartermasters," [19] and the long wait for transports greatly intensified this feeling. In spite of the fact that his old friend Thomas S. Jesup was Quartermaster General, he became increasingly critical of this department. By September 1, when his army was severely handicapped by a shortage of wagons and horseshoes and was suffering for want of many minor supplies, his patience reached an end and he sent to Washington a letter

[17] *Id.* to *id.*, June 10, 1846, *ibid.*, 252; W. W. S. Bliss to Captain John Sanders, May 28, 1846, *ibid.*, 256.

[18] Deputy Quartermaster General Henry Whiting to Quartermaster General Thomas Jesup, July 14 and 23, 1846, *ibid.*, 365–67; Taylor to the Adjutant General, September 1, 1846, *ibid.*, 261.

[19] Taylor to the Adjutant General, August 26, 1845, in *House Executive Documents*, 29 Cong., 1 Sess., No. 196, p. 90.

filled with complaints and accusations which he requested the Adjutant General to lay before General Scott and the Secretary of War.[20] When the Secretary confronted Jesup with Taylor's charges, the Quartermaster General took nearly three months to investigate his own department, then made a report completely exonerating himself and his subordinates and condemning General Taylor for failing to keep the quartermaster's office properly informed as to his requirements.[21] There is some justice to this countercharge, for Taylor sometimes failed to anticipate his needs and then expected the Quartermaster to supply them on short notice. But the major criticism must rest with the Quartermaster's Department which was content to operate during war at much the same leisurely pace as in peace—so leisurely that Taylor complained "the Qr Masters dept is on crutches." [22] The General was not alone in criticizing Jesup. The brilliant young West Point graduate, Lieutenant George B. McClellan, came to the conclusion after a few weeks on the Rio Grande "that the Quartermaster's Department is most woefully conducted—never trust anything to that Department which you can do for yourself." [23] President Polk was astonished at the delays involved in transporting reinforcements to Taylor,[24] and before the war was over he concluded that Jesup was "wholly unfit for his place." [25] Even Jesup, while seeking in one report to put the entire blame on Taylor, admitted in another that "the Quartermaster's department is far from being efficient; the officers are efficient individually, but they are not suffi-

[20] *Id.* to *id.*, September 1, 1846, in *House Executive Documents,* 29 Cong., 2 Sess., No. 119, p. 261.

[21] Thomas S. Jesup to William L. Marcy, December 5, 1846, *ibid.*, 262–64.

[22] Taylor to R. C. Wood, October 12, 1846, in *Letters from the Battlefields,* 63.

[23] William Starr Meyers (ed.), *The Mexican War Diary of George B. McClellan* (Princeton, 1917), 19.

[24] Polk, *Diary,* II, 117.

[25] *Ibid.*, III, 127, 134.

ciently numerous for the highly responsible and laborious duties that devolve upon them." [26]

Taylor's problems of transportation and supply were greatly intensified by the large reinforcements hurried to him in the weeks following the commencement of hostilities. Many of these were militia sent in response to calls from the excitable and eccentric General Gaines at New Orleans without authorization from Washington.[27] They arrived with a minimum of equipment and with little or no means of transportation beyond Brazos Island where they were landed by the Gulf steamers. They were not equipped, said Taylor, to move a barrel of flour a single mile.[28] Taylor was further embarrassed by the fact that the three months' service of these militia would expire before they could be of any real value. Nor was his embarrassment lessened by the belief of some that they had volunteered for six months' duty. The Secretary of War instructed him that there was no legal provision for the employment of militia for a period longer than three months. Any who desired might enlist for a year under the act of May 13 authorizing the President to raise 50,000 volunteers, but volunteers for six months could not be accepted.[29] By June 3 Taylor had nearly 8,000 regular and volunteer troops under his command; [30] six weeks later he had 3,500 regulars and 11,000 volunteers.[31] Many of these were still at Point Isabel while others were encamped between that town and Matamoros.

The thousands of volunteers increased Taylor's problem

[26] Thomas S. Jesup to William L. Marcy, December 27, 1846, in *House Executive Documents,* 29 Cong., 2 Sess., No. 119, pp. 270–71.

[27] *Senate Documents,* 29 Cong., 1 Sess., No. 378, pp. 19–20, 59–61.

[28] Taylor to James Buchanan, August 29, 1847, in *Letters from the Battle-fields,* 176.

[29] Correspondence between Taylor and Secretary of War Marcy, in *House Executive Documents,* 29 Cong., 2 Sess., No. 119, pp. 35–45.

[30] Taylor to the Adjutant General, June 3, 1846, *ibid.,* 33.

[31] *Id.* to N. Young, July 18, 1846, in Division of Manuscripts, Library of Congress.

in regard to discipline and health. As long as his force was composed entirely of regulars he had little difficulty preserving peace and order in the occupied town of Matamoros, but the volunteers gave constant trouble, robbing, stealing, and killing. "Their own officers," recorded Lieutenant Meade, "have no command or control over them, and the General has given up in despair any hope of keeping them in order." [32] Taylor had a strong regard for the rights of private property, and on the day he took possession of Matamoros he announced his determination that the army under his command should not be disgraced by scenes of plunder. He warned that officers found violating his order would be held to answer before a court-martial, that regular soldiers would be brought to trial, while volunteers would "be instantly discharged with disgrace from the service." [33] Three weeks later he wrote to a friend at home that he had not interfered directly or indirectly with private property or the administration of the Mexican laws or customs. Such things "are carried on as if we had never entered their territory." [34] Taylor's regard for property went so far as to forbid the use of private houses for hospital purposes without the consent of the owners. As most of the owners had fled from the city, no such consent could be obtained and the medical officers were hard put to find suitable quarters.[35] The health of the volunteers suffered more than that of the regulars who were by this time somewhat acclimated. Not only diarrhea, dysentery, and other digestive diseases, but also measles, attacked them. Many of the volunteers arrived without tents, and the lack of proper shelter during the rainy season greatly increased their afflictions.[36] Taylor was never enthusiastic about volunteer troops, and

[32] Meade, *George Gordon Meade,* I, 110.

[33] Order No. 62, May 17, 1846, in *House Executive Documents,* 29 Cong., 2 Sess., No. 119, pp. 199–200.

[34] Taylor to "My dear Sir," June 8, 1846, in Taylor Papers.

[35] Mills, Diary, 25.

[36] Duncan, "Medical History of General Taylor's Army," *loc. cit.,* 82.

he especially felt that they had no place in his army. "Volunteers were never intended to invad[e] or carry on war out of the limits of their own country," he wrote, "but should be used, as the constitution intended they should be for enforcing the execution of the laws; & repelling invasion, for which they are admirably suited." [37] Nevertheless he did everything in his power to alleviate their sufferings. Both at Point Isabel, where his son-in-law, Dr. Wood, was the chief medical officer, and at Matamoros extensive hospital facilities were provided, extra civilian physicians were employed, and the sick were made as comfortable as possible.

While the army waited at Matamoros for transportation, a delegation of Louisiana citizens arrived to express to Old Rough and Ready the thanks of their state legislature for his brilliant victories and to inform him that that body was having prepared a beautiful sword which would be presented to him as soon as completed. When their arrival was announced, the General, always opposed to ceremonial fuss and pomp, "observed he would rather go through another battle than make a speech in reply to them." [38] His reception of the delegation was courteous but so simple that at least one of his officers criticized it as not very pleasant or proper. "The Genl. is a scrub son. What are two buckets of champaign for four or five hundred officers. They had not enough to drink a few toasts." [39] The social amenities were better cared for by some of the officers who invited the delegation to dinner at the fine mansion that had been General Arista's headquarters. Governor J. Pinkney Henderson of Texas, who had just arrived to command the Texan troops, and all the volunteer officers were also invited. Wine flowed freely, "the old hero was of course very much toasted, and very highly complimented by all the distinguished personages present; but he was in fine spirits

[37] Taylor to R. C. Wood, September 3, 1846, in *Letters from the Battlefields*, 51.

[38] Meade, *George Gordon Meade*, I, 112.

[39] Mills, Diary, 26.

and seemed to enjoy it all very much, although he commonly takes these things very composedly." [40]

Early in June, Taylor sent a force of three hundred men to occupy the town of Reynosa, sixty miles above Matamoros. This was accomplished without opposition. A month later, several of the steamers having arrived, he began to advance troops and supplies to Camargo, on the San Juan River three miles above its junction with the Rio Grande. Heavy rains late in June had not only made the roads almost impassable, but had also increased the river current and thoroughly soaked the limited supply of firewood for the steamers. In spite of these obstacles the little boats ascended the Rio Grande with thousands of men and tons of provisions,[41] while a few troops marched by the road along the south bank. They marched by night to escape the heat, a broiling heat that cooked meat in open pans.[42] The first troops arrived at Camargo on July 14 and occupied it without resistance. Early in August, Taylor moved his headquarters to that town and began preparations for the advance on Monterrey.[43]

Once again Taylor was faced with the problem of transportation. Now it was not a problem of steamboats, but of mules and wagons. He still needed the steamers to transport supplies from the river's mouth to Camargo, but from that point to Monterrey transportation was by land. Although his army was now many times as numerous as when it left Corpus Christi, he had not received one additional wagon —not even a replacement for those worn out by months of constant travel over rough Texas roads.[44] "At least a thousand wagons ought to be on the route between the Rio

[40] McCall, *Letters from the Frontiers,* 457.

[41] Taylor to the Adjutant General, July 11 and 22, and August 10, 1846, in *House Executive Documents,* 29 Cong., 2 Sess., No. 119, pp. 115–16, 126.

[42] Holland, "Diary of a Texan Volunteer in the Mexican War," *loc. cit.,* 15–19; Grant, *Memoirs,* I, 104.

[43] Taylor to the Adjutant General, August 10, 1846, in *House Executive Documents,* 29 Cong., 2 Sess., No. 119, p. 126.

[44] *Id.* to *id.,* September 1, 1846, *ibid.,* 261; Fry, *Taylor,* 272.

Grande and Monterey," Taylor's quartermaster officer wrote to his chief in Washington. "We have now less than two hundred." [45] While Taylor scoured the country for miles around in search of pack mules and other means of transportation, his troops died by the hundreds from the sickening heat and brackish water.[46] "Camargo is the sickliest place I think in the world," wrote Gideon J. Pillow, Tennessee politician and brigadier general of volunteers, "and it is only matter of surprise & wonder, that I am still alive. I suppose we must have buried a thousand poor volunteers at that river port. Oh how I rejoice to get away from it!" [47] Another Tennessean, a member of the "Bloody First," reported that every day from five to seven members of his regiment were buried. "Hour after hour," he wrote, "was heard the mournful, melancholy sound of the dead march, and the slow, heavy step of the detail that bore some shroudless, coffinless corpse to its long home." This regiment, which left Tennessee a thousand strong, was reduced by sickness and death at Camargo to less than five hundred effective men.[48]

Because his army had been so long idle Taylor decided not to await transportation sufficient for his entire force but to move on Monterrey with six thousand men, half of whom would be regulars and the remainder the best of the volunteers. Even with this limited force it was necessary to leave behind tents and other articles, convenient but not essential, to limit strictly the personal baggage permitted to officers as well as men, and to take rations for a limited number of days.[49] Before leaving Camargo, Taylor organized his regulars into two divisions, the First under General Twiggs and the Second under General Worth. The volunteers who

[45] Assistant Quartermaster General Whiting to Jesup, August 28, 1846, in *House Executive Documents,* 29 Cong., 2 Sess., No. 119, p. 372.

[46] Robinson, *Reminiscences of a Campaign in Mexico,* 109–11.

[47] Gideon J. Pillow to his Wife, December 8, 1846, in Historical Society of Pennsylvania.

[48] Robinson, *Reminiscences of a Campaign in Mexico,* 109–11.

[49] Mills, Diary, 34; Meade, *George Gordon Meade,* I, 123.

advanced with the army were also organized into divisions, one composed entirely of Texas troops under Major General J. Pinkney Henderson, a second composed of regiments from Kentucky, Ohio, Tennessee, and Mississippi under Major General William O. Butler. The troops left at Camargo and farther down the river, Taylor placed under the command of Robert Patterson, Major General of Volunteers.[50] Nearly ten thousand bitterly disappointed troops, mainly volunteers who had rushed to the colors looking for glory and adventure upon the battlefield, were left at Camargo and at Matamoros and in the camps below that town.

By August 19 enough mules had been gathered to move forward the first troops and supplies. Others soon followed, and step by step, slowly but steadily, Taylor's army pushed up the rough roads of the valley of the San Juan toward Monterrey, nestled at the foot of the Sierra Madre. The first half of the march was over hot and dusty wastes, but when they reached Seralvo the country was greatly improved. From that town Taylor wrote, "we are now in sight of high mountains, amidst large brooks of clear cool water running in torrents from them, as well as among springs of running water as pure as it can well be; my tent is near several which affords [*sic*] water enough to supply the city of New York." [51] Enemy cavalry was occasionally sighted and from time to time there were reports of Mexican troops not far away, but no real opposition was encountered. On the nineteenth of September, just one month after the first troops left Camargo, the American army was in front of Monterrey ready to begin its assault.[52]

[50] Taylor to the Adjutant General, September 3, 1846, in *House Executive Documents*, 29 Cong., 2 Sess., No. 119, pp. 134–36.

[51] *Id.* to R. C. Wood, September 10, 1846, in *Letters from the Battlefields*, 56.

[52] *Id.* to the Adjutant General, August 19, September 12 and 17, 1846, in *House Executive Documents*, 29 Cong., 2 Sess., No. 119, pp. 129, 138–39; *id.* to R. C. Wood, September 28, 1846, in *Letters from the Battlefields*, 59–62.

The demoralized Mexican army that evacuated Matamoros had not at first fallen back upon Monterrey but had taken up its position at the town of Linares, situated as was Monterrey at the base of the mountains, but one hundred miles farther east. Late in July, however, when it became clear that Taylor's line of operations was to be up the San Juan Valley, the Mexican forces moved to Monterrey and began preparations to hold that town against the invading Americans. Shortly thereafter General Ampudia arrived with numerous reinforcements and assumed the command. In spite of discord among the Mexican officers and some indecision on the part of Ampudia as to whether the main stand against Taylor should be made at Monterrey or at some point nearer Camargo, work on the fortifications continued through the summer and by the middle of September was well completed.[53]

When Taylor left Camargo he was eager to meet the full strength of the enemy, for he believed defeat for them in another general battle would do more than anything else to bring peace. His chief fear was that the Mexicans would not fight for Monterrey or meet him in force until he had penetrated far beyond it. He expected them to attack his communications and supplies and to attempt in that way to force him back upon the river.[54] By September 10, when his army had covered half the distance to Monterrey, he was still doubtful whether the enemy would attempt to defend the town, though he knew they had "thrown up some slight defences for its protection." He still hoped for battle and a chance to capture their army, artillery, and military stores. About this time Taylor also began to receive reports that Santa Anna, who had just returned to Mexico and resumed the presidency, was marching north with a large force and would reach Monterrey in a few days.[55] A week later, when

[53] Ramsey, *The Other Side,* 62–69.

[54] Taylor to R. C. Wood, August 23, 1846, in *Letters from the Battlefields,* 46.

[55] *Id.* to *id.,* September 10, 1846, *ibid.,* 54; *id.* to the Adjutant General,

Taylor was only twenty-four miles from the town, he still had no authentic information concerning Santa Anna; but his reports were that General Ampudia's force at Monterrey included three thousand regulars and an equal number of volunteers, and he was beginning to think it would be "somewhat strange" if that General did not risk a battle for so important a place as Monterrey.[56]

All doubt that the Mexicans would fight to hold Monterrey was removed on September 19 when their artillery opened fire on the American forces as they approached the town. Taylor promptly fell back and encamped at Walnut Springs, the first convenient location out of range of their shot, while the enemy's position and defenses were carefully reconnoitered. It was soon apparent that the town's position was naturally strong and that it was well fortified with numerous works plentifully supplied with artillery and strongly garrisoned. A strong work known as the citadel, or Black Fort, occupied the center of the defensive line and commanded all the northern approaches. The Bishop's Palace, in reality only the remains of an unfinished building, and several heights in its vicinity had been fortified and controlled the western approach. At the eastern or lower end of the city several smaller but strong works had been constructed. There could be no doubt that the town could be taken, if at all, only after a real battle. Taylor had come to take the town, he had hoped for a fight, and he did not now hesitate.

Unfortunately Taylor was without most of his heavy guns. Presumably because of the shortage of transportation they had been left at Camargo. But only the expectation that no real battle would be offered by the enemy can fully account for such a step. Surely if Taylor had foreseen the opposition he was to face, he would have assigned a portion

September 12, 1846, in *House Executive Documents,* 29 Cong., 2 Sess., No. 119, p. 138.

[56] *Id.* to *id.,* September 17, 1846, *ibid.,* 139; *id.* to R. C. Wood, September 16, 1846; in *Letters from the Battlefields,* 57.

of his limited transportation facilities to the heavy guns or delayed his advance until additional transportation was available.

The reports handed to Taylor late on the evening of the nineteenth by Major Joseph Mansfield and Captain W. G. Williams, the engineer officers who conducted the reconnaissance, convinced the General that the west flank of the enemy could be turned and his communications with the interior cut. By noon of the following day, Sunday, Taylor's plans had been laid and shortly thereafter troops were in motion. While Taylor sought to divert the enemy's attention from the flanking movement by a strong demonstration in front of the town, two thousand troops, the Second Division and a regiment of Texas mounted volunteers, all under the command of General Worth, marched west. By the close of day, Worth's troops had made the necessary detour and had advanced almost within range of the enemy's guns. There they halted for the night. At daybreak on the twenty-first the troops were again in motion and almost at once became engaged with a strong force of Mexican cavalry and infantry. After a brief but desperate fight in which the Americans had the advantage of superior numbers and artillery, the valiant Mexicans were defeated and control of the road that led through the pass to Saltillo was wrested from them. Thus reinforcements and supplies from that direction were prevented from reaching the city.

Worth now turned his attention to the fortifications that protected the western entrances to Monterrey. On the edge of the city the main Saltillo road passed between two high hills. To the south was Federation Hill nearly a thousand feet high and very steep. To the north was Independence Hill, not quite so high but even more precipitous. A branch road from Saltillo entered the city on the south side of Federation Hill. Two well-fortified positions on each of these hilltops gave the Mexicans command of the roads. Until these works were taken, any attempt to enter the city from the west would be almost suicidal. Throughout the afternoon the American troops stormed the batteries on the crest of Federation Hill and at nightfall, after hours of conflict involving regular infantry, artillery, and Texas Riflemen, they were in possession of these strategic works. In spite of stiff opposition from the Mexicans, who were aided by their position on the heights, the loss of life suffered by the attacking troops was small—the wounded and dead together numbered but fifteen.

Throughout the twenty-first, while the troops under Worth were successfully carrying out Taylor's orders on the right of the town, the Commanding General himself was leading the remainder of his little army in a vigorous attack upon the left. It was commenced early in the morning as a diversion for the benefit of Worth's movement, but it rapidly developed into the heaviest and most critical fighting of the day. Only the companies left as the camp guard failed to see action. While two twenty-four-pound howitzers and one ten-inch mortar opened fire on the citadel, Taylor moved his troops forward. The First and Third Regiments of Infantry, a battalion of volunteers from Baltimore and Washington, and Captain Braxton Bragg's field artillery, all under command of Lieutenant Colonel John Garland, were ordered to attack the enemy's defensive works at the east end of the town. The remaining troops, the Fourth Infantry and the Division of Volunteers, took up a position just to the rear of the howitzer and mortar.

Under the murderous direct fire of the near-by batteries and an enfilading fire from the citadel on the right, Garland and his troops advanced. They broke through the fortifications and with reckless courage pushed into the city, hoping to take the batteries from the rear. They soon found themselves in narrow streets and subject to a most destructive fire from guns concealed in the strong stone buildings and behind street barricades. "We . . . had advanced but a short distance when we came suddenly upon an unknown battery, which opened its deadly fire upon us," wrote one of the officers. "From all its embrasures, from every house, from every yard, showers of balls were hurled upon us . . . there was no resisting the deadly, concealed fire, which appeared to come from every direction. On every side we were cut down." [57] For several hours the Americans fought their way from house to house and street to street, but the terrific losses convinced Taylor that it was unwise to continue the battle in the city, and he ordered the troops withdrawn. By this time the Fourth Infantry and three regiments of volunteers, one the Mississippi Rifles under Colonel Jefferson Davis, had been thrown into the assault by Taylor and had captured one of the strong defensive works, Fort Tenería.

A bit later in the day General Taylor ordered portions of Colonel Garland's brigade and the Fourth Infantry into the city again, to carry, if possible, another of the enemy's works, one which had been so persistent and destructive in its fire that the Americans had named it Fort Diablo. Again the American troops were exposed to the galling fire of concealed musketry and artillery. Again, with dauntless courage, they pushed steadily ahead. Although they reached an advanced position and maintained it for some time against fearful odds, they could not reach the "devil's fort," and when their munitions ran low they were once again forced to withdraw.

At the close of day possession of the one fort, Fort Tenería, was all that had been gained. Its cost in brave officers and men had been enormous. The two regiments of regulars in Garland's brigade had been literally cut to pieces. Nearly one third of the Fourth Infantry had fallen. The three regiments of volunteers, especially the one from Tennessee, had also suffered heavily. The total casualties numbered 394.

[57] Henry, *Campaign Sketches,* 194.

Fourteen officers had been killed or mortally wounded. Lieutenants, captains, majors, and colonels had met death as they led their troops forward.

After a long night during which "a cold and pitiless rain fell in drenching torrents" and the groans and cries of the wounded pierced the air, the battle was resumed. Day was just breaking when Worth's forces, in motion since 3 A.M., stormed Independence Hill and the strongly fortified Bishop's Palace. Far on the east side of town, Captain W. S. Henry of the Third Infantry witnessed the assault as he lay on his back in the mud seeking refuge from the spiteful fire of Fort Diablo's guns:

> Just at the gray dawn of day . . . I witnessed the storming of the height. . . . The first intimation we had of it was the discharge of musketry near the top of the hill. Each flash looked like an electric spark. The flashes and the white smoke ascended the hill side steadily, as if worked by machinery. The dark space between the apex of the height and the curling smoke of the musketry became less and less, until the whole became enveloped in smoke, and we knew it was gallantly carried. It was a glorious sight, and quite warmed up our cold and chilled bodies.[58]

Captain Henry was not mistaken. The defenses on the summit of Independence Hill had been carried. Before many hours passed the Mexicans were driven from the Bishop's Palace as well, and all of the western fortifications were in American possession. Again, as on the previous day, General Worth was fortunate in gaining his success with but small loss of life.

On this second day of the battle of Monterrey, action at the east end of town was limited. Taylor ordered no general attack and only minor clashes occurred. At the close of the day and under cover of darkness, however, the Mexicans evacuated several defensive works in this section, thus opening to the attacking force the eastern approaches to the city.

[58] *Ibid.*, 203–204.

When this situation was revealed to Taylor on the morning of the twenty-third, he determined to carry the battle into the heart of the town. Two columns of troops—one from the east and one from the west—entered the city and slowly and painfully fought their way to the main plaza where Ampudia had concentrated his troops and prepared strong defenses. The streets were barricaded with solid masonry walls with embrasures for guns which swept the thoroughfares. All the buildings for two squares on each side of the plaza were occupied by the infantry, loopholes having been made to enable them to fire in any direction. To escape the withering fire of the enemy, the American troops cut their way from house to house with axes and crowbars. Throughout the day Taylor was in the fiercest of the fight. Where the enemy's fire was thickest, there was Old Rough and Ready giving orders and encouragement to his battling troops. Apparently oblivious to danger, at times mounted but frequently on foot, he unhesitatingly pushed forward to the heart of the city. When night fell the invaders were only one square from the plaza. At this point the troops on the east were withdrawn by Taylor, but those on the west held their position through the night. All night long, at half-hour intervals, Worth's guns shelled the closely crowded plaza and the Cathedral which was filled with munitions.[59]

Early the next morning while Taylor was making preparations for another assault, he received a proposal from Ampudia to surrender the city provided he be permitted to leave it with his army, arms, and baggage of every descrip-

[59] This account of the battle of Monterrey is based on the official reports found in *Senate Documents,* 29 Cong., 2 Sess., No. 1, and *House Executive Documents,* 30 Cong., 1 Sess., No. 17; the following letters of Taylor: September 28 to R. C. Wood, in *Letters from the Battlefields,* 59–62, October 9 to J. J. Crittenden, in Crittenden Papers (Division of Manuscripts, Library of Congress); Meade, *George Gordon Meade,* I, 132–37; Mills, Diary, 38–40; Robinson, *Reminiscences of a Campaign in Mexico,* 125–60; Henry, *Campaign Sketches,* 192–216; T. B. Thorpe, *Our Army at Monterey* (Philadelphia, 1847).

tion. Taylor declined this proposition and demanded surrender of the town and army, but promised terms as liberal as possible. He acceded to his opponent's request for a personal interview, which ended, after protracted conversation, in an agreement for each to appoint three officers to settle the terms of capitulation. The terms decided upon by these officers and approved by the commanders required the defeated Mexicans to retire to the interior of Mexico, and permitted the officers to march out with their side arms and private property, the infantry and cavalry with their arms and accoutrements, and the artillery with one field battery not to exceed six pieces. All other public property was to be surrendered to Taylor. Finally, it was stipulated that the American forces would not advance beyond the mountains, behind which the Mexicans were to retire, before the expiration of eight weeks unless such an armistice be disapproved by either government.[60] The next morning Taylor's troops occupied the citadel and three days later took complete possession of the town. As the last brigade of Mexican troops marched for Saltillo the jubilant Americans entered, singing lustily as they swung along the road:

Yankee Doodle came to town,
Riding on a pony,
Stuck a feather in his cap
And called it macaroni.[61]

Taylor knew these terms were liberal and admitted they were not warranted by his instructions. Yet he must have expected that they would receive the approval of the government or he would not have agreed to them. He also apparently thought they required some explanation, for in the following weeks he wrote several long letters defending his action. To Dr. Wood, to Senator J. J. Crittenden of

[60] Taylor to the Adjutant General, September 25, 1846 and enclosures, in *House Executive Documents,* 29 Cong., 2 Sess., No. 119, pp. 68–72.

[61] *Id.* to *id.,* September 28, 1846, *ibid.,* 140; Henry, *Campaign Sketches,* 215.

Kentucky, to Maunsel White and to Major E. G. W. Butler, both of Louisiana, he justified at length his terms of capitulation. To these friends he explained that the whole negotiation was based on the fact that the United States government had made an offer of peace which was then under consideration by the Mexican authorities, and which the officials at Monterrey assured him would be accepted. In such circumstances the further effusion of blood seemed unnecessary and unwise. Moreover, if the attack had been continued, the town would have fallen only after the shedding of much more blood and the sacrifice of many more lives, for the defenders were still in possession of stout fortifications that could have been carried only by storm. While there was a prospect of peace such sacrifice seemed to Taylor unthinkable. He also wished to avoid the destruction of women and children which must have been considerable had the storming process been resorted to. He pointed out that because of the size and position of the town, he had not been able with his force completely to invest it, and Ampudia could have withdrawn most, if not all, of his army under cover of darkness. Finally he explained that the eight weeks' armistice really restricted him but little, for it would take him that long to bring up reinforcements and supplies and prepare again to move.[62] The surprising thing to Taylor was that the Mexicans "should have surrendered a place nearly as strong by nature as Quebeck [*sic*], well fortified, the works armed with 40 pieces of artillery, abundantly supplied with amunition [*sic*] &c., garrisoned by seven thousand regular & 2,000 irregular troops . . . to a force of half its numbers, scantily supplied with provisions, & one or two heavy guns." [63] The

[62] Taylor to R. C. Wood, September 28, 1846, in *Letters from the Battle-, fields*, 59–62; *id.* to J. J. Crittenden, October 9, in Crittenden Papers; *id.* to Maunsel White, October 13, in Southern Historical Collection, University of North Carolina; *id.* to Major E. G. W. Butler, October 19, in Huntington Library.

[63] Taylor to Major E. G. W. Butler, October 19, 1846.

Mexican forces at Monterrey fell short of Taylor's estimate by nearly two thousand, but the general strength of their position and the abundance of their supplies cannot be denied.

These terms had the approval not only of General Taylor, but also, of course, of the three American officers who aided in drafting them—Brigadier General Worth, Major General Henderson of the Texas Volunteers, and Colonel Jefferson Davis of the Mississippi Volunteers.[64] Nevertheless, it is difficult to agree that the military situation justified such liberal terms. If retreat or escape were as easy for the Mexicans as Taylor suggested, why did they not withdraw without seeking terms from the foe? If the defenses were still as strong as claimed, why did he reply to Ampudia's proposal to surrender the town with a demand for the surrender of the army also? Both Ampudia's offer and Taylor's first reaction thereto indicate that the Mexican forces were not in a position to withstand much longer the assault of the American troops. As to the eight weeks' armistice, it seems reasonable to believe that if Taylor had been able to advance from Camargo to Monterrey in half that time, the necessary supplies and reinforcements for a further advance could have been moved up from his depot in much less than two months' time. Clearly Taylor was motivated not by military necessity but by the desire to avoid the further shedding of American blood as well as that of Mexican civilians and, above all, by the hope of peace. Just a month before the fall of Monterrey he had written, "No one can desire peace more than I do." [65] Now he hoped that a spirit of magnanimity toward a prostrate foe would induce him to listen to the peace proposals of the American government.[66]

[64] Rowland (ed.), *Jefferson Davis, Constitutionalist,* I, 63–65, 69.

[65] Taylor to R. C. Wood, August 23, 1846, in *Letters from the Battlefields,* 47.

[66] *Id.* to *id.,* September 28, 1846, *ibid.,* 61; Meade, *George Gordon Meade,* I, 151.

Chapter X

AT ODDS WITH THE ADMINISTRATION

COMMUNICATION between Taylor's headquarters and the War Department was exasperatingly slow. Rough weather on the Gulf frequently delayed boats for days, if not weeks, and the long journey from New Orleans to the nation's capital was by no means rapid. Consequently, it was early November before Taylor received word that his terms of capitulation had not met with approval in Washington. President Polk was anxious to win the war before it became a weapon in the hands of his political opponents or built up a Whig presidential candidate. Therefore he was disgusted that the Mexican army had not been captured but had been allowed to withdraw and prepare for another stand. He promptly submitted the question to the Cabinet and with their unanimous approval notified Taylor that the armistice must be terminated at once.[1] Over the signature of the Secretary of War, Taylor was instructed that the Mexican government had reserved the question of peace for submission to the Mexican Congress in December and that Polk was eager to occupy Tampico and most of the department of Tamaulipas before that time. The President hoped that such additional blows would incline the Congress toward peace.[2]

The President's disapproval of his terms to Ampudia greatly displeased Taylor and turned him against the administration. For several months he had been critical of the

[1] Polk, *Diary,* II, 181–86.

[2] Secretary William L. Marcy to Taylor, October 13, 1846, in *House Executive Documents,* 29 Cong., 1 Sess., No. 119, p. 77.

treatment he had been receiving from Polk and Marcy but had not openly complained. Henceforth he was in almost constant conflict with his superiors. The beginning of his critical attitude toward the administration seems to be found in his long wait for a word of commendation following his victories in May.[3] Not until the end of June did he receive so much as an acknowledgment of his dispatches reporting those battles. Meanwhile he grew impatient because of the lack of transportation facilities and as early as June 21 concluded, "Was I a prominent or ambitious aspirent [*sic*] for civil distinction or honors, I might very readily suppose there was an intention somewhere among the high functionaries to break me down, which am now satisfied will be done." [4] This feeling increased during the summer, and when in November he received Marcy's letter disapproving the terms given at Monterrey, he was convinced that an "intrigue" was going on against him with the object of removing him from command because certain politicians had mentioned him for the presidency.[5] This feeling was not entirely without justification, for though the disapproval of the armistice was not due to a desire to discredit Taylor, it was only "his standing with the people" that saved him from being recalled at this time.[6] It must also be admitted that there was something of an intrigue against Taylor. General Pillow of the volunteers was a close friend of the President and was busily writing him letters to undermine General Taylor. When in early December Pillow learned that the main offensive against Mexico was to be entrusted to Scott and not Taylor, this vain and ambitious schemer wrote: "This gives me joy and congratulation. It is my work." [7] Certainly in part it was Pillow's work. But in part

[3] McCormac, *James K. Polk,* 430–31.

[4] Taylor to R. C. Wood, June 21, 1846, in *Letters from the Battlefields,* 13.

[5] *Id.* to *id.,* November 10, 1846, *ibid.,* 67.

[6] Mary Ann Coleman, *Life of John J. Crittenden* (Philadelphia, 1871), I, 260.

[7] Gideon J. Pillow to his Wife, December 8, 1846, in Historical Society of Pennsylvania.

Taylor was himself responsible for the administration's loss of confidence in him. His capitulation terms at Monterrey were the turning point in his war career.

When Congress assembled at the close of the year and resolutions were introduced thanking Taylor and his army "for their courage, skill, fortitude, and good conduct in storming the city of Monterey" and for the "brilliant victory" which resulted, partisan politics were quickly aroused. President Polk's friends in the House of Representatives insisted upon adding the amendment, "Provided that nothing herein contained shall be construed into an approbation of the terms of the capitulation of Monterey." The Senate, however, with John M. Clayton, Crittenden, Webster, and Calhoun vigorously denouncing this studied insult, refused to concur in the resolution until the objectionable proviso was removed. The enthusiasm and unanimity with which Congress had voted its thanks to Taylor following his triumphs at Palo Alto and Resaca de la Palma were significantly lacking.[8]

At Monterrey, as at Matamoros, Taylor established his own headquarters well outside the city and kept most of the army with him; General Worth with the Second Division, composed entirely of regulars, occupied the town.[9] Some of the men were disgusted that only Worth's division was to have comfortable quarters in the city. Surgeon Mills, Taylor's faithful critic, felt it was "an abominable outrage for which old Taylor should receive one hundred lashes on his bare back, well laid on." [10] Although Taylor issued but a limited number of passes for his men to visit the city and hoped thereby to maintain quiet and order, he found that "shameful atrocities" were committed. The Texas mounted volunteers were especially guilty of misconduct, and the General seized the earliest opportunity to muster them out of service and return them to Texas.

[8] *Congressional Globe,* 29 Cong., 2 Sess., 295–96, 315–18, 558.
[9] Meade, *George Gordon Meade,* I, 147.
[10] Mills, Diary, 41–42.

"With their departure," he wrote, "we may look for a restoration of quiet and order." [11] Taylor's frank statements in his reports that the Texans perpetrated shameful atrocities and seldom made an expedition without unwarrantably killing a Mexican, and his subsequent request that because of the constant recurrence of such atrocities no more Texas troops be sent to his column, caused Senator Sam Houston to charge him with strong prejudice against Texans. Nearly four years later, when Taylor as President opposed Texas' extreme boundary claims, Houston bitterly denounced him on the floor of the Senate and charged that when a general in the field he had unwarrantably assailed, traduced, and defamed the people of Texas and had stigmatized them as the veriest refuse of the community, a dishonor to the army. So much did the Texas senator make of this point that two senators came to Taylor's defense and clearly demonstrated from the reports that he had given the Texans warm praise for their part in the battle of Monterrey and that his subsequent criticisms were due not to prejudice but to the undeniable misconduct of the Texan troops.[12]

For a while following the departure of the Texas troops conditions improved, but some weeks later the "many outrages . . . recently committed . . . upon the persons and property of Mexican citizens," again aroused the General. In the hope of keeping the men closer to camp, he banned the use of every sort of riding animal by any except commissioned officers.[13] Not only in Monterrey but also on the road between that city and Camargo depredations were committed. These also met Taylor's disapproval and in an order read at the head of every company he warned the

[11] Taylor to the Adjutant General, October 6, 1846, in *House Executive Documents,* 29 Cong., 2 Sess., No. 119, p. 146; Mills, Diary, 42.

[12] *Congressional Globe,* 31 Cong., 1 Sess., 1320–21, Appendix, 1024–26, 1034–41.

[13] Order No. 146, November 27, 1846, in *House Executive Documents,* 29 Cong., 2 Sess., No. 119, p. 200.

troops that the good faith of the United States and the army had been pledged to the protection of the rights of all Mexican citizens and that it was to the interest of all "to see that the reputation of neither be disgraced by scenes of plunder and marauding." The troops were well supplied, he maintained, "and nothing can justify the wanton destruction of private property." [14]

Late in November men from the first regiment of Kentucky Volunteers were guilty of a series of apparently unprovoked attacks upon the natives which gave rise to such bitter feeling that Taylor feared for the peace and safety of the entire army. When a group of Mexicans brought to his tent and laid at his feet a crying, bleeding twelve-year-old boy with a broken leg who had been shot while at work in a cornfield, the old General was much aroused and he ordered the entire regiment to the rear in disgrace. When, however, the officers of the regiment promised to find the guilty individuals and to prevent such outrages in the future, Taylor relented and revoked the order.[15]

It may be that in this case and in that of the Texas regiments Taylor was not severe enough and that his orders were not always enforced, but few commanding generals of an invading army have shown such consideration for the rights and welfare of the native population as Taylor did in Mexico. Doubtless this was one reason why the American minister to Mexico three years later found that Taylor was held in high esteem in that country "both as a military man and an upright gentleman, altogether above doing a mean thing, because of his power to do it." [16]

[14] Order No. 149, December 2, 1846, *ibid.*, 221.

[15] Meade, *George Gordon Meade,* I, 161–62; Mills, Diary, 46; draft in Taylor's hand of a letter of December 1, 1846, to the officers of the regiment, in Taylor Papers.

[16] R. P. Letcher to William Meredith, February 13, 1850, in Meredith Papers (Historical Society of Pennsylvania).

Although the climate of Monterrey was vastly superior to that of the valley of the Rio Grande, the health of Taylor's army was none too good. The men still suffered somewhat from diarrhea and dysentery but now were particularly attacked by fevers, both intermittent and remittent. Nearly a third of the troops at Monterrey, including many of the wounded, were affected at one time. Fortunately the fevers were of a mild character and of short duration. "Old Zach," ever a devotee of the simple and temperate life, escaped the disease and continued to enjoy his usual good health.[17] Meanwhile the troops left by Taylor at Matamoros and at the mouth of the river, mainly volunteers with little experience in camp life and with medical officers equally inexperienced, suffered terribly. Late in November one officer claimed that out of every ten men one had died, three had gone home sick, and two, though still in camp, were on the sick report. Thus six out of ten were a total loss to the service.[18]

About the middle of October while Taylor moved new supplies forward to Monterrey, preparatory to the resumption of hostilities should peace negotiations fail, he received instructions from Secretary Marcy, written September 22, three weeks before the fall of Monterrey was known in Washington. In these he was instructed to push south toward San Luis Potosí while another column under Major General Robert Patterson moved against Tampico and the southern portion of Tamaulipas. It was not intended to weaken Taylor's forces, he was informed, but some of the troops on the lower Rio Grande were to be sent with Patterson. The entire expedition was to be under Taylor's supervision, but, to save time, orders had been sent direct to Patterson. Whether the Tampico ex-

17 Duncan, "Medical History of General Taylor's Army," *loc. cit.*, 96–97; Meade, *George Gordon Meade*, I, 145–46.

18 John Sedgwick, *Correspondence of John Sedgwick, Major-General* (New York, 1902–1903), I, 38.

pedition should be by sea or land, or perhaps both, was left to Patterson and Taylor to decide.[19]

These instructions were thoroughly unsatisfactory to General Taylor. He promptly replied that he could and would move forward about seventy-five miles and occupy Saltillo, but that he was far from strong enough to advance on San Luis Potosí which was three hundred miles beyond Saltillo, strongly held by the combined forces of Ampudia and Santa Anna, and close enough to the heart of the republic to receive munitions and reinforcements without difficulty. As Saltillo is about equidistant from the Rio Grande and San Luis, he wrote, "every day's march beyond it lengthens our already long line, and curtails theirs; weakens us, and gives them strength." This movement should not be undertaken with less than twenty thousand effective troops, of whom half should be regulars, and five thousand additional men to hold the country already gained and to guard the line of communications. His present force of nine thousand volunteers and three thousand regulars was entirely inadequate for the proposed movement on San Luis Potosí, to say nothing of a simultaneous movement to Tampico. Instead of this double offensive, Taylor recommended the holding of a defensive line, either the Rio Grande or the Sierra Madre. "The former line," he pointed out, "could be held with a much smaller force than the latter; but even the line of the Sierra Madre could be held with a force greatly less than would be required for an active campaign. Monterey controls the outlet from the interior. A strong garrison at this point, with an advance at Saltillo and small corps at Monclova, Linares, Victoria, and Tampico, would effectually cover the line." If the administration should "determine to strike a decisive blow at Mexico," he added, "it

[19] Secretary William L. Marcy to Taylor, September 22, 1846, in *House Executive Documents,* 29 Cong., 2 Sess., No. 119, pp. 64–66.

is my opinion that the force should land near Vera Cruz or Alvarado; and, after establishing a secure depot, march thence on the capital. The amount of troops required for this service would not fall short . . . of 25,000 men." [20]

Not only was Taylor dissatisfied with the plan of campaign set forth in Marcy's instructions; he was also thoroughly aroused by the Secretary's procedure in sending orders directly to General Patterson. Direct communication by the department with his subordinates on points pertaining exclusively to the general in command was, he protested, a course "pregnant with the worst evils" from which "confusion and disaster alone" could result and "a violation of the integrity of the chief command in the field." "While I remain in command of the army against Mexico, and am therefore justly held responsible by the government and the country for the conduct of its operations," he frankly wrote, "I must claim the right of organizing all detachments from it, and regulating the time and manner of their service." [21] Many of Taylor's officers also viewed Marcy's behavior as outrageous and shared Old Rough and Ready's indignation.[22]

Neither Taylor's suggestion for a defensive line in northern Mexico nor his proposal of a Vera Cruz expedition was new with him in October. As early as July 2 he had given his opinion to the War Department that it would be difficult to operate much beyond Monterrey. At the same time, in a private letter, he advocated holding the Rio Grande and invading Mexico from Vera Cruz.[23] By the middle of August it was well known among Taylor's officers that he believed, unless Mexico soon made peace, the best plan of campaign would be to take Vera Cruz and move on the capital.[24] During the summer and early

20 Taylor to the Adjutant General, October 15, 1846, *ibid.*, 73–75.

21 *Ibid.*, 75–76.

22 Meade, *George Gordon Meade*, I, 145.

23 Taylor to John Ewing, July 3, 1846, in New York Historical Society.

24 Gideon J. Pillow to his Wife, August 16, 1846, in Historical Society of Pennsylvania.

fall Secretary Marcy was also thinking of a Vera Cruz expedition, so Taylor's proposal was no surprise to him.[25]

While the indignant commander went about his work at Monterrey and his mid-October dispatch recommending a defensive line journeyed the long miles to Washington, President Polk discussed campaign strategy with his Cabinet. After hours of debate they reached much the same conclusion as Taylor. Unanimously they decided to invade Mexico from Vera Cruz or some other point on the coast and to order Taylor not to advance beyond Monterrey and the positions necessary to secure that town.[26] Polk had originally hoped to induce the northern provinces of Mexico to declare their independence and to make peace with the United States, but he had now abandoned all hope of this and had concluded that only an expedition into the very heart of the country would bring Mexico to terms.[27] Major Robert W. McLane was taken into the full confidence of the President and sent as special messenger with both oral and written instructions to General Taylor.[28]

It was on the night of November 2 while the General was still thoroughly disgruntled over the Patterson affair that a dispatch bearer arrived at Taylor's headquarters with the administration's disapproval of his terms of capitulation at Monterrey. These instructions by no means improved his humor. "The old man is very angry and flies about like an old hen with one chicken," observed Surgeon Mills.[29] Four days passed before Taylor dispatched a messenger to notify the Mexican commander at San Luis Potosí that the armistice would cease on the thirteenth, the date on which the messenger was expected to reach his destination.[30] Meanwhile Taylor made preparations to

[25] Secretary William L. Marcy to Taylor, July 9, and October 13, 1846, in *House Executive Documents,* 29 Cong., 2 Sess., No. 119, pp. 57–60, 77–79.

[26] Polk, *Diary,* II, 198–99.

[27] McCormac, *James K. Polk,* 451.

[28] Polk, *Diary,* II, 200, 204.

[29] Mills, Diary, 44.

[30] Taylor to the Adjutant General, November 9, 1846, in *House Executive Documents,* 29 Cong., 2 Sess., No. 119, p. 82.

cross the mountains and occupy Saltillo at the other end of the pass. On the morning of the twelfth, as these plans neared completion, Major McLane reached the end of his three weeks' journey and delivered to General Taylor the orders to hold his present line. In spite of these instructions he proceeded with his plans, for he regarded Saltillo as an important outpost of Monterrey and deemed its occupation necessary, partly because it was the capital of Coahuila, but primarily because it controlled the mountain pass and the fertile country beyond, from which considerable foodstuffs might be obtained.[31] When on the thirteenth a portion of the Second Division under General Worth marched for Saltillo, the Commanding General accompanied them. Three days later the town was occupied without opposition or incident worthy of notice. Taylor remained for several days making arrangements with the natives for a supply of breadstuffs and examining the surrounding country. When the citizens attempted to extort exorbitant prices for the provisions Taylor demanded of them, "the old gentleman treated them without ceremony," recorded Lieutenant Meade, "and he ordered to be seized all the supplies that were in the town, ascertained their owners, and then offered them the market prices previous to our arrival, or nothing at all. They very wisely determined to take his prices, and there the affair ended." [32] Leaving Worth and his troops to garrison Saltillo, Taylor returned to Monterrey which he reached on November 23.[33]

While Taylor had been conducting his campaign against Monterrey, other American troops had successfully occupied New Mexico and California, and a column of some 2,500 to 3,000 men commanded by Brigadier General John

[31] *Id.* to *id.*, November 12, 1846, *ibid.*, 94–96.

[32] Meade, *George Gordon Meade*, I, 158.

[33] Taylor to the Adjutant General, November 24, 1846, in *House Executive Documents*, 29 Cong., 2 Sess., No. 119, pp. 96–97; *id.* to R. C. Wood, November 26, 1846, in *Letters from the Battlefields*, 71; *id.* to J. J. Crittenden, December 12, 1846, in Crittenden Papers.

E. Wool had been organized at San Antonio for a movement against Chihuahua. The extension of the war to the Pacific Coast and the occupation of California called forth severe criticism from Taylor. He informed Dr. Wood that he entirely disapproved the administration's California policy and considered "no act of the brittis govt as regards the acquirement of territory in the East, or anywhere else more outrageous than our attempt or intention of taking permanent possession of that country." [34]

When General Wool's Chihuahua expedition was organized late in the summer, it was made a part of Taylor's command. He was not enthusiastic about the arrangement, however. Communication with Wool's column was slow and difficult, and Taylor took little responsibility for it. By the end of October, Wool, having reached the town of Monclova, about 150 miles north of Saltillo, reported to Taylor that the only practicable route to Chihuahua was the very circuitous one by way of Parras which would take him almost to Saltillo, and inquired what was to be gained by going to Chihuahua. Taylor thought little was to be gained and promptly ordered him to remain at Monclova.[35] Meanwhile the department in Washington had also come to doubt the wisdom of this movement and suggested to Taylor that if Wool had not advanced too far on his march to Chihuahua, "it may be advisable that he should at once form a junction with you." [36] This suggestion, which reached Taylor in the middle of November just as he was taking possession of Saltillo, received his full approval. He ordered General Wool to abandon his communications with San Antonio, to move south and occupy Parras, and to establish communications by way of Monterrey and the Rio Grande. At Parras, ninety miles west of Saltillo, he would control a rich agricultural sec-

[34] *Id.* to R. C. Wood, August 23, 1846, in *Letters from the Battlefields,* 49.

[35] *Id.* to the Adjutant General, November 9, 1846, in *House Executive Documents,* 29 Cong., 2 Sess., No. 119, p. 82.

[36] Secretary William L. Marcy to Taylor, October 22, 1846, *ibid.,* 85.

tion from which abundant supplies could be drawn not only for his own troops, but also for those at Saltillo and Monterrey. If a Mexican force should advance from San Luis Potosí his troops could be quickly joined with those at Saltillo to form an army of about five thousand men.[37]

The administration's instructions, delivered to General Taylor by Major McLane on November 12, not only ordered him to hold his present line and authorized him to consolidate General Wool's forces with his own, but also informed him that the expedition to be headed by General Patterson would be increased to four thousand troops and would be sent to Vera Cruz instead of Tampico. Therefore he was instructed to "make the necessary arrangements for having four thousand men (of whom fifteen hundred or two thousand should be regular troops) ready to embark for Vera Cruz . . . at the earliest practicable period." [38] Although the detachment of this force was to be contingent upon Taylor's approval, the whole plan was outlined, the several officers to lead the expedition were "suggested," and it is obvious that Taylor was expected to carry it out. The government was anxious, he was informed, "that nothing should occur to prevent the expedition." [39] Again, as when the Patterson expedition was first planned, orders were sent direct to Patterson.[40]

Taylor believed that a force of four thousand men would be quite inadequate for a descent upon a hostile coast; they might capture the town but they could not hold it. Such an expedition should be large enough to meet any contingency that might arise and to avoid even the smallest chance of failure. No less than ten thousand men

[37] Taylor to the Adjutant General, November 12 and 24, December 8, 1846, *ibid.*, 95, 97, 99.

[38] Marcy to Taylor, October 22, 1846, *ibid.*, 86.

[39] *Ibid.*

[40] Secretary William L. Marcy to Major General Robert Patterson, October 28, 1846, *ibid.*, 88–89.

should be sent against Vera Cruz, and before any march into the interior was undertaken they should be increased to twenty-five thousand. Holding such views, and being unable to spare ten thousand men from his own line of operation, he continued with his plans to occupy Victoria and the lower part of Tamaulipas and to move on Tampico. At the same time he informed Washington that he would hold four thousand troops ready to embark for Vera Cruz whenever an additional six thousand could be sent from the United States.[41] The evacuation of Tampico by the Mexican garrison and the occupation of the town by a United States naval force under Commodore Matthew C. Perry modified his plans but slightly. He still thought it wise to advance to Victoria with a view to examining the country. He particularly desired to ascertain whether the passes through the mountains toward San Luis Potosí and other interior points were passable for an army with wagons and artillery.[42]

It was the middle of December when Taylor was ready to move. Leaving Wool and his force of 2,400 at Parras, Worth and a similar force at Saltillo, and Butler in command of the "reserves" at Monterrey and the line to Camargo, Taylor marched for Victoria. With him marched the division of regulars under Brigadier General Twiggs and several regiments of volunteers commanded by Brigadier General John A. Quitman. At Montemorelos he was to be joined by two additional regiments which would increase his force to 3,500 men. At the same time, Patterson marched south from Matamoros with some 1,500 troops to join Taylor at Victoria.[43]

On the evening of December 17, when the army was

[41] Taylor to the Adjutant General, November 12, 1846, *ibid.*, 95–96.

[42] *Id.* to *id.*, November 26, 1846, *ibid.*, 98.

[43] *Id.* to *id.*, December 8 and 14, 1846, *ibid.*, 98–102. For the march of General Patterson's column see: Furber, *Twelve Months Volunteer: or Journal of a Private . . . in the Campaign in Mexico*, 275–321; Meyers (ed.), *The Mexican War Diary of George B. McClellan*, 23–44.

halted at Montemorelos after a pleasant, easy advance of sixty miles, it was overtaken by a dispatch bearer with information from General Worth that Santa Anna was concentrating his forces to attack Saltillo and Parras. Ordering Quitman to proceed with the volunteers to Victoria, General Taylor and the regulars hastened back to Monterrey only to learn that there was no real threat from Santa Anna. Both the General and the men cursed Worth for their useless exertion, rested a day, and once again started for Victoria.[44] Taylor had advanced but two days' march when he was again overtaken by important dispatches. These included one from General Scott announcing that he was on his way to Mexico to take charge of the operations against Vera Cruz and that he would be obliged to take from Taylor "most of the gallant officers and men (regulars and volunteers)" whom he had "so long and so nobly commanded." Scott informed Taylor that he would ascend the river as far as Camargo in order to be within easy corresponding distance and hoped to reach that town by December 23.[45] Having already been once turned back from his march to Victoria, Taylor was anxious to be on his way. In spite of this new turn of events he marched on. Although Scott did not request Taylor to meet him at Camargo or at any other point, as he might well have done, he did make it clear that he wished to have quick communication with Taylor, and he was justified in feeling that Taylor had treated him cavalierly by turning his back and marching off to distant Victoria.[46] Moreover, there was no imperative need for Taylor to go on. The combined forces of Quitman and Patterson were adequate to meet any probable contingencies at Victoria. Early in Jan-

[44] Taylor to the Adjutant General, December 22, 1846, in *House Executive Documents,* 29 Cong., 2 Sess., No. 119, pp. 104–105; Mills, Diary, 47; Meade, *George Gordon Meade,* I, 168–70.

[45] Scott to Taylor, November 25, 1846, in *House Executive Documents,* 29 Cong., 2 Sess., No. 119, pp. 93–94.

[46] *Id.* to Secretary William L. Marcy, January 16, 1847, in Marcy Papers (Division of Manuscripts, Library of Congress).

uary, Taylor reached his destination and found that Quitman had occupied the town without resistance and that Patterson and his force were safely at hand. Examination of the mountain passes soon disclosed that there was no route west from Victoria that was passable for artillery or wagons. Consequently there was no possibility of moving against San Luis Potosí from Victoria or Tampico, and likewise there was little danger that garrisons at these towns would be attacked from the interior.[47]

No further word was heard from General Scott until January 14 when Taylor, still at Victoria, was startled to learn that because of his absence Scott had given orders to General Butler, Taylor's second in command, detaching nine thousand of his troops for service with Scott. One thousand cavalry, half regulars and half volunteers, eight thousand infantry, half of whom should be regulars, and two field batteries of light artillery were immediately to be concentrated at the mouth of the Rio Grande and at Tampico. All the troops with Taylor, except possibly a small garrison for Victoria and an escort for the General on his return march to Monterrey were to proceed to Tampico; enough others to make up the nine thousand would be ordered to the Rio Grande by Butler. "I am compelled, by diminishing your forces," wrote Scott, "to reduce you for a time to the strict defensive." [48]

Although he promptly obeyed the orders of the Commanding General, Taylor was thoroughly indignant at both the fact and the manner of the heavy withdrawal of troops, and he protested not only to Scott, but also to the President. To Scott he wrote:

> Had you, general, relieved me at once in the whole command, and assigned me to duty under your order, or allowed

[47] Taylor to the Adjutant General, January 7, 1847, in *House Executive Documents,* 29 Cong., 2 Sess., No. 119, p. 107.

[48] Scott to Taylor, January 3, 1847, in *House Executive Documents,* 30 Cong., 1 Sess., No. 60, pp. 848–50; *id.* to Major General W. O. Butler, January 3, 1847, *ibid.,* 851–53.

me to retire from the field, be assured that no complaint would have been heard from me; but while almost every man of my regular force and half the volunteers, (now in respectable discipline) are withdrawn for distant service, it seems that I am expected, with less than a thousand regulars and a volunteer force, partly of new levies, to hold a defensive line, while a large army of more than twenty thousand men is in my front. . . .

I cannot misunderstand the object of the arrangements indicated in your letters. I feel that I have lost the confidence of the government, or it would not have suffered me to remain, up to this time, ignorant of its intentions, with so vitally affecting interests [*sic*] committed to my charge. But, however much I may feel personally mortified and outraged by the course pursued, unprecedented at least, in our own history, I will carry out in good faith, while I remain in Mexico, the views of the government, though I may be sacrificed in the effort.[49]

In a letter to the Adjutant General which he asked to have laid before the Secretary of War and the President, Taylor protested that he had never been officially informed by the department that Scott was coming or that a large portion of his troops were to be transferred. "Having been placed in command of the army, and charged with the operations against Mexico by the orders of the President of the United States, had I chosen to be punctilious, I might have declined to make any detachment from my force without the same authority expressly communicated." He was constrained to believe, he wrote, that he no longer possessed the confidence of the government, and he expressed regret that the President had not relieved him from his position.[50]

To his friends Senator Crittenden and Dr. Wood, Taylor denounced even more frankly the "outrageous course" pursued toward him, called it "an intrigue of Marcy, Scott & Worth," charged Scott with the "greatest duplicity," and indicted the Washington authorities for want

[49] Taylor to Scott, January 15, 1847, *ibid.*, 862–63.
[50] *Id.* to the Adjutant General, January 27, 1847, *ibid.*, 1100–1102.

of common courtesy or decency. That which most offended and aroused him was the failure of the President or the Secretary of War to advise him of the change which was to take place as soon as it was determined on in Washington.[51] Although some months later Taylor was satisfied that the arrangements for stripping him of his troops were the work of Scott and his friends who got the ear of Polk, "without any agency of Mr. Marcy in the matter," [52] the passage of time did nothing to assuage his indignation. In September, after eight months of reflection, he wrote to Crittenden:

> I should like to know why the army which I commanded for more than two years, which I had conducted from the Sabine to the tablelands of [the] Sierra Madre, which had won three important battles . . . under my orders was so unceremoniously taken from me, without the usual courtesy on such occasions, as if intended to add insult to injury; or if it was thought necessary to send another to supplant me, why was it done in the most cruel manner which could be thought of & superseded by one too, who had declined taking it when he thought his doing so would interfere with his prospects for reaching the presidency & why was I not offered a command in that army, even as a subordinate, which I had been so long associated with, that I might have shared its dangers, hardships & triumphs, but I had "done enough" perhaps too much; these are matters however, which can only be explained by those better versed in court intrigues than I am, or wish to be— [53]

Immediately on receiving Scott's order at Victoria, "Old Zach" decided to throw up his command and return to the United States. But on more mature reflection he concluded that such action was exactly what his enemies expected and desired of him, and he determined to disap-

[51] *Id.* to J. J. Crittenden, January 26, 1847, in Coleman, *Crittenden*, I, 270–78; *id.* to R. C. Wood, January 30, 1847, in *Letters from the Battle-fields*, 84.

[52] *Id.* to J. P. Taylor, January 19, 1848, in Taylor Papers.

[53] *Id.* to J. J. Crittenden, September 15, 1847, in Crittenden Papers.

point them. He would remain and do his duty, "no matter under what circumstances," until relieved or superseded in fact as well as in effect.[54]

General Taylor's conclusion that he no longer possessed the confidence of the government was quite correct. Indeed, as early as September 5 Polk had decided that Taylor, though a good subordinate officer, ready to obey orders, was not the man for the chief command of the army, because he lacked "resources or grasp of mind enough to conduct such a campaign," and was "unwilling to express any opinion or to take any responsibility on himself." [55] When, in October, the President learned of Taylor's terms at Monterrey and received Pillow's letters recounting dissatisfaction in the army with Taylor because of these terms and his supposed partiality, he was further convinced that Taylor was not fit to command. But public opinion was in Taylor's favor and there seemed to be no one to put in his place.[56] Polk's own preference was for Senator Thomas Hart Benton, who had been an influential adviser on war plans from the outset. Unfortunately, from the President's point of view, there was no way under the existing laws that the Senator could be given sufficient rank to command, and Congress could not be persuaded to pass the necessary special legislation. By the middle of November, Polk, Marcy, and Benton were even more dissatisfied with Taylor because of his extreme caution in offering suggestions and his failure to give Washington adequate information about the enemy's country, resources, and plans.[57] Moreover, the President had come to regard him as "a bitter political partisan," hostile to the administration, and controlled by cunning and shrewd men.[58] Therefore it was determined that the Vera Cruz

[54] *Id.* to *id.*, January 26, 1847, *loc. cit.; id.* to Wood, February 9, 1847, in *Letters from the Battlefields*, 85.

[55] Polk, *Diary*, II, 119.

[56] *Ibid.*, 181, 211; Coleman, *Crittenden*, I, 260.

[57] Polk, *Diary*, II, 229–32.

[58] *Ibid.*, 229, 236.

expedition, which had been fully decided upon, should be placed in other hands. Unable to appoint Benton and convinced that "anybody would do better than Taylor," the President reluctantly turned to General Scott. Polk had little confidence in him as a military commander and still resented portions of his correspondence with the Secretary of War in May, but Benton and Marcy both urged his appointment and no satisfactory alternative was apparent.[59]

Polk's decision to place the conduct of the Vera Cruz campaign in other hands was fully justified. Taylor had proved himself a practical leader of men and a courageous fighter, but he had not demonstrated such strategical or tactical ability or such executive efficiency as to make him an indispensable general. Added to this was the far more important fact that he so completely distrusted and despised the administration that it was impossible for him to work harmoniously with it. If the administration had lost confidence in him, he had also lost confidence in the administration. Some new arrangement was inevitable. The manner in which the change was made, however, is far less defensible. Admitting that Taylor was unduly suspicious and sensitive, and that Scott was sincerely friendly toward him, there is still reason to believe that a successful general was entitled to more consideration than Taylor received from either Marcy or Scott.

[59] *Ibid.*, 241–43, 250.

Chapter XI

THE BATTLE OF BUENA VISTA

FULLY convinced that "Scott, Marcy & Co." were more eager to destroy him than they were to defeat the enemy, and determined that their efforts should not succeed, Old Rough and Ready returned to Monterrey on January 24. In spite of the fact that he had fewer than six thousand troops at his command and that all but two squadrons of cavalry and a portion of his artillery were inexperienced volunteers,[1] he had no intention of playing a humble, defensive role. Learning that enemy cavalry units were active on the road south of Saltillo where they had captured every member of a large reconnoitering party,[2] he determined to disregard instructions from General Scott to abandon that town and "to make no detachments, except for *reconnoissances* and immediate defence, much beyond Monterey." [3] Instead, he promptly concentrated his troops at Agua Nueva, eighteen miles south of Saltillo on the road to San Luis Potosí, and informed Scott that he would hold that position unless positively ordered to fall back by the government at Washington.[4] He believed that a retreat to Monterrey not only would have a bad effect on the morale of the volunteer troops, but would be an unwise move strategically, for it would open his flanks and communications to attack by the enemy.[5] He was not the

1 Taylor to the Adjutant General, January 26, 1847, in *House Executive Documents,* 30 Cong., 1 Sess., No. 60, pp. 1097–98.

2 *Id.* to *id.,* January 30, 1847, *ibid.,* 1106.

3 Scott to Taylor, January 26, 1847, *ibid.,* 864–65.

4 Taylor to Lieutenant H. L. Scott, February 7, 1847, *ibid.,* 1162–63.

5 *Ibid.;* Taylor to the Adjutant General, February 7, 1847, *ibid.,* 1110–11.

least dismayed by reports that strong enemy forces were advancing upon his position. "Should they offer us battle I shall indulge them," he wrote, "be the consequences what they may." [6] In less restrained language he declared to the correspondent of the New York *Tribune:* "Let them come; damned if they don't go back a good deal faster than they came." [7]

Taylor's decision to move his army forward to Agua Nueva was clearly unwise. He himself soon discovered that his advanced position was a poor place at which to meet the enemy and he withdrew from it. He might well have followed the orders of Scott and abandoned Saltillo. Either at the mountain pass between that town and Monterrey or behind the fortifications of Monterrey itself a stand could have been made with far less chance of defeat and at the cost of fewer lives than in the open field. Certainly at Monterrey his lines of communication and his flanks would have been more easily protected than when he was nearly one hundred miles farther on. But he was eager to show that he was ready to fight if only his troops had not been taken from him. So, he advanced to meet the enemy.[8]

The chief threat to Taylor's army came from the powerful Mexican force gathered at San Luis Potosí by General Antonio López de Santa Anna, the self-styled Napoleon of the West, who over a period of thirty years alternately held the presidential office and sought safety in exile. In the middle of August, 1846, while Taylor was marching against Monterrey, Santa Anna returned to Mexico from one of his periodic exiles. He passed through the blockading naval squadron with the connivance of President Polk who hoped that somehow—though just how is not clear—Santa Anna's presence in Mexico would lead to an early

[6] *Id.* to R. C. Wood, January 30, 1847, in *Letters from the Battlefields,* 84.
[7] Smith, *War with Mexico,* I, 374.
[8] *Ibid.,* 547–48.

and favorable peace.[9] After a few weeks' political skirmishing in the capital, he hurried north to undertake new military operations against the invading Yankees. In the middle of October he established his headquarters at San Luis Potosí and for the ensuing three months was constantly busy gathering men and supplies for his campaign.[10]

In spite of political and financial obstacles Santa Anna made progress, and the town soon resounded with the martial sound of drum and bugle and the staccato shouts of command as the General and his aides drilled the troops that arrived from all parts of Mexico. Early in the new year he had nearly twenty-five thousand troops under his command. They were still none too well equipped or trained, but the country was crying out for action and Santa Anna decided to move.[11] He may also have been influenced to act by a knowledge of Taylor's weakness, for the original copy of General Scott's January 3 letter to Taylor detailing the withdrawal of troops for the Vera Cruz expedition was intercepted by the enemy and may have reached the Mexican commander.[12]

Late in January, Santa Anna's army left San Luis Potosí and headed north for Saltillo, 250 miles away. Through rain and snow and bitter cold, through dust and heat they plodded on. Food became scarce and water was at times completely wanting. But in spite of hunger and thirst, in

[9] "Message from the President of the United States, Transmitting Documents in Relation to the Return of Santa Anna and Paredes to Mexico . . . ," in *House Executive Documents*, 30 Cong., 1 Sess., No. 25; Polk, *Diary*, I, 224–30, III, 286–99; McCormac, *James K. Polk*, 438–41; Wilfrid Hardy Callcott, *Santa Anna: The Story of an Enigma Who Once Was Mexico* (Norman, 1936), 229–38.

[10] Ramsey, *The Other Side*, 83–89; Callcott, *Santa Anna*, 242–44.

[11] Ramsey, *The Other Side*, 89–93; Callcott, *Santa Anna*, 245–50. For the difficulties of Santa Anna in raising and equipping his army see Justin H. Smith (ed.), "Letters of General Antonio López de Santa Anna Relating to the War Between the United States and Mexico, 1846–1848," in American Historical Association, *Annual Report, 1917*, 355–428.

[12] Taylor to the Adjutant General, January 26, 1847, in *House Executive Documents*, 30 Cong., 1 Sess., No. 60, p. 1098.

spite of sickness, death, and large-scale desertion, Santa Anna pressed forward.[13]

It was on February 5 that General Taylor, quite unaware that Santa Anna was on the march, established his headquarters at Agua Nueva. During the following week all of his troops, except the small garrisons left in the rear, moved forward and encamped on this advanced ground. The only regulars remaining in Taylor's army were: two companies of the First Dragoons, under Captain Enoch Steen; two companies of the Second Dragoons, under Captain Charles A. May who had been brevetted major and lieutenant colonel for his distinguished services in the battles of Palo Alto and Resaca de la Palma; the batteries of the Third Artillery commanded by Captain Thomas W. Sherman and Captain Braxton Bragg whose gallant conduct at Monterrey had won him the brevet rank of major; and Captain John M. Washington's battery of the Fourth Artillery. All the rest were volunteers, and for the most part volunteers who had never been tested under fire. These included a regiment of Arkansas cavalry under Colonel Archibald Yell, a former governor of the state, a regiment of Kentucky cavalry under Colonel Humphrey Marshall, a regiment of Kentucky infantry under Colonel William McKee, a regiment of Mississippi Rifles under Colonel Jefferson Davis, two regiments of Indiana infantry commanded by Brigadier General Joseph Lane and Colonels William A. Bowles and James H. Lane, two regiments of Illinois infantry under Colonel John J. Hardin and Colonel William H. Bissell, and two companies of infantry from Texas. In all, just under five thousand officers and men.[14]

Reports now reached Taylor that a large portion of the troops at San Luis Potosí had started south to aid in the defense of Vera Cruz, and he became doubtful that the

[13] Ramsey, *The Other Side,* 114–20; Callcott, *Santa Anna,* 250–51.

[14] *Senate Executive Documents,* 30 Cong., 1 Sess., No. 1, p. 142; and the several reports on the battle printed in this document.

enemy would make even a serious demonstration in his direction. Nevertheless he urged supplies forward as rapidly as possible in order that he would be ready to take advantage of any opportunity that might offer to create a diversion in favor of General Scott.[15] Taylor believed there was no likelihood of an enemy movement against him, but he wisely made careful reconnaissance, and by the twentieth of February he had unquestioned information that instead of being on his way to the defense of Vera Cruz, Santa Anna with his main force was at Encarnacion, about thirty miles in his front with obvious intentions of attacking the weakened American army.

Taylor's position at Agua Nueva was not one to be held by five thousand raw troops against an attacking force three times as numerous. Both flanks were exposed and could surely be turned by an enemy with superior numbers. Nevertheless, and in spite of the fact that this position had been taken when no attack was expected, Taylor, always opposed to retreat, was with difficulty persuaded to abandon it.[16] His objections were finally overcome and early on the afternoon of Sunday, the twenty-first, the army withdrew eleven miles to a strong position, called by the Mexicans La Angostura—the narrows, just south of the hacienda of Buena Vista. Here the road ran through a mountain pass some three miles wide and divided almost in half by a stream. The field of battle was further narrowed by a network of deep and impassable gullies which rendered the western half of the pass quite impracticable for artillery and cavalry. On the east of the road the ground rose gradually toward the base of the mountains, forming an elevated plain of tableland which was intersected at several points by ravines or gorges worn by the torrents of water that rushed from the mountainside during the rainy season. Some of the ravines extended to the

[15] Taylor to the Adjutant General, February 4, 7, and 14, 1847, in *House Executive Documents,* 30 Cong., 1 Sess., No. 60, pp. 1109–13.

[16] Smith, *War with Mexico,* I, 554.

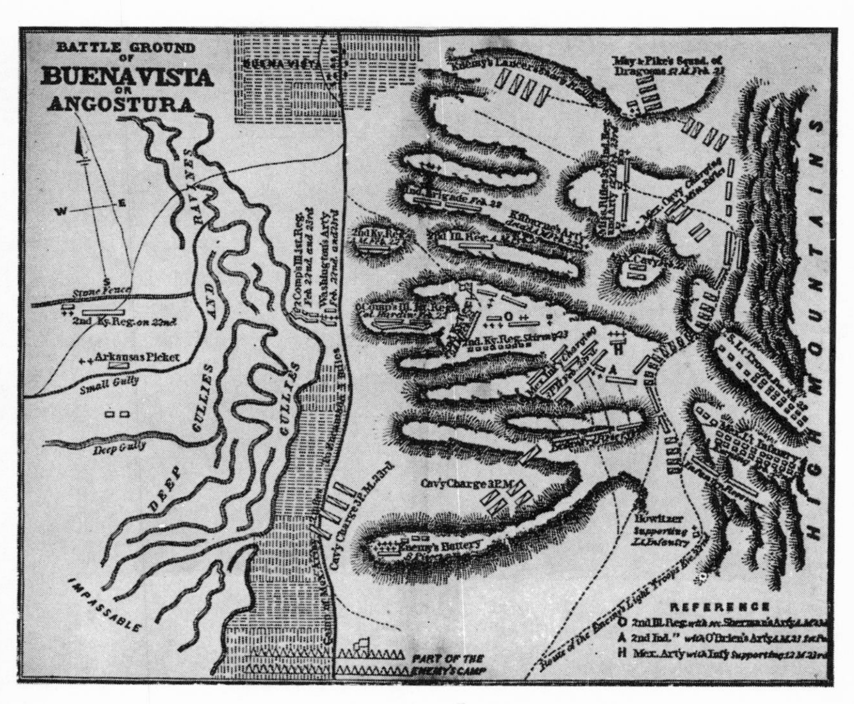

BATTLEGROUND OF BUENA VISTA

Reproduced from W. S. Henry, Campaign Sketches of the War with Mexico *(New York, 1847), p. 312.*

very foot of the mountains, others only part way. At most points these ravines were quite precipitous and almost impassable, but near the foot of the mountains their sides were sloping and could be climbed without great difficulty. Thus at the base of the mountains that formed the eastern boundary of the battlefield there was a rough passageway, generally parallel to the regular road, by which troops could advance from south to north. "The features of the ground," reported Taylor, "were such as nearly to paralyze the artillery and cavalry of the enemy, while his infantry could not derive all the advantage of its numerical superiority." [17]

The battlefield having been selected, Taylor continued on to Saltillo to strengthen the defenses of that town, for a Mexican cavalry force under General Vicente Minón, reported to be three thousand strong, was operating in that vicinity. Meanwhile, through most of the night, the army labored to remove the provisions and equipment that had been gathered at Agua Nueva and to throw up earthworks to strengthen their defensive position.[18] All knew that the morrow would bring battle with the powerful foe, but spirits remained high. One determined soldier entered in his journal: "we will have a dreadful fight, but we can not be whipped by a Mexican Army. It will be too the birthday of our Washington all Americans love the day—I will fight for its glory and honor. I am ready for the conflict. God and victory. The whole army has implicit confidence in General Taylor. All think him a consummate general." [19]

The next morning, when Taylor returned from Saltillo,

[17] Taylor to the Adjutant General, February 24 and March 6, 1847, in *Senate Executive Documents,* 30 Cong., 1 Sess., No. 1, pp. 97, 132; Lew Wallace, *An Autobiography* (New York, 1906), I, 166.

[18] Brigadier General John E. Wool to Major W. W. Bliss, March 4, 1847, in *Senate Executive Documents,* 30 Cong., 1 Sess., No. 1, pp. 144–45.

[19] Eleanor Damon Pace (ed.), "The Diary and Letters of William P. Rogers, 1846–1862," in *Southwestern Historical Quarterly,* XXXII (1928–1929), 274.

he found the advance columns of the enemy halted just beyond cannon shot. At an early hour the Mexicans had reached Agua Nueva, at which place latest reports had located Taylor's forces, only to find them gone. The signs of hasty withdrawal—burned supplies and abandoned wagons—persuaded Santa Anna that the Americans were demoralized and in full retreat. Consequently his weary troops were pushed forward in double time in order to overtake the fleeing Yankees before they recovered morale or position. Late in the morning, having covered nearly fifty miles in twenty-four hours, the Mexicans came upon Taylor's army occupying its well-chosen ground at La Angostura.[20]

When General Taylor arrived at the battlefield he found his troops already ordered into position by General Wool, his second in command. Captain Washington's battery was posted across the road at the narrowest and most strategic point with companies of the First Illinois Regiment protecting each flank. On a hill immediately in rear of Washington's battery the Second Kentucky Infantry was stationed. To the left of this regiment was the Second Illinois Infantry. The Indiana brigade was posted on a ridge just to the rear of this first line, while Captain Steen's dragoons were in reserve still farther to the rear. On the left, well out toward the mountains, the Kentucky and Arkansas cavalry regiments were stationed.[21] These dispositions met Taylor's full approval, and with confidence he awaited the attack.

At eleven o'clock, soon after Taylor arrived on the battlefield, he received from General Santa Anna a demand for unconditional surrender within an hour. "You are surrounded by twenty thousand men, and cannot in any human probability avoid suffering a rout and being cut

[20] Ramsey, *The Other Side*, 121–22; George L. Rives, *The United States and Mexico, 1821–1848* (New York, 1913), II, 348–49.

[21] Brigadier General John E. Wool to Major W. W. Bliss, March 4, 1847, *loc. cit.*, 145.

to pieces with your troops," he was informed. Taylor had no need for time to deliberate. Without hesitation he promptly and plainly rejected the demand.[22]

Santa Anna had already commenced pushing his light infantry, under Ampudia, into the mountains on Taylor's left in an effort to turn that flank, and he continued this movement after his demand for surrender was rejected. Taylor sent a detachment of Kentucky and Arkansas dismounted cavalry and Indiana riflemen, all under Colonel Humphrey Marshall, to oppose this advance. At the same time, in order to prevent the enemy from coming around by the base of the mountain, General Lane with the Second Indiana Regiment and a section of Washington's artillery under Lieutenant John Paul Jones O'Brien[23] was ordered to the extreme left and front of the American line. All through the afternoon, until dark, there was light action on the mountainside. Meanwhile the Mexicans had opened fire with a large howitzer posted in the road and had also attempted an advance on Taylor's right. This latter movement led Taylor to extend his right flank by sending the Kentucky infantry and Bragg's battery to the west of the road. At no time on the twenty-second, however, was the fighting heavy. When darkness fell and the firing ceased, General Taylor, convinced that no serious attack would be made before morning and nervous about the safety of Saltillo, returned to the town with the Mississippi regiment and a squadron of dragoons. That night the troops remained under arms and bivouacked without fires on the ground they occupied at the close of the day.[24]

At daybreak on the twenty-third, action was renewed by the Mexicans on the mountainside and continued

[22] Taylor to the Adjutant General, February 24, 1847, and enclosures, *Senate Executive Documents,* 30 Cong., 1 Sess., No. 1, pp. 97–98.

[23] O'Brien was promoted to Captain in the Quartermaster's Corps on January 18, 1847, but his commission had evidently not reached him.

[24] Taylor to the Adjutant General, March 6, 1847, in *Senate Executive Documents,* 30 Cong., 1 Sess., No. 1, p. 133; Wool to Bliss, March 4, 1847, *ibid.,* 146.

throughout the day with steadily increasing fury. It was a day of long and bloody battle. From dawn to sundown the fight was waged with the outnumbered Americans repulsing attack after attack by the fiercely fighting Mexicans who tried in vain to capture La Angostura and force Taylor's army to flee or surrender. Throughout the day the position of the Americans was critical. As soon as the enemy was checked at one point he threatened elsewhere, and only the rapid and skillful shifting of troops and the utmost courage and energy on the part of the men could save the situation.

Again, as on the previous afternoon, the enemy's main attack was on the American left. A strong demonstration to the right of Taylor's center was "dispersed by a few rapid and well-directed shots from Captain Washington's battery,"[25] but on the left the Mexicans succeeded in driving in the Second Indiana Regiment and O'Brien's guns and opened a route along the base of the mountain by which Santa Anna poured masses of cavalry and infantry toward the American rear. O'Brien and his men courageously stood their ground in the face of the overwhelming power of the enemy until all the cannoneers and horses of one of his three pieces had been killed or disabled and his infantry support withdrawn by the incompetent Colonel Bowles, who ordered his regiment to cease firing and retreat at the very moment General Lane intended they should advance.[26]

It was at this point, with the Indiana regiment fleeing in disorder, with Colonel Marshall's command on the mountainside forced to abandon its position or be cut off from the main body of troops by the Mexican column that was pushing its way toward the American rear, that General Taylor arrived on the battlefield from Saltillo. Someone advised him to fall back and occupy new ground,

[25] Taylor to the Adjutant General, March 6, 1847, *ibid.*, 134.
[26] *Ibid.*, and accompanying reports.

but he replied with determination and courage, "No, we will decide the battle here!" and then, with his usual humanity, added, "I will never, alive, leave my wounded behind." [27] As Old Rough and Ready arrived and "took his position in the center of the field of battle, where he could see and direct the operations," [28] the troops burst into cheers and attacked the enemy with new spirit.[29] While the Second Kentucky and First Illinois infantry regiments and the artillery of Sherman and Bragg drove back the Mexicans who were advancing in the wake of the retreating Indiana troops, the Mississippi regiment which arrived on the field with Taylor, and other troops hastily shifted from the center and the right, savagely fought the Mexican troops threatening the rear. Yet farther to the rear the dragoons and volunteer cavalry clashed with other Mexican forces. A detachment of Mexican cavalry got through and threatened Taylor's supply depot at Buena Vista but was successfully driven off. Attack after attack was repulsed. Hour after hour the battle raged. Finally the flanking movement was checked and the Mexicans were compelled to retreat with the Americans in hot pursuit.

Meanwhile Santa Anna, well aware that Taylor had been forced to weaken his center by dispatching troops to the left and rear, determined to carry that weakened sector by advancing with his whole strength from the left and front. The fighting that ensued, as the greatly outnumbered Americans courageously held their ground, was described by General Wool, who wrote: "This was the hottest as well as the most critical part of the action; and at the moment when our troops were about giving way before the greatly superior force with which they were contending, the batteries of Captains Sherman and Bragg coming up most opportunely from the rear, and under the

[27] *Southern Quarterly Review,* XXXIII (1850–1851), 175–76.
[28] Wool to Bliss, March 4, 1847, *loc. cit.,* 147.
[29] *Southern Quarterly Review,* XXXIII, 176.

immediate direction of the commanding general, by a well directed fire checked and drove back with great loss the enemy who had come close upon the muzzles of their pieces."[30] "Old Zach," with folded arms, sat astride Whitey, his favorite horse, tensely and silently watching the tide of battle. When finally he saw the enemy give way and retreat, his whole body relaxed and his face became wet with tears. Santa Anna's greatest effort had been successfully repulsed.[31] Indeed, though Taylor did not yet know it, the battle had been won.

In the course of the day General Minón and his cavalry, using a narrow mountain pass to the northeast, gained the road between Buena Vista and Saltillo, captured a small number of American troops, and temporarily severed Taylor's line of communications. Upon approaching Saltillo the Mexican force was driven off by the garrison and pursued by a company of Illinois Volunteers and two field pieces until they disappeared in the mountains.[32]

On the main field of action artillery fire continued until dark. Then, drenched by rain that had fallen during the afternoon, the troops spent a second cold and fireless night on the field of battle. This night the General did not return to Saltillo, but remained upon the field with his men. Under cover of darkness the wounded were carried to the rear, a few fresh troops were brought forward from Saltillo, and every possible preparation was made for the resumption of the battle in the morning. Although his men were exhausted and the casualties were heavy, Taylor would not listen to the repeated advice that no more fighting could be done, that only retreat could save his army.

[30] Wool to Bliss, March 4, 1847, *loc. cit.*, 149.

[31] H. Montgomery, *The Life of Major General Zachary Taylor* (New York, 1847), 337–39.

[32] Taylor to the Adjutant General, March 6, 1847, in *Senate Executive Documents,* 30 Cong., 1 Sess., No. 1, p. 136; Captain L. B. Webster to Major John Munroe, February 27, 1847, *ibid.,* 206–207; Lieutenant W. H. Shover to Captain Braxton Bragg, March 3, 1847, *ibid.,* 207–209.

He was determined to hold his ground. Nevertheless, when the morning light disclosed that the Mexican army had fled with the night, Taylor was much relieved. While the battle-worn men shouted with joy, Taylor and Wool threw themselves, with moist eyes, into each other's arms.[33] Scouts soon reported that Santa Anna was at Agua Nueva, but Taylor did not advance. He well knew that the exhaustion of his troops and the disparity of numbers rendered pursuit hazardous and inexpedient.[34] The tired army remained at Buena Vista awaiting another attack. When a few days later the Mexicans abandoned Agua Nueva and headed south, Taylor moved forward with his troops and again occupied the ground from which they had so hastily fled a week before.[35]

The victory of Buena Vista was due in part to the strong defensive position held by the American army and in part to the splendid work of the horse-drawn light artillery which dashed from position to position to pour forth its murderous fire and stem the onward rush of the attacking forces. All of the troops fought with valor and determination, but without the artillery the day would have been lost. "It was always in action at the right place and the right time," declared Taylor.[36] Above all, the victory was due to General Taylor's own courage and his ability to inspire confidence in his men. Hour after hour, astride his white charger, he remained in the thick of the fight. Time and again his aides urged him to seek a more sheltered post, but even when enemy fire pierced his coat Old Rough and Ready refused to retire. He issued few orders and contributed little in the way of tactical knowledge or

[33] Smith, *War with Mexico,* I, 398; *A Campaign in Mexico, or a Glimpse at Life in Camp* (Philadelphia, 1847), 66–68.

[34] Taylor to the Adjutant General, March 6, 1847, *loc. cit.*, 136–37.

[35] *Id.* to J. P. Taylor, March 27, 1847, in Taylor Papers; *A Campaign in Mexico,* 70.

[36] Taylor to the Adjutant General, March 6, 1847, *loc. cit.,* 138.

skill, but he contributed that which was of far greater value, a constant example of valor and energy, courageous, unconquerable leadership.

The most famous anecdote concerning Taylor and the battle of Buena Vista exhibits this indomitable spirit. It may be that the incident never occurred,[37] but it was so widely told that it became a significant element in the public's picture of the General. As recounted in *The General Taylor Almanac for the Year of our Lord 1848,* Captain Bragg and his battery of six-pounders were hard pressed by the enemy on the second afternoon of the battle and the Captain was preparing to retire in order to save his pieces. Major Mansfield of the Engineers Corps, believing it would be fatal for Bragg to abandon his position, sought out General Taylor to urge him not to allow the battery to move. Taylor replied: "No sir! no sir! not at all! Tell him not to move one inch, but to give them grape and canister." A few minutes later Taylor quietly rode up behind Bragg and said, "A little more grape, Captain Bragg!" These few words so inspirited the Captain and his men that they fired with redoubled vigor and repulsed the attackers.[38] According to General S. E. Chamberlain, instead of saying "A little more grape," Taylor exclaimed, "Double-shot your guns and give 'em hell!" [39]

Other stories of Taylor's actions on the field of battle were also told. On one occasion a colonel sent word to Taylor that he was surrounded and wanted instructions. "With convincing energy Taylor replied, 'Go and tell your Colonel that he has got them just where he wants them, and now is the time to give them Jesse;' upon which the adjutant, whose face had been a picture of despair,

[37] According to E. A. Hitchcock, Major Bliss told him in December, 1848, "that the stories of the general in connection with Bragg are all false. He never said 'A little more grape, Captain Bragg,' nor did he say 'Major Bliss and I will support you.' " Hitchcock, *Fifty Years in Camp and Field,* 349.

[38] *The General Taylor Almanac, for the Year of our Lord 1848 . . .* (Philadelphia, 1848), 31.

[39] Smith, *War with Mexico,* I, 559.

clapped spurs to his horse, rushed back and delivered the message at the top of his voice with a spirit that every soldier caught instantly." [40] At another time, seeing a Kentucky regiment stagger, Taylor cried out, "By God, this will not do; this is not the way for Kentuckians to behave." Then, seeing them rally, he rose in his stirrups and shouted, "Hurrah for Old Kentuck! That's the way to do it. Give 'em hell, damn 'em!" [41]

The battle of Buena Vista was not cheaply won. Taylor's army lost 267 killed, 456 wounded, and 23 missing—nearly one sixth of the whole number engaged. The officers, who were constantly in the thick of the fight, suffered most heavily. Sixty-nine, more than one fifth of the officers on the field, were slain or wounded. Colonel Hardin of Illinois, Colonel Yell of Arkansas, and Colonel McKee of Kentucky all fell at the head of their regiments. Lieutenant Colonel Henry Clay, Jr., son of the famous Kentucky statesman, was also among the killed. One of the wounded was Taylor's son-in-law, Colonel Jefferson Davis, who continued to lead his Mississippi regiment until the battle was won. The enemy's losses were even greater. At least 500 of his dead were left upon the field, and Taylor estimated that his casualties would not fall short of 1,500.[42]

In Taylor's official report of the battle he was most generous in his praise of officers and men who "were ever prompt and cheerful in the discharge of every duty, and finally displayed conspicuous steadiness and gallantry in repulsing at great odds a disciplined foe." He was fully conscious of the services rendered by General Wool both before and during the battle and did not hesitate to give him credit for "a large share of our success." Even the volunteers, who usually won little recognition from Taylor, received his commendation. As nine tenths of his army were volunteers, well might they share in the praise.[43]

[40] *Ibid.* [41] *Ibid.*

[42] Taylor to the Adjútant General, March 6, 1847, *loc. cit.*, 138.

[43] *Ibid.*, 138–41.

The only regiment that received criticism instead of praise was the Second Indiana Infantry which had fallen back at such a critical juncture in the fighting. Taylor's censure of this regiment aroused a storm of protest and created for him a situation similar to that produced by his criticism of the Missouri Volunteers in the battle of Okeechobee. Not only the members of the regiment but also their many friends at home regarded his report as a grave injustice to the men concerned and a reflection upon the honor of the state. So keen and widespread was this feeling that it became an issue in the election of 1848 and was partially responsible for Taylor's failure to carry that state.[44]

The people of Indiana had some justification for their attitude. Taylor's statement that the regiment "had fallen back in disorder, being exposed . . . not only to a severe fire of small arms from the front, but also to a murderous cross-fire of grape and canister from a Mexican battery on the left" [45] was accurate but somewhat unfair in its implication. The regiment had fallen back not because its courage had faltered but because Colonel Bowles so ordered. This fact, unknown to Taylor when he wrote his report, was disclosed by a court of inquiry held a few weeks later. Taylor's refusal to amend his report in the light of this new evidence was the first cause of complaint.[46] Most objectionable, however, to the Indianians was Taylor's further statement that the regiment, having fallen back, "could not be rallied, and took no further part in the action, except a handful of men, who under its gallant Colonel, Bowles, joined the Mississippi regiment, and did good service, and those fugitives who, at a later period in the day, assisted in defending the train and depot at Buena Vista." [47] Without question the regiment

[44] Wallace, *An Autobiography*, I, 177–92.
[45] Taylor to the Adjutant General, March 6, 1847, *loc. cit.*, 134.
[46] Wallace, *An Autobiography*, I, 177–81.
[47] Taylor to the Adjutant General, March 6, 1847, *loc. cit.*, 134.

became completely disorganized as it retreated, and many of the men fled as far as the hacienda at Buena Vista, but it is equally clear that far more than a handful returned to the battle. Indeed, few of those who were not disabled by wounds failed to do so.[48] On this point Taylor's censure was certainly too severe.

It was indeed fortunate for General Taylor that Buena Vista was a victory. He had boldly disobeyed his orders in advancing so far, and had he been defeated would unquestionably have been held to answer. Even with victory to his credit he suffered the President's displeasure. Polk blamed Taylor for an unnecessary battle and heavy loss of life and held that only the army's bravery had saved him from disaster.[49] Taylor's own view was that he had "saved the honor of the country & our glorious flag from trailing in the dust." [50] He declared that if he had fallen back to Monterrey, as ordered by General Scott, Santa Anna would have invested that town, and the whole northern part of Mexico would have risen; "every depot on the Rio Grande would have been at once abandoned, taken, or destroyed, all the artillery and cavalry horses and every animal belonging to the trains would have been destroyed or starved, as there was no depot of forage at Monterey, where our volunteer army shut up and disheartened must have either surrendered or been cut to pieces." [51] Responsibility for the bloodshed at Buena Vista he believed rested with Scott and the Secretary of War, and he proposed that the friends of those who fell in that battle "should hold meetings in the several states & call on the president to remove Marcy from his present position as being entirely

[48] Wallace, *An Autobiography*, I, 178–79, 189–90.

[49] Polk, *Diary*, II, 434, 436, 451–52, 462.

[50] Taylor to R. C. Wood, March 20, 1847, in *Letters from the Battlefields*, 90.

[51] *Id.* to James Buchanan, August 29, 1847, *ibid.*, 183. Taylor expressed similar views in a long letter to Senator Crittenden dated March 25, 1846 [1847], in Crittenden Papers, and to his brother, J. P. Taylor, March 27, in Taylor Papers.

incompetent to the situation; as well as to send Scott back to Washington." To Senator Crittenden he suggested that Congress should require Marcy and Scott to explain to the country why he was left with such inadequate forces.[52]

It is difficult to see how any such disaster as Taylor described could have followed from a withdrawal to Monterrey, but fortunately for the General the public was ready to agree with him. While the President found fault with their hero, the people praised him with new enthusiasm. They criticized the administration for stripping him of his seasoned troops and leaving him well-nigh defenseless before powerful enemy forces. All blame for his perilous position they placed upon the administration. All credit for turning defeat into victory they gave to Taylor. The presidential boom for Old Rough and Ready gathered full headway.[53]

The battle of Buena Vista was hardly over when the victorious general received what he regarded as an abusive and contemptible letter from Secretary Marcy reprimanding him in the name of the President for a letter he had written many months before. Early in November Taylor had written a personal letter to General Gaines in which he discussed at length the military operations, both completed and contemplated, questioned the desirability of continuing offensive operations, criticized the administration, and defended his own actions.[54] In January the letter became public when it was printed in the New York *Express* and promptly copied by many other papers. Because of its severe strictures upon the administration and its discussion of the projected Vera Cruz campaign, President Polk's anger was thoroughly aroused and was in no degree lessened by Gaines's prompt admission that Taylor was not responsible for its publication. It was Polk's

[52] Taylor to R. C. Wood, March 20, 1847, *loc. cit.*, 91; *id.* to Crittenden, March 25, [1847], in Crittenden Papers.

[53] *Niles' National Register,* LXXII (1847), 69, 80, 112, 128.

[54] *Ibid.,* LXXI (1846–1847), 342–43.

belief that if the matter were dealt with strictly, both Taylor and Gaines would be subject to arrest and trial for giving aid and comfort to the enemy. After a thorough airing of the matter in the Cabinet, such extreme measures were avoided and the Secretary of War was instructed to reprimand Taylor for his conduct.[55]

This reprimand was neatly administered by making Taylor's letter the occasion for the revival of a paragraph from the 1825 edition of the *General Regulations for the Army* which had been omitted from the compilation published in 1841. The President, Taylor was informed, had directed that this paragraph be republished and the observance of it strictly enjoined upon all officers. It read: "Private letters or reports relative to military marches and operations are frequently mischievous in design, and always disgraceful to the army. They are therefore strictly forbidden; and any officer found guilty of making such report for publication, without special permission, or of placing the writing beyond his control so that it finds its way to the press, within one month after the termination of the campaign to which it relates, shall be dismissed from the service."[56]

While Cabinet members and administration supporters both in and out of Congress joined in the denunciation of Taylor, his political friends, with the election of 1848 in mind, stepped forward to defend his course. Although Taylor viewed the excitement as "much ado about nothing," and regarded the battle of Buena Vista as the best answer to his enemies,[57] he was thoroughly vexed by Marcy's letter. To him it was further evidence of the determination of the administration to "break him down." He frankly replied that there was nothing in his letter

[55] Polk, *Diary*, II, 353–59.

[56] Marcy to Taylor, January 27, 1847, in *House Executive Documents*, 29 Cong., 2 Sess., No. 119, pp. 109–10.

[57] Taylor to R. C. Wood, April 4, 1847, in *Letters from the Battlefields*, 92.

he would not write again in the same circumstances, that he perceived from the newspapers his views as to the general policy to be pursued toward Mexico were shared by many distinguished statesmen, and that his letter could give to the enemy no valuable information he did not already possess. He regretted "the apparent determination of the department" to place him in an "attitude antagonistical to the government," and declared he would continue to devote all his energies to the public good, looking for his "reward to the consciousness of pure motives, and to the final verdict of impartial history." [58]

Taylor's friends in Congress did not permit this reply to remain hidden in the files of the War Department. When the new Congress assembled at the close of the year, the House of Representatives called upon the President for a copy of the letter and ordered ten thousand extra copies printed.[59] There can be little doubt that Polk's objection to the Gaines letter was political rather than military. Nor can there be much doubt that when preparing his answer Taylor had the public in mind. The whole affair was but another item in the growing political controversy between the administration and General Taylor.

For nine months following Buena Vista, Zachary Taylor remained in Mexico in command of the troops in this northern theater. They were months of little activity. While Scott captured Vera Cruz, climbed the mountains to the central plateau, and marched against Mexico City, Taylor held the line of Monterrey. For two weeks immediately following Buena Vista he was confined to his camp with a sore leg caused by the bite of some poisonous insect or a slight wound from a thorn which was neglected and became a "troublesome affair." He continued to feel indisposed for several weeks but by the end of April was

[58] *Id.* to Marcy, March 3, 1847, in *House Executive Documents,* 30 Cong., 1 Sess., No. 60, pp. 809–10.

[59] *Congressional Globe,* 30 Cong., 1 Sess., 301.

entirely recovered and ready for "any duty."[60] During March he was concerned with repeated enemy cavalry attacks upon his supply trains. The contents of more than 150 wagons were captured or destroyed, nearly 100 wagoners and troops were killed, and for a while communication between Monterrey and Camargo was entirely cut off.[61] During May and June he was busy sending home the regiments of twelve months' volunteers whose terms of service were about to expire, and receiving in their stead raw regiments of regulars raised under a recent act of Congress.[62] In his private correspondence he was constantly expressing his readiness to advance farther into the heart of Mexico the moment a proper force was placed at his disposal and the rains replenished the grass and water supply. Yet he seems to have had no real desire to undertake such a movement. In the middle of June, after it had become apparent that few of the new regiments were to be sent to him, and believing that the best means of bringing the Mexicans to peace was to take and keep possession of Mexico City, Taylor advised the administration that his forces were not sufficient to undertake such a movement against San Luis Potosí as General Scott had contemplated and he asked for further instructions. "If I were called upon to make a suggestion on the general subject of operations against Mexico," he wrote, "it would certainly be to hold in this quarter a defensive line, and throw all the remaining troops into the other column."[63]

[60] Taylor to J. P. Taylor, April 25, 1847, in Taylor Papers; *id.* to R. C. Wood, May 9, 1847, in *Letters from the Battlefields,* 100.

[61] *Id.* to the Adjutant General, March 1, 1847, in *Senate Executive Documents,* 30 Cong., 1 Sess., No. 1, p. 99; *id.* to J. J. Crittenden, March 25, 1846 [1847], in Crittenden Papers; *id.* to the Adjutant General, March 20, 22, 28, 1847, in *House Executive Documents,* 30 Cong., 1 Sess., No. 60, pp. 1119–25.

[62] *Id.* to *id.,* May 2 and 9, and June 16, 1847, *ibid.,* 1132–36, 1177; *id.* to J. J. Crittenden, May 15, 1847, in Crittenden Papers.

[63] *Id.* to the Adjutant General, June 16, 1847, in *House Executive Documents,* 30 Cong., 1 Sess., No. 60, p. 1177; *id.* to J. P. Taylor, September [?], 1847, in Taylor Papers; *id.* to J. J. Crittenden, May 15 and September 15, 1847, in Crittenden Papers.

The exact nature of the "defensive line" he did not explain to the administration, but in a private letter of the same date to his friend Colonel William Davenport, he advocated falling back to the Rio Grande where a sufficient force should be stationed to prevent the enemy from crossing.[64] This apparently involved abandonment not only of Saltillo, but of Monterrey as well. Yet, when two months later word came that the President approved his plan and directed him to hold "such a line" as he had suggested,[65] Taylor did not withdraw from either Saltillo or Monterrey. He did, however, promptly reduce his garrisons at all points to the minimum necessary for defensive security, and dispatch between two and three thousand troops to General Scott.[66] All thought of offensive operations in this northern theater was ended. Taylor's part in the Mexican War was over.

Early in 1848 when Scott was recalled from Mexico and President Polk and his advisers were faced with the selection of a new commanding general for the United States army in Mexico City, Taylor was considered. A majority of the Cabinet, including Secretary Marcy, urged his appointment, but Polk "decided positively against it." His stand was due in part to the fact that Taylor was then at his own request on leave in the United States, but primarily to the fact that Polk still desired to have a commanding general who would harmonize his views with the government, and he well remembered that but a year before he had superseded Taylor with Scott only because the former would not co-operate with the administration. Therefore the President blocked the restoration of Taylor to command and selected Major General W. O. Butler for the post. When a few days later Secretary Marcy sought to

64 *Id.* to Colonel William Davenport, June 16, 1847, in Historical Society of Pennsylvania.

65 Marcy to Taylor, July 15, 1847, in *House Executive Documents,* 30 Cong., 1 Sess., No. 60, pp. 1193–94.

66 Taylor to the Adjutant General, August 16, 1847, *ibid.,* 1187–88; *id.* to R. C. Wood, August 25, 1847; in *Letters from the Battlefields,* 125.

reopen the question, Polk declared that the matter had been settled and that he was prepared to assume the full responsibility for the decision.[67]

Without the benefit of West Point training, without experience in organized warfare, General Taylor conducted the campaign against Mexico with a high degree of success. Although always inferior in numbers to the Mexicans, he fought and won four general engagements and in a year's time drove back the enemy nearly five hundred miles. In doing so he demonstrated unusual common sense and practical shrewdness, as well as unquestioned physical and moral courage. "No soldier could face either danger or responsibility more calmly than he," declared Ulysses S. Grant. He "knows not what fear is," was the judgment of George Gordon Meade.[68] He also revealed ability to discern the particular merits of his subordinates and to assign them to duty accordingly, regardless of any personal prejudices he might have. Most important of all, he demonstrated uncommon qualities of leadership; he won the devotion and confidence of his troops and inspired them to victory. Although fearless, rough, and ready, Taylor was not one who gloried in war. His constant hope was that peace, honorable peace, would be quickly made in order that further suffering and bloodshed might be avoided. For him the joys of victory were always tempered by the realization of its cost in human life. In the hour of triumph no one was more concerned with the welfare of the wounded than Taylor, not only his own wounded but also those left on the field of battle by the retreating enemy. The discovery of several hundred starving, wounded Mexicans encamped far in his front following the battle of Buena Vista impelled him to send supplies from his own army which he cheerfully promised to pay for if Washington disapproved.[69]

[67] Polk, *Diary*, III, 278, 281–82, 293–94.
[68] Grant, *Memoirs*, I, 100; Meade, *George Gordon Meade*, I, 101.
[69] Taylor to J. P. Taylor, March 27, 1847, in Taylor Papers.

Taylor's Mexican campaign reveals other characteristics less praiseworthy. Certainly he did not conduct his operations with all possible vigor and speed. When danger seemed imminent, as in the case of the threat to Point Isabel in May, 1846, or that of General Worth's call for help in December, he could and did act promptly and push forward his troops with energy. But with more foresight and more initiative he might have saved weeks during the summer and perhaps have advanced to San Luis Potosí before the end of the year. Taylor failed to organize a systematic spy service and thus lacked adequate information about the Mexican army as well as about the country through which he was to operate.[70] This fault was doubtless due in part to his economy with public funds, but in this instance it was an unwise economy. Never would he have asked for $50,000 for this purpose, as Scott did upon leaving for Mexico.[71] But economy is not the complete explanation of this shortcoming, for he failed to use as he might have the topographical engineers who were on duty with his army. "Did he have his own way," wrote Lieutenant Meade of this corps, "we should be perfectly useless; not from any unfriendly feeling on his part towards us, but from absolute ignorance of what we can be required to do, and perfect inability to make use of the information we do obtain." [72] Justin H. Smith, one of Taylor's severest critics, charged him with violating the best of military precepts by underestimating the strength and power of the enemy and consequently attacking at Monterrey in an almost foolhardy manner.[73] There is some justice to this charge, but on the other hand Taylor was always critical of exaggerated reports of the enemy's

[70] Smith, *War with Mexico,* I, 489–91; William L. Marcy, "Diary and Memoranda of William L. Marcy, 1849–1851," in *American Historical Review,* XXIV (1918–1919), 455.

[71] Scott to Marcy, November 19, 1846, in *House Executive Documents,* 30 Cong., 1 Sess., No. 60, p. 836.

[72] Meade, *George Gordon Meade,* I, 101.

[73] *War with Mexico,* I, 463, II, 316.

strength. Robert E. Lee, who served with Taylor in Mexico, was much impressed by his critical attitude, and years later on a Civil War battlefield met a wild report of Northern strength with a story about Old Rough and Ready. He recounted how, shortly before the battle of Buena Vista, he had been at Taylor's headquarters "when an excited young officer announced that he had seen 20,000 Mexican troops moving up with 250 guns." When that officer, in reply to a question from Taylor, insisted he had actually seen that force, "Old Zach" said, "Captain, if you say you saw it, of course I must believe you; but I would not have believed it if I had seen it myself." [74]

Smith also criticized Taylor for staying too close to headquarters and failing to get out to see things for himself.[75] It is true that he went on no long reconnaissance expeditions, but in the immediate presence of the enemy he was almost constantly in the saddle. It was Grant's judgment that Taylor "moved about the field in which he was operating to see through his own eyes the situation"; that whereas "Scott saw more through the eyes of his staff officers than through his own . . . Taylor saw for himself." [76]

Taylor's campaign revealed no prepared plan of strategy, no careful tactical movements, little understanding of the art of war. Yet these shortcomings proved of little importance when offset by "moral force" and "a broad sort of calculation that enabled him to produce effects which a mere educated soldier could scarcely have obtained." [77]

Throughout the summer and fall of 1847, General Taylor maintained his headquarters at Monterrey. Except for occasional guerrilla activity there was little to relieve the dull monotony of life, and he grew increasingly tired of inaction. Now, as all through the war, he spent many

[74] Douglass S. Freeman, *R. E. Lee: A Biography* (New York, 1934–1935), I, 217.

[75] *War with Mexico,* I, 208.

[76] Grant, *Memoirs,* I, 138–39.

[77] Smith, *War with Mexico,* II, 316.

hours writing long letters to his family. Mrs. Taylor and Betty were at Baton Rouge. Dick, who had paid a brief visit to his father's camp at Matamoros in the summer of 1846, was suffering with rheumatism and was seeking relief at various watering places in the South. Dr. Wood and his family were at the Barracks below New Orleans to which station he had been transferred from Point Isabel in the early spring. His brother, Colonel Joseph P. Taylor, was with him in Mexico as the chief officer of the Commissary Department until the middle of 1847, when poor health, with which he had been suffering during most of the war, led him to seek a transfer to the United States. While in Mexico he was occasionally at the General's camp, but more frequently was at Matamoros or Point Isabel pushing forward supplies.

General Taylor was much concerned for the welfare and comfort of the members of his family and was always ready to advise the proper course of action for each. Particularly when the yellow fever broke out in New Orleans during the summer was he solicitous about their health and anxious that they seek safety in Kentucky or Mississippi. All except Dr. Wood, who could not leave his post, went to East Pascagoula in the latter state and escaped the disease. Taylor also took a lively interest in the progress of his two grandsons, Robert and John Wood, and was much pleased when John decided upon a naval career and received an appointment to Annapolis. By the middle of the summer his family letters were somewhat curtailed by the demands of a rapidly increasing correspondence with political friends and supporters. One letter which must have taken many long hours to write was to the Secretary of State, James Buchanan, in answer to a very courteous one disclaiming any hostility toward him on the part of the Cabinet. This letter, dated "Camp near Monterey, August 29, 1847," reviewed at great length his actions from the time he took command at Fort Jesup in 1844, and was designed to place his "course and conduct in their proper light" before one whose good opinion he desired to possess and deserve. Taylor accepted the friendly advance of Buchanan but his contempt for Marcy and Scott he made perfectly clear.[78] Although in his correspondence Taylor repeatedly denied all interest in the question of the presidency, the constant flow of letters and newspapers which reached him, and which he assiduously read, kept the issue alive. More and more it came to fill his thoughts.[79]

Taylor's correspondence of this period contains many harsh criticisms of other men in public life. His natural kindliness and usual sane judgment had become warped by the months of controversy with the administration and by his ever stronger conviction that he had been shamefully treated. No one who found fault with him or who seemed to him in any way responsible for the decision to relegate him to second place escaped his bitter condemnation. He denounced General Scott not only as "physically disqualified from the effects of gout, dropsey &c. from carrying on properly an active campaign," [80] but also as one who would "stoop to anything however low & contemptable [*sic*] . . . to obtain power or place." [81] His old friend General Jesup he characterized as a "poor misera-

[78] *Letters from the Battlefields,* 173–86. The receipt of Buchanan's communication is mentioned by Taylor to Crittenden in a letter of November 1, 1847, in Crittenden Papers.

[79] *Letters from the Battlefields,* 99–152, contains many letters from Taylor to Dr. R. C. Wood. Eight letters to his brother, J. P. Taylor, written during this period are in the Taylor Papers in the Library of Congress. Both of these groups contain evidence that they are not complete collections as well as references to his correspondence with other members of his family. Few of his letters to Mrs. Taylor or to Betty appear to have survived. Many of his political letters were to Senator J. J. Crittenden and may be found in the Crittenden Papers in the Library of Congress. Letters to Taylor are not available for he made it a practice to destroy them as soon as they were answered.

[80] Taylor to J. J. Crittenden, March 25, 1847, in Crittenden Papers.

[81] *Id.* to R. C. Wood, September 27, 1847, in *Letters from the Battlefields,* 136.

ble creature, & perfect tool of the powers that be." [82] Thomas Ritchie, the editor of the Washington *Union,* the mouthpiece of the administration, Taylor regarded as thoroughly unprincipled and lacking in veracity.[83] He was also very critical of Lewis Cass, Michigan's prominent Democratic senator: "Cass is certainly one of the most unprincipled demagogues in our country, & if his moral or personal courage was equal to his capacity, he would be one of the most dangerous men in the country." [84] Of all the men in public life, it was Polk whom Taylor disliked most. When just before he left Mexico he heard a rumor that Polk was dead, Taylor was thoroughly skeptical of its truth but informed Dr. Wood that though he always regretted to hear of the death of anyone he "would as soon have heard of his [Polk's] death if true, as that of any other individual in the whole Union." [85]

As early as May, 1847, General Taylor made up his mind to return to the United States by the close of the year. If this could be accomplished in no other way, he was almost prepared to resign from the service.[86] Finally on October 4, believing that General Scott's capture of Mexico City would soon terminate the war, he applied for a six months' leave of absence with permission to visit the United States. Not only did he desire to visit his family from whom he had been separated for two and one-half years and to look after his private affairs, but also, he said, the state of his health required "some relaxation from the exposure, fatigue, and anxieties of the field service." Confident that his request would be granted and eager to get out of Mexico as soon as possible, Taylor moved his headquarters to Matamoros in November, and there, on No-

[82] *Id.* to J. P. Taylor, May 9, 1847, in Taylor Papers.

[83] *Id.* to *id.,* May 29, 1847, *ibid.*

[84] *Ibid.*

[85] Taylor to R. C. Wood, November 2, 1847, in *Letters from the Battlefields,* 148.

[86] *Id.* to *id.,* May 9 and 30, 1847, *ibid.,* 99, 105; *id.* to J. P. Taylor, April 25 and May 9, 1847, in Taylor Papers.

vember 23, received the welcome leave. He promptly turned over the command to General Wool and descended the river to Brazos Island. On Friday, November 26, he and his staff boarded the *Monmouth* and sailed for New Orleans.[87]

After a four-day voyage Old Rough and Ready reached the bar at the mouth of the Mississippi, transferred to the *Mary Kingsland* and steamed up the river while the welcoming cheers from the decks of passing boats filled the air. At the Army Barracks, just below New Orleans, Mrs. Taylor and other members of the family were waiting. Here the General disembarked and rested for two days. Then, escorted by the city officials and hundreds of private citizens, the returning hero journeyed the remaining five miles to the city proper. It was a gay pageant as the parade of boats came up the river, crowded with vessels from all parts of the world and flying the flags of almost every nation. As the ships approached the town strains of martial music and joyous peals from a thousand bells filled the air. These soon gave way to the roar of artillery and the long, continuous shouts from the thousands of citizens who had turned out to greet "Old Zach." In the Place d'Armes the mayor officially welcomed Taylor, who made a brief response. Then through a grand triumphal arch of evergreens, topped by the American flag and eagle and bearing in large gilded letters the names of Taylor and his victories, the party marched to the near-by Saint Louis Cathedral where the singing of the *Te Deum,* congratulations from the bishop, and another response from Taylor were heard. The General then mounted Old Whitey and, escorted by the military, fire companies, Masons, Odd Fellows, and numerous other organizations, paraded through the principal streets. In the evening the ceremonies continued with a banquet, fireworks, and appearances by Taylor and his party at each of the city's

[87] *Id.* to the Adjutant General, October 4, November 14, 23, and 25, 1847, in *House Executive Documents,* 30 Cong., 1 Sess., No. 60, pp. 1199, 1211–14.

three theaters. Seldom in the history of this gay old city had such a prolonged and enthusiastic welcome been displayed. The next day Taylor's New Orleans reception was concluded when the governor of Louisiana presented to him the sword which the state legislature had voted in recognition of his victories at Palo Alto and Resaca de la Palma.[88] He tarried another night in the city and then, with the cheers of his fellow citizens still ringing in his ears, he departed for Baton Rouge which was to be his residence for the next year.

[88] A. T. Burnley to J. J. Crittenden, December 12, 1847, in Crittenden Papers; *General Taylor and His Staff* (Philadelphia, 1848), 275–84.

Chapter XII

"MY UNFORTUNATE PLANTATION"

GENERAL TAYLOR welcomed his leave, not only because of the opportunity it afforded to join his family, but also because he greatly desired to give personal attention to his plantation which had suffered severely in the heavy Mississippi floods of recent years. At this time Taylor owned two plantations, but was operating only one. The five-hundred-acre plantation on the border of Louisiana and Mississippi which he had owned for twenty-five years was rented out. Taylor had sold it at the close of 1841 to Henry H. Wall of Wilkinson County, Mississippi, but as the latter failed to make his payments, Taylor was forced to take the property back.[1] Shortly after going to Washington in 1849 Taylor succeeded in disposing of this plantation to Captain John Sims, a neighboring planter, for the low price of $3,000, less than half of what he had paid for it.[2]

Taylor's other plantation, known as Cypress Grove, was a 2,100-acre place in Jefferson County, Mississippi, on the bank of the river between Natchez and Vicksburg. This plantation, including the slaves and other property thereon, he purchased for $95,000 cash in December, 1841, when he was looking forward to an early retirement from the army.[3] Jefferson was distinctly a plantation county.

[1] Copy of Deed of Bargain and Sale, May 3, 1844, in Hardie Collection.

[2] Edward McGehee to Taylor, May 5 and July 16, 1849, in Hardie Collection; T. Henderson and Peale to Edward McGehee, April 29, 1850, *ibid.*

[3] "Agreement between John Hagan of New Orleans and Z. Taylor of the U.S. Army, December 31, 1841," in *The Autograph*, I, No. 1 (November, 1911), 12; "Partition between the Heirs of General Zachary Taylor, December 9, 1850," in Hardie Collection.

Eighty per cent of the population were slaves and few of the whites were without a direct interest in slavery.[4] How many slaves Taylor obtained with the plantation does not appear, but the purchase price indicates that the number was not small. At the time of Taylor's death in 1850 there were 127 Negroes on the plantation; probably most of these came with the land. Classified according to age and sex these included forty-two males and thirty-eight females eighteen years of age and over, three of each sex fifteen to seventeen years, sixteen males and twenty-two females one to fourteen years, and three infants not listed by sex.[5] This number of slaves falls far short of the three hundred constantly referred to during the presidential campaign of 1848 as the number owned by Taylor, but it is large enough to warrant his inclusion among the great planters of the South. In 1850 only 1,733 planters, roughly one half of one per cent of all the slaveholders of the nation, owned more than one hundred slaves. Some two hundred of these were in the state of Mississippi where they amounted to nearly one per cent of the slaveholders.[6] General Taylor's acquisition of this large plantation in the oldest and richest section of the important cotton state of Mississippi definitely identified him with the planting aristocracy.

Zachary Taylor was, of course, an absentee owner. Except while in Mexico he found it possible to visit the plantation about once a year, but the day-by-day operation of it was necessarily in the hands of an overseer or manager. In the spring of 1845 Taylor hired for this position a young man named Thomas W. Ringgold who seems to have been in most respects a satisfactory manager. During the General's long absence in Texas and Mexico,

[4] Charles S. Sydnor, *Slavery in Mississippi* (New York, 1933), map p. ii.

[5] "Partition between the Heirs of General Zachary Taylor, December 9, 1850," in Hardie Collection.

[6] *Agriculture of the United States in 1860, Compiled from the Original Returns of the Eighth Census . . .* (Washington, 1864), 248.

Ringgold kept him informed about conditions at Cypress Grove and in return received Taylor's careful instructions as to operations. Little of this correspondence has survived, so our knowledge of Taylor as a planter and slaveowner is very limited. We do not know to what extent he engaged in the buying and selling of slaves, whether he was troubled with the problem of fugitives, or whether his slaves received average, or better than average, care. The little evidence available, however, reveals him as a thrifty and prudent planter. While urging his manager to use great care in feeding and to make the foodstuffs raised on the plantation go as far as possible, Taylor cautioned him, "at the same time it is bad economy not to keep all work animals in good order," and advised him to plant oats early in the spring to make up for the shortage of corn. In 1847 when Taylor's cotton crop was hard hit by the flood waters he was very desirous that such cotton as matured should be picked and ginned with care, and he reminded Ringgold that "it is a good rule in planting never to lose anything after it is made, no matter how small the value; there is fully as much if not more in economy of planting than there is in making." In general, he instructed his manager that he wished the servants "well fed and cared for, as well as the stock of every kind well looked after, and in fact everything made the most of." [7]

Cypress Grove was primarily a cotton plantation, but General Taylor was careful to make it as nearly self-sufficient as possible. It usually produced enough corn, peas, vegetables, and meat to feed the slaves and work animals. Sometimes there was beef or mutton to be sold. Another product, and one which proved increasingly important as year after year the cotton crop suffered from the high waters of the Mississippi, was the wood cut in the great cypress swamp and hauled to the riverbank for the steam-

[7] Taylor to Thomas W. Ringgold, September 15, 1847, in Massachusetts Historical Society, *Proceedings*, LXII (1928–1929), 141–43; *id.* to Thomas W. Ringgold, June 9, 1846, in New York Historical Society.

boats. When wood brought three dollars a cord, as it did at times, Taylor regarded it as twice as profitable to employ his hands at cutting and hauling wood as at cultivating cotton. He estimated that when the swamp was dry enough to work in, forty men could put thirty cords of wood per day on the bank.[8] Shortly after returning from Mexico, Taylor planned to erect a steam sawmill on the plantation. But James Thornton who was to have had an interest in it withdrew and the project was temporarily abandoned. Two years later, however, the mill had been set up and was busy night and day.[9]

Some of General Taylor's ideas about plantation management he expressed in a letter to his brother Hancock in 1833 when the latter moved from his plantation to the old family home on the Muddy Fork of Beargrass Creek. The operation of a plantation on the outskirts of the growing city of Louisville differed considerably from that of a Mississippi cotton plantation, but the basic similarity of the problems makes the letter of interest. After expressing the hope that Hancock would succeed in getting a good manager for his lower plantation, Zachary continued:

It strikes me was I in your place, I would enclose the whole of the land, lay off what is cleared into four fields, with the exception of a large garden, & would raise nothing for sale but corn, wheat or barley & vegitables [*sic*], milk or butter whichever was most profitable; the corn I intended for sale I would cut up, & as far as practicable would feed it out foder [*sic*] & all to catle [*sic*] belonging to the butchers on the farm, as well with the view to the manure, as to profit. Your manager should at any rate attend markets once a week, if not oftener, & should daily send to market during the vegitable & fruit season, he should keep a regular account of everything raised, sold & purchased on, & for the establishment, & you should settle with him

[8] *Id.* to *id.*, September 15, 1847, *loc. cit.*

[9] *Id.* to J. P. Taylor, March 10 and May 15, 1848, in Taylor Papers; *id.* to Richard Taylor, June 12, 1850, in Hardie Collection.

at least every two months. By adopting a course of this kind & pursuing it [you] will make your manager much more attentive to your interest, than perhaps he otherwise would be.[10]

When Taylor returned from Mexico he was much disturbed because his only son had not yet found a profession or business which he desired to enter. The General not only regarded idleness as "discreditable," but believed it to be "the foundation of all evil." [11] For some time he had been anxious that Dick, who reached his twenty-first birthday in 1847, should not longer remain idle. "Let him select his own calling," he wrote to Mrs. Taylor from Mexico in December, 1846, "& I will be contented with the same, be it what it may. I will do all in my power to further his views and wishes; only let him be engaged in some pursuit or other, & I will be content. Anything but idleness!" [12] A year later Dick had still made no decision so his father decided to try him at planting. "If we can do no better," he suggested just before leaving Mexico, "I want him to go to the plantation & have a general supervision of the establishment, until he understands the operation or principles of planting, when I will set him up in that way on his own acct." [13] This plan was promptly carried out and on the first of January, 1848, Dick was placed in charge of Cypress Grove. Two months later when the General returned to the plantation he was gratified to find everything going on as well as he could wish and he became satisfied that Dick would make "a first rate planter." [14]

During this spring visit to Cypress Grove, Taylor took time for a brief trip to the plantations of Jefferson and

[10] *Id.* to Hancock Taylor, March 4, 1833, in New York Historical Society.

[11] *Id.* to Mrs. Taylor, December 22, 1846, in *The Autograph*, I, No. 6 (July–August, 1912), 128–29.

[12] *Ibid.*

[13] Taylor to R. C. Wood, November 17, 1847, in *Letters from the Battlefields*, 152.

[14] *Id.* to J. P. Taylor, March 10, 1848, in Taylor Papers.

Joseph Davis, located some fifty miles to the north and easily reached by the Vicksburg steamers. Jefferson Davis was in Washington at the time but Taylor spent a delightful day inspecting Hurricane and Brierfield and visiting with Mr. and Mrs. Joseph Davis and other members of the family. He was especially pleased with Hurricane which impressed him as a most desirable and handsomely arranged plantation—"a little paradise." [15]

A less satisfactory aspect of this March visit to Cypress Grove was the settlement of a boundary dispute involving about 160 acres of land. On his way south to Baton Rouge, Taylor stopped at Natchez where the controversy was disposed of by arbitration with the decision adverse to his claims.[16]

The Cypress Grove plantation turned out to be a disappointing and unfortunate investment for General Taylor. He made the purchase at a time when the price of cotton, the chief crop of the plantation, averaged 8.1 cents per pound, lower than ever before in the history of the country. Perhaps he expected that the high prices of the previous decade which had made Mississippi planters prosperous would soon return. If so, he was disappointed. The next four years saw the price go even lower—reaching 5.9 cents in 1844. In only two of the eight years that Taylor operated the plantation did cotton bring over 10 cents a pound. The average price for the entire period was just under 8 cents. These prices represent the average and if Taylor were fortunate in his market he may have done a little better, but even slightly higher prices would give small profit unless the crops were large.[17]

Unfortunately Taylor's crops were not large. Almost every spring for a decade following the purchase of his new plantation the river rose well above normal high

[15] *Id.* to Jefferson Davis, April 20, 1848, in Historical Society of Pennsylvania.

[16] *Mississippi Free Trader,* March 29, 1848 (weekly edition).

[17] Sydnor, *Slavery in Mississippi,* 183.

water. For years the mark set by the great flood of 1828 had been the gauge by which all others were measured. In 1842, at Natchez, just below Cypress Grove, the river rose to within eighteen inches of the 1828 mark and the following year missed it by only four. In 1844 several months of very heavy rain throughout the Valley created one of the most memorable floods ever known on the Mississippi. The high mark was approximately that of 1828, but because of the extent and duration of the flood immense injury was done to towns and plantations. Again in 1847 and 1849 the river was unusually high and great stretches of land were inundated.[18]

The repeated damage suffered at Cypress Grove as the floodwaters swept over the lower portions of it led Taylor to refer to it as "my unfortunate plantation." As early as the summer of 1843 he wrote to his brother Joseph that because of the unusually high water in the Mississippi for two successive years "the large purchase I made on said river in the winter of 41 has proved a most unfortunate one, & I fear owing this circumstance that I will when they are properly looked into, find my affairs in a very embarrassed situation so much so, that it will take several years of great industry, & economy to get them once more in a healthy state." He had not yet learned the extent of the damage done by the floodwaters of that season but declared he would be content "if it does not exceed one half the crop." [19] Two years later, just after returning from a brief visit to his plantation, Zachary informed his brother that for the last four years his affairs had been regularly going from bad to worse, "so much so, that I can hardly say or rather am afraid to state what my losses have been." [20] For Taylor the spring of 1850 was the most disastrous of all. In early March the river reached the 1828

[18] John W. Monette, "The Mississippi Floods," in *Mississippi Historical Society Publications* (Oxford), VII (1903), 454–72.

[19] Taylor to Joseph P. Taylor, June 17, 1843, in Taylor Papers.

[20] *Id.* to *id.*, January 29, 1845, *ibid.*

level, fell a bit, but remained high till the end of May when new floodwaters from the many tributaries raised it to a new high.[21] Cypress Grove and neighboring plantations suffered as never before. President Taylor, in far-off Washington and sorely tried by the persistent harassment of his Congressional opponents, was much distressed. In despair he wrote to Dick: "Something must be done or inevitable ruin must be the consequence, and I must say from my great distance from Louisiana and Mississippi, I hardly know what to do, or advise to be done, or what disposition is to be made of the servants. . . . I don't know but it would be good policy to dispose of the whole establishment, or if that can't be done the servants and let the land take care of itself. Misfortune on misfortune have followed me in such rapid succession from floods and otherwise for the last six or eight years, I feel almost heartbroken and brokendown." [22]

In the same letter in which he wrote so despairingly, President Taylor authorized Dick to purchase a Louisiana sugar plantation provided he was satisfied with it and would take the control and management of it. Dick promptly acted on this authority. He bought the thousand-acre Fashion plantation and sixty-four slaves located about twenty miles above New Orleans in St. Charles Parish. Although purchased by Dick, his father was clearly interested in it and assumed that the financial obligation was one that he would have to meet. The purchase price of $115,000 was to be paid in five somewhat unequal yearly payments including an initial sum of $19,500. Further evidence that Taylor looked upon the new plantation as a joint enterprise is found in his instructions to take to Fashion all slaves not needed to care for Cypress Grove and to keep the sawmill running. He estimated that with eighty-five or ninety good hands six hundred to eight hun-

21 Monette, "The Mississippi Floods," *loc. cit.*, 472.

22 Taylor to Richard Taylor, May 9, 1850, copy in Hardie Collection.

dred hogshead of sugar could be produced annually and that this should yield a profit, over and above expenses, of $20,000.[23] "The great art in planting, it seems to me," he wrote to Dick when approving the purchase, "is a proper rotation of crops sugar following corn & peas; the land to be improved as much as it can be don[e] conveniently, well prepared before planting & nicely cultivated; ditching for the purpose of draining is all important on all lands & more particularly so, on on [*sic*] the lowlands on the Mississippi." [24]

President Taylor did not live to share in the operation of Fashion plantation. Two months after authorizing its purchase he died. Dick's two sisters were unwilling to share the responsibility for the purchase and by agreement among the three of them he became sole owner of the plantation which he successfully operated until civil war brought devastation and seizure.[25]

The ante-bellum cotton planters of the South found the services of a factor or merchant indispensable. Zachary Taylor was no exception and throughout his planting career the business and financial aspects of his activities were handled by Maunsel White and Company, a substantial New Orleans merchant house. Year after year the cotton crop was sold through this firm and the proceeds held by it to make purchases in Taylor's behalf or to be paid out as Taylor drew upon them. One of White's last reports indicates that during the year ending June 30, 1849, he received for Taylor's account $18,379.39 and paid out $19,734.61 and that he was carrying a balance of slightly

[23] *Id.* to *id.*, June 12, 1850, and a June 11 draft of this letter in Taylor's own hand, both in the Hardie Collection (the June 11 draft contains information not included in the letter of the 12th); Jackson B. Davis, "The Life of Richard Taylor," M. A. thesis, Louisiana State University, published in summary form in *Louisiana Historical Quarterly,* XXIV (1941), 47–126. Davis assumes that Richard Taylor purchased Fashion on his own but does not explain where he obtained the necessary funds.

[24] Taylor to Richard Taylor, June 12, 1850, in Hardie Collection.

[25] "Partition between the Heirs of General Zachary Taylor, December 9, 1850," in Hardie Collection.

over $50,000.[26] At the time of Taylor's death this balance had been reduced to approximately $19,000, chiefly, no doubt, as a result of the purchase of Fashion.[27] The relationship between factor and planter was usually a most intimate one. Certainly this was true in the case of Taylor and White. The General regarded White as one of his oldest and best friends and took a sincere interest in his well-being. When Taylor feared that overwork was undermining White's constitution he did not hesitate to advise him that the preservation of his health was of more importance to his family and friends than any other consideration and that he "must look well to the proper care of it." [28]

The army must have had first place in Taylor's affections or he would not have continued in that service year after year in the face of slow promotion and frontier hardships. But he was a child of the plantation and loved the soil and growing things. Throughout his life he was keenly interested in planting and to the end of his days was constantly looking forward to the time when he could devote his full attention to it.

[26] "Report of Maunsel White and Co. for the year ending June 30, 1849," in Hardie Collection.

[27] "Partition between the Heirs of General Zachary Taylor, December 9, 1850," in Hardie Collection.

[28] Taylor to Maunsel White, October 13, 1846, in Southern Historical Collection, University of North Carolina.

Chapter XIII

PRESIDENTIAL ELECTION OF 1848

NO other President of the United States, with the possible exception of Grover Cleveland, rose as rapidly as Zachary Taylor from obscurity to the White House. So suddenly was he thrust upon the American people that if the Whig national convention of 1844 had been told that four years later their party would nominate Zachary Taylor for President, the delegates would have been amused and mystified. Some of them would have had difficulty identifying him. Many, certainly, would have recalled him as an army officer active in the Florida war, but none would ever have thought of him as a presidential candidate. Moreover, if his name had been presented, few if any of the delegates would have thought his ability or training fitted him for the office. Perhaps somewhere in the country a few followers of Andrew Jackson would have believed that Taylor, like any other honest American, would make a satisfactory President, but surely the Whig national convention of 1844 would have been incredulous.

No one would have been more skeptical of such a prophecy than Zachary Taylor himself. Ever since his entry into the army in 1808 he had been stationed at distant frontier posts well removed from the realm of politics and political controversy. By his own admission he never voted in a presidential election.[1] Except in 1824 when he was on recruiting duty at Cincinnati and Louisville he was on the frontier at election time, and in that year he

[1] Taylor to J. J. Crittenden, September 15, 1847, in Crittenden Papers.

apparently failed to cast a ballot. Through newspapers and correspondence he kept somewhat informed as to the course of events and he occasionally took some interest in legislation affecting the army, but a political career for himself never entered his thoughts. His one interest, other than the army, was planting, and he fully expected to turn to that whenever he returned to civil life.

Taylor's sudden emergence into the political limelight was the direct result of the military fame won during the first year of the war with Mexico. When at the outset of the war he won the unexpected victories at Palo Alto and Resaca de la Palma against forces that far outnumbered his own, and thus rescued his army from a situation that the American press had depicted as full of danger and peril, politicians and newspaper editors in both major parties began to talk of Old Rough and Ready for the presidency. As soon as the news of these victories reached the United States, New Jersey citizens, without distinction of party, assembled and declared him their candidate for President two years hence.[2] A similar assemblage in New York refrained from nominating him only because he informed them that he had no aspirations for the high office.[3] As early as June 18, 1846, Thurlow Weed, editor of the Albany *Evening Journal* and powerful Whig politician of New York state, suggested editorially that Taylor might be the next President of the country. About this same time, according to his autobiography, Weed met Colonel Joseph P. Taylor on board a Hudson River steamboat en route to join his brother in Mexico and through him sent word to the General that if he would for the time being avoid politics, answer no letters, and concentrate on military affairs, he could be elected President in 1848.[4]

[2] *Niles' National Register,* LXX (1846), 256; Montgomery, *Life of Taylor,* 374.

[3] *Niles' National Register,* LXXI (1846–1847), 20–21.

[4] Harriet A. Weed (ed.), *Autobiography of Thurlow Weed* (Boston, 1883),

General Taylor's immediate reaction to this presidential talk, of which he was kept well informed through newspapers and letters from the United States, was one of indifference if not opposition. The earliest reference to the subject in his own correspondence appears to be in a letter of June 21, 1846, to Dr. Wood in which he said President Polk and General Scott "need have no apprehensions of being interfered with by me for that high office, which I would decline if proffered, & I could reach it without opposition." [5] A few weeks later he informed his friend Nathaniel Young of Newcastle, Delaware, that he was not and never would be an aspirant for the presidency. "My opinion has always been against the elevation of a Military Chief to that position," he wrote. "We must have a statesman able to control the people at home and elevate the credit of the country abroad." [6] His opposition to military chiefs, however, could not have been very strong for in August while again expressing his desire "to have nothing to do with that high office," he hoped General Scott would be the Whig candidate in 1848.[7]

In spite of the administration's criticism of the capitulation terms granted by Taylor at Monterrey, his capture of that town stimulated the Taylor-for-president talk. The growing popular interest in him and his own increasing conviction that the administration was seeking to "break him down" and to destroy him as a presidential possibility made Taylor more receptive to the idea. He no longer talked of declining the office if proffered, but declared: "I will not say I would not serve if the good people were to be imprudent enough as to elect me." [8] This position

---

571–72. During the war Weed wrote, at least occasionally, to Col. Taylor, who passed the letters on to his brother to read. Taylor to J. P. Taylor, May 9, 1847, in Taylor Papers.

[5] *Letters from the Battlefields,* 14.

[6] Taylor to N. Young, July 18, 1846, in Division of Manuscripts, Library of Congress.

[7] *Id.* to R. C. Wood, August 4, 1846, in *Letters from the Battlefields,* 35.

[8] *Id.* to *id.,* December 10, 1846, *ibid.,* 76.

he announced to his son-in-law in December, and a month later after the transfer of his most seasoned troops to General Scott, which he regarded as such an outrageous and insulting procedure, he also made it known to Senator J. J. Crittenden of Kentucky who was one of the leading advocates of his candidacy.[9] He still insisted that he had no interest in reaching the presidency; that he hoped some Whig statesman, schooled in civil matters, honest, capable, and faithful to the Constitution, would be chosen; that he would much prefer to retire to his plantation.[10] Clay, Crittenden himself, Associate Justice John McLean of the Supreme Court and father-in-law of Colonel Taylor, and John M. Clayton all received his approval. In spite of these assertions it was clear that Taylor was now ready to respond to the call of the people. Indeed, as the feeling of gross injustice rankled within him he evinced a growing determination not to be shoved aside—a readiness to "undergo political martyrdom rather than see Genl. Scott or Cass elected." [11]

Taylor's presidential boom was quite moderate until his victory at Buena Vista. But that triumph over Santa Anna's large and powerful army, won in the face of the supposed efforts of the administration to tie his hands and leave him to the mercies of the enemy, caused his popularity to spread like wildfire and produced a spontaneous and irresistible demand for his candidacy. State and local meetings representative of both parties and sections of the country enthusiastically nominated Old Rough and Ready. Innumerable newspapers placed his name at the head of their editorial columns as the candi-

[9] *Id.* to J. J. Crittenden, January 26, 1847, in Coleman, *Life of Crittenden,* I, 270.

[10] *Id.* to R. C. Wood, December 10, 1846, and May 9, 1847, in *Letters from the Battlefields,* 76, 99; *id.* to J. J. Crittenden, May 15, 1847, in Crittenden Papers.

[11] *Id.* to R. C. Wood, July 20, 1847, in *Letters from the Battlefields,* 118.

date of their choice.[12] Rough and Ready clubs and Rough and Ready newspapers sprang into existence. The "Taylor fever" swept the country. One New Yorker reported in August that the ice carts and other vehicles driven about the city carried the portrait of General Taylor "well painted on the tail board, and under neath, 'Rough and Ready.' . . . It is on the butcher's stall, it is in the market places. It is on the fish stands, it is on cigar boxes and divers other places." [13]

From the outset Taylor's strength was greatest with the Whigs. His cause was never taken up with enthusiasm by the Democratic leaders. Many of the rank and file of the party urged his nomination and some of the Calhoun Democrats, opponents of Polk's war policy, looked with favor upon the military hero as a candidate who could defeat the war President. Throughout 1847 there continued to be talk of making him the Democratic nominee, but as the months passed and his name became more and more closely associated with the Whig party, that suggestion was less frequently heard.[14]

Many Whig politicians, tired of defeat with Henry Clay, were quick to seize upon Taylor as a candidate. They had experienced a brief triumph in 1840 with one military hero, William Henry Harrison, and were more than ready to try their luck with another one in 1848. Not only did Clay's political opponents advocate Taylor's candidacy, but many men who had been his ardent supporters in past years transferred their support to the Gen-

[12] Louisville *Courier,* April 10 and 24, 1847; *Niles' National Register,* LXXII (1847), 97, 112, 128, 294, 340, 375.

[13] J. B. Mower to John McLean, August 16, 1847, in McLean Papers (Division of Manuscripts, Library of Congress).

[14] Numerous letters in J. Franklin Jameson (ed.), *Correspondence of John C. Calhoun,* in American Historical Association, *Annual Report, 1899,* Vol. II (Washington, 1900), and Chauncey S. Boucher and Robert P. Brooks (eds.), "Correspondence Addressed to John C. Calhoun, 1837–1849," *ibid., 1929* (Washington, 1930), 125–533.

eral. These latter still proclaimed there was no man they would rather see President than Clay but they believed he could not be elected, and they preferred victory with Taylor to defeat with Clay. This was true of Senator Crittenden, a long-time friend and champion of Henry Clay, who became one of the first and warmest advocates of Taylor's candidacy. Early in the war he opened a correspondence with the General which was carried on until the latter entered the White House.[15] Friendly relations between Crittenden and Taylor were increased when the Senator's son Thomas spent several months at Taylor's headquarters in the early part of 1847 and served as an unofficial member of his staff at Buena Vista.[16] The fact that Thomas Crittenden's mother, the first wife of the Senator, was a Lee and a distant relative of Taylor added to the pleasure the General found in the young man's company. Taylor welcomed the correspondence with Senator Crittenden and relied on his political counsel more than on that of any other individual.[17] "Advise me freely and fully," he urged; "keep me constantly advised as regards the best course for me to pursue as regards the presidency." [18]

Another Whig statesman who early pushed Taylor's cause was Alexander H. Stephens of Georgia. Under his leadership the Whig convention of that state formally nominated Taylor in July, 1847. More important was his work in organizing in Congress a Taylor club, known as the Young Indians. At the outset the members were only seven in number, Stephens and Robert Toombs of Georgia, Truman Smith of Connecticut, Abraham Lincoln of Illinois, and three Virginians, William Ballard Preston, Thomas S. Flournoy, and John S. Pendleton. This group with some later additions, never faltered in their determina-

[15] Taylor's letters to Crittenden are in the Crittenden Papers (Division of Manuscripts, Library of Congress).

[16] Taylor to J. J. Crittenden, January 26, March 25, and May 15, 1847, in Crittenden Papers.

[17] *Id.* to *id.*, November 1, 1847, *ibid.* [18] *Id.* to *id.*, May 15, 1847, *ibid.*

Courtesy of the Library of Congress

JOHN JORDAN CRITTENDEN

tion to make Taylor the Whig candidate. So important was their work that Stephens was perhaps justified in asserting in later years that it was he who made Taylor President.[19]

In spite of the strong sentiment for Taylor there were many Whigs who opposed his nomination. In the North many objected to him as a slaveowner and gave their support to Daniel Webster, to Thomas Corwin, or to John McLean. Although the latter was married to Taylor's niece, he did not support the General's candidacy, but remained to the end a very active contender for the nomination. McLean regarded Taylor as a modest man of good sense and sterling integrity, but like many other Whigs he objected to Taylor because he was a military man without experience in political affairs.[20] Many persons still supported Clay who was unquestionably the most popular candidate, next to Taylor. Other Whig leaders such as Crittenden and John M. Clayton had their supporters, as did also General Scott. Indeed, Scott's victorious battles of August and September boomed his presidential chances and checked the Taylor fever.

The most serious threat to General Taylor's presidential chances was not from other candidates, but from his own pen. Contrary to the advice of Thurlow Weed and Crittenden to refrain from writing political letters he responded to requests for his views and opinions. Three days after promising Crittenden that his good advice would be conformed to for the most part and that he would be very guarded in what he wrote,[21] Taylor penned a reply to a letter from the editor of the Cincinnati *Signal* which, when published in that Democratic paper, seriously dampened Whig enthusiasm for his cause. The editor of the *Signal* had enclosed an editorial from his paper stating

[19] Myrta Lockett Avary (ed.), *Recollections of Alexander H. Stephens* (New York, 1910), 21–22.

[20] John McLean to Caleb B. Smith, April 15 and 26, May 6, 1848, in Caleb B. Smith Papers (Division of Manuscripts, Library of Congress).

[21] Taylor to J. J. Crittenden, May 15, 1847, in Crittenden Papers.

his views on important issues and urging the nomination of Taylor as an independent no-party candidate. He advocated the extension of the Ordinance of 1787 to the southwest beyond the Rio Grande and proposed that no legislation designed to accomplish this "high and permanent" object should be "baffled by presidential vetoes." The editorial also declared that as the national debt incurred in the prosecution of the war would necessitate an increased tariff and would prevent the distribution of proceeds from public land sales, neither of these questions would need to be an issue in the forthcoming election. Furthermore it was not to be expected that the Whigs would again urge a United States bank until the independent treasury had been given a fair trial. In his reply to the editor's request for his opinions on these subjects Taylor began by saying that his military duties did not leave him time to answer such important questions, but before closing he expressed his approval of the sentiments and views embraced in the editorial.[22]

Approval of these views seemed to many persons to mark Taylor as a Democrat rather than a Whig and caused much cooling off toward him.[23] The situation was made much worse a few weeks later when Taylor informed a correspondent, Edward Delony, that he could not state his views on the necessity or constitutionality of a United States bank or a protective tariff because he did not have time to investigate those subjects,[24] and in another letter declined for the same reason to comment on a set of resolutions adopted by the Democrats of Clarksville, Tennes-

[22] *Id.* to James W. Taylor, May 18, 1847, in *Niles' National Register,* LXXII (1847), 288, 295.

[23] James E. Harvey to Willie P. Mangum, August 17, 1847, in Mangum Papers (Division of Manuscripts, Library of Congress); Thomas B. Stevenson to J. J. Crittenden, September 7, 1848, in Crittenden Papers (this letter is misdated; it should probably be September 7, 1847); *Niles' National Register,* LXXII (1847), 294.

[24] Taylor to Edward Delony, June 9, 1847, *Niles' National Register,* LXXII (1847), 288.

see, denouncing a national bank, protective tariffs, the distribution of proceeds from public lands, and internal improvements by the national government.[25] Whigs throughout the nation found it difficult to understand how Taylor, if he were a Whig, would need time to investigate these subjects on which the party's principles were well known. Many who had warmly supported him before he commenced letter writing began to "treat his pretensions with absolute derision." [26]

Taylor's first reaction to the storm of criticism called forth by these letters was disdainful indifference. "I do not care a fig about the office," he wrote, "so they the editors & others may publish my letters & make as many comments on them as they please." [27] Within a few weeks, however, he was assuring his son-in-law and Senator Crittenden that in the future he would be more guarded in his replies to political letters and that he would mark all such communications private and clearly state they were not to be published.[28] Taylor believed courtesy necessitated replies to some communications but recognized that attempts to correct misinterpretations of his views would make matters worse rather than better and he wisely determined to let them pass unnoticed. In spite of the best of intentions Taylor's brief and naïve letters frequently were made public and often contained sentences that were seized upon by his opponents. Throughout the campaign one of the most difficult tasks of those who were guiding the Taylor movement was to prevent the General's quill from destroying the popularity gained for him by his sword.

[25] *Id.* to Dr. C. L. Wilcox and others, July 20, 1847, *ibid.*, LXXIII (1847–1848), 63.

[26] Thomas B. Stevenson to J. J. Crittenden, September 7, 1848, in Crittenden Papers.

[27] Taylor to R. C. Wood, September 14, 1847, in *Letters from the Battlefields*, 130.

[28] *Id.* to *id.*, October 5, 1847, *ibid.*, 139; *id.* to J. J. Crittenden, November 1, 1847, in Crittenden Papers.

When Taylor left Mexico late in 1847, after months of inactivity and time for reflection on his position in the approaching political campaign, he was still reluctant to be a candidate. He knew that he would be just as content in a cabin as in the White House and saw no reason why he should seek an office that would neither lengthen his days nor add to his happiness.[29] A week before leaving Monterrey for home he wrote to Crittenden: "I can say to you in all sincerity, it will be with the greatest reluctance I will embark in the approaching contest for the Presidency, & still indulge the hope that something will yet occur between this & the first of November 1848 to obviate the necessity of my being a candidate." [30] The aspect of the presidency he most dreaded was the patronage problem. He knew there would not be enough offices for all who would wish or expect them and that many applicants would be disappointed and would attribute their lack of success "to personal considerations, or some other equally absurd" cause. "Could I gratify & give all places who wanted them; & make everyone rich or happy," he said, "it would do away [with] one of the greatest objections I have to said office." [31] He not only expressed his desire that Crittenden feel entirely free to support Clay or any other candidate behind whom the Whig party could unite, but also authorized the Senator to withdraw his name from the canvass if at any time he reached the conclusion it would be for the best interests of the party or the country to do so. "Country first, & friendship second," he wrote.[32]

Although at this time General Taylor was seemingly quite willing to see Clay the party candidate, he was not ready to follow the advice of Clay's friends, some of whom

[29] *Id.* to R. C. Wood, September 27, 1847, in *Letters from the Battlefields*, 137.

[30] *Id.* to J. J. Crittenden, November 1, 1847, in Crittenden Papers.

[31] *Ibid.*

[32] *Ibid.*

urged him publicly to decline in favor of the veteran statesman, while others suggested that he be the vice-presidential candidate on a ticket with Clay. He took the position that he could not decline in favor of his rival for he was not a candidate. Only his friends who had placed his name before the people could withdraw it. Moreover, he would not presume to tell the American people whom to elect.[33]

Taylor's reluctance to participate in the presidential contest was increased when, upon his return to the United States, he found Mrs. Taylor in "very delicate health" and "decidedly opposed" to his having anything to do with political matters.[34] He joined her at Baton Rouge where he remained, except for an occasional visit to New Orleans and other near-by towns or to his plantation, until he departed for the White House more than a year later. He received numerous invitations from individuals, including Senator Crittenden and Henry Clay, and from state legislatures and officials to visit them, but all were declined, partly because he had informed the War Department that he could be reached at Baton Rouge if his services were needed, but primarily because he had been granted leave to visit his family and attend to his private affairs. If he now traveled to distant cities, he might well be charged with using his leave for electioneering purposes, and this he desired to avoid.[35]

Attention to private affairs proved very difficult, however, because of the constant stream of visitors who came to see and converse with the hero of Buena Vista and presidential candidate. Many were his friends; others were

[33] Taylor to J. P. Taylor, September, [1847], in Taylor Papers; *id.* to J. J. Crittenden, September 15, 1847, in Crittenden Papers.

[34] *Id.* to J. J. Crittenden, January 3, 1848, in Crittenden Papers; *id.* to J. P. Taylor, January 19, 1848, in Taylor Papers.

[35] *Id.* to Orlando Brown, March 15, 1848, in Kentucky Historical Society; *id.* to J. J. Crittenden, January 3 and March 25, 1848, in Crittenden Papers; Washington *Daily Union,* January 4, 1848.

mere curiosity seekers.[36] Taylor's activities were also interfered with by an attack of neuralgia or rheumatism in his right leg which, accompanied by a slight fever, confined him to the house for five weeks. The pain, occasionally so acute as to prevent him from putting his foot to the floor, frequently kept him awake at night. By the first of March he was sufficiently recovered to get about without the aid of a crutch or cane and shortly thereafter made a trip to his plantation.[37] Sculptors and portrait painters also consumed his time. In April he was sitting to three artists eight hours daily, and at one time, shortly before, had been in the hands of six. Political correspondence also demanded attention. At least some of the thirty or more letters received each week seemed to him to require replies.[38]

Shortly after his return to the United States, Taylor's attitude toward his place in the presidential contest underwent an important modification. Influenced by the urgings of many former Clay supporters who called upon him at Baton Rouge, he decided not to retire from the canvass if Clay or someone else were chosen as the Whig candidate, but to remain in the field, letting those who had brought him forward for the presidency drop him. The authority which he had shortly before given to Crittenden to withdraw his name whenever such a step seemed to be for the best interests of the party or the country he now canceled.[39] This decision may have been due in part to the advice of Albert T. Burnley, a long-time Kentucky friend of Crittenden, whose activities extended to Louisiana and Texas. He was close to Taylor during these pre-

[36] Taylor to J. J. Crittenden, January 3, 1848, in Crittenden Papers; *id.* to Jefferson Davis, April 20, 1848, in Historical Society of Pennsylvania.

[37] *Id.* to J. J. Crittenden, February 13, 1848, in Crittenden Papers; *id.* to R. C. Wood, February 18 and 28, 1848, in *Letters from the Battlefields,* 154–56; *id.* to J. P. Taylor, March 10, 1848, in Taylor Papers.

[38] *Id.* to Jefferson Davis, April 20, 1848, in Historical Society of Pennsylvania.

[39] *Id.* to J. J. Crittenden, January 3, 1848, in Crittenden Papers.

GENERAL TAYLOR'S RESIDENCE AT BATON ROUGE WHEN ELECTED PRESIDENT IN 1848. NOW THE GROUNDS OF THE STATE CAPITOL

From an old number of Harper's Magazine, *November, 1854. Courtesy Hill Memorial Library, Louisiana State University.*

election months and rejoiced at his determination to remain in the field.[40] A few of his supporters were pleased by this new policy, but the majority of the Whig leaders were thoroughly disgusted. It seemed to them to be proof that the General did not have the interests of the party at heart and was not a trustworthy Whig.

Unquestionably Taylor was not a strong party man. Although he was convinced that a few more years of Democratic rule would leave nothing of the Constitution but its name,[41] and at times declared his readiness to support any candidate who could defeat the Democrats, at other times he stated that if he were given the power to select the chief magistrate, he would, if he knew the individual, select the man, be he Whig or Democrat, who would perpetuate our institutions as given us by the founders and restore the government as nearly as possible to the purity with which it was conducted by our first Presidents.[42] Moreover, ever since his name was first mentioned for the presidency he had insisted that he would not be the candidate of a party. Again and again he had declared he could not enter the White House as the president of a party but only as the president of the whole nation. For this reason he opposed a national nominating convention and urged that local and state gatherings with little emphasis upon party be left free to make their own nominations. He believed national conventions stirred up party asperity and controversy "which have so long prevailed to the great injury, & in many instances to the disgrace of the Country." [43] Moreover, he saw no possibility of a Whig victory

[40] Albert T. Burnley to J. J. Crittenden, December 12, 1847, in Crittenden Papers; George R. Poage, *Henry Clay and the Whig Party* (Chapel Hill, 1936), 176.

[41] Taylor to Orlando Brown, March 15, 1848, in Kentucky Historical Society; *id.* to J. J. Crittenden, March 25, 1848, in Crittenden Papers.

[42] *Id.* to J. P. Taylor, May 9, 1847, in Taylor Papers; *id.* to J. J. Crittenden, May 15, 1847, in Crittenden Papers.

[43] *Id.* to *id.,* November 1, 1847, in Crittenden Papers. See also *id.* to Brantz Mayer, September 25, 1847, in Historical Society of Pennsylvania;

on a strict party vote. He recognized that the party was normally a minority one and that a Whig candidate could win only if the election were as nonpartisan as possible, only if he received support from the moderate Democrats. For these reasons, and because he could not give such pledges as he was sure a convention would require of him, he declared he could not be a convention candidate.[44] Clearly he wanted to defeat the Democrats, but he wanted the victors to be nonpartisans devoted to the welfare of the nation and not of a party.

In this spirit Taylor accepted the nomination of any and all local meetings, regardless of party, provided no pledges of policy were demanded of him. His position was most clearly set forth in a letter of January 30, 1848, to Peter Sken Smith of Philadelphia, which soon found its way into the newspapers and attracted wide attention. He had, he said, no desire to dictate to the American people the manner in which they should nominate him, but on one point his position was immutable—he was not to be brought forward as the candidate of any party nor the exponent of any party doctrines. "In conclusion," he wrote, "I have to repeat, that if I were nominated for the presidency, by any body of my fellow-citizens, designated by any name they might choose to adopt, I should esteem it an honor, and would accept such nomination provided it had been made entirely independent of party considerations." [45] This letter which caused one Whig leader to declare "the man is certainly demented," [46] greatly strengthened the position of those Whig politicians who had been claiming for months that Taylor should

---

id. to Orlando Brown, December 18, 1847, March 15, 1848, in Kentucky Historical Society; *id.* to J. J. Crittenden, September 15, 1847, in Crittenden Papers.

[44] *Id.* to *id.*, February 13 and March 25, 1848, in Crittenden Papers.

[45] *Id.* to Peter Sken Smith, January 30, 1848, in Washington *Daily Union*, February 26, 1848.

[46] Caleb B. Smith to John McLean, April 10, 1848, in McLean Papers.

not be the Whig candidate because he was not a Whig. He would not support Whig principles; he would remain in the field regardless of the outcome of the Whig convention; he would accept the nomination of any political group.

Taylor's supporters within the party still regarded him as the candidate with the best chances of carrying the party to victory and they set about to counteract the influence of these no-party declarations. In Washington, Crittenden, Stephens, and Toombs drafted a letter covering not only this point, but also the chief issues likely to arise during the campaign.[47] Major Bliss who was in the capital at the time carried it south to Taylor, and under date of April 22 it soon appeared in the press as a letter to his brother-in-law, Captain J. S. Allison of Louisville.[48] Throughout the campaign it was famous as the first Allison letter. How much the General may have altered the draft sent from Washington is not known, but he was not one to sign communications without making certain that the contents met his approval. Moreover, as most of the ideas expressed therein may be found in his frank letters to Crittenden, there is no reason to doubt that this letter, though drafted by others, is a sincere statement of his views. After stating that he had not always replied to requests for his opinion on the many issues, large and small, before the country, the letter continued:

> I confess, whilst I have great cardinal principles, which will regulate my political life, I am not sufficiently familiar with all the minute details of political legislation to give solemn pledges to exert my influence, if I were President, to carry out this, or defeat that measure. I have no concealments. I hold no opinion which I would not readily proclaim to my assembled countrymen; but crude impressions upon matters of policy,

[47] Taylor to J. P. Taylor, May 15, 1848, in Taylor Papers; Coleman, *Life of Crittenden*, I, 294; Poage, *Henry Clay and the Whig Party*, 177.

[48] Washington *Daily Union*, May 3, 1848; *Niles' National Register*, LXXIV (1848–1849), 8.

which may be right to-day and wrong to-morrow, are, perhaps, not the best test of fitness for office. One who cannot be trusted without pledges, cannot be confided in merely on account of them.

After this general statement of his position, he declared, "I am a Whig, but not an ultra Whig. If elected I would not be the mere President of a party. I would endeavor to act independent of party domination. I should feel bound to administer the government untrammelled by party schemes." On the subject of the presidential veto he expressed the conviction that for some years the executive had exercised an "undue and injurious influence upon the legislative department of the government" and that the veto power should be exercised only "in cases of clear violation of the constitution, or manifest haste and want of consideration by Congress." Having taken this position on the veto it was natural to assert that on the subjects of the tariff, currency, and internal improvements the chief executive should carry out the will of the people as expressed through their representatives in Congress. As to the Mexican War he declared:

> I sincerely rejoice at the prospect of peace. My life has been devoted to arms, yet I look upon war at all times and under all circumstances as a national calamity, to be avoided if compatible with national honor. The principles of our government as well as its true policy, are opposed to the subjugation of other nations, and the embarrassment of other countries by conquest. In the language of the great Washington, "Why should we quit our own to stand on foreign ground?" In the Mexican war our national honor has been vindicated, amply vindicated, and in dictating terms of peace we may well afford to be forbearing and even magnanimous to our foes.

This declaration of principles would perhaps have satisfied most of the Whig politicians, but unfortunately for the plans of Crittenden and Stephens there appeared in the newspapers almost simultaneously another letter of

Taylor's, dated two days before the Allison letter, in which he not only stated that he would refuse a nomination by the Whig convention unless he were "left free of all pledges, and permitted to maintain the position of independence of all parties in which the people and my own duty have placed me," but also declared that the newspaper statements that he would withdraw from the campaign if Clay were nominated by the Whig national convention were wholly false. "It has not been my intention, at any moment," he wrote in this letter to the editor of the Richmond *Republican,* "to change my position, or to withdraw my name from the canvass, whoever may be the nominee of the National Convention, either of the whig or democratic party." [49] Taylor had apparently forgotten he had at one time given Crittenden discretionary power to withdraw his name and had at the same time written Clay he was "ready to stand aside" if he or any other Whig "were the choice of the party." [50] Not only did he state to the editors of the Richmond *Republican* that it had never been his intention to withdraw, but he also stated in his private correspondence that he had no recollection of ever pledging himself to decline the canvass if Henry Clay were the candidate.[51]

Taylor's advice against the holding of a national convention carried little weight with the party leaders who called upon delegates to assemble in Philadelphia on June 7.[52] Thus the issue for the Whigs during the spring months was who would win the support of that convention. The contest was still primarily between Taylor and Clay who in April abandoned the passive attitude he had thus far maintained and announced his willingness to run again.

[49] Taylor to O. P. Baldwin or Robert H. Gallaher, April 20, 1848, in Washington *Daily Union,* May 4, 1848.

[50] Taylor to Henry Clay, November 4, 1847, in Calvin Colton (ed.), *Works of Henry Clay* (New York, 1904), V, 548–49.

[51] *Id.* to J. P. Taylor, March 10, 1848, in Taylor Papers; *id.* to Orlando Brown, March 15, 1848, in Kentucky Historical Society.

[52] Washington *Daily Union,* February 5, 1848.

The only hope of other candidates was that a convention deadlocked over the two leaders might turn to a compromise candidate. Indeed the contest between the Clay and Taylor camps became so warm that a compromise choice did not seem unlikely. This was the hope of McLean's supporters and it may also have been the plan of the famous editor of the New York *Tribune,* Horace Greeley. Publicly he supported the candidacy of Clay and in his private correspondence seems to have been sincerely interested in his success,[53] but many observers believed that he supported Clay only to kill off Taylor and make way for an antislavery candidate—perhaps McLean, Corwin, or Seward.[54] Thurlow Weed also was aware of the possible opportunity for a compromise candidate and on the eve of the convention was reported to be working for Seward as the chief candidate or as the running mate of Clayton or Crittenden.[55]

On the appointed day the Whig delegates assembled in Philadelphia in the spacious and elegant hall of the Chinese Museum. Matters of organization and other preliminaries occupied the first and most of the second day. Amidst storm and tumult various efforts were made to pass resolutions pledging the party or the candidate to some principle, but without success. No platform or declaration of principle of any sort was adopted. The evening of the second day the all-important task of selecting a candidate was commenced. On the first ballot Taylor received 111 votes to 97 for Clay, 43 for Scott, 22 for Webster, four for Clayton, and two for McLean. Taylor's strength was chiefly in the slave states from which he received 86 votes to 22 for Clay. After a second ballot on

[53] Horace Greeley to Henry Clay, November 30, 1847, and May 29, 1848, in Clay Papers (Division of Manuscripts, Library of Congress).

[54] Thomas Dowling to John McLean, October 30, 1847, J. B. Mower to John McLean, February 15, and March 13, 1848, in McLean Papers; Poage, *Henry Clay and the Whig Party,* 163.

[55] J. B. Mower to John McLean, April 19, May 15, and June 5, 1848, in McLean Papers.

which Taylor picked up seven votes while his chief rival dropped 12, the convention adjourned for the night. Conferences among Taylor's opponents were without result and when on the next day balloting was resumed the General added 15 votes to make his total 133, only 8 short of the necessary majority. At this point Judge Saunders of the Louisiana delegation announced that General Taylor had authorized him to state that he would be satisfied with any nomination made by the convention and that his friends could withdraw his name at any time. By the act of uniting with this convention, declared Saunders, "his friends withdraw his name from the canvass, unless he be the nominee of this convention." Another ballot was taken and, amidst the cheers of Taylor men and howls of protest from the antislavery delegates of New England and Ohio, Old Rough and Ready was declared nominated with 171 votes. His main support was still in the slave states whose delegates gave him 106 votes, but he received at least one vote from every state in the Union. Scarcely had the result been announced before Charles Allen, delegate from Massachusetts, sprang to his feet and dramatically declared, "The Whig party is here and this day dissolved. You have put one ounce too much on the strong back of Northern endurance." Whereupon Allen and at least one other "Conscience Whig" from New England walked out of the hall and began preparations for a new antislavery party. When order was restored the convention turned to the selection of a nominee for Vice-President and on the second ballot named Millard Fillmore of New York.[56]

In the opinion of some observers Judge Saunders' statement was the determining factor in winning the nomination for Taylor,[57] but Horace Greeley believed his success

[56] *Niles' National Register,* LXXIV (1848–1849), 349, 354–58; *The Campaign* (Washington, 1848), No. 3 (June 14, 1848), 42–43, No. 4 (June 21, 1848), 57–59; Washington *Daily Union,* June 8, 11, and 15, 1848.

[57] Washington *Republic,* June 13, 1849.

was assured from the first. "The first three ballots," he said, "were simply so many acts of a farce, played off to enable tenderfooted delegates to break through the instructions of their constituents gradually. . . . If it had been necessary to General Taylor's nomination to give him 140 votes on the first ballot, he would have got them." [58]

Not until several days after the convention completed its work was Taylor aware that he had been nominated. He was busy on his plantation when the river steamer *General Taylor,* en route from Memphis to New Orleans, brought the news. The shouts of the passengers called him down to the landing where he received unofficial notice of his nomination. With little sign of emotion he exchanged greetings with the captain, acknowledged the cheers of the passengers, and returned to his cabin.[59] He felt "neither pride [n]or exultation" but was deeply moved by the honor done him and by the realization that the convention delegates, most of whom had no personal acquaintance with him, had selected him as a suitable candidate for the highest office in the land without requiring pledges or promises of any kind.[60] After another week on the plantation Taylor returned to Baton Rouge where he found Mrs. Taylor far from happy over his nomination but hopeful that as he had been nominated he would be elected.[61]

Because the convention had adopted no platform of principles Taylor's letter of acceptance was awaited with special interest, but week after week passed without its appearance. The delay proved to be due to his refusal to pay the postage on the increasing quantity of mail ad-

[58] Quoted in Poage, *Henry Clay and the Whig Party,* 180.

[59] New Orleans *Daily Delta,* June 15, 1848.

[60] Taylor to Jefferson Davis, July 10, 1848, in Rowland (ed.), *Jefferson Davis, Constitutionalist,* I, 208–10; *id.* to R. C. Wood, June 22, 1848, in *Letters from the Battlefields,* 158–59.

[61] French, *Two Wars,* 96.

dressed to him, for prepaid postage was not yet the rule. When Taylor learned that the official notice of his nomination was among the letters sent to the dead-letter office, he asked for their return and in due time they arrived back in Baton Rouge. Before their arrival, however, he received a duplicate letter from the chairman of the convention which he answered under date of July 15. This delay, and especially Taylor's part in it, was a subject of amusement and attack for his opponents all through the campaign.[62] When his acceptance was finally given to the public early in August, it did nothing to supply the want of a platform. After expressing his thanks for the honor conferred upon him and his own distrust of his fitness for the office, he pledged himself, should he be elected, to endeavor to discharge his new duties so as to meet the just expectations of his fellow citizens and "preserve undiminished the prosperity and reputation of our common country." [63]

Immediately following the convention Taylor was also faced with the need for some explanation of Judge Saunders' statement to that body. It seemed so inconsistent with his declared intention not to withdraw from the campaign that many doubted that he had actually authorized it. The Taylor Democrats who had been supporting him as a noparty candidate were particularly eager to know whether Saunders had correctly represented his point of view. Taylor's first inclination, resulting doubtless from his own understanding of the situation, was to declare that Saunders had exceeded his authority, that he was still an independent candidate, that he was no more the Whig candidate than he was the candidate of other groups that had nominated him. But a hurried visit from Balie Peyton, Logan Hunton, and A. C. Bullitt apparently persuaded him to approve publicly the course taken by Saunders and

62 Washington *Daily Union,* July 22, 23, 25, and 26, and August 1, 1848.
63 *Niles' National Register,* LXXIV (1848–1849), 69.

to deny that he ever had any other thought.[64] This stand was so resented by a group of Baltimore Independents who had been working for Taylor that they disbanded their organization. They, like many other Independents and Taylor Democrats, felt not only that he had abandoned his own original position, but also that his uncertainty and vacillation were signs of weakness.[65]

The Whig politicians, happy in the thought that they had forced Taylor into a position as a definite Whig candidate, were rudely shocked when, a few weeks later, he "thankfully accepted" nomination by a Charleston meeting of Democrats and Independents. This acceptance was doubly distasteful to the Whigs because the meeting had named as Taylor's running mate the vice-presidential candidate chosen by the Democrats at their national convention.[66] When news of this acceptance reached New York, the home state of Millard Fillmore, the Whig candidate for Vice-President, there was widespread spontaneous indignation and a demand that Taylor be displaced as the Whig candidate. Half an hour after the telegraph brought the news to Albany a call was out for a mass meeting to be held in the hall of the capitol building. The crowd that assembled in response to this call freely voiced its indignation, but in the end, guided by the master politician Thurlow Weed, refrained from taking any action injurious to Taylor or the Whig cause.[67] A few weeks later the New York Whigs were somewhat appeased by Taylor's public reference to Fillmore as a "distinguished citizen of New York, whose acknowledged abilities and sound conservative opinions might have justly entitled him to the first place on the ticket." This statement was contained

[64] Washington *Daily Union,* July 4 and 8, 1848; *The Campaign,* No. 7 (July 12, 1848), 103–104.

[65] *The Campaign,* No. 8 (July 19, 1848), 113–14; Washington *Daily Union,* September 23, 1848.

[66] Washington *Daily Union,* August 30, 1848.

[67] Thurlow Weed Barnes, *Memoir of Thurlow Weed* (Boston, 1884), 169–71; Washington *Daily Union,* August 30, 1848.

in a second letter to Captain Allison which was prepared by Thurlow Weed as a final effort to place Taylor before the people as a true Whig. In this letter, drafted by Weed and approved by Fillmore, Taylor reviewed his stand on the presidential contest from the beginning, declared that he was a Whig and had on all proper occasions professed himself to be one, and that he had not refused nominations by political opponents because he thought he had no more right to do that than to refuse the vote of a Democrat at the polls. He sought to soften the effect of his frequent statement that he was not a party candidate by saying that he was not a party candidate "in that straightened and sectarian sense" which would prevent his being president of the whole people.[68] This clever attempt to reconcile Taylor's no-party statements with his position as the candidate of the Whig party had the desired effect at least in a measure, and many wavering Whigs fell in line to march to the White House behind Old Rough and Ready.

Taylor's chief opponent in the campaign was Lewis Cass, veteran Michigan statesman, "Father of the West," who bore the title of General as a result of his services in the War of 1812. As he was the original champion of the application of popular sovereignty to the problem of slavery in the territories, and as he had been nominated upon a platform framed to suit the South, his nomination called forth cries of rage and disappointment from the antislavery Democrats of the North. He was also opposed by a faction of New York Democrats known as Barnburners. In August these two groups of dissatisfied Democrats met in Buffalo with the free-soil Whigs and the representatives of the Liberty party, which had been in the field for nearly a decade, and nominated Martin Van Buren and Charles Francis Adams upon a platform pledged to pro-

[68] Taylor to J. S. Allison, September 4, 1848, in *Niles' National Register*, LXXIV (1848–1849), 200–201; Weed, *Autobiography*, 579.

hibit the extension of slavery and to abolish it wherever the power of Congress extended. So clearly was Van Buren's name associated with the Democratic party and so new was he to the antislavery fold that he did not appeal strongly to the free-soil Whigs. In the important state of New York, however, this weakness was more than offset by his strength with the Barnburners. Thus the campaign became a three-cornered contest with the Free-Soil party holding the balance of power in several Northern states.[69]

In comparison with the exciting presidential campaigns of 1840 and 1844 the contest among Van Buren, Cass, and Taylor aroused little enthusiasm. So many Northern Whigs were dissatisfied with Taylor and so many Democrats, Southern and Northern, were opposed to Cass that neither party was able to face the country with united strength.[70] Calhoun withheld his support from Cass, and Clay refused to help in any way to elect Taylor. He refused to permit a New York meeting to enter him in the contest as a fourth candidate,[71] but he wanted no responsibility for Taylor's administration and to the end of the campaign declined to endorse his candidacy.[72] Daniel Webster early decided not to cast in his lot with the Free-Soil movement, nor to do anything else that would oppose the regular Whig nominee, but not until late in the campaign did he publicly appeal for the election of Taylor. Then he did so in such lukewarm fashion that his appeal was of doubtful value. Because of Taylor's lack of politi-

[69] *The Campaign,* No. 1 (May 31, 1848), 16, No. 2 (June 7, 1848), 19–21; Theodore C. Smith, *The Liberty and Free-Soil Parties in the Northwest* (New York, 1897), 124, 138–42; Andrew C. McLaughlin, *Lewis Cass* (Boston, 1891), 232–40, 255.

[70] For Southern opposition to Cass see Jameson (ed.), *Correspondence of John C. Calhoun, loc. cit.,* and Boucher and Brooks (eds.), "Correspondence Addressed to John C. Calhoun, 1837–1849," *loc. cit.*

[71] Clay to James Brooks, September 8, 1848, in Washington *Daily Union,* September 29, 1848; Clay to James Lynch, September 20, 1848, in Colton (ed.), *Works of Henry Clay,* V, 575.

[72] Clay to Thomas B. Stevenson, September 4 and October 9, 1848, in Colton (ed.), *Works of Henry Clay,* III, 483, 485.

cal experience Webster frankly denounced his nomination as "one not fit to be made." Yet he urged all Whigs to vote for him as preferable to Cass or Van Buren.[73] Horace Greeley talked of escaping to some quiet farm or to Europe, but in the end turned the *Tribune* to Taylor's support.[74]

The one issue in which the people were interested and which could have aroused enthusiasm was that of the extension of slavery. But on this question the two leading candidates carefully avoided taking a clear stand. Since the early months of the Mexican War, Congress had repeatedly considered in one form or another the proposition known as the Wilmot Proviso—prohibiting slavery in any territory acquired from Mexico. It had not been enacted into law, but it was still the demand of antislavery leaders who hoped to secure its adoption by the new administration if not before. Cass had clearly announced his belief that the question of slavery in the territories should be settled by squatter sovereignty, but many Southern Democrats were not convinced that he would refuse to sign a bill embodying the proviso if it were presented to him. At no time during the campaign did he remove this uncertainty. General Taylor's stand on this important issue was even more confusing. As a planter and owner of more than one hundred slaves he was expected to oppose the Wilmot Proviso. And though he would not so declare himself, he was presented in the South as one who could be counted upon to protect Southern interests and rights. As such he appealed not only to the Southern Whigs but also to many Democrats. The only statement made by Taylor that threw any light upon his stand was his oft-

[73] Daniel Webster to Fletcher Webster, June 16 and 19, 1848, in Claude H. Van Tyne (ed.), *Letters of Daniel Webster* (New York, 1902), 368–69; *id.* to E. Rockwood Hoar, August 23, 1848, *ibid.*, 372; *id.* to R. M. Blatchford, September 18, 1848, in Fletcher Webster (ed.), *The Private Correspondence of Daniel Webster* (Boston, 1857), II, 285–86; George Ticknor Curtis, *Life of Daniel Webster* (New York, 1870), II, 344–47.

[74] Horace Greeley to Henry Clay, June 21, 1848, in Clay Papers.

repeated declaration that the presidential veto should be exercised only in "cases of clear violation of the constitution, or manifest haste and want of consideration by Congress." [75] This enabled Northern Whigs to declare that he would not veto the Wilmot Proviso and that the antislavery cause could be best served by putting Taylor in the White House and electing congressmen pledged to enact the Proviso into law.[76] On this understanding many of the less fanatical opponents of slavery campaigned and voted for him. But thousands of Free-Soilers, especially in Ohio, gave their support to Van Buren and prevented Taylor from carrying any of the Northwest states. Throughout the campaign the opposing interpretations of his views on the slavery question were widely denounced by Democratic newspapers and orators as "Taylor's Two Faces." [77]

Taylor's silence on the Wilmot Proviso was due in part to his sincere belief that it should be left to Congress but also in part to a realization that discussion of it would array the people of the two sections against each other and endanger the Union. To Jefferson Davis, to whom he most fully expressed his slavery views, he wrote in the spring of 1848, "this Wilmot question should never have been agitated, nature has so arranged matters as regards the ceded territory, which will prevent the existence of Slavery in any portion of it; for no one will while in his senses carry his slaves there unless he wishes to get them out of the reach of some civil process; this proviso was gotten up with no other object but to array the North against the

[75] Taylor to J. S. Allison, April 22, 1848, in *Niles' National Register*, LXXIV (1848–1849), 8.

[76] George E. Baker (ed.), *The Works of William H. Seward* (Boston, 1887), III, 290, 299, 304; Smith, *Liberty and Free Soil Parties*, 149–50.

[77] Washington *Daily Union*, July 14, September 22 and 24, October 4, 8, 10, and 27, and November 4, 1848; *General Taylor's Two Faces* (Published under authority of the National and Jackson Democratic Association Committee).

South, & I much fear its injurious effects before it [is] finally disposed of; but I hope for the best." [78]

Because the intemperate zeal of the fanatics, north and south, made impossible a proper and calm discussion of the slavery question either in or out of Congress, Taylor regarded the subject as the most important one faced by the country since the organization of the government. He saw no objection to reasonable discussion of Southern institutions by the people of the North, but if they "go beyond that point where resistance becomes right and proper," he wrote to Davis, "let the South act promptly, boldly and decisively, with arms in their hands if necessary, as the Union in that case will be blown to atoms, or will be no longer worth preserving. But I pray to God this state of things will not occur in my day, or in your or that of our children or children's children, if ever." It was Taylor's sincere intention, if elected, to observe scrupulously the right of both slave and free states, to do justice "to and in every part of the country, North, East, South and West, in accordance to the provision of the constitution," which he regarded as the best and only course to preserve the Union.[79] That disagreement as to the proper interpretation or application of the Constitution was one of the main obstacles to any solution of the problem, he apparently quite overlooked.

Closely connected with the question of slavery was that of the acquisition of territory from Mexico. During the preconvention period of the campaign the issue was how much territory should be demanded of Mexico in the peace treaty. Partly because he favored a peace based on justice and magnanimity, but also because he foresaw the bitter sectional struggle that would follow annexation, Taylor opposed taking more territory than would be sufficient to

[78] Taylor to Jefferson Davis, April 20, 1848, in Historical Society of Pennsylvania.

[79] *Id.* to *id.*, August 16, 1847, in Library of Congress.

compensate American citizens for claims against Mexico. In his judgment this should include no land west of the Rio Grande or south of 36° 30′, the Missouri Compromise line. Consequently he looked with disfavor upon the territorial provisions of the Treaty of Guadalupe Hidalgo and opposed the movement which developed at the close of the war for the acquisition of all of Mexico.[80] Later in the campaign the question of territorial acquisition was again raised by reports of American filibustering expeditions against the northern provinces of Mexico. This movement was of necessity secret, but it was widely rumored that an officer of conspicuous gallantry, fine talents, great experience, popularity, and political knowledge was the chief and leader in the enterprise. Although President Polk replied to a Senate call for information on the scheme that none was in his possession, his Secretary of State viewed the project as a serious threat to the peace of the nation.[81] When the reported movement was called to Taylor's attention he privately expressed his thorough opposition to it and to any further annexation, but publicly he refrained from comment.[82]

Taylor's opposition to a foreign policy of aggression was in marked contrast to that of his chief opponent, Lewis Cass, who had a reputation as an imperialist. During the campaign, it is true, he was more restrained in his demands; but his earlier support of extreme American claims in Oregon and Texas, his well-known anti-British views, and his open advocacy of territorial expansion at

80 *Id.* to J. J. Crittenden, November 1, 1847, in Crittenden Papers; *id.* to J. P. Taylor, January 19, 1848, in Taylor Papers; Bailie Peyton to J. J. Crittenden, January 25, 1848, in Crittenden Papers; Taylor to Orlando Brown, March 15, 1848, in Kentucky Historical Society; *id.* to Jefferson Davis, April 20, 1848, in Historical Society of Pennsylvania.

81 John F. Crampton to Palmerston, August 14 and 28, 1848, in Public Record Office, Foreign Office 5:486 (Library of Congress Photostats); *Congressional Globe,* 30 Cong., 1 Sess., 1050.

82 Truman Smith to J. J. Crittenden, September 23, 1848, in Crittenden Papers; Taylor to John M. Clayton, September 4, 1848, in Clayton Papers (Division of Manuscripts, Library of Congress).

the expense of Mexico seemed a clear indication of his foreign policy. When on this ground the London *Times* expressed a preference for Taylor as "the fittest and best man to be President of the United States," the Democrats denounced him as the candidate of the *Times*.[83] Taylor's own supporters, however, presented him to the public as a man of peace. They made the most of his opposition to aggression and frequently referred to his statement that he looked upon "war at all times and under all circumstances as a national calamity" and the subjugation of other nations as contrary to American principles of government.

Throughout the campaign General Taylor's stand on the presidential veto was denounced by his opponents as a pledge "not to perform his official duties as enjoined by the constitution." [84] Such certainly was not his intention. He merely opposed the excessive use of the veto inaugurated by Andrew Jackson and advocated a return to the policy of earlier presidents. His position he clearly stated in the summer of 1847 when he wrote:

> It appears to me that no president should hesitate a moment to veto any law formed by Congress which conflicted with the provisions of the constitution, but [in] matters of expediency great forbearance should be used and only after the most mature consideration. It appears to me, and has for some time, that we are considering an office of chief magistrate, and will soon make it so, of too much importance, instead of its being what it was intended to be, a co-ordinate branch of the government. It is rapidly swallowing up the other two and should be closely looked to by the people, let each of the three great departments revolve within their proper circle and [all] will go right.[85]

This statement shows no disregard of the Constitution, but the wisdom of the policy set forth may be open to

[83] *The Campaign*, No. 10 (August 2, 1848), 156.
[84] *Ibid.*, No. 24 (October 27, 1848), 369–70.
[85] Taylor to Jefferson Davis, August 16, 1847, in Library of Congress.

question. It is not unfair to ask, as did James Fenimore Cooper, whether a President is better qualified to judge of what is or is not constitutional than of what is or is not expedient? Whether it is not more important for the President to veto inexpedient legislation than unconstitutional bills, because the latter will presumably be voided by the Supreme Court whereas the former, if not vetoed, becomes law and stands until repealed? [86] Moreover, how important a part the President should take in the formulation of policy was as debatable a question in Taylor's day as it has been ever since. Shall he lead, or shall he merely execute?

To a great degree it was this conception in regard to the proper share of the executive in the government that influenced Taylor to withhold his opinions on the issues before the country. On most of the issues he had definite views—he believed the United States bank was dead and would not be revived in his time, that the tariff would be increased only for revenue, that internal improvements would go on in spite of presidential vetoes, and that Congress would never permit a slave state to be created out of the Mexican cession [87]—but he did not believe that a presidential candidate should express his opinion "on subjects which must or ought to come before the National Legislature." [88] Because he believed that the President has nothing to do with the making of laws he could declare, when declining to give his views to an unnamed correspondent, "my opinions, even if I were the president of the United States, are neither important nor necessary." [89] To the end of the campaign little definite information as to Taylor's stand was available other than that he would not

[86] J. Fenimore Cooper to Samuel L. Harris, September 5, 1848, in *The Autograph,* I, No. 2 (December, 1911), 22–24.

[87] Taylor to R. C. Wood, September 27, 1847, in *Letters from the Battlefields,* 134; *id.* to Jefferson Davis, July 27, 1847, in Charles B. Going, *David Wilmot: Free-Soiler* (New York, 1924), 234–35.

[88] *Id.* to J. J. Crittenden, November 1, 1847, in Crittenden Papers.

[89] Washington *Daily Union,* October 14, 1848.

attempt to influence congressional legislation and would use the veto only in extraordinary cases; that he would execute the laws faithfully and would "support the constitution as near as practicable, as [it] was construed by our first chief magistrates, who had so large a share in creating & putting it in motion." [90]

In the absence of any vital campaign issues it is not surprising that the Democratic arguments against Taylor concerned points of little or no importance. Because the London *Times* spoke of him approvingly he was denounced as the British candidate,[91] and because he accepted support from Native Americans he was declared to be hostile to Roman Catholics and foreign-born citizens.[92] His numerous letters were seized upon as evidence of his lack of education and inability to write correct English; [93] yet he was described as a large and opulent slaveholder, the candidate of the party of privilege who could not be the people's president.[94] When the Whigs charged Cass with receiving thousands of dollars in extra pay for services as Indian Superintendent at the same time he drew pay as Governor of Michigan Territory, the Democrats replied by showing that since Taylor entered the army in 1808 he had received in pay and extra allowances $168,285.88.[95] Moreover, because of his refusal to pay postage on mail addressed to him and because of his simple habits of dress he was denounced as stingy.[96] The

[90] Taylor to R. C. Wood, July 13, 1847, in *Letters from the Battlefields,* 113.

[91] *The Campaign,* No. 10 (August 2, 1848), 156.

[92] Washington *Daily Union,* September 28, 1848.

[93] *The Campaign Democrat* (Louisville, Ky.), September, 1848; Washington *Daily Union,* September 19 and 20, 1848.

[94] *The Campaign,* No. 3 (June 14), 33.

[95] Washington *Daily Union,* October 25, 1848; *Allowances and Extra Pay, A Plain Statement of Fact From the Record . . .* (Published under authority of the National and Jackson Democratic Association Committee); *The Campaign,* No. 17 (September 20), 257–59, No. 23 (October 25), 353–54, No. 24 (October 27), 370–71.

[96] Gideon Welles, Diary, July 29, 1848, in the Huntington Library; *The Campaign Democrat,* September, 1848.

Democrats attempted to offset Taylor's military popularity by reminding those who had served as volunteers that he had severely criticized their conduct during the war, and by playing up Cass's record in the War of 1812 and the Mexican War services of General W. O. Butler, his running mate.[97] But most of all the Democrats called attention to General Taylor's political inexperience, his own frequently expressed doubts as to his qualifications, and his vacillating stand on his relationship to the Whig party.[98]

The Whig campaign was directed by Truman Smith, Connecticut congressman and chairman of the Whig executive committee of the two houses of Congress. Although his vote at the Whig convention was cast for Clay, he had been an original member of Stephens' club of Young Indians and had worked for Taylor's nomination for months. He voted for Clay only because his instructions required it. The Democrats not unjustly referred to Smith as the "principal schemer, spokesman, and general circular-letter writer for the Whig party," the "franker-general of their documents." [99] He himself described his work to Alexander H. Stephens to whom he wrote early in October: "I returned to this city on the 5th of the last month and have ever since been busy in distributing documents right & left and in carrying on an extreme correspondence with all parts of the country. . . . We have sent off for the last three weeks from 15 to 20 thousand 'documents' . . . per diem and we are making Uncle Caves [100] mail bags absolutely groan. New speeches which we have circulated have consisted of Claytons Stewarts Toombs & yours—otherwise

[97] *The Campaign,* No. 19 (October 4), 301, No. 20 (October 11), 312–13, No. 21 (October 18), 326–27.

[98] *The Campaign Democrat,* September, 1848; Washington *Daily Union,* July 4, August 3, October 6 and 8, 1848; *The Campaign,* No. 4 (June 21), 51–55, No. 11 (August 9), 160–61.

[99] Washington *Daily Union,* September 28, 1848.

[100] Cave Johnson, Tennessee politician, was Postmaster General in Polk's administration.

we have confined ourselves exclusively to Life of Taylor in English & German & several well got up pamphlets, or tracts such as the last platform, V. Buren Platform, Moral & intellectual character of Taylor &c." [101] Gideon Welles, a member of Polk's administration, thought Smith's persistent labors in Taylor's behalf both before and after his nomination would never be fully appreciated.[102] At least one Whig, however, declared "he was the murat of our hosts, and his 'white plume' nodded along the whole line of the Taylor battalions. God bless him!" [103]

Whig speeches and pamphlets answered some of the charges or arguments against Taylor but placed their emphasis upon the General's character, good judgment, and sound sense, and maintained that an honest, faithful, and soundly American heart is a man's best qualification for the presidency. Whig campaigners constantly compared their candidate to George Washington, another military man, another nonpartisan President.[104]

Except for the writing of an occasional letter General Taylor took no part in the campaign. He remained close to Baton Rouge, giving attention to his private interests and performing the duties of commander of the Western Division of the army to which command he had been assigned early in the summer at the expiration of his six months' leave.[105] Invitations to appear in various states he

[101] Truman Smith to Alexander H. Stephens, October 2, 1848, in Stephens Papers (Division of Manuscripts, Library of Congress).

[102] Welles, Diary, [Undated entry for late October or early November, 1848], in the Huntington Library.

[103] Thomas Dowling to Caleb B. Smith, December 8, 1848, in Caleb B. Smith Papers (Division of Manuscripts, Library of Congress).

[104] Coleman, *Crittenden*, I, 306–13; *A Sketch of the Life and Public Services of General Zachary Taylor* . . . (Washington, July, 1848); *Gen. Taylor's Moral, Intellectual, & Professional Character As Drawn by the Hon. John J. Crittenden* [and others] . . . (Washington, 1848); *Reasons Good and True For Supporting the Nomination of General Zachary Taylor* (no place or date of publication).

[105] Taylor to the Adjutant General, May 29, 1848; R. P. Thian, *Notes Illustrating the Military Geography of the United States* . . . (Washington, 1881), 31.

declined because he considered it "undignified" for a presidential candidate to travel about the country attending political meetings.[106] He refrained from making any public dénunciation of the Polk administration and assiduously avoided everything that tended to bring him into hostile collision with it.[107] He was still eager to defeat the Democrats for it was his belief that they would, if continued in office, soon put an end "to our glorious institutions, at any rate to their purity, so much so, they will hardly be worth preserving." [108] Yet personally, he insisted, he had little desire to enter upon the duties of the presidency and declared defeat would bring no mortification. He assured his Democratic son-in-law, Jefferson Davis, that he was much more interested in Davis' political future than in his own and urged him freely to follow that course which his good judgment indicated.[109] As late as August 8 he professed complete indifference toward the outcome of the election and expressed the hope that persons who were displeased by his course in connection with the Whig convention would vote for someone else and even nominate another candidate.[110] This same spirit continued after the election when he disclaimed any feeling of exultation or gratification at his success and declared that he looked upon the presidency "more as a bed of thorns than one of roses." His one satisfaction in the outcome of the election was in the fact that the sovereign people had signally rebuked the Polk administration which he still felt had "resorted to every measure" to break him down when in front

[106] Taylor to J. J. Crittenden, September 23, 1848, in New York Historical Society.

[107] *Id.* to J. M. Clayton, October 2, 1848, in Clayton Papers.

[108] *Id.* to J. J. Crittenden, September 23, 1848, in New York Historical Society.

[109] *Id.* to Jefferson Davis, July 10, 1848, in Rowland (ed.), *Jefferson Davis, Constitutionalist,* I, 208–10. Davis supported Cass but spoke so highly of Taylor as a man and a soldier that some Democrats accused him of actually working for Taylor's election.

[110] *Id.* to R. T. Allison, August 8, 1848, in *Letters from the Battlefields,* 164–65.

of the enemy, and to destroy him "by the vilest slanders of the most unprincipled demagogues this or any other nation ever was cursed with," and had pursued him with the relentlessness of bloodhounds.[111]

It may be that Taylor's claimed indifference as to the outcome of the election and his frequently declared preference for private life did not express his true feelings. Few persons could be as disinterested in the presidency as Taylor claimed to be. Yet, unless one wishes to maintain that he "doth protest too much," the consistency with which he held to this position is almost convincing. Moreover, his statements have a ring of sincerity to them that make it difficult to believe that his political reticence was merely a pose. He seems to have been entirely ready to leave the whole question to the decision of the people.

In 1848, for the first time in the nation's history, in accordance with the congressional act of 1845, the presidential electors were chosen in all states on the same day —November 7, the Tuesday after the first Monday. In South Carolina, where the old method of selection was followed, the state legislature made the choice. In every other state the people went to the polls and cast their ballots for electors pledged to Taylor, Cass, or Van Buren. The electromagnetic telegraph, successfully demonstrated by S. F. B. Morse four years before, flashed the returns to the waiting populace and by Friday the outcome was clear—Old Rough and Ready was again victorious.

He received 1,360,099 popular votes to 1,220,544 for Cass and 291,263 for Van Buren. Of the electoral votes he received 163 and the Democratic candidate 127. In the North, Taylor carried four of the New England states and New York, New Jersey, and Pennsylvania. Of the slave states, Delaware, Maryland, North Carolina, Georgia, Florida, Louisiana, Tennessee, and Kentucky gave him their votes. His margin of victory was much narrower than

[111] *Id.* to R. C. Wood, December 10, 1848, *ibid.*, 167.

had been anticipated at the time of his nomination. Had the election been held a year earlier it seems probable that General Taylor would have been swept into office by an overwhelming vote, but by November, 1848, more than a year and a half had elapsed since his final victory at Buena Vista and the Taylor fever had nearly burned itself out. Moreover, his nomination by the Whigs and his loss of the fight to remain an independent candidate cost him much of his early bipartisan support. Only in the South did he draw many votes from the Democrats.[112] These enabled him to carry Georgia and Louisiana, two states lost by Clay, the Whig candidate in 1844. But this was not important to his success, for he could have lost both of these states and still have won the election. His success was due to his ability to hold nearly the full Whig strength and to carry New York and Pennsylvania in addition. The loss of either of these states would have meant defeat in the election. Whatever the outcome might have been in New York in a contest between Taylor and Cass, with Van Buren in the field Taylor was the easy victor. In Pennsylvania the Free-Soil party was not a controlling factor. There Taylor won because he received the support of the Native Americans and of the coal and iron interests.[113] The one state lost by Taylor, but carried by the Whig candidate four years earlier, was Ohio in which the strong antislavery objections to a Southern planter could not be overcome in spite of strenuous campaigning by Thomas Corwin, Thomas Ewing, William H. Seward, and other Whig speakers from Ohio and near-by states.[114]

112 James F. Cooper to Howell Cobb, November 11, 1848, in U. B. Phillips (ed.), *The Correspondence of Robert Toombs, Alexander H. Stephens and Howell Cobb,* in American Historical Association, *Annual Report, 1911,* Vol. II (Washington, 1913), 137; *The Campaign,* No. 26 (April 11, 1849), 401.

113 James Buchanan to George Bancroft, December 11, 1848, in J. B. Moore (ed.), *The Works of James Buchanan* (Philadelphia, 1908–1911), XI, 480.

114 William Bebb to J. J. Crittenden, November 24, 1848, in Crittenden Papers.

Old Rough and Ready had been victorious in another campaign, but victory did not bring him peace. Instead it brought him sixteen months of tiresome struggle with the burdens and cares of an office he had not sought and for which he had no liking. It brought him discouragement, disillusionment, and death.

Chapter XIV

THE SPOILS OF VICTORY

AT the close of January, 1849, General Zachary Taylor resigned from the United States Army in which he had served for forty years, bade farewell to his neighbors, and started for Washington. To the people of Baton Rouge and vicinity who gathered on the grounds of his home to wish him success he spoke briefly:

> Gentlemen, I can assure you it is with feelings of no ordinary character that I meet with my fellow citizens on this occasion, many of whom I have been associated with for more than a quarter of a century. Had I consulted my own wishes, I should have preferred to retain the office I am now about to vacate, and remained among you; but the people have, without any solicitation, seen fit to elevate me to another, and although I fear I am not qualified to discharge the great and important duties imposed upon me, yet be assured, fellow citizens, I shall endeavor to fulfill them without regard to fear, favor, or affection for any one.
>
> Permit me, my friends, at parting, to invoke God's blessing upon you all, and may He grant that you and your families may enjoy a long life and prosperity—Farewell.[1]

Up the Mississippi to his plantation where he tarried a few days, on to Memphis, Nashville, Louisville, and Frankfort traveled the President-elect—the hero of Buena Vista. Governors, mayors, legislators, politicians, and great crowds of plain citizens cheered him on his way. Taylor was naturally in a friendly mood and he met the crowds cheerfully, shook hands until exhausted, kissed the ladies,

[1] New York *Weekly Tribune,* February 10, 1849.

greeted the children, and responded briefly to the speeches of welcome. He thanked the crowds for their generous greetings, praised the gallant soldiers who had made possible his military victories, assured the people that he had not sought the presidency but would serve them faithfully with an eye single to the interests of the whole country, promised them that errors and mistakes would be those of the head and not of the heart, and besought their continued indulgent and generous interpretation of his acts. At Memphis he reasserted his opposition to war and stated his conviction that "he was the greatest public benefactor who could preserve peace, with the least human sacrifice." At Nashville, in a somewhat different mood, he declared, "we are emphatically a nation of soldiers. . . . The duty of defending the country is calculated as the first a freeman should learn, and the last he should forget." [2]

Mrs. Taylor did not accompany her husband on his triumphal journey. In order to escape the cheering crowds for which she had neither strength nor inclination, she traveled to the national capital by a more southern route in the company of Colonel Bliss, who by his marriage to Betty Taylor in early December had become the General's son-in-law as well as his indispensable adjutant. Taylor's immediate party included Balie Peyton, A. C. Bullitt of the New Orleans *Picayune*, Judah P. Benjamin and several other Louisiana politicians, Major R. S. Garnett who had been a member of his staff in Mexico, and Dr. Charles McCormick, army surgeon. In addition, he was accompanied by such a throng of curious and enthusiastic supporters that at times two boats were lashed together to accommodate the crowd.[3]

At Louisville, Taylor's reception was especially enthusiastic. The streets were one mass of human beings while windows and roofs of near-by buildings were crammed

[2] *Ibid.*, February 24, 1849.

[3] Louisville *Weekly Courier*, February 10 and 17, 1849; Taylor to R. C. Wood, December 10, 1848, in *Letters from the Battlefields*, 169.

with spectators. Here he not only participated in the public events but took time to visit with his sister and other relatives whom he had not seen since 1840 when he was last in that city. At Frankfort he was received by his friend Crittenden, who had but recently assumed the office of Governor of the state, and by the two houses of the legislature which held brief ceremonies in his honor.[4]

From the Kentucky capital Taylor and his party continued their journey by boat to Madison, Indiana; Cincinnati, Ohio; and Wheeling, Virginia. At Madison the General fell on the wharf and painfully injured his side, but insisted upon proceeding according to schedule. Fifteen miles below Wheeling the steamer was completely blocked by ice and the presidential party had to transfer to sleighs. At Wheeling, Taylor boarded the "cars," the Baltimore and Ohio Railroad, and proceeded over the mountains, on to Baltimore, and to the national capital.[5]

The President-elect arrived in Washington about eight-thirty on Friday evening, February 23, the anniversary of the victory of Buena Vista. He was welcomed by an immense, cheering crowd which escorted him through the streets to Willard's Hotel where Mrs. Taylor, Betty, and Colonel Bliss awaited him.[6] One young member of the crowd wrote to his sister the next day:

> Well, Old Zach has come at last and I suppose no one ever met with a more cordial reception than our citizens gave him last night. I hurried over my supper and started out of the door, and directly I was out of it I heard a hum all around me, as of a great many people. I hurried on to Penn. Av. and saw

[4] Louisville *Weekly Courier,* February 10 and 17, 1849; Frankfort *Daily Commonwealth,* February 15, 1849.

[5] Frankfort *Daily Commonwealth,* February 19, 1849; New York *Weekly Tribune,* February 24, 1849. Today the line from Frederick, Maryland, to Washington, D.C., normally eliminates Baltimore from such an itinerary, but this line had not been constructed in 1849 and Taylor necessarily passed through that city.

[6] Washington *Daily Union,* February 23 and 24, 1849; Welles, Diary, entry for February 24, 1849, in the Huntington Library.

thousands of persons hurrying to one spot, viz, the depot; I of course joined in and such hurrahing, and pushing and knocking down, I never saw before. We at last arrived at the depot and there we saw every description of fireworks, & firearms waiting for the whistle of the cars, to be let off.

Nearly two hours later when Taylor and his party arrived they were welcomed with roaring cannon and flaming Roman candles and skyrockets. Because of the milling, shouting thousands who blocked his way it was another hour before " 'Old Zach' managed to get to the carriage, and then commenced the move for Willard's Hotel; I thought the mob would have torn the horses and carriage into a thousand pieces, some were on the wheels, some *under* them, some had hold of the traces and all were aiming to have a peep at the old Hero."

Finally Taylor reached Willard's where another throng awaited him. With difficulty he made his way into the hotel for a brief rest before reappearing to greet the enthusiastic crowd. Vividly the young correspondent continued:

The General was so much fatigued, he couldn't come out for some time but when he did come, the shout that rent the air and continued for ten minutes would have drowned the roar of the cannon of "Buena Vista." At length he raised his hand, and you could then have heard the fall of a pin; I did not think it possible that such uproar could have been changed into such silence in so short a time. He then commenced but was so fatigued and excited, that he could hardly utter a word, and had to stop before he had finished. He is not so ugly as I had expected to see him, but yet cannot be called *handsome;* and although rather low in stature, has as commanding an appearance, as I ever saw.[7]

Tired and worn by the month-long journey from Baton Rouge and the strain of the vigorous reception at Washington, and still suffering from his fall at Madison, Taylor

[7] John Pegrum to Mary E. Pegrum, February 24, 1849, in Brock Collection, Huntington Library.

kept to his rooms over the week end. He was "too much indisposed" to call upon President Polk on Saturday as planned or to receive many friends.[8] One of the few visitors was Daniel Webster, veteran Whig statesman. He spent a half hour with Taylor on Saturday evening and found him "pleasant and social enough and by no means of such a harsh and stern countenance as the pictures represent him." [9] By Monday the General was well enough to receive a congressional committee who officially informed him of his election by the electoral college. Then, accompanied by Jefferson Davis, Senator Clayton, and a few other friends, he made a half-hour call at the White House.[10] The next evening Robert C. Winthrop, Massachusetts congressman, presented him to a group of fifty or sixty invited friends, including many Whig leaders.[11] On Thursday evening he was the guest of honor at a White House dinner given by President and Mrs. Polk. Among the thirty or forty other guests were Millard Fillmore, Colonel and Mrs. Bliss, Jefferson Davis, Judah P. Benjamin and a few other Louisiana associates of Taylor, his friend Senator John Bell of Tennessee and Mrs. Bell, Justice John Catron of the Supreme Court and Mrs. Catron, the Cabinet members and their wives, and Lewis Cass, the defeated presidential candidate. Politics were strictly avoided and Polk thought the dinner passed off well.[12] Most of Taylor's time during these days before inauguration was spent in receiving crowds of visitors and in conferring with Whig leaders about Cabinet appointments and to some extent about his brief inaugural address.[13]

8 Washington *Daily Union,* February 25, 1849; Polk, *Diary,* IV, 351.

9 Van Tyne (ed.), *Letters of Daniel Webster,* 374–75.

10 Washington *Daily Union,* February 27, 1849; Polk, *Diary,* IV, 352–53.

11 Robert C. Winthrop to J. M. Clayton, [February 26, 1849], in Clayton Papers.

12 Polk *Diary,* IV, 358–59; Washington *Daily Union,* March 2, 1849.

13 Washington *Daily Union,* March 1 and 2, 1849; Frederic Bancroft, *The Life of William H. Seward* (New York, 1900), I, 207.

As the fourth of March fell on Sunday, it was Monday, March 5, when Zachary Taylor was inaugurated. Whether he was President before he took the oath of office or whether Senator David R. Atchison, president pro tempore of the Senate, was "President for a Single Day" or whether there was no President for that day is a constitutional question of little practical importance. The issue was not raised at the time for no problems demanded immediate attention and neither Taylor nor Atchison attempted to act. Only in recent years has the controversy developed. The most thorough defense of Atchison's claim falls just short of being convincing. If anyone was President from Sunday noon to Monday noon, it was Taylor. He could not "enter upon the execution of his office" until he took the required oath, but if an emergency had required action, he could quickly have taken the oath and performed the necessary acts.[14]

A raw wind blew from the east. Overhead was a gloomy, snow-spitting sky. An imposing procession headed by President Taylor in an open carriage drawn by four gray horses and escorted by a bodyguard of one hundred horsemen left Willard's and advanced up Pennsylvania Avenue. At the Irving Hotel the outgoing President joined Taylor, and side by side they rode to the capitol. There, from a specially erected platform in front of the east portico, and before thirty thousand persons, one of the largest of in-

[14] George H. Haynes, in his note "President of the United States for a Single Day," in *American Historical Review,* XXX (1924–1925), 308–10, contends that Atchison was not President. Theodore C. Atchison, in "David R. Atchison: A Study in American Politics," in *Missouri Historical Review,* XXIV (1929–1930), 502–15, takes the opposite view. The chief weaknesses in the latter's position seem to be two: (1) it is not clear how the president *pro tempore* elected by the Senate of the second session of the Thirtieth Congress could hold that office beyond the life of that Congress which the author of the article recognizes as expiring at midnight of March 3; (2) if each President's term expires at midnight of March 3, as contended, then on every inauguration day prior to the passage of the Presidential Succession Act in 1886, the same situation existed and the president *pro tempore* of the Senate was President of the United States for some twelve hours. His assumption, however, seems to be that this situation existed only in 1849.

auguration crowds,[15] Taylor read his inaugural address and took the oath of office administered by Chief Justice Roger B. Taney.[16] In a tone almost inaudible and, thought Polk, "very badly as to his pronunciation and manner," Taylor declared the principles that would control his administration:

> . . . I am conscious that the position which I have been called to fill . . . is surrounded by fearful responsibilities. Happily, however, . . . I shall not be without able cooperation . . . . it shall be my endeavor to call to my assistance . . . individuals whose talents, integrity, and purity of character will furnish ample guaranties for the faithful and honorable performance of the trusts to be committed to their charge . . . . my guide will be the Constitution. . . . For the interpretation of that instrument I shall look to the decisions of the judicial tribunals established by its authority and to the practice of the Government under the earlier Presidents, who had so large a share in its formation . . . . abstain from entangling alliances with foreign nations . . . . [seek] the cultivation of peaceful and friendly relations with all other powers . . . . exhaust every resort of honorable diplomacy before appealing to arms. In the conduct of our foreign relations I shall conform to these views. . . . So far as it is possible to be informed, I shall make honesty, capacity, and fidelity indispensable prerequisites to the bestowal of office, and the absence of either of these qualities shall be deemed sufficient cause for removal.
>
> It shall be my study to recommend such constitutional measures to Congress as may be necessary and proper to secure encouragement and protection to the great interests of agriculture, commerce, and manufactures, to improve our rivers and harbors, to provide for the speedy extinguishment of the public debt, to enforce a strict accountability on the part of all officers of the Government and the utmost economy in all public expenditures; but it is for the wisdom of Congress itself . . . to regulate these and other matters of domestic policy. I shall look with confidence to the enlightened patriotism of that body to

[15] Washington *Daily Union,* March 6, 1849.
[16] Polk, *Diary,* IV, 374–75; Poore, *Reminiscences,* I, 353–54.

Courtesy of the Library of Congress

VIEW OF THE CAPITOL AT WASHINGTON, 1850

adopt such measures of conciliation as may harmonize conflicting interests and tend to perpetuate that Union which should be the paramount object of our hopes and affections. . . .

In conclusion I congratulate you, my fellow-citizens, upon the high state of prosperity to which the goodness of Divine Providence has conducted our common country. Let us invoke a continuance of the same protecting care . . . and let us seek to deserve that continuance. . . .[17]

While the cannon roared and the people cheered, President Taylor and former President Polk re-entered the carriage and together rode down Pennsylvania Avenue to the latter's hotel. There Polk took his leave, and Taylor went on to the White House.[18] That evening he visited briefly the two inauguration balls, one at Jackson Hall, the other in a large new ballroom on Judiciary Square near the City Hall. In spite of a ten-dollar admission charge this hall was packed by three thousand celebrating Whigs. A future president who attended the latter ball was Abraham Lincoln, ardent supporter of Taylor in the election campaign and one of the congressional managers of the ball. Lincoln seems to have enjoyed the affair far more than did the guest of honor, for he remained until three or four o'clock in the morning.[19]

Taylor's first task as President was the nomination of the men who were to head the executive departments and constitute his Cabinet. This problem had naturally received his attention for months, and most of the selections had been made by inauguration day. Several last-minute changes and one addition were made, however, and only on March 6 was his official family completed. The addi-

[17] Richardson, *Messages and Papers of the Presidents,* V, 4–6.

[18] Polk, *Diary,* IV, 375.

[19] Washington *Daily Union,* March 7, 1849; Charles O. Paullin, "Abraham Lincoln in Congress, 1847–1849," in *Journal of the Illinois State Historical Society* (Springfield), XIV (1921–1922), 88; New York *Weekly Tribune,* March 17, 1849.

tion was necessitated by one of the last acts of the Polk administration, an act of March 3, creating the Home Department, soon to be known as the Department of the Interior. The list of nominations sent to the Senate read: John M. Clayton, senator from Delaware, to be Secretary of State; William Meredith, a Pennsylvania lawyer, to be Secretary of the Treasury; George Crawford, former governor of Georgia, to be Secretary of War; William Ballard Preston, congressman from Virginia, to be Secretary of the Navy; Reverdy Johnson, senator from Maryland, to be Attorney General; Jacob Collamer, congressman from Vermont, to be Postmaster General; and Thomas Ewing, veteran Whig politician of Ohio, to be Secretary of the Home Department. These appointments were promptly approved by the Senate and within a few days all had entered upon their duties.[20]

The task of selecting his Cabinet had given Taylor much trouble. He knew personally very few of the many party leaders who were potential Cabinet members; therefore, he had to rely for the most part upon information and advice from his friends. This he did reluctantly, for he much preferred not to be dependent upon the judgment of others, even though they were his friends.[21] So troubled was he by this, the first phase of the much-dreaded patronage problem, that a few weeks after the election he vainly wished he could put the presidency in other hands and have nothing further to do with it.[22] "My troubles & trials have commenced," he wrote to Dr. Wood early in December; "every mail which reaches here are [*sic*] filled with applications for office & those connected with me, are particularly anxious." He could not entertain applications from relatives, he continued, nor in fact from others for to do so would break him down in less

20 *Senate Journal,* 30 Cong., 3 Sess.

21 A. T. Burnley to J. J. Crittenden, January 12, 1849 [misdated 1848], in Crittenden Papers.

22 Hitchcock, *Fifty Years in Camp and Field,* 348.

than six months. "I am no[t] going into office for the purpose of proscribing people for opinion sake," he insisted, "but to be the president of the country— There will be no doubt many who will have to go, for good & sufficient causes, which I very much regret, & wish there was no necessity for removing any one." [23]

In spite of his desire to be the president of the whole nation rather than of a party Taylor early decided, even before leaving Mexico, that if elected he would form a cabinet entirely of Whigs. Democrats would not be proscribed, but his official advisers would be Whigs.[24] Before leaving Louisiana he decided that his Cabinet must be "harmonious, honorable, patriotic, talented & *hard working* . . . [and] of irreproachable private character." By this time he had also pretty well determined upon the geographical distribution of the members. He favored one each from New England, Pennsylvania, Delaware, Georgia, one from Virginia or North Carolina, and one from Kentucky or Tennessee.[25] As Taylor left Baton Rouge for Washington the individuals most definitely in his mind were Crittenden, Preston, Crawford, and Horace Binney of Philadelphia, whom he favored for the treasury post. But only Crittenden, the one man in whom Taylor had complete confidence, had been offered a place—presumably any place he wanted.[26] Taylor knew there was doubt whether his friend would accept, but he still had hopes and was much chagrined and disappointed when he reached Frankfort and learned of Crittenden's decision not to serve. What reason he gave Taylor is not known, but Crittenden apparently felt he ought not to abandon so soon the office to which the people of Kentucky had elected

[23] Taylor to R. C. Wood, December 10, 1848, in *Letters from the Battlefields,* 168–69.

[24] *Id.* to J. J. Crittenden, May 15, 1847, in Crittenden Papers; *id.* to *id.,* July 1, 1848, in Coleman, *Crittenden,* I, 316.

[25] A. T. Burnley to J. J. Crittenden, January 12, 1849, in Crittenden Papers.

[26] *Ibid.*

him, and also believed that by remaining out of the Cabinet he would be in a better position to conciliate the Clay Whigs who were still bitter because their idol had been shoved aside.[27]

Crittenden's decision not to become a member of Taylor's Cabinet was a serious blow to the General's administration. All sections of the country had confidence in the Kentucky statesman and there was almost unanimous agreement that he should have a leading place in the new administration. The very fact of his decision not to hold office under the man he had done so much to make President weakened Taylor's position, and his absence from the Cabinet left that body too weak to hold the respect of the country. Moreover, his absence left Taylor without a close friend in his Cabinet to whom he could turn in time of trouble. Had Crittenden accepted the Secretaryship of State, many of the difficulties of Taylor's administration might have been avoided. The American people who had elected Taylor had every right to expect that Crittenden, one of the earliest, firmest, and most influential of the advocates of Taylor for President, would help guide the administration through the storms which everyone realized were ahead. No one stated this more clearly than Alexander H. Stephens. Early in February he wrote to Crittenden insisting that he must take the head of Taylor's Cabinet. "It is a matter about which you can not hesitate—you owe it to him—to yourself—to your friends and to the country—I tell you the 'crisis' Requires it—those who took the Responsibility of advocating the nomination and election of General Taylor must not *flinch* from the equal and perhaps greater Responsibility of standing by and defending his administration." [28] Al-

[27] John M. Clayton to J. J. Crittenden, December 13, 1848, in Crittenden Papers; Thomas B. Stevenson to Caleb B. Smith, February 16, 1849, in Caleb B. Smith Papers; John D. Defrees to Caleb B. Smith, February 18, 1849, *ibid.*

[28] Alexander H. Stephens to J. J. Crittenden, February 6, 1849, in Crittenden Papers.

though Crittenden did flinch, the responsibility was his and he could not escape it. The blame for the shortcomings of Taylor's brief term must rest in part upon his head.

Crittenden was, nevertheless, interested in the success of Taylor's administration and continued to exert some influence upon it. His influence, however, was indirect and far less important than it would have been had he been at the head of the Cabinet. He steadfastly refused to go personally to Washington, though at various critical times Whig leaders urged him to do so. Apparently he also refrained from writing to the President. However, he was in constant correspondence with Taylor's Secretary of State who leaned heavily upon his advice,[29] and from time to time he made known his views through Kentucky politicians who visited the capital carrying full instructions from him.[30] Moreover, his friend and secretary, Orlando Brown, went to Washington to become Commissioner of Indian Affairs, and through him Crittenden kept in close touch with the President. As Brown entered upon his new duties Crittenden urged him to avail himself of every opportunity to cultivate "the acquaintance, the friendship, and the confidence of General Taylor." "I desire this," wrote Crittenden, "for your sake, for his sake, and for the sake of the country. Such relations with him will be honorable to you, and will, I am certain, be useful to him . . . . he will be glad to have some one with whom he may *talk* outside of the cold, formal limits of the cabinet. That's as *natural* as the desire to break out of prison. You are exactly the man to occupy that relation with him, all circumstances favor it, and nothing but negligence, or something worse, will prevent your falling into that posi-

[29] The correspondence between Crittenden and Clayton is in the papers of the two men in the Division of Manuscripts, Library of Congress.

[30] J. J. Crittenden to J. M. Clayton, July 20, 1849, in Clayton Papers; *id.* to Thomas Ewing, June 4, 1849, in Ewing Papers (Division of Manuscripts, Library of Congress).

tion." [31] Already known to Taylor as a member of an old Louisville family and as a warm supporter with whom he had had a pleasant and confidential correspondence shortly after his return from Mexico, Orlando Brown had no difficulty establishing the cordial relationship that Crittenden suggested. Although Taylor talked frankly and confidentially with Brown, he made him a confidant and not an adviser. This fact, added to Brown's failure to obtain any real influence with the members of the Cabinet, greatly lessened his value to Crittenden and further proved that only at the head of the Cabinet could the latter make a real contribution to the success of the administration.[32]

While in Kentucky en route to Washington, Taylor discussed Cabinet appointments quite fully with Crittenden, but the latter's refusal to serve so mortified the President-elect that it may be doubted whether he was much influenced by his friend's counsel. Crittenden's "judgment and heart were set upon the appointment" of Robert P. Letcher, former governor of Kentucky, whom he urged upon General Taylor with considerable insistence for the office of Postmaster General. On the ground that he had already offered to Kentucky a Cabinet post which had been declined, Taylor turned a deaf ear to this plea.[33]

Upon Governor Crittenden's refusal to take a place in the Cabinet, General Taylor telegraphed an invitation to Senator John M. Clayton of Delaware to become his Secretary of State.[34] Crittenden was thoroughly in favor of Clayton's appointment [35] and doubtless urged it, but Taylor was already favorably inclined toward Clayton before leaving Louisiana. Clayton had steadfastly defended the

[31] *Id.* to Orlando Brown, July 3, 1849, in Coleman, Crittenden, I, 340–43.

[32] Orlando Brown to J. J. Crittenden, June 23 and 27, 1849, and April 19, 1850, in Crittenden Papers; Poage, *Henry Clay and the Whig Party,* 187–88.

[33] J. J. Crittenden to J. M. Clayton, February 17, 1849, in Clayton Papers.

[34] James C. Hall to *id.,* February 16, 1849, *ibid.*

[35] J. J. Crittenden to *id.,* November 14 and December 19, 1848, *ibid.;* J. M. Clayton to J. J. Crittenden, December 13, 1848, in Crittenden Papers.

General when his terms of capitulation at Monterrey were under fire in the Senate in February, 1847, and had again spoken in his behalf on the Senate floor in the summer of 1848.[36] Taylor appreciated these efforts and was more than ready to have him as a member of his official family.[37] Clayton was a brilliant lawyer with twenty years of experience in national politics and was supported for the first place in Taylor's Cabinet by many Whig politicians.[38] Yet, at least two important Taylor supporters, Robert Toombs and Truman Smith, were firmly opposed to his selection. When the administration was only a few weeks old Toombs characterized Clayton's appointment as a "fatal step," and spoke of exceedingly numerous complaints against him from Taylor's firmest and most loyal friends.[39] Smith was reported as saying about the same time, "if Genl. Taylor only knew what I know of that rascal he would go straight from his house to the State Department and kick his backsides out, and tell him to be gone forever." [40] What information Smith had about Clayton is not clear, but it may have concerned his excessive use of alcohol, for it was Smith's opinion that Clayton was "fast using himself up" by very heavy drinking.[41] There is no clear evidence to support this charge, but Clayton's death a few years later from kidney disease at least raises a suspicion that Smith was right. Why he did not pass on to the President this information, or any other information he had about Clayton, is also unexplained.

[36] *Congressional Globe,* 29 Cong., 2 Sess., 315–18; *ibid.,* 30 Cong., 1 Sess., 898–99.

[37] William D. Perisson to J. M. Clayton, December 3, 1848, and Henry A. Steele to *id.,* December 22, 1848, in Clayton Papers.

[38] Alexander H. Stephens to J. J. Crittenden, December 6, 1848, in Crittenden Papers; James Buchanan to George Bancroft, January 8, 1849, in Moore (ed.), *Works of James Buchanan,* XI, 482–83.

[39] Robert Toombs to Mrs. Chapman Coleman, June 22, 1849, in Crittenden Papers.

[40] Gideon Welles, Diary, entry for June 12, 1849, in the Huntington Library.

[41] *Ibid.*

Nor is it clear that knowledge that his Secretary of State was a heavy drinker would have caused Taylor to "kick his backsides out." Although Taylor was presented during the campaign as one who never touched alcohol,[42] he served wine frequently, if not regularly, at his dinner table and kept a good supply of whiskey at his headquarters.[43] Certainly he was opposed, however, to anything like drunkenness and would not have tolerated that in a Cabinet member.

As Taylor left Kentucky for Washington he still favored Binney for the Treasury and Crawford for the War Department, and apparently he had decided upon Abbott Lawrence of Massachusetts for Secretary of the Navy.[44] He made no offers other than the one to Clayton, however, until he reached the capital. There his selection of Crawford and Lawrence met with approval, but his Secretary of State, who for two months had been looking for the proper Pennsylvanian to be Secretary of the Treasury, persuaded Taylor to appoint William Meredith instead of Horace Binney.[45] Crawford and Meredith accepted, but Lawrence declined, ostensibly on the ground of health but probably because he desired to head the Treasury Department.[46] Taylor then selected for the Navy post William Ballard Preston whom he had been planning to name as his Attorney General but who some of his advisers declared would look like a fool in the Supreme Court alongside such men as Webster and Reverdy Johnson.[47]

42 *Gen. Taylor's Moral, Intellectual, & Professional Character, as Drawn by the Hon. John J. Crittenden* [and others] . . . , 2, 4.

43 Taylor to J. P. Taylor, March 27, 1847, in Taylor Papers; C. F. Hoffman, *A Winter in the Far West* (London, 1835), II, 8.

44 Thomas B. Stevenson to Caleb B. Smith, February 16, 1849, in Caleb B. Smith Papers.

45 Poore, *Reminiscences,* 351; John M. Clayton to William Meredith, February 28, 1849, in Meredith Papers (Historical Society of Pennsylvania); Washington *Daily Union,* June 10, 1849.

46 Poore, *Reminiscences,* 350; Washington *Daily Union,* March 6, 1849; William R. Lawrence (ed.), *Extracts from the Diary and Correspondence of the Late Amos Lawrence* (Boston, 1855), 266–67.

47 Poore, *Reminiscences,* 352.

Courtesy of the Library of Congress

PRESIDENT TAYLOR, VICE-PRESIDENT FILLMORE AND THE CABINET

Top Row: Zachary Taylor, President; Millard Fillmore, Vice-President. Center row: William M. Meredith, Secretary of the Treasury; John M. Clayton, Secretary of State; George W. Crawford, Secretary of War. Bottom row: Reverdy Johnson, Attorney General; Jacob Collamer, Postmaster General; William Ballard Preston, Secretary of the Navy.

The second of these outstanding Whig lawyers, Johnson, was then called upon to take the Attorney Generalship. The Ohio Whigs strongly supported Thomas Ewing for a Cabinet place. He was at one stage slated to be Postmaster General,[48] but when the Home Department was created and Truman Smith declined that post,[49] Ewing was transferred to the new department and Jacob Collamer was appointed Postmaster General. What influence, other than Taylor's desire to have a New Englander in his Cabinet, led to his selection is not evident. He, like Johnson, Ewing, and Meredith, was the selection of Clayton and other Whig leaders in Washington rather than of Taylor himself.

When on March 7 Taylor's Cabinet appointments became known, there was considerable surprise and some feeling that a group of greater strength might have been formed. The absence of Clay, Webster, Crittenden, and Lawrence was noted.[50] Taylor had, of course, sought the services of the two latter without success. Although Clay had endeavored to maintain friendly relations with the General,[51] Taylor could hardly invite into his Cabinet one who had refused to the very end to support his candidacy. Moreover, in the circumstances, Clay could scarcely have accepted such an invitation had it been given. In view of Webster's support, tardy and reluctant though it was, Taylor might have offered him a place. Yet nothing less than the first place could have been offered, and that seemed rightfully to belong to someone whose support had been

48 William Bebb to J. J. Crittenden, November 24, 1848, in Crittenden Papers; Memorial signed by forty-one members of the Ohio Legislature, February 6, 1849, in Clayton Papers; Washington *Daily Union,* March 2, 1849.

49 William H. Seward to J. M. Clayton [undated, but some time late in February or early in March, 1849], in Clayton Papers; Washington *Daily Union,* March 23, 1849.

50 John F. Crampton to Palmerston, March 18, 1849, in Public Record Office, Foreign Office 5:498 (Library of Congress Photostats); Colton (ed.), *Works of Henry Clay,* V, 586.

51 Taylor to Henry Clay, November 17, 1848, in Colton (ed.), *Works of Henry Clay,* V, 580–81; Louisville *Chronicle,* February 1, 1849.

more enthusiastic. Moreover, because of Webster's vigorous antislavery views, his appointment would have been displeasing to Southern Whigs and would have deprived Taylor of much of their support. The absence of these party leaders from the Cabinet may be explained, but the fact remains that without them Taylor was severely handicapped. This was clearly evident to Sir Henry Bulwer when he arrived some months later to represent the British government in Washington. He early reported to the Foreign Office "the administration does not contain any of the great leaders of the Whig Party, and consequently has not that confidence in itself nor that authority over others which would give it the energy necessary to stem any strong current of public opinion." [52]

Almost from the day he entered upon his new duties until his death sixteen months later, President Taylor had Cabinet trouble. This was due in part to want of competent leadership. Taylor was so inexperienced that he could not furnish it himself, and it quickly became apparent that neither Clayton nor any other member of the Cabinet could do so. Indeed, by November, Clayton's standing was so low with his colleagues that Robert P. Letcher, who was in Washington as Crittenden's confidential representative trying to prevent a collapse of the Cabinet, reported that every member of the Cabinet wanted Clayton out.[53] Even before that Clayton had offered to resign if Crittenden would take his place, but the latter still refused.[54] It was Taylor's own inexperience that led to the widespread report that he regarded his Cabinet as a sort of executive junto, that he had one vote like every other member of the Cabinet and was governed by the majority vote of that group even when it ran counter to his own

[52] Sir Henry Bulwer to Palmerston, January 6, 1850, in P.R.O., F.O. 5:511 (Library of Congress Photostats).

[53] Robert P. Letcher to J. J. Crittenden, November 17, 1849, in Coleman, *Crittenden,* I, 348–50.

[54] J. J. Crittenden to J. M. Clayton, July 20, 1849, in Clayton Papers.

opinions and convictions.[55] Taylor necessarily relied upon the advice of his counselors to a greater degree than more experienced executives had been accustomed to do, but not to the extent that the opposition charged. In spite of the efforts of Taylor's friends to kill the idea that his was a Cabinet administration and to picture him as the active, moving, energetic cause of all things,[56] the charge that "the cabinet is the president" persisted and made that body especially vulnerable to attack.

Taylor's Cabinet difficulties were also due in part to the split in the Whig party. Never a homogeneous or united party, by 1849 it was so sharply divided over the slavery question that only the most skillful leadership could have maintained a measure of harmony. The Whigs had quite successfully evaded the slavery issue during the campaign but they could not do so indefinitely. Although his Cabinet contained four members from the slave states to only three from the North, Taylor soon fell under the influence of the antislavery wing of the party and lost the support of the Southern Whigs. Robert Toombs, one of Taylor's strongest supporters in the South at the time of his inauguration, declared a year later that the chief cause for the alienation of the Southern Whigs was the fact that during the summer of 1849 the Cabinet "threw the *entire patronage* of the North into the hands of Seward and his party," and thus gave Seward control of the New York Whig organization, forced the whole Northern Whig party into the extreme antislavery position of Seward, and "sacked the South." [57] Although Seward's control was not so complete as Toombs charged, he had an important influence which he obtained at the very outset of the ad-

[55] Welles, Diary, May 26, 1849, in the Huntington Library; J. J. Crittenden to J. M. Clayton, July 8, 1849, in Clayton Papers; Washington *Daily Union,* May 22 and 26, June 8, 21, and 27, and July 24, 1849.

[56] J. J. Crittenden to J. M. Clayton, July 8, 1849, in Clayton Papers; Nathan Sargent to J. J. Crittenden, July 15, 1849, in Crittenden Papers.

[57] Robert Toombs to J. J. Crittenden, April 25, 1850, in Coleman, *Crittenden,* I, 364–66.

ministration. During the winter of 1848 while in Baltimore on professional business, Seward established cordial relations with Colonel Joseph P. Taylor who was stationed there, and immediately upon the President-elect's arrival in Washington gained a place as one of his advisers.[58] During the last days of Polk's administration Seward conferred with Taylor on pending legislation for the organization of California and carried the views of the incoming President to other party leaders. At first President Taylor was inclined to be guided in the matter of New York appointments by the wishes of Seward's rival, Vice-President Fillmore; but within a few weeks, partly through Thurlow Weed's intervention and partly through Seward's own success in establishing friendly, and in some instances confidential, relations with every member of Taylor's Cabinet except Crawford, the New York senator obtained a large influence in all questions of patronage.[59] Such a situation led Toombs to regard the Northern members of the Cabinet as "odious" and Clayton as "a dead body tied to the concern." [60]

Not only did the Whigs from the lower South withhold support from the administration, but so also did Clay and Webster. Leading Taylor Whigs had urged Crittenden to prevent the election of Clay to fill Crittenden's unexpired term in the Senate because they were confident that his policy would be rule or ruin. But Crittenden, long a friend of Clay, and eager to reunite the party, did not interfere in his election.[61] Although President Taylor appointed Clay's son, James B. Clay, to the post of chargé

[58] Bancroft, *Seward,* I, 206–207; Van Tyne (ed.), *Letters of Daniel Webster,* 376–78.

[59] Washington *Daily Union,* April 3 and 5, and June 3 and 7, 1849; Poage, *Henry Clay and the Whig Party,* 184–86; and numerous communications in the papers of Clayton, Meredith, and Ewing.

[60] Robert Toombs to J. J. Crittenden, April 25, 1850, in Coleman, *Crittenden,* I, 364–66.

[61] *Id.* to *id.,* December 3, 1848; Reverdy Johnson to *id.,* December 12, 1848; William L. Dayton to *id.,* December 14, 1848; all in Crittenden Papers.

d'affaires in Portugal no real reconciliation between the Clay and the Taylor Whigs could be made. When Congress met in December the inability of the Whigs to work together was immediately evident, and as the months passed the President and his Cabinet found themselves virtually an administration without a party. It was even reported that some Whig congressmen were ready to absent themselves when "strength is needed to pass the appropriation Bills that Gen. T. may have practical evidence that his cabinet are friendless." [62]

President Taylor's Cabinet troubles were due in part also to the difficulties of the patronage problem. If, as frequently maintained, offices are the force that binds a party together, they may, unless wisely filled, become a source of friction and division. Clearly, unless the friends of persons appointed are more numerous and influential than the supporters of the many disappointed applicants, the administration may be weakened rather than strengthened by its distribution of the spoils of victory. And when a party is split into factions as the Whigs were in 1849, when a President is elected by the support of such divergent interests as Taylor was, the dangers of the patronage question are greatly increased. It was well-nigh impossible to satisfy both the Northern and Southern wings of the party or both factions in such important states as New York and Pennsylvania.

Although Taylor had been elected in part because of his oft-repeated statements that he would not be a party president but the president of the whole country, and that his appointments to office would not be on a partisan basis, few except loyal Whigs received offices at the hands of his administration. Consequently Taylor Democrats were soon alienated,[63] and the regular Democrats seized upon the op-

[62] Theodore Barnett to Caleb Smith, April 24, 1850, in Caleb B. Smith Papers.

[63] Charlston Potts to William Meredith, May 17, 1849, in Meredith Papers

portunity to charge the President with breaking his solemn pledges and instituting a policy far more proscriptive than that of Polk. Day after day during the spring of 1849 Ritchie of the Washington *Daily Union* attacked the administration on this score. After the first of June the attacks became less frequent, yet no less severe. Taylor himself was denounced for incapacity and wanton disregard of his pledges and promises, but the blame was placed mainly on his Cabinet. "A ferocious and proscriptive Ewing" and "a tortuous and unscrupulous Collamer" were singled out for special censure, while the whole Cabinet were condemned as "low-minded, unprincipled, and shameless politicians, who are intent only on revenging themselves upon their enemies, and seizing the 'spoils of victory.' "[64]

While the Democrats decried the partisan policy of the administration, many Whigs loudly and bitterly complained of its timidity in making removals. The demand for office was more widespread than any witnessed since Andrew Jackson's supporters swarmed into Washington twenty years before and it was not easily satisfied. So insistent were many of the office seekers, reported Clayton, that if the President "does not *kick* a man down-stairs he goes away and declares he *promised him* an office."[65] Taylor and the Cabinet did not hurry to sweep the Democrats from office, and many supporters who were kept waiting became unfriendly.[66] Gradually, however, the administration's removal policy was formulated, and Democratic postmasters, public land officers, United States attorneys and marshals, collectors and surveyors of ports, and consuls were forced out to make way for the office-hungry Whigs.

[64] Washington *Daily Union,* May 15, 1849.

[65] J. M. Clayton to J. J. Crittenden, July 11, 1849, in Coleman, *Crittenden,* I, 344.

[66] Governor William F. Johnston to William Meredith, April 30, 1849, in Meredith Papers; James E. Harvey to William Meredith, July 27, 1849, *ibid.;* Philadelphia *Public Ledger,* March 26 and 30, 1849.

Before Taylor's death 540 of the 929 Federal officials whose appointments were made by the President with the advice and consent of the Senate had been removed. No previous administration had displaced so large a number.[67] In addition, thousands of Democratic officers in the departments at Washington and in the Federal offices throughout the country, subordinate officials whose appointments did not require Senate action, gave way to the friends of the administration.

When Congress met in December, 1849, President Taylor's patronage policy was savagely attacked by James W. Bradbury, Democratic senator from Maine. Because Taylor had stated in his inaugural address that want of honesty, capacity, or fidelity would be cause for removal, Bradbury insisted that by implication every man who had been removed was accused of dishonesty, incapacity, or infidelity. Therefore he requested the adoption of a resolution calling upon the President to lay before the Senate "all charges which have been preferred or filed in any of the Departments against individuals who have been removed from office since the 4th day of March last, with a specification of the cases, if any, in which the officers charged have had opportunity to be heard, and a statement of the number of removals made under each Department." Bradbury spoke at length in support of his resolution and charged President Taylor with violation of his pre-election promises and the sacred pledge of his inaugural.[68]

The chief defense of the President was made by Senator Truman Smith who marshaled an array of statistics to prove that so completely had the Democrats dominated the offices at the close of the Polk administration that the removals of Taylor had done no more than equalize the position of the two parties. Not to have done this, claimed

[67] Carl Russell Fish, "Removal of Officials by the Presidents of the United States," in American Historical Association, *Annual Report, 1899* (Washington, 1900), I, 67–86.

[68] *Congressional Globe,* 31 Cong., 1 Sess., 74, 160, Appendix, 47–51.

Smith, would have been proscription of the Whigs, a continuation of the proscriptive policy pursued by the Democrats for twenty years. He also insisted that this policy was in no way inconsistent with Taylor's pre-election promises, chief of which was to make no pledges but to enter the White House untrammeled and free to act as he found best at the time. Moreover, Smith maintained, the President had opposed an extreme policy of removal and had frequently heeded the appeals of Democratic senators for the retention of incumbents.[69]

The long and exhaustive defense by the Connecticut senator was at times almost convincing. Certainly it put the policy of the administration in the best possible light, but it could not remove completely the justice of the charge that removals and appointments were made on a partisan basis and that as President, Taylor was more partisan than his campaign statements had led the people to expect he would be. Bradbury's resolution was debated by the Senate from time to time over a period of six months, but it had not been brought to a vote by the time Taylor's death relegated it to the discard.[70]

Doubtless the Cabinet was in large measure responsible for persuading Taylor to reward his Whig friends, and it was natural for the opposition to attack them on this score. But an additional influence in this direction was that of Thurlow Weed who discussed the matter with the President on several occasions shortly after he took office and convinced him that the overthrow of Democratic supremacy required more than the election of a Whig President and the appointment of a Whig Cabinet. So completely was Taylor won over to the partisan point of view that he declared, as Weed recalled it, "I did not think it either wise, or just to kick away the ladder by which I ascended to the presidency; colonels, majors, captains, lieutenants,

[69] *Ibid.,* Appendix, 480–96.
[70] *Ibid.,* 31 Cong., 1 Sess., 806, 899, 1063, 1081, 1113, 1125, 1130, 1361.

sergeants, and corporals are just as necessary to success in politics as they are to the discipline and efficiency of an army." After one of his conversations with the President on this subject, Weed further reported, the two called at the Treasury Department where Taylor inquired of Secretary Meredith whether "our friends are getting their share of the offices," and urged him to appoint only loyal Whigs.[71]

Taylor by no means relegated all patronage questions to his Cabinet as the Democratic press charged.[72] Many appointments must perforce have been left to department heads, but there is abundant evidence that the President took an active interest in others. He personally conferred with applicants for office and with congressmen who came to plead their cause, and he evinced familiarity with the qualifications of the candidates. Moreover, on occasion, he sought information from his own friends in distant cities to guide him in making decisions.[73] In all cases he was ready to listen to the advice of his Cabinet members, and certainly at times he altered his decisions to suit their views. Clayton persuaded him to appoint Thomas Crittenden rather than Governor Edward Kent of Maine to the lucrative Liverpool consulate,[74] and Taylor's objections to William D. Lewis for the post of collector of the port of Philadelphia were finally overcome and he was given the appointment.[75]

Taylor's administration was only a month old when rumors of dissension in the Cabinet were heard and the re-

[71] Barnes, *Memoir of Thurlow Weed,* 175.

[72] Washington *Daily Union,* March 10, 1849.

[73] L. C. Levin to [Wm. D. Lewis], April 26 and 29, and May 2, 1849, in Levin Papers, Huntington Library; James Cooper to Henry White, March 20, 1849, in Meredith Papers; Daniel Webster to Fletcher Webster, March 29 and April 12, 1849, in Van Tyne (ed.), *Letters of Daniel Webster,* 376–79; Orlando Brown to J. J. Crittenden, July 24, 1849, in Crittenden Papers; J. Prescott Hall to J. M. Clayton, May 4, 1849, in Clayton Papers.

[74] J. M. Clayton to J. J. Crittenden, April 8, 1849, in Crittenden Papers.

[75] James Cooper to Henry White, March 20, 1849, and William D. Lewis to William Meredith, May 10, 1849, in Meredith Papers.

port whispered that Clayton would retire. Although at this time the Secretary of State insisted the Cabinet was united and that he had no thought of leaving it, three months later the criticism was so insistent that he offered to resign if Crittenden would take his place.[76] By this time the Democratic *Union* was crying that the mission "of the present imbecile and blundering cabinet is ended," [77] and even so loyal a supporter of the President as A. T. Burnley was convinced that the Cabinet was "incompetent" or "incapacitated by outside circumstances" so that it "must go out" if General Taylor's administration were to be saved.[78] Crittenden still favored Letcher for Postmaster General and urged that he be substituted for Collamer.[79] Others suggested that the Home Department be abolished to get rid of Ewing.[80] In the middle of November, almost on the eve of the meeting of Congress, the opposition to Clayton included so many of his own colleagues that a disruption of the Cabinet seemed inevitable. It was rumored that both Clay and Webster were to enter the Cabinet, the former to be Secretary of State and the latter to head the Treasury Department. Several all-night conferences, however, smoothed matters over for a period, and Taylor was able to face Congress without an open break in his official family. But few persons doubted that it would come sooner or later.[81] When Congress assembled, dissensions among the Whigs, between the slavery and antislavery Whigs, and between the Clay and Taylor Whigs immediately broke out, and talk of a new Cabinet was resumed. Humphrey Marshall, Kentucky con-

[76] J. J. Crittenden to J. M. Clayton, April 11 and July 20, 1849, in Clayton Papers; J. M. Clayton to J. J. Crittenden, April 18, 1849, in Crittenden Papers.

[77] Washington *Daily Union*, August 14, 1849.

[78] A. T. Burnley to J. J. Crittenden, July 24, 1849, in Crittenden Papers.

[79] J. J. Crittenden to J. M. Clayton, September 1, 1849, in Clayton Papers.

[80] Charles Sumner to Francis Lieber, October 13, 1849, in Huntington Library.

[81] R. P. Letcher to J. J. Crittenden, November 17 and 26, 1849, in Coleman, *Crittenden*, I, 348–50, 352.

gressman, assured Crittenden that if Clayton and Ewing remained there was not the remotest prospect of success for the administration. "The first has no friends, so far as I know," he wrote, "who would walk a square to save him and the last is especially odious to the Democratic side of the House." [82] C. S. Morehead of North Carolina, chairman of the Philadelphia convention that nominated Taylor, concluded "there is but one safe course for General Taylor to pursue, and that is to reconstruct his whole cabinet. I am perfectly satisfied that he cannot carry on the government with his present ministers." [83]

Just at this time, at the close of President Taylor's first year in office, when dissatisfaction with his Cabinet was widespread, a first-class scandal involving three Cabinet members added new fuel to the fires of criticism. "The Cabinet is doomed," announced the *Union*. "Nothing can now save it. . . . It must go out, 'bag and baggage,' individually and as a unit." [84]

Taylor's Secretary of War, George W. Crawford, had served since 1833 as the counsel and agent of the heirs of George Galphin, a pre-Revolutionary Indian trader, and in their behalf had pressed a large claim against the United States government. Finally, in the summer of 1848 Congress authorized payment and Polk's Secretary of the Treasury paid the principal of the claim, $43,518.97. Whereupon Crawford, who was employed on a contingent basis of one-half the proceeds, promptly filed a claim for interest from colonial times, but no action was taken on this point before the end of Polk's administration. When the new administration took office the claim for interest was pushed before Secretary Meredith by Judge Joseph Bryan who was retained to assist Crawford, now Secretary of War. Crawford did not make known to his colleagues

[82] Humphrey Marshall to *id.*, March 10, 1850, in Crittenden Papers.

[83] C. S. Morehead to *id.*, March 30, 1850, in Coleman, Crittenden, I, 362–63.

[84] Washington *Daily Union*, April 14, 1850.

his connection with the claim nor his interest in it, but he did on several occasions urge that it be decided without delay. When the Comptroller of the Treasury advised against its allowance on the ground that it was not the policy of the government to allow interest on its debts, Meredith turned to Attorney General Johnson for an opinion. Johnson ruled that the Act of 1848 not only authorized the payment of interest, but practically required it. On the strength of this opinion Secretary Meredith proceeded to pay interest amounting to nearly $200,000, half of which went into the pocket of his colleague Crawford.[85]

Shortly after taking office Crawford called upon President Taylor and informed him that this claim for interest was before the Treasury Department and that he was still interested in it on a contingent basis as he had been for more than fifteen years. Apparently he did not inform the President of the amount of the claim or the extent of his interest therein. Politically inexperienced, with no suspicion of the dynamite in the situation, and with thorough confidence in the integrity of his Cabinet, Taylor replied that in his opinion "none of the preëxisting individual rights of Governor Crawford had been curtailed by his acceptance of office." The claim did not become a subject of Cabinet deliberation and apparently did not again come to the President's attention until after it had been paid and had attracted public notice. Then, in a second conference with Crawford, he again expressed the view that the Secretary of War had not lost his rights as agent and stated that if the claim were a just one, "under the law of Congress it should have been paid, no matter who were the parties interested in it." The credit and good faith of the government were involved, Taylor said, and he as

[85] *Congressional Globe,* 31 Cong., 1 Sess., Appendix, 546–49; William P. Brandon, "The Galphin Claim," in *Georgia Historical Quarterly* (Savannah), XV (1931), 113–29.

President would not have been justified in suspending examination and decision of the claim by the Treasury Department.[86]

Logically Taylor was right. The claimants were entitled to a decision on their claim for interest, even though one of the interested parties had become a member of the government. But any familiarity with politics or with human nature ought to have warned Taylor that the payment by his administration of a claim in which one of his official family had a financial interest, especially when that claim had been rejected by the preceding administration, could not fail to call forth charges of conspiracy and corruption. Crawford particularly was at fault. It is true that he early called the matter to the President's attention, but he did not inform Taylor of the size of the claim and apparently left him with the impression that it was pending before Congress rather than before the Treasury Department. Moreover, as an experienced politician Crawford ought to have realized that a vigilant opposition would attack such a transaction and make it a source of unending embarrassment to the administration. As one of Taylor's advisers he ought to have warned him of the danger involved. Crawford might well have presented the whole matter to the Cabinet that they might advise the President, though on this point it could be maintained that by keeping secret his connection with the claim he was preventing any charge of undue influence.

A congressional investigation, instituted at Crawford's request as soon as the Democratic attacks upon him commenced, and conducted by a committee of five Democrats and four Whigs, failed to discover that the Secretary of War had used his official position to influence the decision on the claim, or that Meredith or Johnson was aware until the claim had been adjudicated that he had an interest in it. The Democratic majority of the committee, how-

[86] *Congressional Globe*, 31 Cong., 1 Sess., Appendix, 548.

ever, believed that the Act of 1848 had not authorized the payment of interest and that "its payment was not 'in conformity with law' or 'precedent,' " and they urged Congress to adopt a resolution to that effect. They also proposed two other resolutions: first, that the original Galphin claim "was not a just demand against the United States," and second, that the Act of 1848 "made it the duty of the Secretary of the Treasury to pay the principal of said claim." [87]

The report of the committee was presented on May 17, but only on July 1 did Congress commence serious consideration of it. Then a full week was devoted to it; the three resolutions were thoroughly and warmly debated and the three Cabinet officers involved were boldly censured. Whigs as well as Democrats joined in the hue and cry. In spite of a sturdy defense of the administration led by Stephens and Toombs of Georgia and Charles E. Clarke of New York, all three resolutions were adopted by the House on July 8. By a vote of 142 to 49 they declared the Galphin claim was not a just demand. The second resolution, that the Act of Congress required the Secretary of the Treasury to pay the principal, carried 112 to 66 and the view that the act did not authorize the payment of interest was upheld 118 to 71.[88] Many Democrats felt that these resolutions did not contain a sufficient censure of the administration, and in the course of the debates repeated attempts were made to amend them. Resolutions disapproving Attorney General Johnson's opinion in favor of the allowance of interest, disapproving the payment by Secretary Meredith, and dissenting from the correctness of President Taylor's statement to Crawford that his position as a member of the Cabinet did not deprive him of his rights as agent for the claim were adopted as amend-

[87] *Ibid.*, 31 Cong., 1 Sess., 1019–21; *ibid.*, Appendix, 548.

[88] *Ibid.*, 31 Cong., 1 Sess., 1019–21, 1280, 1322–54; *ibid.*, Appendix, 616, 624, 823, 829, 843, 886, 895, 930.

ments to an amendment, only to be lost when the amendment itself failed to carry.[89] The President's critics were not easily defeated. They resorted to every possible parliamentary maneuver to renew these amendments and managed to keep them before the House in one form or another for several days. These efforts to make the censure of Taylor and his advisers more severe were still in progress, with a real possibility of success, when they were checked by the news that the President lay dangerously ill in the White House and was not expected to live. When, nearly a week later, the House resumed its normal course the proposed amendments were withdrawn and this scheme to discredit President Taylor's administration came to an end.[90]

Although the investigating committee found no evidence of corruption in the settlement of the Galphin claim, the affair had an ugly side to it which furnished occasion for renewed criticism of the Cabinet. The three officers involved had been fairly free from attack during the first year of the administration, but now they too were denounced. Clayton, Ewing, and Collamer had long been condemned. Now Meredith, Crawford, and Johnson were added to the list. Only Preston of the Navy Department remained without serious opposition. Secretary Ewing continued to be a subject of bitter attack by the administration critics. Charges of improper use of the patronage and of the reopening of claims previously denied had long been hinted in the partisan press and bruited about the streets. In April, 1850, while still in an investigating mood, the Democratic House took notice of these criticisms and authorized an inquiry into his activities. The report of the committee, made after Ewing was out of office, was of little significance, but the April debate on the resolution

[89] The vote on the resolution dissenting from the correctness of Taylor's statement to Crawford was 91 to 86 and on the resolution covering both Johnson's opinion and the interest payment by Meredith 119 to 66.

[90] *Congressional Globe*, 31 Cong., 1 Sess., 1350–51, 1354, 1358–60, 1371–72.

of inquiry furnished ample opportunity to censure Taylor's Secretary of the Interior.[91]

During the spring weeks even the *Republic,* a newspaper established in Washington at the outset of Taylor's term as the administration and party organ, grew critical of the Cabinet and gave but weak support to the President. It was owned by A. T. Burnley, G. S. Gideon, and its two editors, A. C. Bullitt and John O. Sargent. Bullitt was a former editor of the New Orleans *Picayune* who had come to Washington at Taylor's personal request.[92] During 1849 the *Republic* loyally supported President Taylor, kept him constantly in view as the people's President, and defended his Cabinet against the endless attacks of Ritchie's *Union* with almost as much heat and spirit as Ritchie himself displayed. By early 1850, however, the two editors, who were alone responsible for the *Republic*'s policy, concluded that the Cabinet was an impossible combination, so that the paper's support of the administration became halfhearted. In spite of "long and affectionate" conversations between Taylor and Bullitt the editors could not be won over. Consequently, when the payment of interest on the Galphin claim called forth a new flood of criticism, the President determined upon the establishment of a new paper which would zealously and enthusiastically support his Cabinet and administration.[93] A. T. Burnley hastened to Washington where he conferred with his associates, with President Taylor, and with Secretaries Clayton and Meredith. Burnley was opposed to the editorial policy of the *Republic* and informed the editors that unless it were changed the paper must become at once an opposition organ. But he too failed to win over the editors. Finding that the Cabinet members

[91] *Ibid.,* 782–91, 1746.

[92] A. T. Burnley to J. J. Crittenden, January 12, 1849 [misdated 1848], in Crittenden Papers; Washington *Republic,* May 21, 1850.

[93] Orlando Brown to J. J. Crittenden, April 19, 1850, in Crittenden Papers.

had no plans for financing a new journal, he undertook to buy out Bullitt and Sargent and after a week of difficult negotiations came to terms with them.[94] To Crittenden, who was keenly interested in the problem, Burnley explained the terms: "The understanding is they have sold out to me, but I tell you in confidence, as I am incapable of speculating on two friends whose confidence in me is so great, I shall make their fate & my fate in this enterprise *the same.* I shall furnish them with what money they want now & periodically, & tell them to call on the 4th of March 1853, & I will inform them what the *terms* are on which I bought them out." [95] Burnley and Gideon, who continued to have a financial interest in the *Republic,* hired as editor Allan A. Hall of Nashville. Under his editorship the paper gave full satisfaction to President Taylor during the closing weeks of his administration. In announcing their retirement Bullitt and Sargent frankly declared that it was due to "personal differences" between themselves and members of the Cabinet, "that are inconsistent with the relations in which we stand towards President Taylor and the Whig party," and their desire to place no obstacle in the way of party harmony.[96]

President Taylor was cruelly disappointed by the widespread criticism of his trusted advisers, and regarded it, as indeed it was frequently intended, as criticism of himself. Moreover, he was offended by the persistent opposition to his territorial policy which came from members of his own party, and by the absence of any warm defenders either in Congress or among the men of the press. Mindful that he had not sought the office, and conscious of his own integrity and desire to promote the welfare of the whole nation, he saw no justification for the attacks; indeed, he was deeply wounded by them. In the midst of the Gal-

[94] *Id.* to *id.,* May 9 and 15, 1850, *ibid.;* A. T. Burnley to *id.,* May 8, 1850, *ibid.*

[95] A. T. Burnley to *id.,* May 15, 1850, ibid.

[96] Washington *Republic,* May 14, 1850.

phin investigation and the controversy with the editors of the *Republic* he disclosed his feelings in a long evening visit with Orlando Brown, the former secretary of Crittenden and now, as head of the Bureau of Indian Affairs, his chief representative in Washington. Of this presidential visit Brown wrote to Crittenden:

The President called to see me last evening and in a conversation of several hours fully disclosed to me his feelings and his purposes. He spoke as a proud, a brave and a deeply injured man alone can speak of an unmerited wrong and unprovoked persecution. I listened to his recital of the annoyances by which he had been harrassed, of the contumely that had been heaped upon him—of the contemptuous disparagements which were showered on him from high places, till my heart was sad and my eyes filled with tears. But when, almost with the eloquence, certainly with an equal depth of agony, of Lear he spoke of his being exposed without defense to this pitiless storm *I felt* like I could now see how keener than a serpent's tongue was the ingratitude of our race. But General Taylor is the unconquerable man. When he was through with the recital of his injuries, the soldier awoke within him and he exclaimed that he always kept his flag flying in front of his tent and would never strike it—that he had never turned a back to friend or foe and that by God he would not do it now.[97]

Determined not to strike his colors, the President steadfastly resisted all efforts during the spring of 1850 to force a change in his Cabinet. As long as the members were not guilty of incompetence or corruption he would keep them. Not they, but their critics, would be thrown overboard.[98] But by early summer, if Thurlow Weed's recollections may be relied upon, Taylor had come to recognize that the reflections cast upon the Cabinet by the Galphin claim necessitated its reconstruction. Weed talked with him at length on the subject and persuaded him to

[97] Orlando Brown to J. J. Crittenden, April 19, 1850, in Crittenden Papers.
[98] *Ibid.;* Thomas Corwin to Caleb Smith, April 25, 1850, and Theodore Barnett to *id.*, April 24 and May 14, 1850, in Caleb B. Smith Papers.

get rid of all but Ewing and Collamer who doubtless pleased Weed by their very partisan distribution of the patronage. Weed also persuaded Taylor to make Hamilton Fish his new Secretary of the Treasury and advised him concerning men for the other departments.[99] Secretary Clayton was apparently ready to step aside and open the way for reorganization. A letter of resignation dated June 18, written in his own hand and signed, remains in his papers. Whether it had been sent to the President and returned or was held for future use is not known, but he was clearly ready to relinquish his difficult post. Before any reconstruction was undertaken, in fact before Weed's conferences with Taylor were completed, death intervened and the task of forming a new Cabinet fell to other hands.

[99] Weed, *Autobiography*, 589–92.

Chapter XV

PEACE—BUT NOT AT ANY PRICE

THE critical problems of Taylor's administration were domestic, but several troublesome and somewhat significant questions developed in the sphere of foreign relations. This was a field in which he was wholly without experience. Yet his part in the annexation of Texas, in the preliminaries of the war with Mexico, and in the war itself had given him a close association with diplomatic affairs and had caused him to reflect upon the general subject of international relations. He became a sincere advocate of honest friendship with all nations, strict neutrality in the affairs of other countries, and amicable adjustment of international controversies. These views he carried with him into the presidency where, however, they conflicted with his narrow, stubborn insistence upon American rights and dignity, so much so that they frequently lost out to the latter. In spite of his inexperience he took an active interest in the conduct of the nation's foreign affairs. He was constantly consulted by Secretary Clayton, not only on important developments, but at times on rather minor points as well, and on several occasions he exercised a significant influence on negotiations.

One of Taylor's correspondents during his months in the White House was Edward Everett, the president of Harvard University and former minister to Great Britain, who frequently shared with Taylor letters from distinguished transatlantic friends. Taylor read with interest these communications which threw light on affairs and conditions in Europe, and he never failed to urge Everett to send him more. "It is impossible in this country," Taylor wrote, "to appreciate the difficulties which beset the continental governments of Europe, watched as they are by strong and jealous neighbors, and we are perhaps too prone to condemn acts which may be the result as you remark of 'political necessity.' "[1] In his first reply to Everett, written but a few weeks after the election, Taylor briefly indicated his desire for a peaceful foreign policy:

> I regret most truly the present disturbed state of Europe, & I wish instead of discord & anarchy they might be blessed with a share of the peace and prosperity which rest upon our happy land. I agree with you that much caution will be necessary in the management of our relations with European powers and those of our own continent. It is the evident duty of our Government watchfully to guard against connexion with the turmoils of other nations & against any step calculated to compromise the neutrality of the country or its peaceful relations with all the world.[2]

There is no clear evidence that Taylor influenced the diplomatic appointments of his administration, but the important posts were filled with men who unquestionably had his approval. Abbott Lawrence, whom he had sought for his Cabinet, was sent to England; and William C. Rives, whom Truman Smith had hoped to see Secretary of State, was returned to Paris where he had represented the United States twenty years before. Crittenden's friend, Robert P. Letcher, was appointed minister to Mexico, and another Kentuckian, James Clay, was sent to Portugal as chargé d'affaires. Balie Peyton, who had been almost constantly at Taylor's side since 1846 when he had led a regiment of volunteers to Mexico, was named minister to Chile.

In the course of the presidential campaign an inquiry

[1] Taylor to Edward Everett, July 13, 1849, in Massachusetts Historical Society.

[2] *Id.* to *id.*, December 13, 1849, *ibid.*

from Clayton and Truman Smith as to his views about a reported filibustering expedition into Mexico called forth from Taylor the assertion, "I consider our neutrality laws and particularly our treaty obligations as perhaps the most important that can demand the attention and action of the Executive," and elicited the promise to employ all the means at his disposal to uphold the neutrality laws of the country.[3] This promise proved to be no mere pre-election pledge to be forgotten as quickly as possible, but rather a cardinal principle of Taylor's foreign policy.

Widespread economic distress and deep political discontent in Canada gave rise in 1849 to a strong movement for annexation to the United States as the only remedy for the "insufferable ills" with which the country was afflicted. The enthusiastic support of this movement by the American people, who were still fired with the spirit of manifest destiny, and the inflammatory articles in the press created some fear on the part of British authorities that filibustering expeditions would be organized on American soil to aid the Canadians in a revolt against the mother country—fear that the revolutionary fires of 1776 would be rekindled and that Canada, and perhaps New Brunswick and Nova Scotia as well, would follow the example of the thirteen rebellious colonies. John F. Crampton, British chargé d'affaires in Washington, promptly inquired of the newly inaugurated Taylor administration what its attitude would be toward such proceedings on the border. He was assured that the President was determined to enforce the neutrality laws of the nation, and was ready to send General Scott and an adequate military force to the border to prevent the execution of any schemes of violence against Canada.[4] The fearless and determined manner in which President Taylor followed a particular course when once he had made up his mind that it was his duty to

[3] *Id.* to John M. Clayton, September 4, [1848], in Clayton Papers.

[4] John F. Crampton to Lord Palmerston, April 2 and 15, 1849, in P. R. O., F. O. 5:499 (Library of Congress Photostats).

pursue it inclined Crampton to attach a great deal of importance to these assurances. In reporting them to his home government he wrote: "Should circumstances, unfortunately, render such a precaution necessary, it is satisfactory to reflect that there have been few Presidents of the United States whose personal influence would give greater effect to a measure of the sort than would that of General Taylor." [5] Although annexation sentiment continued, no filibustering expedition was organized and it did not become necessary for Taylor to send troops to the border.

Another opportunity to adhere to the policy of strict neutrality arose in connection with the efforts of the government of the newly formed German Confederation to acquire in the United States an armed vessel for use in its war against Denmark. At the close of 1848, during an armistice in the war, the government of the Confederation determined to build a navy and turned to the United States for officers and ships. The Polk administration, eager to co-operate to the fullest, sent Commodore F. A. Parker to Europe to consult with the German officials, and authorized the commandant of the Brooklyn navy yard to make the facilities of that yard available for equipping as a vessel of war the merchant steamer, *United States,* recently purchased by a German agent. The prospect of renewed war between the German states and Denmark eventually induced Polk to decline making American officers available for service in the German navy, but work on the *United States* was rapidly nearing completion when his administration gave way to that of Taylor.[6] Determined to fulfill with strict impartiality the duties of a neutral, the new administration promptly terminated all work upon the vessel at the navy yard and ordered Ameri-

[5] *Id.* to *id.,* April 2, 1849, *ibid.*

[6] "Correspondence Between the Department of State and the Minister of the German Empire," in *Senate Executive Documents,* 31 Cong., 1 Sess., No. 1, pp. 18–28.

can naval officers to "abstain from any further participation, either by advising or otherwise, in the preparation and equipment of the steamship." [7] Although the armistice between the German Confederation and Denmark was still in effect, peace had not been made and President Taylor sought from Baron von Roenne, the German minister in Washington, "solemn assurance" in writing that the vessel would not be employed against any power with which the United States was at peace.[8] In spite of the repeated protests of von Roenne that the whole proceeding had been undertaken with the knowledge and approval of the government of the United States, and therefore could not be a violation of the Neutrality Act of 1818, President Taylor adhered to his decision, a decision in which he was strengthened by the renewal of hostilities in Europe. Von Roenne was unwilling to give the assurance demanded by the President, but eventually the ship was allowed to depart after bond had been given, double the value of the vessel, its cargo and armament, that it would not commit hostilities against any people with whom the United States was at peace.[9] Shortly after the steamer reached Europe the two belligerents made peace and any danger that the bond would be violated was ended.

Although their actions in this matter were entirely justified by international law and the American Neutrality Act of 1818, the President and his Secretary of State were vigorously attacked by the Democratic *Union.* In long outbursts editor Ritchie insisted that American citizens had a perfect right to sell ships to foreign nations and that nothing but a desire to reflect upon the Polk administration could have induced a reversal of its policy.[10] In truth,

[7] William B. Preston to Captain Isaac McKeever, March 19, 1849, and *id.* to Commodore M. C. Perry, March 19, 1849, *ibid.*, 28.

[8] John M. Clayton to Baron Von Roenne, April 10, 1849, *ibid.*, 32–33.

[9] *Ibid.*, 34–48.

[10] Washington *Daily Union,* June 16 and 20, 1849.

Taylor's action grew out of his belief that the strict observance of neutral duties was one of the most important functions of the executive.

A third and even more significant opportunity to prevent the use of American soil as a base of operations against a friendly nation developed in connection with Cuba, the richest and most important of Spain's remaining American colonies. Situated less than two hundred miles south of the Florida peninsula, Cuba had long been an object of deep concern to American statesmen, many of whom believed that inevitably the island would in time become a part of the United States. No one stated this view more convincingly than John Quincy Adams who, when Secretary of State, boldly announced, "there are laws of political as well as of physical gravitation and if an apple, severed by the tempest from its native tree, cannot choose but fall to the ground, Cuba, forcibly disjoined from its own unnatural connection with Spain and incapable of self support can gravitate only towards the North American Union, which by the same law of nature, cannot cast her off from its bosom." [11] Americans were content to wait and, meanwhile, to give assurances to Spain that the full power of the country would be used to prevent any other nation from seizing the island.[12] By the close of the Mexican War, however, the demand for Cuba was exceedingly strong. The spirit of manifest destiny was at work; the acquisition of California and Oregon had created a nationwide interest in the status of Cuba so strategically located for all transisthmian routes; and the desire of some Southerners for more slave states in order to maintain the balance in Congress made annexationist schemes especially popular in that section. The expansionist Polk adminis-

[11] John Quincy Adams to Hugh Nelson, April 28, 1823, in John Bassett Moore (ed.), *Digest of International Law* (Washington, 1906), I, 583–84.

[12] Moore, *Digest of International Law,* VI, 451.

tration, eager to satisfy this demand, endeavored to purchase Cuba, but Spain indignantly rejected the proposition.[13]

Perhaps no American was more actively interested in the acquisition of Cuba than John L. O'Sullivan, New York journalist and champion of manifest destiny. He was the first to suggest to President Polk the idea of purchasing Cuba [14] and he subsequently urged this action upon Polk and his Secretary of State with great earnestness.[15] When Polk's efforts to buy the island failed, O'Sullivan became an ardent supporter of filibustering expeditions to Cuba.[16]

Meanwhile Cuba was growing increasingly restless under Spanish rule, and many of her ardent patriots were preparing for independence. One of the chief of these was Narciso López, a native of Venezuela, a general in the Spanish army, and a former Spanish official in Cuba. He and many other Cuban patriots found refuge in the United States where they sought aid for their revolutionary enterprises from the many friends of liberty. Their chief support came, however, from annexationists, such as O'Sullivan, who were ready to work for Cuban independence in the belief that annexation would soon follow. In New York, in Baltimore, in New Orleans, and in other ports of the United States little groups of Cubans and their American associates were soon busy preparing to strike for Cuba's freedom. Such was the situation when Taylor

[13] For interesting articles showing the favor with which some Americans looked upon the annexation of Cuba see *The United States Magazine and Democratic Review* (New York), XXVI (1850), 97, and XXIX (1851), 291. See also the discussion of this subject in Herminio Portell Vilá, *Historia de Cuba En Sus Relaciones Con Los Estados Unidos y España* (La Habana, 1938–1941), I, Chapter VII, and the documents in William R. Manning (ed.), *Diplomatic Correspondence of the United States: Inter-American Affairs, 1831–1860* (Washington, 1932–1939), XI, 54–64, 443–59.

[14] Polk, *Diary*, III, 493.

[15] *Ibid.*, 446, 476–80; O'Sullivan to James Buchanan, March 19, 1848, quoted in Portell Vilá, *Historia de Cuba*, I, 371–74.

[16] O'Sullivan to John C. Calhoun, August 24, 1849, in American Historical Association, *Annual Report, 1899*, II, 1202–1203.

came into office determined to enforce the neutrality laws of the country.

Early in August it was discovered that hundreds of men were being recruited in various parts of the country and that a filibustering expedition was being organized on Round Island near the mouth of the Mississippi. Although Taylor did not know it, O'Sullivan was writing to John C. Calhoun urging him to strain every nerve in support of the undertaking. "The South ought . . . to flock down there [Cuba] in 'open boats,' the moment they hear the tocsin," he wrote. "They ought not only to go, but *to go at once*. . . . It can easily be done legally. They can go as emigrants, California adventurers *via* Cuba. . . . All going may rely on generous compensation from opulent Cuba, once liberated. But independent of such motives there are considerations enough of a different character which I should think ought to rouse all the youth and manhood of the Southern States in particular to rush down to help the Cuban Revolution." [17]

It was not clear to the authorities whether the expedition was aimed at Cuba or Mexico, but the principle involved would be the same in either case, and Taylor lost no time in warning all citizens of the United States that participation in an armed expedition against a friendly nation was "in the highest degree, criminal, as tending to endanger the peace and compromit the honor of this nation." He exhorted "all good citizens, as they regard our national reputation, as they respect their own laws and the laws of nations, as they value the blessings of peace and the welfare of their country, to discountenance and prevent, by all lawful means, any such enterprise," and called upon every civil and military officer of the nation to arrest any offenders against the neutrality laws of the United States.[18] Taylor hastened to back up this proclamation

[17] *Ibid.*

[18] Proclamation, August 11, 1849, in *Senate Executive Documents,* 31 Cong., 1 Sess., No. 1, p. 17.

with force and dispatched Commodore Parker and the ships under his command at Pensacola to aid the United States attorney at New Orleans in breaking up the Round Island expedition. The watchful presence of the navy successfully blocked the sailing of the adventurers, and in due time most of them abandoned the enterprise.[19]

At almost the same time, J. Prescott Hall, the United States attorney in New York, and his assistant, William M. Evarts, were winning the commendation of the President for "the prompt, energetic and judicious manner" in which they responded to his proclamation and detained two vessels ready to sail with arms, munitions, and men to join in the Cuban expedition.[20]

The energetic action of President Taylor and his subordinates prevented the sailing of this first López filibustering expedition, but the leaders were soon busy with new plans. Angel Calderón de la Barca, the Spanish minister to the United States, frequently protested to Clayton that preparations were under way for an armed expedition to Cuba. He had little concrete evidence to present, but Clayton and President Taylor both gave careful attention to his protests and repeatedly assured him of their firm resolution to prevent the violation of American neutrality laws.[21] The Federal officials in New York and New Orleans were constantly instructed to keep the strictest watch for any movement directed against Cuba, and "to take due care that the laws of the land were not, in any respect, violated, either by our own citizens or such foreigners as

[19] "Message of the President of the United States, Transmitting Reports . . . as to Alleged Revolutionary Movements in Cuba," June 1, 1850, in *Senate Executive Documents,* 31 Cong., 1 Sess., No. 57, pp. 67–116.

[20] John M. Clayton to J. Prescott Hall, August 10, September 6, 7, and 19, 1849, *ibid.,* 7, 14, 15, 17; J. Prescott Hall to John M. Clayton, September 8, 1849, *ibid.,* 17. For the activities in New York see Brainerd Dyer, *The Public Career of William M. Evarts* (Berkeley, 1933), 14–16.

[21] Manning, *Diplomatic Correspondence,* XI, 71–76, 82–85, 470, 473, 476–81, 485, 495.

come here to violate our hospitality and abuse our free institutions." [22]

Nevertheless, by the spring of 1850 the adventurers were ready for a second attempt. The watchful officials in New York discouraged action by the Cuban sympathizers in that city, but in New Orleans a large expedition was set on foot. General López and his associates, acting under expert legal advice, proceeded with such circumspection that Logan Hunton, the United States attorney at New Orleans, found no violation of the law and offered no interference when early in May three vessels departed with men and munitions. The expedition consisted of some six hundred men recruited in Kentucky, Mississippi, and Louisiana. Many more were said to be awaiting transportation, and the Washington authorities thought that eventually six to ten thousand men might be involved.[23]

President Taylor was indignant that his proclamation had been so flagrantly violated, and by his direction five naval vessels were promptly dispatched to Cuban waters to prevent the landing of any armed expedition from the United States.[24] In spite of this measure the steamer *Creole,* one of the vessels of the filibusters, succeeded in putting ashore on the coast of Cuba about five hundred of the adventurers with General López at their head. After capturing the town of Cárdenas, burning the governor's palace and losing some thirty of their number in clashes with the Spanish troops, the invaders sought refuge on their ship which hurriedly departed for Key West with an armed Spanish steamer in hot pursuit. The United

[22] J. Prescott Hall to John M. Clayton, June 28, 1850, *ibid.,* XI, 94.

[23] Don A. Calderon de la Barca to *id.,* May 8, 1850, *ibid.,* 23–24; Logan Hunton to *id.,* May 14, 1850, *ibid.,* 24–25.

[24] Sir Henry L. Bulwer to Lord Palmerston, May 16, 1850, in P. R. O., F. O. 5:512 (Library of Congress Photostats); John M. Clayton to Don A. Calderon de la Barca, May 18, 1850, in *Senate Executive Documents,* 31 Cong., 1 Sess., No. 57, pp. 29–31; instructions of Secretary Preston, *ibid.,* 54–62.

States government promptly confiscated the *Creole* and arrested López, but subsequent attempts to convict him and other leading filibusters of violation of American laws were frustrated by the widespread public sympathy for their cause and the innumerable technical loopholes in the legislation of 1818. President Taylor had no wish to prosecute the rank and file of the expedition, but he earnestly desired to bring to justice the organizers and the officers. He believed that the honor of the country was involved and he called for energetic measures against the offenders. Legal proceedings were instituted against many of the leaders, but the difficulties of furnishing satisfactory legal proof of "organization," "enlistment," and "intent," and the sympathetic attitude of Southern juries prevented any convictions.[25]

A group of the adventurers, fifty-two in number, were captured by the Spanish on a small Mexican island off the coast of Yucatan where they had been left by the main expedition because they refused to participate further in the enterprise. They were removed to Havana, denounced as pirates, and threatened with summary execution. Although in his proclamation of the previous August, President Taylor had clearly warned all persons participating in any such enterprise that they would forfeit their claim to the protection of their country, he now came to their aid. Because these men had not landed or made any attempt to land on Cuban soil, Clayton insisted, they had committed no offense in the eyes of Cuba or Spain and he desired, in demanding their release, to present a virtual ultimatum offering no alternative but war. When other members of the Cabinet opposed such an uncompromising position and Clayton threatened to resign, President Taylor, "in defiance of three-fourths of his advisers, gave the plan his approval, declaring that if the prisoners were put

[25] *Ibid.*, 43–46; Robert G. Caldwell, *The Lopez Expeditions to Cuba, 1848–1851* (Princeton, 1915), 78–79.

to death he would immediately send a war message to Congress." [26] The President resolved, said Clayton, "that the Eagle must and shall protect them against any punishment but that which the tribunals of their own nation may award." [27] Thus originated a bitter controversy between the United States and Spain which for a time seriously threatened to engulf the two nations in war. Although Spain refused to yield to Clayton's demand and placed the prisoners on trial before a maritime court, all but three were found not guilty on the ground that they had been deceived as to the purpose of the expedition. Moreover, the three found guilty were soon pardoned and returned to the United States.[28]

President Taylor's strict enforcement of the Neutrality Act of 1818 was unpopular with the large group of Americans who favored Cuban independence or annexation of the island to the United States. They denounced his breaking up of the Round Island expedition as an outrage and his sending of naval vessels to Cuban waters to intercept the filibusters of 1850 as an unconstitutional usurpation of power and a violation of international law.[29] On the floor of the Senate, David L. Yulee of Florida angrily charged the President with making war without the authority of Congress, and with stretching his powers "beyond the limits of a just neutrality to crush a movement conceived in the spirit of freedom, and to bolster the authority of a grinding despotism." [30]

[26] Mary W. Williams, "John Middleton Clayton," in Samuel Flagg Bemis (ed.), *The American Secretaries of State and Their Diplomacy* (New York, 1927–1929), VI, 38–39; John M. Clayton to Robert B. Campbell, June 1, 1850, in *Senate Executive Documents,* 31 Cong., 1 Sess., No. 57, pp. 48–49.

[27] John M. Clayton to Robert B. Campbell, June 1, 1850, *loc. cit.*

[28] The correspondence bearing on this phase of the expedition may be found in Manning (ed.), *Diplomatic Correspondence,* XI, 78–90, 493–580; *Senate Executive Documents,* 31 Cong., 2 Sess., No. 41; *House Executive Documents,* 32 Cong., 1 Sess., No. 83.

[29] Washington *Daily Union,* October 10 and 11, 1849; Portell Vilá, *Historia de Cuba,* I, 445.

[30] *Congressional Globe,* 31 Cong., 1 Sess., 1032–33.

To this day Cuban historians contend that Taylor's policy postponed the independence of their country for half a century, and they bitterly criticize him for taking an interest in the independence movements of far-off Europe and at the same time opposing the efforts of near-by Cubans to win freedom and liberty. Herminio Portell Vilá, accepting a statement of Senator Henry S. Foote of Mississippi that Taylor was "decidedly in favor of the annexation of Cuba," [31] charges that it was this desire to make the island American territory that accounts for the President's opposition to López and Cuban independence.[32] Taylor may have been in favor of the acquisition of Cuba in the sense that he was not opposed to it, though even that is not clear, but certainly his Cuban policy was not dictated by any burning desire to annex that island. He was far from being an expansionist, and his minister to Spain was early instructed that the administration did not desire to renew the proposition made by Polk for the purchase of Cuba, and that if the Spanish government of its own accord made any offer of sale he should content himself with transmitting the offer to Washington for consideration.[33] At the same time President Taylor was just as determined as his predecessors that the island should "never be ceded by Spain to any other power than the United States," and the minister was informed that the news of such a cession would be "the instant signal for war." [34]

A minor incident in the relations of the United States and Cuba was the case of Juan Francisco García y Rey. Although not in itself of great importance, the newspapers stirred up considerable feeling over the case and for a

[31] *Ibid.*, 30 Cong., 2 Sess., 162.

[32] Portell Vilá, *Historia de Cuba,* I, 407–50.

[33] John M. Clayton to Daniel M. Barringer, August 2, 1849, in Manning (ed.), *Diplomatic Correspondence,* XI, 69–71.

[34] *Ibid.*

brief period it promised to become a serious controversy. García, a Havana jailer who fled to the United States after aiding two prisoners to escape and who became associated in some degree with the filibustering movement at New Orleans, was abducted by the Spanish consul in that city and shipped back to Havana for punishment. The newspapers clamored for the arrest of the consul for violation of American sovereignty and Clayton instructed the United States consul at Havana that if the circumstances proved to be as alleged, President Taylor "would not hesitate to recommend immediate war." [35] By the middle of August, Secretary Clayton was convinced that the consul was implicated and he so informed President Taylor, who was in the midst of his tour of Pennsylvania. "I fully coincide with you in the opinion," Taylor replied, "that the honor of the country demands the most ample atonement for the outrage and that the most decided measures be taken to demand the release of Garcia and his restoration to this country." [36] Serious controversy was avoided when the Cuban authorities pardoned García and sent him back to the United States. Whereupon Taylor and Clayton dropped their demand for "ample atonement." The Democratic opposition, always ready to find fault with the administration, bitterly complained that justice had been secured for García but not for the nation.

As previously indicated, President Taylor's desire to maintain friendly relations with all nations came into conflict with his stubborn insistence upon the rights and honor of the country, even in questionable cases. So inflexible was his position in two controversies that friendly relations with France and Portugal were badly strained.

[35] John M. Clayton to Robert B. Campbell, July 28, 1849, quoted in Portell Vilá, *Historia de Cuba,* I, 419–20.

[36] John M. Clayton to Taylor, August 18, 1849, Taylor to John M. Clayton, August 29, 1849, in Clayton Papers; *Senate Executive Documents,* 31 Cong., 1 Sess., No. 13; Caldwell, *The Lopez Expeditions to Cuba,* 51–54.

His Secretary of State was perhaps primarily to blame for the serious situations that developed, but Taylor firmly supported his stand in both instances.

The trouble with France began at the very outset of Taylor's administration. It grew out of correspondence between Secretary Clayton and William Tell Poussin, the French minister to the United States, over a small claim for damages suffered by a Frenchman at the hands of the American army in Mexico. Although no significant principle was at stake, this correspondence, commenced as soon as Clayton assumed office, rapidly became acrimonious. By April 21 it reached a point where Clayton, acting under instructions from the President, summoned Poussin to return from New York and upon his arrival informed him that his last note was highly objectionable and might well be withdrawn. Poussin did withdraw the communication, eliminated the most offensive part, and returned it to Clayton.[37]

A few weeks later Clayton rejected another French claim without perhaps giving it all the consideration it deserved. Poussin, still smarting from his recent clash with the Secretary of State, promptly protested in a note which Clayton regarded as impugning the honor and dignity of the United States. Instead of dismissing Poussin or asking for his recall, the administration decided to lay the whole correspondence before the French government without any request for specific action. This step was taken with the full approval of President Taylor and probably at his suggestion. After examining the documents Alexis de Tocqueville, the French Foreign Minister, though expressing regret at the turn affairs had taken, criticized Clayton for the use of undiplomatic language and revealed no clear intention to recall Poussin. President Taylor, surprised

[37] Williams, "John Middleton Clayton," *loc. cit.*, 19–21. The whole correspondence was printed in many of the newspapers of the period. See New York *Weekly Tribune*, September 29, 1849.

and disappointed at Tocqueville's attitude, promptly instructed Clayton to dismiss the French minister. At the same time Clayton sharply censured Tocqueville for his indulgence of Poussin's disrespectful language.[38]

The inflexible and somewhat unfriendly attitude of the administration toward the French minister may have been intensified by an influence of a purely personal nature. Such, at least, was the belief of the British chargé in Washington. "There is an unlucky circumstance, too, of a private and personal nature to M. Poussin," he wrote when informing his government of the dismissal of the French diplomat, "which did not, I fear, tend to diminish that tone of 'acerbity' which M. de Tocqueville remarks, pervades the correspondence in question; I mean the fact, that the ladies of General Taylor's family thought that they had good grounds for declining that social intercourse with Madame Poussin which they maintain with the ladies of the other members of the Diplomatick Body at Washington." [39] There is no other evidence of this social conflict, but it may easily have been a factor in the controversy.

The French government was deeply wounded by the drastic action of Taylor's administration and refused to receive William C. Rives, the new United States minister then in Paris, until satisfactory explanations were made. Secretary Clayton was inclined to be conciliatory and to offer some loophole through which the French government might back out with dignity, but Taylor, sensitive and proud, stubbornly insisted that no explanation be given. Although much disturbed by the widening breach with France, Clayton carried out the President's instructions. But so apprehensive of war was he that only after long night hours of mental anguish—"the most terrific

[38] Williams, "John Middleton Clayton," *loc. cit.*, 21–27; New York *Weekly Tribune,* September 29, 1849.

[39] John F. Crampton to Lord Palmerston, September 23, 1849, in P. R. O., F. O. 5:500 (Library of Congress Photostats).

and agonizing pains," reported R. P. Letcher, who gave him aid and encouragement—did he succeed in drafting a note that met Taylor's requirements but was not too harsh.[40]

Fortunately, at the very time that Taylor and his Cabinet were deciding upon an uncompromising reply to Tocqueville, Louis Napoleon suddenly dismissed his ministers and received Rives in a cordial interview. Eager to be free to participate in European politics without the restrictions of an American war, the French ruler had not hesitated to take the necessary step to preserve peace. Now that his point had been won President Taylor was ready to co-operate in the restoration of friendly relations. In his annual message to Congress a few weeks later, he referred to the strong ties of amity that had long bound the United States to her sister republic; and when in March a new French minister arrived in Washington, Taylor received him with unusual cordiality.

The dismissal of the French minister caused great excitement in the United States and even affected the public funds. Day after day, for two weeks, this diplomatic controversy was heatedly discussed in the press. Clayton's attempt to explain and defend the administration's action by making public most of his correspondence with Poussin only added fuel to the fire. Needless to say Democratic editors seized upon this unnecessary break with France as another opportunity to attack Taylor and his Cabinet. Coming as it did close upon the controversy with the German minister, the excitement over the abduction of García, and the interference with the Round Island expedition, it was new proof to Ritchie of the *Union* that "the President and the Cabinet are utterly incompetent to conduct the affairs of this great nation." [41]

[40] R. P. Letcher to J. J. Crittenden, November 8, 1849, in Crittenden Papers; Williams, "John Middleton Clayton," *loc. cit.*, 28.

[41] Washington *Daily Union*, September 29, 1849. See the files of the *Union*

The other instance of insistence upon American rights even to the point of a breach of diplomatic relations grew out of several claims against Portugal. One claim extended back to the War of 1812 when an American privateer, the *General Armstrong,* was destroyed by the British in Portuguese waters. The United States demanded damages on the ground that Portugal had violated her neutral duties. The other claims, of much more recent origin, were also for damages to American ships and cargoes. Promptly upon entering office Clayton took up these claims and pushed them with great vigor. He informed the Portuguese government that further delay in the settlement of the claims would be regarded as a rejection of them, and he warned that President Taylor contemplated laying the whole subject before Congress. But, in spite of Clayton's efforts, little satisfaction was obtained. At the end of a year Portugal had rejected the *General Armstrong* claim and had promised to pay all of the others which should be found just. The Taylor administration was thoroughly dissatisfied with this promise and early in March, 1850, determined to make a final demand for settlement. A naval vessel was dispatched to Lisbon with instructions to James Clay, the American chargé, to inform Portugal that unless a satisfactory answer were received within twenty days he would demand his passports and that meanwhile the warship would remain in the harbor. The sailing of the naval vessel was delayed, possibly to give Portugal time to reflect upon the seriousness of the crisis, and it was not until the middle of June that the ship and instructions reached Lisbon. Clay promptly submitted the twenty-day ultimatum. On July 7 the Portuguese government agreed to arbitrate the *General Armstrong* claim and under protest to pay all others. Having been informed that Taylor would not submit the claims to arbitration, Clay viewed the Portu-

---

and the Washington *Republic,* particularly for the period September 20 to October 6.

guese reply as unsatisfactory and requested his passports. Thus, almost at the very hour that death terminated the Taylor administration, its uncompromising attitude brought it to an impasse with a second nation.[42]

Although inclined to push controversies with some countries to the danger point, the Taylor administration made no attempt to twist the British lion's tail. The more cautious and courteous conduct of relations with Great Britain may have been due in part to a realization of that nation's power and influence. It may also have resulted from President Taylor's appreciation of the common heritage of the two peoples. When at the outset of his administration he received the diplomatic corps he made a deep impression upon the British chargé d'affaires by his "friendly and even affectionate" discussion of the satisfactory state of affairs between the two nations. "We [Englishmen and Americans] are of the same bone and sinew," Taylor remarked, as he shook Crampton warmly by the hand, "and there is, I thank God, now no reason why we should not also be of one heart and one mind." [43]

The most important event in Anglo-American diplomacy during Taylor's administration was the negotiation of the Clayton-Bulwer Treaty by which the United States and Great Britain agreed never to exercise exclusive control over an isthmian canal through Central America, never to erect any fortifications in the vicinity thereof, and never to "occupy, or fortify, or colonize, or assume or exercise any dominion over Nicaragua, Costa Rica, the Mosquito Coast, or any part of Central America." It was further agreed that the canal should be open to the subjects or citizens of the two nations on terms of equality.[44] Although regarded by Secretary Clayton as a diplomatic

[42] Williams, "John Middleton Clayton," *loc. cit.*, 32–37; *House Executive Documents*, 32 Cong., 1 Sess., No. 53.

[43] John F. Crampton to Lord Palmerston, March 18, 1849, in P. R. O., F. O. 5:498 (Library of Congress Photostats).

[44] *United States Statutes at Large*, IX, 995–98.

triumph and approved by the Senate with only eleven dissenting votes, it soon became one of the most unpopular treaties in the nation's history. Its unpopularity was due in part to the fact that it seemed to be in conflict with the principles of the Monroe Doctrine and in part to the fact that in the years after the Civil War, when the American policy regarding a canal envisaged a waterway under the exclusive control of the United States, this treaty stood in the way. Also, at the time of its negotiation it was unpopular with the advocates of manifest destiny because it cut off the possibility of extending United States dominion into Central America.

The American people had long been interested in an interoceanic canal, and at the time of Taylor's presidency this interest was intensified by the recent territorial acquisitions on the Pacific Coast and the resultant transportation problem. The most popular canal route was through Nicaragua by way of the San Juan River and Lake Nicaragua, and an American company was actively seeking canal rights from that country. Consequently, the United States was much concerned in 1848 when Great Britain seized the mouth of the San Juan in the name of the Mosquito Indians over whom the British had long claimed a protectorate and whose territory they now began to insist extended south of that point. Nicaragua vainly protested this expansion at her expense and appealed to the United States for aid. The Polk administration sent an agent to Central America to investigate but offered no official remonstrance and made no attempt to resist the seizure. However, before this agent, Elijah Hise, was recalled by President Taylor he signed a treaty with Nicaragua securing for the United States the exclusive right to build a canal by the Nicaraguan route and to fortify the same. In exchange the United States undertook to protect and defend Nicaraguan sovereignty over all territory rightfully in her possession. Although no such treaty had been sought by the Taylor administration it proved to be a lever in its hands for use against the British. Taylor did not send it to the Senate for ratification, but held it for submission whenever circumstances should seem to warrant.[45]

Taylor's Secretary of State had long taken an interest in the project of a canal which he regarded as of paramount importance to the commercial interests of the United States. Promptly upon taking office he commenced negotiations to prevent British domination of any territory through which the canal would pass and to secure from Nicaragua the necessary right of way. He did not seek for the United States the exclusive control of any transisthmian route. Such monopoly he feared would arouse the jealousies of other nations and give rise to bloody and expensive wars. Now, as for many years past, he advocated a canal open on equal terms to all nations who would agree to the necessary treaties, a canal free from oppressive exactions either from the government within whose territorial limits it should lie or from the company constructing and owning it. He was perfectly willing to share with Great Britain control of the canal route but he was determined that she should not, through her Mosquito protectorate nor in any other way, exercise an undue influence. Because the Nicaraguan route was regarded as the most practicable, Clayton's concern centered upon it; but it was his desire to apply the same principles to the isthmus of Panama, to the isthmus of Tehuantepec, and to any other route between the two oceans. President Taylor fully shared these views and joined Clayton in presenting them. Entering Clayton's office upon other business when the Secretary was engaged in a long conference on Central American affairs with the British chargé d'affaires, Taylor "waived all ceremony," Cramp-

[45] Williams, "John Middleton Clayton," *loc. cit.*, 41–42; Elijah Hise to John M. Clayton, September 15, 1849, in Manning (ed.), *Diplomatic Correspondence*, III, 375–86.

ton reported to his government, "and joined in our conversation with great frankness and every appearance of a wish to make proof of the most friendly feelings towards Her Majesty's Government by evincing a disposition to deal with entire openness with regard to the affair in question." After explaining Clayton's views on an isthmian canal, Crampton continued: "In the whole of these observations General Taylor cordially concurred; the attempts, he remarked, which were making, and would be made in many quarters to produce a misunderstanding or a collision between the two governments on this matter were, in his opinion, only to be met by perfect frankness and fair dealing; it was his earnest wish, therefore, that the matter should be laid in this spirit before Your Lordship; and he expressed an anxious wish that the question might be promptly arranged equally to the honour and advantage of both countries." [46]

Clayton early made clear to Lord Palmerston, the British Secretary of State for Foreign Affairs, that the United States regarded Nicaragua as the true sovereign of the San Juan River territory and could not countenance Britain's seizure of it. He also made known the administration's opposition to Britain's claim to exercise protection over the Mosquito Indians and to the claim of a semi-independent status for them. At the same time he left no doubt that the President desired to avoid collision with Great Britain and was sincerely anxious to maintain the most cordial good understanding between the two governments.[47] When preliminary exchanges disclosed that though Palmerston could not agree with these views he was ready to co-operate in obtaining a canal dedicated to

[46] John F. Crampton to Lord Palmerston, October 1, 1849, in P. R. O., F. O. 5:501 (Library of Congress Photostats). A copy of this dispatch was submitted to Clayton; see Crampton to Clayton, October 2, 1849, in Clayton Papers.

[47] John M. Clayton to George Bancroft, May 2, 1849, in Manning (ed.), *Diplomatic Correspondence*, VII, 33–36; William C. Rives to John M. Clayton, September 25, 1849, *ibid.*, 312–17.

the use of all nations, Clayton proposed that the two countries enter into a treaty guaranteeing the independence of Honduras, Nicaragua, and Costa Rica, providing for the transfer to Nicaragua, for a price, of any Mosquito territory through which the canal might pass, and agreeing not to colonize, settle, annex, or fortify any part of Central America. In concluding the lengthy communication in which he instructed Abbott Lawrence, the United States minister, to propose such a treaty and to present the administration's views on the whole canal problem, Clayton said:

> The President is firm in his purpose, and will never consent that Great Britain shall under any pretext enjoy any exclusive possession within the territory of Nicaragua. If we adopt the treaty negotiated by Mr. Hise, and Great Britain should persevere in her assertion of the Mosquito title, I know not how we can avoid a collision consistently with our national honor. If, on the other hand, Great Britain should, as the President sincerely hopes she will, meet our proposition in the spirit in which it is made, the two greatest commercial nations of the world, instead of contending in hostility with each other, will engage in the accomplishment of an object which may redound more to the true glory of each of them than the most successful war in which either could engage.[48]

Without approving the detailed stipulation of such a treaty Lord Palmerston replied that the British government would "feel great pleasure in combining and cooperating" with the United States to secure the protection of a canal open to the commerce of all nations.[49] Negotiations, however, were suddenly complicated by developments in Central America. The success of Ephraim George Squire, whom Taylor sent to replace Hise, in obtaining from Nicaragua a charter of incorporation for a canal company and a new treaty whereby the United States

[48] John M. Clayton to Abbott Lawrence, October 20, 1849, *ibid.*, 52; Abbott Lawrence to Lord Palmerston, November 8, 1849, *ibid.*, 319–20.

[49] Lord Palmerston to Abbott Lawrence, November 13, 1849, *ibid.*, 323.

guaranteed the neutrality of the canal and recognized Nicaraguan sovereignty over the entire route placed the United States in a strong position. On the other hand, the seizure of Tigre Island at the Pacific end of the canal route by the British navy gave Great Britain control of both ends of the proposed canal and aroused a storm of indignation in the United States. The fact that this seizure was made in the face of a second treaty negotiated by Squire —a treaty with Honduras ceding Tigre Island to the United States for eighteen months—greatly increased the indignation.[50]

Clayton, anxious to complete the treaty negotiations before a congressional debate on the subject should destroy all chances of agreement, turned to Sir Henry Lytton Bulwer, the new British minister, who arrived in Washington just at the end of the year. Bulwer proved quite co-operative. Although lacking specific instructions on this subject he entered upon negotiations which within a few weeks resulted in the draft of a treaty designed to settle all dispute or discussion concerning the canal route through Nicaragua, while avoiding the question of Great Britain's protectorate over the Mosquito Indians and the rival territorial claims of Nicaragua and the Mosquitos.[51] Clayton reluctantly abandoned his earlier insistence that Great Britain definitely renounce her Mosquito protectorate. He believed he had indirectly accomplished this purpose, however, by including the word "occupy" in the joint pledge not to "occupy, or fortify, or colonize, or assume or exercise any dominion over Nicaragua, Costa Rica, the Mosquito Coast, or any part of Central America." [52]

On February 3 the two diplomats completed their work and affixed their signatures. While Bulwer hurried a copy

[50] Ephraim George Squire to John M. Clayton, September 10, 1849, *ibid.*, III, 360–74; *id.* to *id.*, October 10, 1849, *ibid.*, 393–407; *id.* to *id.*, October 25, 1849, *ibid.*, 418–23.

[51] Sir Henry L. Bulwer to Lord Palmerston, January 6 and February 3, 1850, in P. R. O., F. O. 5:511 (Library of Congress Photostats).

[52] Williams, "John Middleton Clayton," *loc. cit.*, 54–55.

to Palmerston and awaited his approval, Clayton presented the treaty to the Cabinet and promptly discovered that he might well have consulted them before. President Taylor and some of the Cabinet members were dissatisfied because Britain's Mosquito protectorate remained and they feared that Great Britain, "altho' agreeing not to occupy &c. directly for herself," might "consider herself at liberty to occupy &c. in right of the Mosquito King." Taylor insisted that the treaty should be a dead letter until Great Britain agreed to insert an explanatory article or clause pledging not to do indirectly what she could not do directly.[53] When these views were made known to the British minister he urged his government to make as much concession as possible because the administration, he reported, was in great difficulties, and, moreover, the question was becoming more perplexing the longer it remained unsettled and actually had in it the seeds of war.[54] Palmerston authorized Bulwer to sign the treaty as agreed to on February 3 and to present a note disclaiming any intention on the part of Britain to use her Mosquito protectorate to accomplish any of the things she had agreed not to do. This seemed to meet the objections of the Cabinet but not of President Taylor. He now insisted that Bulwer be notified that the United States did not recognize the title of the Mosquito Indians to the territory of the San Juan River. A note to this effect, prepared in a session of the Cabinet, was sent to Bulwer under date of April 6 with the statement that the President regarded it as indispensable to a proper definition of his position before signing the treaty. "He will not suffer it to be signed on any other terms," Clayton added.[55]

[53] John M. Clayton to Abbott Lawrence, February 15, 1850, draft in Clayton Papers.

[54] Sir Henry L. Bulwer to Lord Palmerston, February 18, 1850, in P. R. O., F. O. 5:511 (Library of Congress Photostats).

[55] John M. Clayton to Sir Henry L. Bulwer, April 6, 1850, draft in Clayton Papers.

Bulwer took strong exception to this note because it so definitely introduced the question of the Mosquito protectorate which it had been agreed at the outset to avoid. For ten days it appeared that the treaty might be abandoned, but after several long communications had been exchanged and conferences held, a solution was reached. Taylor finally consented to withdraw the note of April 6 and Bulwer agreed to embody in the treaty itself, rather than in an accompanying note, the pledge not to make use of any Central American protectorate or alliance to accomplish the objects forbidden by the treaty. On these terms the treaty was signed April 19, 1850.[56] A month later, after warm debate, the Senate gave its approval to the agreement, but before ratifications were exchanged new difficulties as to the proper interpretation of its provisions arose which again threatened to put an end to the project. Finally, after declarations and counterdeclarations and an all-night conference, an understanding was reached and ratifications were exchanged about dawn on July 5.[57]

Although in later years the Clayton-Bulwer Treaty was an obstacle in the way of an American canal under American control, at the time of its negotiation it served the important purpose of checking British expansion in Central America and preventing the Nicaraguan route from falling into the hands of a European power. "It liberates all Central America from foreign aggression," declared Clayton, "and it will . . . be hailed as a declaration of Central American independence." [58] A strict interpretation of the Monroe Doctrine might not have permitted England to participate in the protection of an American

[56] *Id.* to *id.*, April 8, 1850, *ibid.;* Sir Henry L. Bulwer to John M. Clayton, April 9 and 18, *ibid.;* Williams, "John Middleton Clayton," *loc. cit.*, 60–63.

[57] Williams, "John Middleton Clayton," *loc. cit.*, 66–69; Sir Henry L. Bulwer to John M. Clayton, June 29, 1850, in Manning (ed.), *Diplomatic Correspondence,* VII, 397; John M. Clayton to Sir Henry L. Bulwer, July 4, 1850, *ibid.*, 63–64.

[58] John M. Clayton to William C. Rives, April 27, 1850, in Manning (ed.), *Diplomatic Correspondence,* VI, 456.

canal, but Clayton did not regard that doctrine as an established principle of the American government and frankly admitted that it was not the policy of the Taylor administration.[59] While recognizing that the United States had paramount interests in an interoceanic canal the administration looked upon it as a great highway for the benefit of mankind. Consequently Britain's guarantee of the neutralization of the canal was welcomed, and a stipulation that other nations should be invited to make similar commitments was inserted in the treaty. In this spirit Clayton promptly commenced efforts to secure such an agreement with France, but he left office before anything could be accomplished. Clearly the Clayton-Bulwer Treaty was drafted, not with an eye to America's defense needs in the twentieth century, but for the promotion of peaceful international commerce.

Other problems in Anglo-American relations, but less critical than the Central American rivalry, resulted from the repeal of the English corn laws and the inauguration by the British government between 1846 and 1849 of a free-trade policy. The economic interests of Canada and other British North American colonies were so hard hit by the loss of preferential treatment in British markets that economic distress and political discontent resulted. While many influential Canadians advocated annexation to the United States as the remedy for their ills, as noted early in this chapter, others started vigorous agitation for free access to the markets of the United States on a reciprocal basis. This latter policy was supported by the Canadian government, including Lord Elgin, the Governor General, who constantly urged the officials in London to bend every effort to obtain better trade relations with the United States. Only in that way, believed Elgin and many others, could economic conditions be improved

[59] John F. Crampton to Lord Palmerston, October 15, 1849, in P. R. O., F. O. 5:501 (Library of Congress Photostats); Clayton's speech in the Senate, March 9, 1853, in *Congressional Globe*, 32 Cong., 2 Sess., Appendix, 254.

and annexation defeated. Negotiations looking to this end were commenced during Polk's administration and, though Polk and his Secretary of the Treasury, Robert J. Walker, looked with favor upon the proposition, no arrangement was concluded. Shortly after Taylor took office Crampton reopened the question. The new administration, led by such stanch advocates of protection as Clayton, Meredith, and Ewing, declined to consider any reciprocity treaty. Moreover, President Taylor believed that the matter should be left to Congress, for it involved the tariff laws and therefore the House of Representatives was entitled to share in any decision concerning it. He promised to submit the question to Congress and to abide by its decision. At no time, however, did the President or the Cabinet support or advocate legislation of this nature. Taylor made no mention of Canada or reciprocity in his annual message, and only in May, 1850, after Congress had of its own accord commenced a consideration of the subject did he submit to it Clayton's correspondence thereon. Meanwhile, however, he had appointed a special agent, Israel D. Andrews, to visit the British North American colonies in order to gather statistics and general information concerning their commerce; moreover, Clayton had secured from Great Britain a promise to open the St. Lawrence River to the navigation of American ships, provided reciprocal free trade were agreed upon. Congress, however, was too much absorbed in the great slavery controversy to act upon the question of trade with the nation's northern neighbors.[60]

Taylor likewise left to Congress the several questions

[60] *House Executive Documents*, 31 Cong., 1 Sess., No. 64; John F. Crampton to Lord Palmerston, July 9, 1849, in P. R. O., F. O. 5:500; Sir Henry L. Bulwer to *id.*, January 6 and June 3, 1850, *ibid.*, 511, 513 (Library of Congress Photostats). For full discussions of the reciprocity problems see C. C. Tansill, *The Canadian Reciprocity Treaty of 1854* (Baltimore, 1922); Donald C. Masters, *The Reciprocity Treaty of 1854* (London, 1937); and C. D. Allin and G. M. Jones, *Annexation, Preferential Trade and Reciprocity* (Toronto, 1912).

arising out of the repeal in 1849 of the two-century-old British navigation laws. Under an 1817 act of Congress this step on the part of the British government opened American ports to British ships on equal terms with those of the United States. But whether this meant that British vessels might engage in the trade between Atlantic and Pacific ports or whether such was a part of the coasting trade and therefore closed to all foreign ships, and whether British-built ships might be admitted to American registry, were proper subjects, Taylor insisted, for legislative consideration. He therefore submitted them to Congress, but carefully refrained from making any recommendation as to action. On these problems, as on reciprocity, Congress made no decision at this time.[61]

President Taylor's decision to view such matters as legislative problems was a natural result of his conviction that recent administrations had magnified the power and importance of the executive department far beyond the intention of the fathers of the Constitution and his own determination not to encroach upon the powers of Congress. But as already indicated the tariff policy of the Whig party was doubtless another influence in this direction.

With a single exception the few remaining diplomatic problems seem to have aroused no special concern on the part of the President. In his annual message he revealed an interest in American relations with Mexico, South America, and the Hawaiian Islands, but the negotiation of a treaty of commerce with Hawaii and of a claims convention with Brazil and discussions with Mexico over the Treaty of Guadalupe Hidalgo he apparently left entirely to Secretary Clayton. However, the desperate struggle of the Hungarians to rid themselves of Austria's autocratic rule gained his attention and interest. Believing that the United States could not be an unconcerned spectator of

[61] John M. Clayton to Sir Henry L. Bulwer, January 14, 1850, in P. R. O., F. O. 5:511 (Library of Congress Photostats); *House Executive Documents*, 31 Cong., 1 Sess., No. 46.

revolutionary events in Europe, and hopeful that the revolution would be successful, he determined to be the very first to recognize the new state.

President Taylor was by no means alone in his sympathetic attitude toward Hungary's fight for independence. The great majority of Americans shared his interest. Some of the more enthusiastic citizens gathered in mass meetings and adopted resolutions urging the administration to recognize the independence of Hungary.[62] So widespread was popular interest in this and other mid-century revolutions in Europe that American poets turned to the subject and Thomas Buchanan Read wrote

> Oh, joy to the world! the hour is come,
> When the nations to freedom awake.[63]

In Congress, Representative Alexander W. Buel of Michigan declared that Hungary would not look in vain upon the talents and patriotism of that body for support in her misfortunes. "It is the province, the mission, aye, the destiny of my country," he proclaimed, "to become a propagandist of its own principles and institutions, until the language of history shall inscribe upon every throne of the earth, 'FUIT.' "[64]

As his secret agent to visit Hungary in order to make known his intention of extending recognition as soon as it appeared that a permanent government had been set up President Taylor appointed A. Dudley Mann. This diplomat was at the time an attaché of the American legation in Paris and had previously served on special missions to Central Europe. Unfortunately for the Hungarians, Austria received aid from Russia and the revolt was

[62] Philadelphia *Public Ledger*, July 6, 1849; Merle E. Curti, *Austria and the United States, 1848–1852* (Northampton, 1926), 141; John G. Gazley, *American Opinion of German Unification, 1848–1871* (New York, 1926), 51–58.

[63] Gazley, *American Opinion of German Unification, 1848–1871*, 19.

[64] *Congressional Globe*, 31 Cong., 1 Sess., Appendix, 144.

crushed. By the time Mann reached Hungary recognition was out of the question.[65] Although the matter seemed to be closed Taylor did not hesitate to declare in his annual message what his intentions had been and to state that the feelings of the United States "were strongly enlisted in the cause, and by the sufferings of a brave people, who had made a gallant, though unsuccessful, effort to be free." [66] Nor did the protests of the Austrian chargé d'affaires against this, Taylor's nearest approach to meddling in the affairs of another nation, restrain him from giving a cordial welcome to a group of the leading Hungarian refugees when they were presented to him in Washington in January, 1850. "The oppressed of every land," Taylor promised them, "will here find the same protection that we ourselves enjoy. Here your rights, and liberties, and religion will be respected and maintained." [67]

Most Americans were pleased with Taylor's Hungarian policy and felt that he had done all that could be done in the circumstances, but there were, as always, a few individuals who were dissatisfied. By failing to recognize the independence of Hungary before the revolution was crushed, "the President and his Cabinet departed from the settled policy of the country, disappointed the friends of freedom and did violence to the sympathies and wishes of the American people," Representative Buel charged on the floor of Congress.[68]

When in March, in response to a request from the Senate, the administration's instructions to Mann were made public, Hülsemann, the Austrian chargé d'affaires in Washington, filed a bitter protest. His government had

[65] Clayton's instructions to Mann are in *Senate Executive Documents,* 31 Cong., 1 Sess., No. 43; and his reports in *Senate Executive Documents,* 61 Cong., 2 Sess., No. 279, and *Senate Executive Documents,* 65 Cong., 2 Sess., No. 282.

[66] *Annual Message,* December 4, 1849, in Richardson, *Messages and Papers of the Presidents,* V, 12.

[67] Washington *Republic,* January 16, 1850.

[68] *Congressional Globe,* 31 Cong., 1 Sess., Appendix, 146.

been displeased when it first learned of the Mann mission, and Taylor's reference to the Hungarian revolution in his annual message had increased the resentment. Equally offensive was Senator Cass's proposal that diplomatic relations with Austria be suspended as a rebuke to that country for her "atrocious acts of despotism, by which human liberty and life have been sacrificed." [69] Now the whole matter was to be further aired by the publication of the instructions to the special agent. The Austrian government, in order that silence might not be interpreted as acquiescence in the American policy, instructed Hülsemann to make known its view that the Mann mission was an unjustified interference in the internal affairs of that country.[70] This protest called forth from Daniel Webster, who had succeeded Clayton in the State Department, his famous note of December 21, 1850, in which he vigorously defended the actions of the Taylor administration and the right of the United States to take an active interest in the European struggles for freedom.[71]

Although Taylor and Clayton in their conduct of American foreign relations occasionally reflected too clearly the stubborn pride of the young and growing United States, on the whole they successfully maintained honest friendship with all nations. They adhered to the policy of strict neutrality in the affairs of other countries, avoided serious trouble with Spain over Cuba, and furthered friendly relations with Great Britain. At most points the more experienced Secretary of State led the way, but on occasion Taylor boldly took command and contributed in no small measure to the successful conduct of the nation's foreign affairs.

[69] *Ibid.*, 54.
[70] Curti, *Austria and the United States, 1848–1852*, 161–63.
[71] *Senate Executive Documents*, 31 Cong., 2 Sess., No. 9.

Chapter XVI

A NATIONAL CRISIS

IN 1820 the bitter sectional debates over the Missouri Compromise sounded in the ears of Thomas Jefferson like a fire bell ringing in the night. Nearly thirty years later, as Zachary Taylor said good-bye to his friends at Baton Rouge and traveled north and east to Washington, the bell was ringing more violently, more ominously, than ever before. The issue of the extension of slavery, raised anew by the acquisition of Texas and Oregon and the Mexican cession, once again threatened to dissolve the Union. While Northern legislatures were adopting resolutions asserting the right of Congress to exclude slavery from the territories and the desirability of its doing so, in the South state legislatures, special conventions, and Southern congressmen led by John C. Calhoun, were calling for united resistance to Northern aggression. Disunion, secession, separation, resistance at all hazards, civil war, a Southern confederacy—these words fell from the lips of loyal Americans, both north and south, with increasing frequency and feeling.

South Carolina and Mississippi were most extreme in their outcries, but even Virginia, normally moderate and cautious, was boldly asserting that Congressional acceptance of the Wilmot Proviso would force the people of that state to choose between "abject submission to aggression and outrage, on the one hand, or determined resistance on the other, at all hazards and to the last extremity." No

ZACHARY TAYLOR AS PRESIDENT OF THE UNITED STATES

Reproduced from a lithograph by F. D'Avignon after a daguerreotype by Brady. Courtesy of the Library of Congress.

doubt was entertained by the legislature that resistance, not submission, would be the people's choice.[1]

For two and a half years Congress had struggled with the Wilmot Proviso in one form or another, as they battled over the question of slavery in the territories. Finally in August, 1848, Oregon had been organized as a free territory, but California and the rest of the Mexican cession were still unorganized when Polk's administration came to an end. In vain did Taylor's Southern supporters, led by Toombs, Stephens, and Preston, seek some solution to this problem during the closing months of the Thirtieth Congress which expired on March 4, 1849—a solution that would free the incoming Whig administration from this source of friction and strife. Equally fruitless were Taylor's own efforts to exert some influence through William H. Seward, senator-elect from New York. As the final hours of Congress were slipping away in hopeless controversy Taylor urged that some solution—any solution—of the California problem be reached. But his efforts were unavailing.[2]

When Taylor took office there were five vexatious problems—bleeding wounds, Henry Clay called them—disturbing the harmony and threatening the well-being if not the very existence of the Union. These problems, all the result of sectional conflict over slavery, were: the organization of California as a territory or state, with or without slavery; the organization of the remainder of the Mexican cession; a boundary dispute between Texas and the inhabitants of the New Mexico area; the demand of the South for a more effective fugitive-slave law; the demand of the antislavery forces of the North for the abolition of the slave trade, if not slavery itself, in the District of Columbia.

[1] Henry T. Shanks, *The Secession Movement in Virginia, 1847–1861* (Richmond, 1934), 22–26. These resolutions were originally adopted in March, 1847, but they were reaffirmed and strengthened in January, 1849.

[2] Washington *Daily Union,* March 29, April 3 and 5, 1849.

Most in need of immediate attention was the first of these issues. The discovery of gold in California early in 1848 had set the whole country ablaze with excitement and started a stream of fortune seekers to the West Coast. The rapid increase in population made acute the need for civil government in California, and though Polk repeatedly urged action upon Congress, slavery blocked the way. The South would not authorize the organization of a free territory or state; the North would not consent to the extension of slavery.

As Taylor and Polk rode away from the Capitol on inauguration day California was discussed. Taylor startled the outgoing President with the suggestion that California and Oregon were too distant to become members of the Union and that it would be better for them to be organized into a separate, independent state.[3] But this view was soon discarded. Before he had been a month in office Taylor dispatched Thomas Butler King, Whig congressman from Georgia, to make known to the people of California the President's desire that they form a state constitution and government, and petition Congress for admission as a state.[4] Congress had failed to provide a territorial government and had omitted to authorize the organization of a state government. Therefore Taylor proposed that the people wait no longer, but take matters into their own hands. He believed it of no importance whether the first steps toward the formation of a new state were taken by invitation of Congress or on the initiative of the people. The final decision remained with Congress. The people of California, he believed, had a right to assemble in convention, adopt a form of government, and seek from Congress admission to the Union.

This plan did not originate with the President. Secre-

[3] Polk, *Diary,* IV, 375.

[4] President Taylor's California Message, January 21, 1850, in *House Executive Documents,* 31 Cong., 1 Sess., No. 17, p. 1; John M. Clayton to Thomas Butler King, April 3, 1849, *ibid.,* 9–11.

tary Clayton, with perhaps some support from Preston, was its author. Early in the last session of the Thirtieth Congress, Clayton had proposed to Crittenden that the best solution of the territorial problem would be to skip the territorial stage and organize states which should be admitted with such constitutions as they adopted.[5] At that time he had hoped Congress would authorize the organization of states, but when it did not, he doubtless conceived the idea of acting without such authority. Clayton's original proposal received the warm endorsement of Crittenden both at the time it was made and after Clayton had become Secretary of State.[6] When in April, Crittenden urged him to do everything possible to carry out this plan, Clayton, who had finished the instructions to King but a few days before, replied: "As to California & New Mexico, I have been *wide awake*. Everything is done as you would wish it. The plan I proposed to you last winter will be carried out fully. The States will be admitted —free and Whig!" [7] During the previous session of Congress, Preston, then one of Virginia's representatives in the House, also urged the immediate organization of California as a state. Now as a member of Taylor's Cabinet he doubtless supported the administration's California policy.[8]

But whether suggested by Clayton or Preston, or by some other adviser, this policy fully met the President's approval and was adhered to by him during the ensuing months with great persistence. Before going to Washington he had taken the ground that Congress ought not to legislate about slavery in the new territory.[9] He had long

[5] John M. Clayton to J. J. Crittenden, December 13, 1849, in Crittenden Papers.

[6] J. J. Crittenden to John M. Clayton, December 19, 1848, and April 11, 1849, in Clayton Papers.

[7] John M. Clayton to J. J. Crittenden, April 18, 1849, in Crittenden Papers.

[8] *Congressional Globe*, 30 Cong., 2 Sess., 477–80.

[9] Hitchcock, *Fifty Years in Camp and Field*, 348.

viewed the Wilmot Proviso as of no importance except as a source of sectional conflict and he believed that it never should have been proposed. Therefore Taylor welcomed an opportunity to disregard it. In the debates in Congress a year later it was charged that he adopted this policy because he lacked moral courage and was unwilling to accept the responsibility of approving or vetoing a bill that contained the proviso. He adopted this California policy, however, not because it would enable him to shun responsibility, but because he believed it would permit the nation to escape bitter controversy on the subject of slavery in California.

Even before Taylor's special messenger reached his destination, the Californians, with the full approval of the military authorities, had made plans for a state organization and had started to carry them into effect. Encouraged by the knowledge that their plans accorded with the President's wishes they worked rapidly. By the close of the year a constitution had been drafted and ratified by the people and officials had been elected. On December 20, Brigadier General Bennet Riley, with the approval of Secretary of War Crawford, surrendered his powers as governor of California to the recently elected civilian governor, and the state government came into full operation.[10] There remained, however, the all-important question: Would Congress, which alone was authorized by the United States Constitution to admit new members to the Union, accept this "state," which had been carved out of United States territory without waiting for a congressional enabling act?

That portion of the Mexican cession east of California, known as New Mexico, was also in need of a civil government, but the need was not so pressing. The Mexican population in this region was not numerous and there was no gold strike to draw American pioneers in large num-

[10] For the formation of the California government and the special mission of Thomas Butler King see: *House Executive Documents,* 31 Cong., 1 Sess., No. 17, and *Senate Executive Documents,* 31 Cong., 1 Sess., No. 52.

bers. Therefore President Taylor did not act with the same promptness in the case of New Mexico, but when he did he followed the same policy as in California. In November, Lieutenant Colonel George A. McCall, about to join his regiment in New Mexico, was instructed that the people of New Mexico need not await congressional action before organizing a government, and that if they took any steps toward this object he and the other officers with whom he was associated should advance, not thwart, these efforts. "It is their right to appear before Congress and ask for admission into the Union," his instructions declared.[11]

President Taylor desired to have New Mexico organized as a state not only to spare Congress and the country the agitation of the question of slavery in that territory, but also because there was a difficult boundary dispute between Texas and the New Mexicans. Taylor foresaw that if this problem were left to Congress for settlement it would inevitably become involved in the bitter slavery controversy. The South would insist upon Texas' claim to the Rio Grande as her western boundary, for that would give the largest limits to that slave state. The North would oppose this claim and insist upon the organization of New Mexico as a free state or territory. On the other hand, if New Mexico could be organized as a state the boundary dispute could be submitted to the Supreme Court and settled as a legal rather than a political or sectional problem.

When Congress assembled in December, President Taylor reported in his annual message that California had created a state government and was expected shortly to apply for admission to the Union, and that similar action by the people of New Mexico was looked for at no very distant period. He entreated Congress to await the action of these two groups and thus avoid "all causes of uneasi-

[11] George W. Crawford to George A. McCall, November 19, 1849, in *House Executive Documents,* 31 Cong., 1 Sess., No. 17, pp. 280–81.

ness," and urged them to preserve "confidence and kind feeling." "With a view of maintaining the harmony and tranquillity so dear to all," he further advised, "we should abstain from the introduction of those exciting topics of a sectional character which have hitherto produced painful apprehensions in the public mind." [12] Any doubt as to where this son of Virginia and Kentucky, this planter from Louisiana and Mississippi, stood in reference to the threat of disunion that had been ringing through the country for more than a year should have been removed by his closing paragraph—a paragraph added, it was claimed, in defiance of a request from Calhoun that the message be silent on this critical point.[13] "But attachment to the Union of the States," he said, "should be habitually fostered in every American heart. . . . In my judgment its dissolution would be the greatest of calamities, and to avert that should be the study of every American. Upon its preservation must depend our own happiness and that of countless generations to come. Whatever dangers may threaten it, I shall stand by it and maintain it in its integrity to the full extent of the obligations imposed and the powers conferred upon me by the Constitution." [14]

Before Taylor's annual message with its advice on the maintenance of harmony and tranquillity could be received, the House of Representatives had engaged in a three weeks' contest over the election of the speaker, in the course of which the bitter sectional hostility was given every opportunity to express itself, and the threat of disunion was defiantly hurled by Toombs.[15] This contest was

[12] *Senate Executive Documents,* 31 Cong., 1 Sess., No. 1, p. 11.

[13] Ben Perley Poore claimed (*Reminiscences,* 354–55) that it was Taylor's inaugural address to which a paragraph was added in defiance of Calhoun, but the final paragraph of the annual message is more clearly on this subject and seems more in the nature of an appendix. Moreover, that it was the annual message is borne out by the testimony of Senator Thomas Hart Benton in his *Thirty Years' View* (New York, 1881), II, 740.

[14] *Senate Executive Documents,* 31 Cong., 1 Sess., No. 1, p. 16.

[15] *Congressional Globe,* 31 Cong., 1 Sess., 2–66.

significant not only because it removed the lid from the boiling cauldron of sectional jealousies and hatreds, but also because it opened the split in the Whig party that was to leave Taylor helpless before his enemies. When on the eve of the meeting of Congress the party caucus refused to pledge opposition to the Wilmot Proviso, Southern Whigs, led by Toombs and Stephens, withdrew from the caucus and declined to give their support to Robert C. Winthrop of Massachusetts who had been selected as the party's candidate for speaker.[16] Toombs and Stephens had worked for the nomination and election of Taylor in 1848 in the firm belief that Southern interests would not suffer at the hands of a Southern planter. During the weeks preceding Taylor's inauguration they had opposed Calhoun's attempt to organize the South, because, as Toombs declared to the assembled Southern congressmen, "we did not expect an administration which we had brought into power would do any act or permit any act to be done which it would become necessary for our safety to rebel at." [17] But when a year later they returned to Washington for the opening of the new Congress, and found how powerful was Seward's influence, and when they failed to secure from Taylor a pledge to veto any bill containing the Wilmot Proviso, they felt compelled to cast their lot with the Southern Democrats. They determined to oppose the Proviso regardless of any effect upon Taylor and his administration and, so far as Toombs was concerned, "even to the extent of a dissolution of the Union." [18]

President Taylor's recommendation that California be admitted just as soon as she presented the antislavery constitution which she had already adopted, aroused the full

[16] Richard H. Shryock, *Georgia and the Union in 1850* (Durham, 1926), 238; Ulrich B. Phillips, *The Life of Robert Toombs* (New York, 1913), 66–73.

[17] Robert Toombs to J. J. Crittenden, January 22, 1849, in Crittenden Papers.

[18] *Id.* to *id.*, April 23, 1850, *ibid.*; Avary, *Recollections of Alexander H. Stephens*, 25–26.

opposition of the slave-state politicians. There were at the time an equal number of slave states and free states—fifteen of each—and the Southerners were determined not to admit California, not to surrender their power to block any hostile legislation in the Senate, without first obtaining a satisfactory solution of every slavery problem before the country. "We shall never be stronger than we are today," cried Henry W. Hilliard of Alabama on the floor of Congress, "and we must therefore settle today the interests of the great future. . . . We are strong enough now to repel the aggressions which threaten us, and to secure ample protection for our future safety." [19] On the same day, in the Senate, Henry S. Foote of Mississippi, expressing the same point of view, declared that the admission of California except as a part of a general settlement of all problems growing out of the institution of slavery would "demand" secession.[20] Calhoun, believing that the South had "borne the wrongs and insults of the North long enough" urged resistance to the admission of California "until restoration of all our rights, or disunion, one or the other, is the consequence." [21]

It is not surprising that Southern congressmen holding such views assailed Taylor for urging California to prepare for admission without waiting for authority from Congress. Scarcely had the annual message been read when resolutions were introduced in both the House and the Senate calling upon the President for information as to events in California and New Mexico, and particularly as to any agents or officers sent by the President or other executive departments to aid or advise the people of those territories as to the formation of state governments. The clear implication was that the President, through his agents, had been responsible for the organization of government in Cali-

[19] *Congressional Globe,* 31 Cong., 1 Sess., 359.
[20] *Ibid.,* 365–67.
[21] John C. Calhoun to Mrs. T. G. Clemson, December 31, 1849, in Jameson (ed.), *Correspondence of John C. Calhoun, loc. cit.,* 778.

fornia and had controlled it step by step.[22] These resolutions, both sets of which were adopted, called forth from Taylor a special message and nearly a thousand pages of documents.[23] The message, submitted to the House on January 21, 1850, had been circulated among the Cabinet by Clayton, who doubtless had the largest share in its preparation.[24] In it Taylor acknowledged sending agents to California and New Mexico to make known his desire that the residents of those territories organize state governments and petition Congress for admission into the Union, but he denied exercising any influence or control in their subsequent activities. He pointed out that on the contrary he had made it clear in his instructions that any such government must "be the result of their own deliberate choice, and originate with themselves without the interference of the Executive." His earnest desire to avoid "occasions of bitter and angry dissensions among the people of the United States," he said, was his principal motive in advising early applications for statehood. Once again he entreated Congress to admit California as soon as her constitution was presented and to await similar action by the people of New Mexico.

Now that they had over the President's own signature an acknowledgment that he had sent King to California and McCall to New Mexico, the congressional opposition lost no time in pouring forth their angry condemnation of the executive. The attack was commenced as soon as the special message of January 21 was received and was invigorated three weeks later when Taylor submitted to Congress California's constitution. All through the late winter weeks and the spring months it continued. His whole proceeding was denounced as a "crime against the constitution of the

22 *Congressional Globe,* 31 Cong., 1 Sess., 78, 87, 90, 110.

23 *House Executive Documents,* 31 Cong., 1 Sess., No. 17.

24 An undated note in Clayton's hand in the Meredith Papers indicates that the Secretary of the Treasury was requested to make alterations in the message and to pass it on to Ewing.

land," because it usurped legislative powers and in fact amounted to aiding and abetting revolution.[25] Without a shred of evidence to support it, the charge was hurled that the President had instructed King to notify the Californians that they must adopt an antislavery constitution.[26] He was also condemned on the ground that his policy violated the rights of the South by excluding Southerners and their property from the wide expanse of California.[27] Few speakers made any attempt to place the blame for this crime upon any other head than that of the President. One who did was Congressman James A. Seddon of Virginia who denounced the administration's California policy with much warmth but declared he did not hold President Taylor responsible for it. He blamed the Cabinet, rather than the "honest, brave old soldier" whose training had been in arms and not in the council chamber or halls of legislation. He called upon Taylor in the name of his Southern heritage to renounce his past policy and to scatter the cloud of fanatics, abolitionists, and Free-Soilers which threatened the country.[28]

Meanwhile numerous plans for the adjustment of these sectional issues were presented by members of Congress. Senators Clay, Bell, and Foote each introduced lengthy resolutions on the subject.[29] The proposals of Foote, Mississippi's outspoken champion of Southern rights, were thoroughly unacceptable to the North. The resolutions presented by Bell of Tennessee were less comprehensive and dealt only with the problems of the Southwest. Most comprehensive in scope and compromising in spirit were the resolutions introduced by the aged senator from Kentucky, Henry Clay. With the experience of more than forty years of public life to guide him, and with a well-established reputation as a compromiser to sustain him, he

[25] *Congressional Globe,* 31 Cong., 1 Sess., 348–49.
[26] *Ibid.*
[27] *Ibid.,* Appendix, 74–78. [28] *Ibid.,* 78.
[29] *Ibid.,* 31 Cong., 1 Sess., 244–47, 323–24, 436–39.

determined to attempt an amicable adjustment of all the slavery controversies as the only means of preserving the peace of the Union; he determined to present a "great national scheme of compromise and harmony." His resolutions, submitted after consultation with numerous colleagues, called for the admission of California with no congressional restriction as to slavery, the organization of territorial governments for the remainder of the Mexican cession "without the adoption of any restriction or condition on the subject of slavery," relinquishment by Texas of her extreme boundary claims in return for a payment of a portion of her public debt by the United States, the abolition of the slave trade in the District of Columbia but noninterference with slavery in that District, more effectual provision for the return of fugitive slaves and, finally, an assertion that Congress was powerless "to obstruct trade in slaves between the slave-holding states." [30]

For two months Clay's resolutions were the main consideration of the Senate. But whether senators spoke to the resolutions of Clay, Bell, or Foote or to some other resolution or bill touching the slavery problem, senator after senator discussed the great national crisis in all its varied aspects. Almost all other legislation was paralyzed by the all-engrossing debate which at times became so bitter that pistols were drawn and lives were threatened.[31] Great public figures rapidly nearing the end of their days, including Webster, Calhoun, Cass, Benton, and Clay himself, participated in the discussions. Calhoun, almost at the grave, too weak to speak, had no choice but to permit a colleague to read his plea for Southern rights. Younger men not yet at the height of their fame, but soon to reach it—Foote, Douglas, Chase, Seward, and Jefferson Davis—joined in the debate.

[30] *Ibid.*, 244–47, 365–68.

[31] James S. Pike, *First Blows of the Civi War: The Ten Years of Preliminary Conflict in the United States, From 1850 to 1860* (New York, 1879), 27–32.

It was in the midst of these speeches, toward the end of February when the secession danger reached its peak, that Daniel Webster decided to support the cause of compromise. A few days later, in a Senate chamber crowded with privileged persons, the great Massachusetts orator delivered his famous Seventh of March Speech. "Not as a Massachusetts man, nor as a Northern man, but as an American," the "God-like Daniel" appealed "for the preservation of the Union." While his antislavery constituents stood aghast, the friends of compromise applauded Webster's bold stand. His influence, added to that of the Great Pacificator, seemed to guarantee the success of compromise and to ensure the amicable adjustment of the national crisis. Although the threat of immediate disunion waned, a long and bitter fight ensued before an agreement was reached.[32]

While this debate was carried on in public the details of the compromise measures which were to be adopted many months later were worked out in secret. "All the Union men, North and South, Whigs and Democrats, for a period of six months," Stephen A. Douglas later said, "were assembled in caucus every day, with Clay in the chair, Cass upon his right hand, Webster upon his left hand, and the Whigs and Democrats arranged on either side." [33] Douglas himself, chairman of the Senate Committee on Territories, played a significant role in all these discussions and maneuvers. The bills finally adopted embodied his ideas to a larger extent than they did those of Clay or any other individual, and "all were carried through the Senate under his leadership and through the House by his friends." [34] Important though Douglas' con-

[32] Herbert D. Foster, "Webster's Seventh of March Speech and the Secession Movement, 1850," in *American Historical Review,* XXVII (1921–1922), 260; *Congressional Globe,* 31 Cong., 1 Sess., 476.

[33] James F. Rhodes, *History of the United States from the Compromise of 1850* (New York, 1893), I, 173 n.

[34] Frank H. Hodder, "The Authorship of the Compromise of 1850," in *Mississippi Valley Historical Review,* XXII (1935–1936), 536.

tributions were, the public looked upon Clay as the leader of the compromise movement. President Taylor also regarded him as chiefly responsible for the efforts to substitute a congressional plan for the proposed executive solution of the crisis and viewed the contest which developed as one between himself and the Kentucky senator.

During the last week of February, before Webster had spoken and while the secession tide was running high, President Taylor had a dramatic opportunity to reassert his inflexible opposition to dismemberment of the Union. On Saturday, February 23, he was waited upon by three Southern Whig congressmen, Stephens and Toombs of Georgia, and Thomas L. Clingman of North Carolina. Early in the week they had led a filibuster through one day and much of the following night to prevent favorable action on the President's recommendation that California be admitted.[35] Now they had come to argue him out of his position. But Taylor stood his ground with all the firmness ever exhibited in the face of the enemy. When he insisted that he would approve any constitutional bill passed by Congress and would faithfully execute the laws of the country, his callers talked of secession and a dissolution of the Union. Whereupon Old Rough and Ready wrathfully informed the congressmen that "if it became necessary, in executing the laws, he would take command of the army himself, and that, if they were taken in rebellion against the Union, he would hang them with less reluctance than he had hung deserters and spies in Mexico!" [36]

A few minutes later when Senator Hannibal Hamlin called upon the President he met the three angry congressmen hurrying from the White House. When he entered the President's office "General Taylor was rushing around the room like a caged lion," fiercely muttering to himself

[35] *Congressional Globe,* 31 Cong., 1 Sess., 375–85.
[36] Barnes, *Memoir of Thurlow Weed,* 176–77.

and shaking his fist at imaginary foes. "Did you see those damned traitors?" the President excitedly asked, and promptly repeated his threat to hang them and to put himself at the head of the army.[37]

When Senator Hamlin departed, after a very brief interview, Thurlow Weed was admitted to the President's room. He, too, found the old gentleman still much excited and pacing to and fro. After relating his experience with the Southern congressmen, Taylor referred to the letter he had written to Jefferson Davis in the summer of 1847 in which he had counseled the South to "act promptly, boldly and decisively, with arms in their hands" if Northern aggressions became unbearable.[38] At that time, he said, he had relied upon the assurances of Southern statesmen that the North was aggressive and the Constitution was in danger, "but that since it had become his duty to look carefully into the merits of the controversy, he had satisfied himself that the exactions and purposes of the South were intolerant and revolutionary." [39] In the South, not the North, lay the danger to the Union.

With the passage of time Taylor calmed down, but he did not weaken in his determination to maintain the Union. When a week later Congressman Horace Mann dined at the White House the President frankly talked of the danger of secession and stated that Thomas Jefferson had pointed out the way to quell any such movement—"which was to send a fleet to blockade their harbors, levy duties on all goods going in, and prevent any goods from coming out. I can save the Union without shedding a drop of blood. It is not true, as reported at the North, that I

[37] Charles E. Hamlin, *The Life and Times of Hannibal Hamlin* (Cambridge, 1899), 201. Nearly thirty years later Senator Clingman denied that he had ever participated in such a conference with Taylor. *Selections from the Speeches and Writings of Hon. Thomas L. Clingman . . .* (Raleigh, 1877), 273.

[38] Taylor to Jefferson Davis, August 16, 1847, in Library of Congress.

[39] Barnes, *Memoir of Thurlow Weed,* 177.

said I would march an army and subdue them: there would be no need of any." [40]

Clay's compromise proposals faced the opposition not only of Calhoun and many other Southern leaders and of the antislavery forces of the North led by Seward, but also of the White House. Having announced his own plan and possessing, as Webster said, "that quality, which, when a man is right, we call firmness, and when he is wrong, we denominate obstinacy," [41] the President determined to stand by it as the only acceptable solution of the slavery problems. Moreover, deeply jealous of Clay because of the praise heaped upon him for his compromise efforts, Taylor became unusually resolute in his position.[42] As the weeks passed without the admission of California he became convinced that his plan had been blocked by Clay's meddling. The more the old senator and his compromise proposals became the center of attention the more determined Old Rough and Ready became that his plan—the President's plan—should not be sidetracked merely to add to the glory of Clay. By the middle of March their relations were "civil but cold." [43] When late in April, the senator passed Taylor on the Avenue without speaking, the President believed that he had been deliberately cut. Clay's subsequent apology and insistence that he had been unaware that he was passing the President appeased Taylor but little.[44] Henceforth "Old Zach" growled at Clay openly.

Although the breach between the chief executive and

[40] Mary Mann, *Life of Horace Mann* (Boston, 1891), I, 292–93.

[41] Daniel Webster to Mr. Haven, September 12, 1850, in Curtis, *Life of Daniel Webster*, II, 473.

[42] Stephen A. Douglas believed that Taylor's jealousy and hatred of Clay made him oppose the compromise. Poage, *Henry Clay and the Whig Party*, 213 n.

[43] Henry Clay to James Harlan, March 16, 1850, in Colton (ed.), *Works of Henry Clay*, V, 603.

[44] Poage, *Henry Clay and the Whig Party*, 204–205.

the veteran statesman was known to all it did not become an open break until the latter part of May. By that time the special Committee of Thirteen, of which Clay was chairman, had reported three bills. One was concerned with the fugitive-slave problem, and a second prohibited the slave trade in the District of Columbia. The third bill provided for the admission of California, the settlement of the Texas boundary, and the organization of Utah and New Mexico as territories with the slavery question left to the decision of the people of these territories at the time of their admission as states. This third bill, which Taylor denounced as an "omnibus bill," Clay had agreed to reluctantly. He preferred to deal with these several problems in separate bills but the Southern members of the committee feared that this arrangement would give the President an opportunity to sign the California bill and veto the others. Therefore they insisted that these issues be dealt with in one bill.[45]

On May 21, speaking in behalf of these compromise measures, Clay threw off all restraint. With deep feeling, scorn, contempt, and derision he attacked the President's plan and challenged any friend of Taylor to rise and support it. "He displayed the spirit and the fire of youth," the New York *Tribune* correspondent wrote. "Deep, pervading passion spoke in his impetuous gestures and his purple countenance. . . . His voice was never more flexible or more trumpet-toned. . . . His features gleamed with demoniac energy. Withering blasts came from his mouth." [46] Not until his physical powers were exhausted and he had no choice but to give up the attack did the Kentucky senator close his speech.

Clay denounced the President's plan because it would leave four of the nation's five wounds to bleed more profusely than ever and would leave the people of New Mex-

[45] *Senate Reports,* 31 Cong., 1 Sess., No. 123.
[46] Pike, *First Blows of the Civil War,* 72.

Courtesy of the Library of Congress

HENRY CLAY

ico under a military government for an indefinite period, and he condemned Taylor for his unwillingness to co-operate in the spirit of compromise.[47] When several weeks later Senator Bell called Clay to task for this withering attack upon the President, Clay insisted that he had made it only after the administration had made war, "open war, undisguised war," upon the compromise bill, after the heads of departments had denounced the measure, and "the President himself in derision had called it the omnibus bill." [48] Taylor, it is true, had made clear his opposition to the compromise plan, and had insisted upon a change in the editorship of the *Republic,* in part because Bullitt was too friendly to Clay's proposal. Some of the Cabinet had also announced their disapproval of the compromise. Further than this Taylor and the administration had not gone. "Open war, undisguised war" was inaugurated not by Taylor, but by Clay himself.

Other senators, especially James M. Mason of Virginia and Lewis Cass of Michigan, joined in the attack on the President and his plan.[49] Not, however, until the first week in July was any serious defense of Taylor offered. Then Senator Bell, speaking on parts of three days, answered Clay, Mason, and Cass, and ably defended Taylor against the charges of usurpation of power, of cowardly shrinking from personal and political responsibility, and of advocating a sit-still and do-nothing policy. He especially reprimanded Clay for his attack of May 21 and charged him with exercising a moral despotism. The issue between Clay and the President, he said, is the old question whether Mahomet will go to the mountain, or the mountain shall come to Mahomet.[50] If Taylor, lying mortally ill at the other end of the Avenue before the speech

[47] *Congressional Globe,* 31 Cong., 1 Sess., Appendix, 614–16.

[48] *Ibid.,* 1091.

[49] *Ibid.,* 649–53, 803–10.

[50] *Ibid.,* 1088–1106. For a useful discussion of Bell's part in the Compromise of 1850 see Joseph H. Parks, "John Bell and the Compromise of 1850," in *Journal of Southern History,* IX, 328–56.

was concluded, learned of this warm and friendly defense, he must have been rejoiced thereby. For weeks he had been waiting for someone to raise a voice in his behalf. Now, at last, almost at the end, it had been heard.

Late in the spring the national crisis was intensified when a Southern convention assembled at Nashville "to devise and adopt some mode of resistance" to Northern aggressions. Although instituted by the radicals of Mississippi and South Carolina, the convention fortunately took no extreme action. After adopting rather harmless resolutions and issuing an address to the Southern people, the delegates adjourned to await congressional action upon the compromise bill.[51]

A far more serious complication in the crisis was the action of the New Mexicans, who in May, in accordance with Taylor's suggestion and at the call of the military officer in command at Santa Fé, held a constitutional convention. There was immediate excitement in Texas where steps had already been taken to organize the disputed area as counties of that state. A special session of the legislature was announced, and there was talk of sending troops to defend Texas territory as well as talk of withdrawing from the Union on the ground that her boundaries as of the time of annexation had been violated.[52] When in June news of the convention reached Washington, Congress was much disturbed. Senator Foote, with the President clearly in mind, boldly declared, "whoever be the man that has either planned, instigated, or sanctioned this vile scheme, [he] is not a patriot, but an insidious traitor to the public weal, an enemy to his country, whose perfidy and ineffable profligacy I hope may ere long be branded with indelible

[51] Cleo Hearon, *Mississippi and the Compromise of 1850* (University, 1914), 64–65.

[52] William C. Binkley, "The Question of Texan Jurisdiction in New Mexico Under the United States, 1848–1850," in *Southwestern Historical Quarterly*, XXIV (1920–1921), 30.

infamy." [53] Twice within a two weeks' period the Senate called upon Taylor for information as to his part in the proceedings. Southern members of Congress began to caucus and on July 1 appointed C. M. Conrad of Louisiana, Humphrey Marshall of Kentucky, and Robert Toombs, all warm supporters of Taylor in 1848, to wait upon him and to urge that he abandon his menacing attitude toward Texas and his insistence upon the admission of California and New Mexico as states. Taylor received the three congressmen and heard their arguments but "he refused to yield an inch." He insisted that as soon as New Mexico's constitution reached him he would recommend her admission as a state, and he let it be known that he was contemplating orders to the United States forces at Santa Fé to repel by arms any attempt by Texas to take control of New Mexico. When Secretary Crawford argued against such a step, fearing that it would lead to civil war, Taylor, "coolly remarked" that he would sign the necessary order himself.[54]

He was ready not only to sign orders but to take personal command of the forces if necessary. Late in June when Lieutenant Alfred Pleasanton who had served with Taylor in Mexico, was ordered to join his regiment in New Mexico, he called upon the President. After expressing his satisfaction that Pleasanton was going to New Mexico where officers of experience and judgment were needed, and stating his belief that the Southern congressmen were trying to bring on civil war, President Taylor continued, as Pleasanton remembered the conversation many years later:

[53] *Congressional Globe,* 31 Cong., 1 Sess., Appendix, 990.

[54] J. F. H. Claiborne, *Life and Correspondence of John A. Quitman* (New York, 1860), II, 32–33. It was Senator T. L. Clingman's recollection thirty years later that these three congressmen called upon Taylor not as a group but as individuals. *Selections from the Speeches and Writings of Hon. Thomas L. Clingman,* 272.

I have ordered the troops in New Mexico to be reinforced, and directed that no armed force from Texas be permitted to go into that territory. Tell Colonel Monroe (commanding in New Mexico) he has my entire confidence, and if he has not force enough out there to support him (and then his features assumed the firmest and most determined expression), I will be with you myself; but I will be there before those people shall go into that country or have a foot of that territory. The whole business is infamous, and must be put down.[55]

Early in July, Alexander H. Stephens also called on President Taylor and protested against the use of Federal troops in the Texas controversy. When he obtained no satisfaction from Taylor he joined Toombs in trying to influence the President through Secretary Preston, but with no more success. When Stephens threatened to impeach Taylor if he ordered additional troops to New Mexico, Preston promptly closed the interview.[56] A final threat by Stephens appeared in the *National Intelligencer* of the next day in the form of a letter to the editors. "The first Federal gun that shall be fired against the people of Texas, without the authority of law," he proclaimed, "will be the signal for the freeman from the Delaware to the Rio Grande to rally to the rescue . . . . the cause of Texas, in such a conflict, will be the cause of the entire South . . . . you may yet live to see that fifteen states of this Union, with seven millions of people, 'who knowing their rights dare maintain them,' cannot be easily conquered!"[57]

Old Rough and Ready was not to be moved. He had made up his mind before going to Washington that Texas was not justified in her extreme claims,[58] and these threats

[55] A. Pleasanton to Thurlow Weed, September 22, 1876, in Barnes, *Memoir of Thurlow Weed*, 180. For conditions in New Mexico at this period see Ralph E. Twitchell, *The History of the Military Occupation of the Territory of New Mexico from 1846 to 1851 by the Government of the United States* . . . (Denver, 1909).

[56] Avary, *Recollections of Alexander H. Stephens*, 26.

[57] Phillips (ed.), *The Correspondence of Robert Toombs, Alexander H. Stephens, and Howell Cobb, loc. cit.*, 192–93.

[58] Hitchcock, *Fifty Years in Camp and Field*, 348.

but strengthened his determination to oppose a seizure of the territory by Texas. He claimed no right to settle the boundary controversy; that was the duty of Congress or the Supreme Court. Meanwhile the disputed territory, he believed, should remain in the possession of the United States which had acquired it through the Mexican War.

The deadlock between the President and Clay lasted until broken by death. As long as Taylor lived, his opposition combined with that of the extremists, both north and south, doomed the compromise to failure. Likewise the opposition of the South, sustained by the compromisers, made impossible the adoption of the President's plan. Late in the summer, after Taylor had passed from the scene, and after the omnibus feature, which Douglas rightly claimed "united the opponents instead of securing the friends" of the various provisions, had been done away with, Congress passed and President Fillmore signed the five measures known as the Compromise of 1850.[59]

As Taylor's plan would have left many of the most important slavery problems to be solved, if solved at all, by a Congress in which the antislavery forces were strengthened by the senators and representatives from California and perhaps New Mexico, it is easy to understand why Southerners resisted it and why a Free-Soiler like Horace Mann approved it.[60] It is not so easy to explain why the President was so adamant in his opposition to the compromise proposals of Clay and his committee. Those proposals included Taylor's first recommendation—the admission of California with the constitution adopted and submitted by her. They did not, it is true, embody the President's second recommendation—nonaction in the case of New Mexico until she too were ready to apply for statehood. But the compromise proposals did call for the organization of New Mexico as a territory without restric-

[59] Hodder, "The Authorship of the Compromise of 1850," *loc. cit.*, 529, 532–36.

[60] Mann, *Life of Horace Mann*, I, 307.

tion as to slavery, and for her subsequent admission as a state with or without slavery as her constitution might provide. This arrangement could not, of course, satisfy the advocates of the Wilmot Proviso, but Taylor might have accepted it as reaching the same end as his plan though somewhat more slowly. As he told Daniel Webster in a final conversation, however, he was determined "that California should not come in at all, rather than that she should come in bringing the Territories on her back." [61] He believed that California was entitled to admission and that it should not be made contingent upon any other action.

President Taylor might have supported the compromise not only because it did no serious violence to his own proposals, but also because to have done so would have accorded with his fundamental policy of noninterference by the executive in legislative matters. In the pre-election months he had repeatedly declared that "the personal opinions of the individual who may happen to occupy the Executive chair ought not to control the action of Congress upon questions of domestic policy." [62] Moreover, in his inaugural address he had not only expressed confidence that Congress would adopt such measures of conciliation as would perpetuate the Union, but he had promised zealously to unite "in any action calculated to promote an object so near the heart of everyone who truly loves his country." His stubborn insistence that his recommendations as to California and New Mexico be followed clearly constituted an attempt to control the action of Congress, and his persistent opposition to the compromise proposals ran counter to his inaugural pledge.

Only on the basis of personal pride and jealous hatred of Clay can Taylor's firm stand be explained. The bitter denunciation of his part in California's application for

[61] Curtis, *Life of Daniel Webster,* II, 473.

[62] Taylor to J. S. Allison, April 22, 1848, in *Niles' National Register,* LXXIV (1848–1849), 8.

statehood aroused his indignation at the very opening of Congress. Never one to retire under fire, he promptly determined to stand his ground. The more his proposal was attacked the more resolute he became. When Henry Clay introduced proposals that threatened to replace the President's plan and received generous praise for his efforts, Taylor was frankly displeased. He had been warned that Clay was returning to the Senate to rule or ruin. Here seemed to be the evidence. He had sought friendly relations with Clay. He had given Clay's son a good appointment. But now, instead of supporting the administration, Clay apparently desired to discredit it and to obtain for himself the glory of a third compromise. Many persons believed, and doubtless informed Taylor, that Clay was the chief cause of all the administration's difficulties, that Clay had been piqued by the decision of the Whigs to thrust him aside and had come to Washington resolved to show that he was still the most powerful figure in the party.[63] Consequently all of Taylor's pride, all of his prejudice, all of his stubbornness was aroused. "Old Zach" could no more surrender to Clay than to Santa Anna on the field of Buena Vista.

President Taylor was also influenced to adhere to his own policy by the threatening Southern talk of secession if California were admitted without redressing the grievances of the South. Believing that issues should be settled upon the basis of right, he would not abandon his plan in the face of threats. They but stirred his fighting spirit. As a soldier he had no fear of a contest of arms with Texas, or with any portion of the South. It is extremely doubtful that he foresaw how bloody a civil war would engulf the nation if the dissatisfied Southerners should take up

[63] Richard Hawes to J. J. Crittenden, May 2, 1850, in Crittenden Papers; Sargent, *Public Men and Events,* II, 356. James S. Pike, Washington correspondent of the New York *Tribune* was outspoken in his denunciation of Clay for making war on the President. See Pike, *First Blows of the Civil War,* 20–25, 53.

arms, but he was determined that the Union should be preserved and that its basis should not be compromise.

The acrimonious slavery debates so completely absorbed the time and attention of Congress that other domestic issues were almost ignored. In Taylor's first and only annual message, which was finally sent to Congress after the bitter speakership fight was ended, he called attention to several important problems requiring legislative action, but Congress gave little heed. His recommendations were buried beneath the avalanche of slavery speeches that filled the legislative halls day after day and week after week, or, in a few instances, they were acted upon after only the briefest consideration. The needs of the newly acquired western lands led Taylor to recommend the establishment of a branch mint in California and the appointment of commissions to examine the validity of land titles in New Mexico and California, to explore the mineral deposits of the new lands and to make a reconnaissance of the proposed routes for a transcontinental railroad, and to report concerning the practicability of such a road as well as on the probable cost of its construction and maintenance.[64]

Taylor's long service in the United States Army naturally gave him an interest in its needs and problems. As the recent territorial acquisitions had greatly increased the demands upon the army, he urged that it be adequately strengthened so that it could efficiently perform its new frontier duties. He also seized the opportunity to recommend two steps which he had long favored. On numerous occasions in the past he had deplored the continued service of officers disabled by age or disease—officers who were absent from their posts for long periods and unable, even when present, to perform their duties effectively. Now he urged that provision be made for the retirement of such officers not only from the army but also from the

[64] *Senate Executive Documents,* 31 Cong., 1 Sess., No. 1, p. 12.

navy. Brevet commissions, which he had so long viewed as a source of friction and embarrassment, he recommended should be designated as honorary rewards carrying no extra pay or authority. This was the suggestion he had made to individual senators nearly twenty years before, and now that he was the Commander-in-Chief of the Army he urged it upon Congress at his first opportunity.[65]

Jefferson Davis, in accordance with Taylor's wishes, introduced into the Senate a bill for the retirement of army officers and successfully piloted it through that body. As the bill did not receive the approval of the House it did not become law.[66] Brief consideration was given to the President's proposal concerning brevet commissions, but again no legislation was enacted.[67] The military requirements of the frontier were so immediate, however, that his recommendation that the army be strengthened could not be ignored. In spite of Taylor's knowledge of army needs based on forty years of service, mainly on the frontier, there was opposition to his proposal and it received favorable action only after warm debate. At the close of the Mexican War, Congress had reduced the army and had fixed the number of privates in each company at fifty for the dragoons, sixty-four for the mounted rifles, and forty-two for the artillery and infantry.[68] Taylor's recommendation was to authorize the President to recruit each company up to seventy-four. Thus the size of the army could be nearly doubled without increasing the number of officers. Taylor knew that it was also necessary to increase the number of mounted troops in order to meet successfully the skillful horsemen of the western Indian tribes. He believed that this could be done most eco-

[65] *Ibid.*, 13; and the report of the Secretary of War, *ibid.*, 91.
[66] *Congressional Globe*, 31 Cong., 1 Sess., 88, 98, 158, 1761, 1767, 1833.
[67] *Ibid.*, 238, 421.
[68] *Senate Executive Documents*, 31 Cong., 1 Sess., No. 1, p. 99.

nomically and efficiently by mounting a portion of the infantry whenever the situation warranted it, and he recommended accordingly.[69]

On the floor of Congress the President's proposals were opposed by economy-minded representatives who could see no need for increasing the army when hundreds of troops were stationed at eastern forts where there was no danger or threat of danger. Even when better-informed congressmen pointed out that forts and arsenals could not be abandoned in time of peace if they were to be kept ready for war, these opponents stood their ground. Objection also came from another source. Representative Volney E. Howard of Texas was bitterly opposed to Taylor's proposal to mount infantry troops when needed. He insisted that the President already had ample authority to call into service mounted volunteers from the states and that because of his failure to do so "the responsibility of the blood that has been spilt upon the frontiers is on the head of General Taylor." [70] He urged that instead of authorizing the President to mount regular infantry he be required to use two regiments of mounted volunteers—rangers—mounted and equipped at their own expense. The twofold opposition was strong enough to delay the passage of the bill for several weeks, but too weak to prevent final approval of Taylor's proposals.[71]

Ever interested in agriculture and believing that every statesman and legislator should strive to "elevate the social condition of the agriculturist, to increase his prosperity, and to extend his means of usefulness to his country," President Taylor declared that the aid given to agriculture in the past had been wholly inadequate. To correct this situation he recommended the creation of an agricultural bureau to be connected with the Department of

[69] *Ibid.*, 13, 91.

[70] *Congressional Globe*, 31 Cong., 1 Sess., 1050.

[71] *Ibid.*, 395, 884, 1045–54, 1059–61; *United States Statutes at Large*, IX, 438–39.

the Interior.[72] In spite of widespread interest in this proposal Congress took no steps to carry it out.

None of his recommendations, except those on the various aspects of the slavery question, attracted so much attention as that on the tariff. The Walker Tariff of 1846, based on the principle of tariff for revenue only, was quite unsatisfactory to the manufacturing interests of the country. They eagerly looked forward to increased protection under the Whig administration in spite of Taylor's noncommittal statements in his campaign letters and inaugural address. The tariff views expressed in his annual message, though carefully phrased to avoid offense to the commercial and agricultural interests, were on the whole satisfactory to the protectionists. He frankly stated, "I do not doubt the right or duty of Congress to encourage domestic industry, which is the great source of national as well as individual wealth and prosperity" and he recommended the establishment of a system of specific duties "at rates high enough to afford substantial and sufficient encouragement to our own industry and at the same time so adjusted as to insure stability." [73] Any doubt as to where he or the administration stood on the tariff question was removed by Secretary Meredith's report, an extreme protectionist manifesto, to which Taylor referred Congress for further details of the proposed revision.[74] Such a complicated and controversial subject as a general revision of the tariff could not wisely be introduced into a Congress already quarreling so bitterly that its members carried guns for self-protection. So the tariff question was passed by.

Only on the territorial question did President Taylor depart from his declared policy, reasserted in his annual message, of leaving Congress free to act without executive control or dictation. On these other matters, having made

72 *Senate Executive Documents,* 31 Cong., 1 Sess., No. 1, p. 11.
73 *Ibid.,* 10.
74 *Senate Executive Documents,* 31 Cong., 1 Sess., No. 2.

his recommendations, he awaited the decisions of the legislative branch. Had he lived he doubtless would have recurred to them in subsequent annual messages and perhaps at the end of four years he could have claimed a share in a considerable body of worth-while legislation.

Chapter XVII

A SOLDIER IN THE WHITE HOUSE

ZACHARY TAYLOR the individual is almost lost in the steady political controversy of his months in the White House. Occasionally there is a glimpse of the old soldier astride his favorite mount, riding the wooded roads of the District, or out for a morning walk, high silk hat perched on the back of his head and a roomy, comfortable black broadcloth suit draped over his short and awkward figure.[1] At other times he is seen giving a genuine and friendly welcome to White House visitors—the diplomatic corps, all in their official uniforms and headed by their dean, Don Carlos Maria de Alvear, minister of the Argentine Federation; a group of forty United States Army officers in full uniform; a delegation of Osage Indians; a group of surviving officers of the War of 1812; and the hundreds of individual Americans eager to see and meet their President.

During his early months in the White House, President Taylor received callers on Friday evenings and on Tuesday and Friday afternoons from noon until two o'clock. At the end of the year, after the session of Congress commenced and the executive duties became heavier, the Friday afternoon hour was dropped. Visitors at other hours were not, however, rigidly excluded. At least one New York visitor to the nation's capital got his evenings confused and called at the White House on a nonreception evening. Nevertheless, he was received most kindly and

1 Poore, *Reminiscences,* I, 357; New York *Weekly Tribune,* September 22, 1849.

courteously by the President and the family circle and he went away delighted.[2] Richard H. Stanton, Democratic congressman from Kentucky, called on "Old Zach" one morning shortly before the new Congress assembled and found him "polite, cordial and talkative. He talked about cotton and hemp crops, but not a word on the subject of politics. Any other topic suits him better than matters of state. I confess he is rather more polished and entertains gentlemen with more ease, than I expected; but there is nothing more about him than there is about any well-bred gentleman." [3]

A less favorable impression was made upon George W. Julian, Indiana congressman, who soon after arriving in Washington wrote home that Taylor was "an old ninny," "an outrageously ugly, uncultivated, uninformed man; & sure enough a *mere* military chieftain. He cant [*sic*] converse in decent language, mispronouncing words, stuttering, stammering, & frequently making break-down in the middle of a sentence. Certainly he could not write a decent letter nor make a decent speech on any subject." [4]

A glimpse of one of President Taylor's first White House dinners is afforded by Gideon Welles, one of the thirty or more guests present. The Cabinet, the heads of the War and Navy Department bureaus, Senators Webster, Benton and Corwin, Balie Peyton, A. C. Bullitt, and some of the members of Taylor's own staff and household constituted the party. Welles, head of the Navy Bureau of Provisions and Clothing under Polk and not yet removed, arrived early and though not personally known to the President, was cordially received. He found Taylor "af-

[2] Washington *Daily Union,* March 11, 14, and 15, 1849; Washington *Republic,* November 7 and December 31, 1849; Welles, Diary, April 9, 1849, in Huntington Library; C. H. Davis to John M. Clayton, May 9, 1849, in Clayton Papers.

[3] R. H. Stanton to John M. Stevenson, November 27, 1849, in Stevenson Papers (Division of Manuscripts, Library of Congress).

[4] George W. Julian to Isaac Julian, January 25, 1850, in Giddings-Julian Papers (Division of Manuscripts, Library of Congress).

Courtesy of the Library of Congress

AN EARLY PICTURE OF THE WHITE HOUSE

fable and unassuming," "guileless and very rightly disposed." "He put on no airs," recorded Welles, "and could wear none were he to attempt it. His manner as we met alone was acceptable if not dignified. He seemed to feel much gratified to see me, looked up in my face with a bland & welcome [?] but not pleasant or rather not pretty smile, which was almost a laugh—as much as to say I am very glad to see you and hope you feel glad also. It put me at once at my ease. As he took my hand he called me by name, and how he knew it I know not." Taylor led his guest to a seat by the fire where they chatted of the weather and the view down the Potomac from the White House until other guests arrived. All in all, Welles found the evening "pleasant" and the dinner "magnificent." [5]

Nearly a year later Horace Mann dined at the White House and sat on the President's left, "with only one lady between, and had considerable conversation with him," and concluded, "He really is a most simple-minded old man. He has the least show or pretension about him of any man I ever saw; talks as artlessly as a child about affairs of State, and does not seem to pretend to a knowledge of anything of which he is ignorant. He is a remarkable man in some respects; and it is remarkable that such a man should be President of the United States." [6]

The social life of the White House was directed by the President's youngest daughter, Betty Bliss, who was a gracious and popular hostess. Mrs. Taylor's strength had failed rapidly and she could not participate in the formal social functions. She was always present at family dinners in which a few friends might share and she occasionally joined her husband in receiving some special group of visitors, but the active duties of mistress of the White House devolved upon her daughter. Mrs. Jefferson Davis later remembered that the most pleasant part of her visits to

[5] Entry for April 6, 1849.
[6] Mann, *Life of Horace Mann,* I, 292–93.

the White House was the time spent in "Mrs. Taylor's bright and pretty room where the invalid, full of interest in the passing show in which she had not strength to take her part, talked most agreeably and kindly to the many friends who were admitted to her presence." [7]

Taylor was fortunate in having so capable a daughter to take charge of the domestic and social affairs of the White House. It was also his good fortune to have his son-in-law, Colonel Bliss, as his secretary. Bliss's many years of experience as Taylor's adjutant, his understanding of the General's habits of mind, a knowledge of his weaknesses as well as of his points of strength, and the thorough and efficient manner in which the Colonel always performed his duties made him an invaluable aid to Taylor in his new position. There is no evidence that Bliss had as much influence over Taylor as the editor of the Washington *Union* occasionally asserted in column-length editorial attacks upon him, but also there is no reason to doubt that the President found him a very helpful friend and adviser.[8]

The newspapers also reveal glimpses of "Old Zach" during a two weeks' period in July attending the funeral of President Madison's widow, the famous Dolly Todd; mourning the loss of his body servant, Charles, a young Negro who had served him all through the Mexican War; listening to student speeches at the annual exhibition of the Washington Seminary; and handing out medals and awards at the commencement exercises of the Convent of the Visitation and of Georgetown College.[9]

During the summer months the Washington public had another opportunity to see and greet the President. On Saturday afternoons the military bands played at the White House grounds and Taylor frequently mingled with the crowds that were freely admitted. Miss Fredrika Bremer,

[7] *Letters from the Battlefields,* ix; Washington *Daily Union,* April 26 and July 7, 1849.

[8] Washington *Daily Union,* August 30 and November 25, 1849.

[9] Washington *Republic,* July 17, 21, 26, 27, and 31, 1849.

famous Swedish novelist traveling in the United States, met President Taylor on such an occasion, and found him "kind and agreeable, both in appearance and manner, and . . . simply, almost negligently, dressed. . . . His demeanor struck me as civil rather than military. . . . The president was delighted with the children who leaped about so joyously and so free from care." Miss Bremer was much impressed not only by the beauty and gaiety of the scene but also by the distinctly "republican character" of the occasion.[10]

During his first summer in the White House, President Taylor planned a six weeks' trip through the states of the Northeast, through Pennsylvania and New York, and into New England as far as Boston. The *Republic* announced that his purpose was to see that section of the country, its people, its resources and its needs, that he went to see, not to be seen, and had no desire for public receptions.[11] However, the many public gatherings arranged and the protective tariff views expressed in his Pennsylvania speeches clearly indicate that the trip was not without its political aspects. When a delegation of Pittsburgh manufacturers informed him that it was impossible for them to operate under the existing tariff, Taylor replied that one great object of his tour was to converse freely with the people of the country and to become personally acquainted with their needs and wishes. He informed them that he and Secretary Meredith had been giving their attention to the tariff, that some articles demanded protection, and that he was prepared to recommend to Congress improvements in the existing tariff, improvements designed to encourage all the great interests of the country and ensure stability.[12]

Accompanied by the marshal of the Federal District, who

[10] Fredrika Bremer, *The Homes of the New World; Impressions of America* (New York, 1853), I, 444.

[11] September 10, 1849.

[12] Philadelphia *Public Ledger*, August 23, 1849; *The Economist* (London), VII (September 22, 1849), 1050.

escorted him as far as Baltimore, Taylor left Washington on August 9. He declined the use of the luxurious special car which had been prepared for him, and cheerfully mingled with the passengers in the regular coach. At Baltimore he was joined by Dr. Wood, and as he crossed the border into Pennsylvania he was met by Governor William F. Johnston who traveled with him through the state for two weeks. To York, to Lancaster where Thaddeus Stevens and James Buchanan joined in a spirited welcome, to Harrisburg, Carlisle, Chambersburg, Bedford Springs, Pittsburgh, and Erie journeyed Taylor, Wood, and Johnston. Everywhere great crowds gathered to give the President an enthusiastic welcome. He shook hands with as many friends and admirers as strength and time permitted, and at various points he made brief speeches reasserting his aim to be the President of the whole country. Some of his hearers were disappointed by his obvious shortcomings as a public speaker, but for the most part he was received uncritically as the hero of Buena Vista, Old Rough and Ready.[13]

Unfortunately Taylor's trip was marred by illness which seized him only a few days after he left Washington and finally forced him to abandon the second half of his tour into New York and New England. At Harrisburg and Carlisle he was attacked by what was at first thought to be cholera, but he rapidly improved and, though weak, he insisted on continuing his tour. At Erie on August 25 he was again attacked by severe diarrhea and a raging fever, so alarming in their effects that for two days Dr. Wood and consulting physicians feared for his life, and Mrs. Taylor and Betty were summoned from Washington. But again the old soldier recovered and on September 1 left by boat for Niagara Falls and Buffalo. After several days there, in the company of Vice-President Fillmore, he

[13] Washington *Republic,* Washington *Daily Union,* and Philadelphia *Public Ledger,* August 10 to September 10, 1849.

yielded to the entreaties of his Cabinet and returned to Washington.[14] He tarried long enough at Albany to dine with Governor Hamilton Fish, and at New York City to breakfast with Simeon Draper. Except for these brief stops the homeward journey was completed as rapidly as possible.[15]

A month later, apparently fully restored in health, the President made an unannounced and unostentatious visit to Baltimore. Always interested in agriculture, he had expected to attend the New York Agricultural Fair. Having missed it, he made the short journey to Baltimore and spent two days visiting the Fair and Cattle Show and the Maryland Institute Fair and thoroughly enjoyed the trip.[16]

Taylor's only other trip away from the capital was in the following February when he went to Richmond to participate in the celebration of Washington's birthday and the laying of the cornerstone of a monument to the memory of the first President. Virginia received her native son with enthusiasm and made his two-day visit a gala affair. He was welcomed at the depot by a large crowd on the afternoon of the twenty-first, and was escorted to the capitol where he was presented to the members of the legislature. That evening he was the guest of honor at a brilliant reception at the governor's mansion. On the twenty-second he headed the mile-long procession through crowded streets to Capitol Square where at noon the ceremonies took place. As always Taylor's speech was very brief and without particular significance. He thanked the presiding officer for his kind allusions to his military services and, as was his custom, gave the credit and the honor for such success as he had achieved to the brave men who had fought with him. He expressed his delight at being

[14] *Ibid.;* R. C. Wood to John M. Clayton, August 29, 1849, in Clayton Papers; John M. Clayton to Taylor, August 29, 1849, draft, *ibid.*

[15] New York *Weekly Tribune,* September 15, 1849.

[16] Baltimore *American and Commercial Daily Advertiser,* October 11 and 13, 1849.

once again in Virginia and his appreciation of the cordial reception given him. No reference was made to the sectional conflict threatening the nation's peace nor to the efforts then under way in Congress to find a satisfactory compromise. His homeward journey on the twenty-third was interrupted by a stop at Fredericksburg where he was the honor guest at a festive dinner celebration, following which he continued to Aquia Creek where he boarded the steamer for Washington.[17]

In Virginia as in Pennsylvania and Baltimore, Taylor's simplicity and cordiality won instant favor. Early morning shoppers in both Richmond and Baltimore were surprised to find the town's distinguished guest at the market, keenly interested in the supplies of meats, fruits, and vegetables. Little as he liked the insistent attentions of the curious populace, his good humor and kindness of heart prevailed, and the many persons who approached him were greeted with a promptly extended hand and a pleasant word.[18] It was perfectly clear that his elevation to the presidency had not turned his head, that he was the same simple, honest old soldier who brushed aside all pomp and ceremony and delighted to chat with the men from the ranks.

Taylor's life in Washington was not a particularly happy one. It was not the type of life he was accustomed to. He would have much preferred a quiet station on the frontier or retirement to his Mississippi plantation. Nor was he used to the give and take of political life. The constant criticism of his trusted advisers, the condemnation of his patronage policy, of his handling of foreign affairs, and of his proposals concerning California and New Mexico were keenly felt. Proud and sensitive, he took very much to heart the attacks and the ridicule of the opposition. The failure of his own party to stand by him hurt perhaps the worst

[17] Richmond *Daily Whig*, February 22, 25, and 26, 1850; Washington *Republic*, February 23 and 25, 1850.

[18] Baltimore *American and Commercial Daily Advertiser*, October 13, 1849; Richmond *Daily Whig*, February 25, 1850.

of all. The lack of support from Clay and Webster, the defection of Toombs and Stephens, the lukewarmness of the *Republic* wounded him deeply. In the late spring of 1850 when his struggle with Clay was at its height and when the investigation of the Galphin claim was in progress—when all his enemies seemed to be gathering around—he clearly began to show the effects of the constant harassment. After an interview with the President early in May, Burnley declared he looked defeated and haggard.[19] A day or two later Orlando Brown, calling soon after breakfast, "found him looking badly—as if he did not sleep well and was unhappy." [20] But the old warrior was not easily conquered. He kept up the fight for another two months.

On July 4 President Taylor participated in the ceremonies connected with the laying of the cornerstone of the Washington Monument. The Declaration of Independence was read, Senator Foote delivered an "able, sensible and patriotic" oration, the bands filled the breezes with martial music, and the President and other distinguished guests were presented.[21] The day was oppressively hot and the exercises long. The President, who had complained of dizziness and headache before leaving his carriage at the Monument, returned to the White House weary and fatigued. He drank freely of iced milk and ate generous quantities of cherries. Shortly after dinner he became seriously ill.[22] Although there were rumors that the President was indisposed, the public was given no news of his illness until five days later. On July 9 the *Republic* carried a brief bulletin, issued by his physician the previous night at eleven o'clock, which stated: "The President is laboring under a bilious remittent fever, following an attack of serious cholera morbus; and is considered by his physicians seriously ill."

With this announcement great crowds gathered about

[19] A. T. Burnley to J. J. Crittenden, May 8, 1850, in Crittenden Papers.
[20] Orlando Brown to *id.*, May 9, 1850, *ibid.*
[21] Washington *Republic,* July 6, 1850.
[22] *Letters from the Battlefields,* xxiv–xxv.

the White House and in hushed silence awaited reports on his condition. Shortly before noon Daniel Webster called and was told that though the President had had a very bad night and had been exceedingly ill that morning, he was then more easy and more composed. With alarming suddenness, however, the fever returned. Appearances of congestion became obvious. Webster had hardly reached the Senate chamber before word came to him that it was unlikely that President Taylor would live through the day. News of the President's serious condition rapidly spread on Capitol Hill. Bitter sectional politics were temporarily forgotten as the two branches of Congress adjourned to await the sad event.[23] The scene in the Senate as Webster moved adjournment was described by a visitor who later recorded that, as she sat listening to a long and tedious proslavery speech by Senator Butler of South Carolina, she

> perceived a thrill, as if from a noiseless electric shock, had passed through the assembly; a number of fresh persons entered by the principal doors, and at once Daniel Webster was seen to stand beside the speaking senator, indicating with a deprecatory gesture that he must interrupt him on account of some important business. The orator bowed and was silent; a stillness as of death reigned in the house, and all eyes were fixed upon Webster, who himself stood silent for a few seconds, as if to prepare the assembly for tidings of serious import. He then spoke slowly, and with that deep and impressive voice which is peculiar to him.[24]

That night, July 9, at half past ten President Taylor died. His final words to the members of his family, his Cabinet, and the few friends gathered in his chamber were: "I am about to die. I expect the summons very soon. I have endeavored to discharge all my official duties faithfully. I regret nothing, but am sorry that I am about to leave my friends." [25]

[23] *Congressional Globe,* 31 Cong., 1 Sess., 1363.
[24] Bremer, *The Homes of the New World,* I, 448.
[25] *Letters from the Battlefields,* xxv.

On Friday, July 12, the departed President's body lay in state in the East Room of the White House while thousands of his fellow Americans in unending procession silently filed past. The next morning the crowded city awoke at sunrise to the first of many funeral salutes fired throughout the morning. At noon the Reverend Smith Pyne, Rector of St. John's Church, conducted services at the White House. When these were concluded the long procession to the Congressional Cemetery started on its sad journey. Close behind the corpse trod "Old Whitey," General Taylor's favorite mount. Many military units and more than one hundred carriages stretched the procession the full length of Pennsylvania Avenue as with far more pomp and ceremony than the simple soldier would have chosen, his body was carried to the burial ground,[26] to rest there on the hill above the Potomac until fall. Then as the brilliant leaves of autumn were fast falling, the earthly remains of Zachary Taylor were quietly removed to Kentucky and entombed at the family cemetery on the Beargrass Creek plantation.[27] There beside his wife, surrounded by many relatives, and close by the hundreds of soldiers since laid to rest in the adjoining military cemetery, he lies today.

The day following the death of President Taylor the Senate and House of Representatives laid aside their party and sectional bitterness and paid tribute to their fallen chief. During the days and weeks that followed similar eulogies were pronounced from many a pulpit and platform in every corner of the land. With few exceptions the speakers emphasized the fact that Taylor was first and foremost a military man. Some claimed he was a military genius; all pronounced him brave and courageous. Few of the speakers, however, dwelt long upon his military career;

26 Washington *Republic,* July 12 and 15, 1850; *Obituary Addresses Delivered on the Occasion of the Death of Zachary Taylor . . .* (Washington, 1850), 100–103.

27 W. W. S. Bliss to Richard Taylor, October 18, 1850, in Hardie Collection.

they preferred to stress his outstanding qualities and characteristics. They spoke of his stern integrity, his unyielding firmness, his frankness, his moderation, and his modesty. Taking their text from his final words they praised his lifelong attention to duty, his unmixed and selfless devotion to the welfare of the country. Charles M. Conrad, Louisiana congressman, who but a few days before had vainly endeavored to persuade the President to alter his territorial policy, declared the traits and qualities that endeared him to his friends and inspired the nation with confidence were "unaffected modesty, combined with extraordinary firmness, a stern sense of duty, and of justice tempered and softened by a spirit of universal benevolence, an inflexible integrity, a truthfulness that knew no dissimulation, a sincerity and frankness which rendered concealment or disguise absolutely impossible." [28] Meanwhile in the Senate chamber Daniel Webster in summing up Zachary Taylor's outstanding characteristics simply stated that he left "on the minds of the country a strong impression, first, of his absolute honesty and integrity of character; next, of his sound, practical good sense; and lastly, of the mildness, kindness, and friendliness of his temper towards all his countrymen." [29]

In reporting to his home government the death of President Taylor, the British minister in Washington expressed his unbiased observation: "His general abilities were good; his experience in public life and political affairs small; his mind not uncultivated; he seems to have possessed some military genius, and to have been uniformly fortunate in war.

"Firmness, which his opponents called obstinacy, was his predominant characteristic. His intentions were always good; his word could always be relied upon; his manners were downright, simple, straightforward; his name was

[28] *Congressional Globe,* 31 Cong., 1 Sess., 1366.
[29] *Ibid.,* 1364.

popular throughout the Union, and he died almost universally respected and lamented." [30]

In his eulogy in the House of Representatives, Congressman Conrad justly asserted that Taylor's biographer would have "no great follies to conceal, or faults to excuse, or crimes to palliate or condemn." "There is no dark passage in *his* life," he said, "which justice will be called upon to condemn, or morality to reprove, or humanity to deplore." [31] Yet the biographer must recognize that Zachary Taylor had his share of human frailties. It was General Scott's judgment that he was "quite ignorant for his rank, and quite bigoted in his ignorance"; that "few men have ever had a more comfortable, labor-saving contempt for learning of every kind"; and that "he had no vice but prejudice." [32] Another critic of Taylor from among his military associates and one who knew him more intimately than Scott was Ethan Allen Hitchcock. At the time of Taylor's death Hitchcock described him as "a man of strong and blind prejudices . . . strong-minded . . . uneducated . . . very ambitious." "He hated bitterly," wrote Hitchcock, "but neither his hatreds nor his friendships were intelligently formed. They were mere passions." [33]

That Taylor was ambitious and prejudiced the biographer can agree, but that he was ignorant or had a contempt for learning is at least open to question. Jefferson Davis regarded him as one of the most deeply read and profoundly learned men in military history that he had ever known.[34] Taylor not only encouraged his children to study French and to read English history, the plays of Shakespeare and the Bible,[35] but he saw to it that Dick received the best clas-

[30] Sir Henry Bulwer to Lord Palmerston, July 11, 1850, in P. R. O., F. O. 5:513 (Library of Congress Photostats).

[31] *Congressional Globe,* 31 Cong., 1 Sess., 1367.

[32] Scott, *Memoirs,* II, 382–84.

[33] Hitchcock, *Fifty Years in Camp and Field,* 366–67.

[34] Jefferson Davis to Hancock Taylor, September 3, 1883, in Hardie Collection.

[35] Taylor to Miss M. E. Taylor, December 15, 1845, in *The Autograph,* I, No. 3 (January–February, 1912), 48–49.

sical training to be had. When he learned that his grandson, John Wood, had chosen the military profession the General urged him not to neglect his studies for "there is nothing more important to insure a young man a high standing either in the army or navy than literary attainments." [36] Taylor's own letters, frequently written under the most difficult circumstances, are filled with errors of spelling and grammar, it is true; but the vocabulary, the many well-turned phrases, and the references to history and literary works clearly indicate that they are the letters of a man not unfamiliar with good literature.

Zachary Taylor was a product of the American frontier. The story of his life is the story of that frontier during half a century. It is the story of Kentucky in the critical years immediately after the Revolution when heroic pioneers battled hostile Indians and founded a new state; of the Old Northwest in the War of 1812; of savage battles with the red men from the woods of Wisconsin to the everglades of Florida; of years of stern and patient duty on the western military frontier; of manifest destiny and American expansion in the Southwest. Taylor's story is the American story of a youth with little formal education and little of the influence of wealth or powerful friends steadily making his way up the ladder of success to the highest office in the land. As a son of the frontier Taylor possessed in full measure the outstanding characteristics generated by frontier conditions. He was courageous and self-reliant; he was democratic; he was patriotic and nationalistic. A hard-working, successful officer rather than a military genius; an honest servant of the people rather than a great statesman; a truly representative American of the early nineteenth century—this was Zachary Taylor, Old Rough and Ready, forty years a soldier and sixteen months the President of his country.

[36] Taylor to R. C. Wood, October 5, 1847, in *Letters from the Battlefields,* 138.

APPENDIX

GENERAL ZACHARY TAYLOR'S ESTATE

On three occasions during his life Zachary Taylor, about to enter upon duties unusually dangerous, made provision for the distribution of his estate. These testamentary papers, attested copies of which are in the possession of Mrs. Alice Stauffer Hardie of New Orleans, clearly disclose Taylor's property interests and are printed below.

Testamentary Paper No. 1
November 20, 1837

Being about to enter on a campaign in Florida, should it be my lot to fall by the enemy, or a victim to the climate, I direct the following disposition to be made of my property viz:

FIRST, I leave to my dear wife *Margaret Taylor* forever, and to do with as she may think proper, my servants *Charles, Tom, Dicy, Jane* and her children, all my bank stock in the Bank of Louisville, or Louisville Bank, and in the Northern Bank of Kentucky, the stock in the former to be increased or made up to one hundred shares; but should the Legislature of Kentucky at their next session fail to sanction the course pursued by the officers of said Bank in regard to the suspension of specie payments, and said bank has to wind up its concerns, I direct the stock to be made equal to ten thousand dollars which I leave her instead of the one hundred shares of bank stock, with all the household and kitchen furniture, I may die possessed of. Also during her life, and at her death to go to my daughter *Mary Elizabeth Taylor,* that portion of the land lying in the pre-emption purchased by me of the heirs of *William Flemming,* which may be assigned me in a division with the heirs of *William Taylor,* being in the county of Jefferson and State of Kentucky, on which, if my wife wishes it, I direct that a small and comfortable dwelling for her accommodation with the necessary outbuildings be erected, the cost of the whole not to exceed four thousand dollars. But should the land referred to be sold by my agent Capt. J. S. Allison, who is authorized to do so, then the purchase money to be placed at interest, well secured, the interest be paid annually and to go to my wife as long as she may live, and at her death the principal to my daughter *Mary Elizabeth;* but should my wife at any time think proper to dispose of said land, she is authorized to do so, the purchase money to be placed at interest as above directed, and the interest to go to my wife during her life, afterwards the principal to my said daughter *Mary Elizabeth.*

SECOND, I leave to my daughter, *Ann M. Wood* and her children thirty thousand dollars as follows: All the money in the hands of my merchants in New Orleans, Messrs. *Maunsel White* & Company on the first day of March next, or after the sale of my present crop of cotton and the expenses of my plantation, including the wages of Mr. *Thornton,* are paid, which must be twenty thousand dollars and upwards, the land that may be allotted me within the limits of the settlement I purchased of the heirs of *Wm. Flemming* on the Ohio river in the county of Jefferson, and State of Kentucky, which I estimate at seven thousand dollars, if not sold; but if disposed of by my agent, as authorized, the amount arising from the same, and the balance to be made up to thirty thousand dollars out of any money that may be due me at the time of my death.

THIRD, I leave to my daughter, *Mary Elizabeth Taylor* and the heirs of her body forever, all my real estate in the city of Louisville consisting of three large store houses on Wall street, and the ground on which they are erected, and the part of a lot on Market Street or Jefferson, which I got of Dr. *Galt,* with the servant girl *Matilda,* now on the plantation, daughter of Alcy; but should my daughter *Mary Elizabeth* die without children, or leaving a child, [*sic*] then the above property to be equally divided between her mother and sister *Ann M. Wood.*

4TH, I direct my plantation, situated a part in the Parish of West Feliciana and State of Louisiana, and in the County of Wilkinson and State of Mississippi, with my negros [*sic*] thereon, in addition to the stock and everything appertaining to the same, shall not be broken up or disposed of, all of which, with the exception of the servant girl *Matilda* previously named and set apart to my daughter, *Mary Elizabeth,* I leave to my son *Richard Taylor* and his heirs forever, on his arrival at the age of twenty one years, with an encumbrance of five hundred dollars to be paid his mother annually during her life. During his minority I direct the plantation aforesaid and servants be placed under the management of some humane and careful individual, the net proceeds arising from the same to be appropriated as follows: 1st, the payments of all my just debts which are but few; 2nd, to make up the one hundred shares of bank stock or ten thousand dollars devised to my wife as directed, to carry into effect and defray the expenses of the buildings referred to, as well as every other named, if there are not other means to do so, defray the expenses of a classical education for my son *Richard,* as well as what may be necessary for board, clothing &c during his minority, and to enable him to study a profession, should he wish to do so, to pay my wife five hundred dollars annually, the residue, whatever it may be, to be equally divided between my two daughters, *Ann M. Wood* and *Mary Elizabeth Taylor.* Should my son *Richard* die before he reaches the age of twenty-one years and without leaving children then the property devised to him to be equally divided between his two sisters *A. M. Wood* and *Mary Elizabeth,* subject to the payment of five hundred dollars annually to my wife during her life.

I appoint my wife *Margaret Taylor,* my brother Capt. J. P. Taylor, of the U. S. Army, and my brothers-in-law, Capt. J. S. Allison of Louisville, Kentucky, and Joseph Smith of Wilkinson County, State of Mississippi my Executrix and Executors to see that the foregoing disposition of my property is carried into effect.

[signed] Z. Taylor

Tampa Bay, Fort Brooke
East Florida, November 20th, 1837

Witnessed

J. P. Taylor
Geo. H. Griffin
W. R. Jouett

A true copy from the original which is wholly in the handwriting of the Testator.

W. W. S. Bliss

Baltimore, Md.
August 1/50

Testamentary Paper No. 2
March 10, 1846

Being about to take possession of the Country to the Rio Grande which may lead to a war with Mexico, and as life at best is at all times uncertain, in the event of my being cut off by the enemy or by disease before joining my family, I wish the following disposition made of my property, viz:

FIRST, I give to my dear and excellent wife, *Margaret Taylor,* all my real estate in the city of Louisville and State of Kentucky, consisting of three large store or warehouses on Wall Street, and one small lot or part of a lot, I purchased of Dr. Wm. C. Galt, situated, I believe, in Jefferson Street, with the following servants, slaves for life, *Charles Porter, Tom, Dicy, Jane* and her two children, *William* & *Caroline,* with my stock in the Bank of Louisville, consisting of one hundred shares, with our household furniture of every kind and description, forever, to dispose of the same in any way or at any time she may think proper.

I give to my son *Richard Taylor,* twenty thousand dollars to be paid him on the first of January next, 1847, out of any money I may have at that time in the hands of my merchants, Messrs. *Maunsel White & Co.* of New Orleans, with my plantation lying and being in the Parish of West Feliciana and State of Louisiana, and in Wilkinson County, State of Mississippi, adjoining the lands of Capt. *Jno. Sims* and others, forever, to dispose of the same when and as he may think best.

I give to my daughter *Mary Elizabeth Taylor* eleven thousand dollars, also to be paid her on the first day of January, 1847, out of the proceeds of my present years crop; but should that not amount to that sum, the same to be made up, first, by any money that may be in the hands of my merchants *M. White & Co.* after paying my son the legacy above referred to, and if that should not suffice, to be made good to her, principal and interest, out of the first clear profits accruing out of my crops, as I wish my plantation not to be broken up or disturbed, but carried on as at present, with the servant woman *Mary* and all her children, slaves for life, who I purchased of Capt. *N. C. Macval* [?], who I do not consider attached to the plantation, forever, to dispose of as she may think proper.

I leave to my daughter *Ann M. Wood,* sixteen shares of Louisville Gas stock, fifty dollars per share, transferred to me by Capt. *J. S. Allison,* with five shares in the Northern Bank of Kentucky, with all the money I may have, or may be due me in Kentucky and elsewhere, after my debts are paid, there being only one small one due, on account of my securityship for *Thos H. Cheu* [?], in which Judge *Edward McGehee* is also bound or concerned.

After paying out of my crops as fast as it can be done, to my daughter *Ann M. Wood,* fifteen thousand dollars, including what she may receive as above stated, in Stock &c. and nine thousand dollars to my daughter *Mary Elizabeth Taylor* in addition to the eleven thousand previously stated, to be paid them annually, in such proportions according to the amount that may be coming to them, making up to them the sums specified; I wish my plantation kept up and all the servants together for the period of ten years, and the proceeds arising from the same equally divided between my three children, *Ann M. Wood, Mary E.* & *Richard Taylor.* At the end of the ten years, the plantation to be sold, and the sum it sells for, with the stock of every kind, except the servants, to be disposed of, divided equally among my children as above. I wish the servants well and humanely treated, the old ones well provided [*sic*] and taken care of, and none to be overworked.

I hereby appoint my friend Judge *Edward McGehee* of Wilkinson County and State of Mississippi my Executor, and who, I hope, will act and will see my wishes carried into effect.

(signed) Z. Taylor

Corpus Christi, Texas)
March 10th, 1846)

The servants at the end of the ten years will be equally divided among my children. No division will be made of the proceeds of the crops of the plantation until the several legacies are made good, when the[y] will be annually divided. This was broken open by me after sealing.

[signed] Z. T.

A true copy from the original which is wholly in the handwriting of the Testator.

W. W. S. Bliss

Baltimore, Md.)
August 2nd/50)

Testamentary Paper No. 3
July 20, 1846

Life being at all times uncertain; and more especially as regards one in my situation, therefore in the event of my being cut off by the hand of the enemy, disease or in any other way, before joining my family, I wish the following disposition made of my property.

I give to my excellent wife, *Margaret Taylor,* all my real estate in the city of Louisville, State of Kentucky, consisting of three large store or warehouses on Wall Street, and one small lot, or part of a lot I purchased of Dr. *William C. Galt,* I believe on Jefferson Street, with my stock in the Louisville Bank or Bank of Louisville, consisting of one hundred shares, and my stock in the Northern Bank of Kentucky, consisting of five shares with the following servants, slaves for life, *Charles Porter, Tom, Dicy, Jane* and her two children *William & Caroline,* with all the household furniture of every kind I may die possessed of, forever, to dispose of when, and as she may think best or proper.

I give to my son *Richard* twenty-one thousand dollars to be paid him on the first day of January next, 1847, out of any money then in the hands of my merchants in New Orleans, Messrs. *Maunsel White & Co.* with the plantation I recently cultivated in the Parish of West Feliciana and State of Louisiana, and in the County of Wilkinson, state of Mississippi, now rented out, adjoining the lands of Capt. *John Sims, John Wiker,* Esq. and others, forever, to dispose of as whenever [*sic*] he may think proper to do so.

I give to my daughter *Mary Elizabeth,* eleven thousand dollars, to be paid her on the first day of January next, 1847, out of any money which may be in the hands of my merchants as aforesaid, after paying my son *Richard* the legacy previously stated, and out of the proceeds of my present years crop, with the servant woman *Mary,* a slave for life, I purchased of Capt. *N. C. Macval,* and her four children, forever, to dispose of as she may think proper. But should the money in the hands of my merchants not be sufficient, in addition to the proceeds of my present crop, after paying the first named legacy, then the eleven thousand dollars to be made good to her, out of the first money arising out of the net proceeds of my crops, with ten per cent interest until paid.

I leave to my daughter *Ann M. Wood,* sixteen shares of stock in the Louisville Gas Bank, with whatever money may be due me at the time of my death, as well as any money that may be in the hands of my merchants at that time, after the disposal of my present years crop and the payment of the legacies referred to, as well as to make up to her, in addition to what she may receive, ten thousand dollars with interest on the same at ten per cent per annum until paid, out of the net proceeds of my plantation.

I wish my plantation and servants kept together for ten years, and after paying the several legacies referred to, the net proceeds of my crops to be equally divided between my two daughters, *Ann M. Wood* and *Mary Elizabeth* until they receive the sum of twenty thousand dollars including what has been previously left them; after which the net proceeds of the crops to be equally divided between the three *Ann, Mary E.* and *Richard,* until the end of the said ten years, when the property to be equally divided among the three, as above named.

I wish my debts paid, there being only one of about a thousand dollars, due on account of security for the late *Thos. H. Cheu* [?], in which Judge *Edward McGehee* of Wilkinson, Mississippi, is concerned, who has the management of the same; I having paid a portion of it.

I wish the servants only moderately worked and kindly treated, and the old ones taken care of and made comfortable, which I hope my children will have attended to.

I leave my friend, Judge *Edward McGehee* of Wilkinson County & State of Mississippi, my Executor to see my wishes carried into effect, which I hope he will not hesitate in doing.

[Signed] Z. Taylor

Matamoras, Mexico)
July 20th 1846)

Note. There is now in the hands of my merchants, Messrs. Maunsel White & Co. about twenty thousand dollars at interest; due me from Capt. Allison I think about seven hundred, and a thousand or more from others, with interest on bank stock say seven hundred dollars, and rent of houses one thousand (more?),[1] which in addition to my crop of the present year which ought to neat 12 or 14 thousand, ought to amount

[1] This parenthetical addition is in Bliss's Copy and probably was added by him.

to about seven [teen] [2] thousand dollars, and no doubt will do so, on the first day of January next and particularly when the crop is all disposed of.

(signed) Z. Taylor

A true copy from the original, which is wholly in the handwriting of the Testator.

W. W. S. Bliss

Baltimore, Md.
Aug. 2d 1850

The above testamentary paper of July 20, 1846, was the last made by Zachary Taylor and was followed as closely as possible in the division of his property. Several important changes in Taylor's property holdings and financial affairs between 1846 and his death necessitated certain modifications in its provisions. He no longer owned the smaller plantation on the border of Louisiana and Mississippi; he had made the initial payment of $19,500 on Fashion, the Louisiana sugar plantation purchased for Richard; apparently he had disposed of his sixteen shares of stock in the Louisville Gas Bank; and while in Washington he had purchased $15,000 worth of other bank stock.

Mrs. Taylor and the three children agreed to distribute General Taylor's estate by giving to Mrs. Taylor as nearly as possible the property mentioned for her in the testamentary paper of July 20, 1846, and to the three children the remainder of the estate which they partitioned among themselves in a separate agreement. According to these documents, attested copies of which are also in the possession of Mrs. Stauffer, Taylor's estate was distributed as follows:

To Mrs. Taylor

1. One hundred and five shares of stock in the Bank of Louisville, valued at $10,500.00
2. $1716.46, proceeds from the sale of household furniture
3. Three warehouses and 1 lot in Louisville [Taylor refused an offer of $4,000.00 each for two of these warehouses in 1849.]
4. Five servants, slaves for life.

[2] This bracketed addition is in Bliss's Copy.

To be partitioned among the children

1. A certain plantation hereinafter more fully described, called the Cypress Grove Plantation valued amongst themselves at the sum of twenty thousand dollars	$20,000.00
2. One hundred and thirty one slaves, whose names and ages are hereinafter fully set forth and the values detailed, the whole worth as per agreement between the parties fifty six thousand six hundred and fifty dollars	56,650.00
3. Cash in the hands of Messrs. Maunsel White & Co. of this city Eighteen thousand six hundred and one dollars and seventy seven cents	18,601.77
4. Ninety five shares in the capital stock of the Bank of Louisville, valued at nine thousand five hundred dollars	9,500.00
5. Thirty shares in the capital stock of the Northern Bank of Kentucky valued at three thousand dollars	3,000.00
6. One hundred shares in the capital stock of the Western Bank of Baltimore valued at two thousand dollars	2,000.00
7. Cash in the hands of Colonel Bliss administrator, under letters taken by him in the Orphans Court at Washington, seven thousand and eighteen dollars and twenty five cents	7,018.25
Making the total amount for division one hundred and sixteen thousand seven hundred and seventy dollars and two cents	$116,770.02

The property received by Mrs. Taylor amounted to $25,000 or more, which added to that divided by the three children made Taylor's total estate somewhat over $140,000. This total does not take into consideration his payment on Fashion plantation which the children agreed to regard as part of Richard's inheritance.

CRITICAL ESSAY ON AUTHORITIES

Manuscript Material

There is no great body of Zachary Taylor papers. It was not Taylor's custom to make copies of his own letters or to preserve letters received. On the contrary, he normally destroyed incoming correspondence as soon as it was answered. The largest collection of Taylor letters is that in the War Department files at the National Archives. Unfortunately not even this group is complete. Many letters and reports from Taylor, listed in the department's index of letters received, are not to be found in the files. Nevertheless, this is the most important source for Taylor's military career.

The Manuscript Division of the Library of Congress possesses a small collection of Zachary Taylor Papers, consisting mainly of letters to his brother, Joseph P. Taylor. This collection and a group of some forty letters written during the Mexican War, primarily to his son-in-law, Dr. Robert C. Wood, which is now in the Henry E. Huntington Library at San Marino, California, are the two largest collections of private letters from Taylor's pen and are invaluable. The latter collection was edited by William H. Samson and privately printed under the title *Letters of Zachary Taylor from the Battlefields of the Mexican War* . . . (Rochester, 1908). Additional Taylor letters are to be found in other collections in the Library of Congress, especially in the papers of John Jordan Crittenden, Ethan Allen Hitchcock, and Thomas S. Jesup, and in widely scattered collections of various state and local historical societies. The Kentucky Historical Society, the Historical Society of Pennsylvania, the Filson Club, the Missouri Historical Society, the New York Historical Society, the Massachusetts Historical Society, the Wisconsin State Historical Society, the Huntington Library, and the University of North Carolina Library all made available Taylor letters or material.

For the presidential election of 1848 and Taylor's administration, the papers and correspondence of other men in public life were used. Taylor's own letters are exceedingly scarce for the period of his presidency.

Many a biographer has been distressed by missing manuscripts. The biographer of Zachary Taylor is no exception. Not only are important documents missing from the War Department Archives, but two collections of great promise could not be located. Mr. Trist Wood of New Orleans, great-grandson of the General, informed the writer that his cousin, the late Mrs. W. R. Stauffer, formerly possessed "a suitcase full" of correspondence between Taylor and Jefferson Davis but that it had disappeared. Mrs. Stauffer's daughter, Mrs. Alice S. Hardie, who possesses many valuable Taylor manuscripts which she generously made available, has no knowledge of the missing suitcase. That some such collection did exist is clear from the fact that in *The War with Mexico* (New York, 1919), Justin H. Smith cites Taylor-Davis correspondence in the possession of Mrs. Stauffer. The second missing collection, also referred to by Mr. Wood, is a "chest of manuscripts" given by Betty Taylor Bliss to her stepson. Following the death of Colonel Bliss she married her cousin Philip Pendleton Dandridge, whose son by a former marriage presumably received the chest. Members of the Dandridge family, however, were not able to furnish further information.

Published Diaries and Correspondence

The printed correspondence of many of Taylor's associates in military or political life throws light on various aspects of his career. Logan Esarey (ed.), *Messages and Letters of William Henry Harrison,* in *Indiana Historical Collections,* VII, IX (Indianapolis, 1922), is of value in connection with Taylor's activities in the War of 1812. Also useful for his early military career are: James A. Padgett, "The Letters of Colonel Richard Taylor and Commodore Richard Taylor to James Madison, Together with a Sketch of Their Lives," in *Register of the Kentucky State Historical Society* (Frankfort), XXXVI (1938), 330–44, and the same author's "Letters of James Taylor to the Presidents of the United States," *ibid.,* XXXIV (1936), 103–30, 251–78, 318–46.

For the period of the Mexican War the following collections give important aid: George A. McCall, *Letters from the Frontiers* (Philadelphia, 1868); John Sedgwick, *Correspondence of John Sedgwick, Major-General,* 2 vols. (New York, 1902–1903); E. Kirby Smith, *To Mexico with Scott: Letters of Captain E.*

Kirby Smith to His Wife (Cambridge, 1917); Justin H. Smith (ed.), "Letters of General Antonio López de Santa Anna Relating to the War Between the United States and Mexico, 1846–1848," in American Historical Association, *Annual Report, 1917* (Washington, 1920), 355–428; William H. Samson (ed.), *Letters of Zachary Taylor from the Battlefields of the Mexican War; Reprinted from the Originals in the Collection of Mr. William K. Bixby of St. Louis, Mo. . . .* (Rochester, 1908); Otto B. Engelmann (ed.), "The Second Illinois in the Mexican War, Mexican War Letters of Adolph Engelmann, 1846–1847," in *Journal of the Illinois State Historical Society* (Springfield), XXVI (1933–1934), 357–452.

Helpful in the study of the problems of Taylor's political career are Chauncey S. Boucher and Robert P. Brooks (eds.), "Correspondence Addressed to John C. Calhoun, 1837–1849," in American Historical Association, *Annual Report, 1929* (Washington, 1930), 125–533; J. Franklin Jameson (ed.), *Correspondence of John C. Calhoun, ibid., Annual Report, 1899,* Vol. II (Washington, 1900); Ulrich B. Phillips (ed.), *The Correspondence of Robert Toombs, Alexander H. Stephens and Howell Cobb, ibid., Annual Report, 1911,* Vol. II (Washington 1913); Calvin Colton (ed.), *The Works of Henry Clay, Comprising His Life, Correspondence and Speeches,* 10 vols. (New York, 1904); William R. Manning (ed.), *Diplomatic Correspondence of the United States. Inter-American Affairs, 1831–1860,* 12 vols. (Washington, 1932–1939); Dunbar Rowland (ed.), *Jefferson Davis, Constitutionalist, His Letters, Papers and Speeches,* 10 vols. (Jackson, Miss., 1923); C. H. Van Tyne (ed.), *Letters of Daniel Webster* (New York, 1902); and Fletcher Webster (ed.), *The Private Correspondence of Daniel Webster,* 2 vols. (Boston, 1857). "Some Letters of John Gibson," in *Indiana Magazine of History* (Bloomington), I (1905), 129–31, shed light on Taylor's activities in the Old Northwest.

Numerous published diaries and journals contribute valuable information about Taylor or the events with which he was connected. Thomas G. Anderson, "Anderson's Journal at Fort McKay, 1814," in *Wisconsin Historical Collections* (Madison), IX (1909 reprint), 207–61, is helpful in the study of Taylor's part in the War of 1812. For his part in the Mexican War the following are of value: Rhoda van Bibber Tanner Doubleday (ed.), *Journals of the Late Brevet Major Philip Norbourne Barbour, Captain in the 3rd Regiment, United*

States Infantry, and his Wife, Martha Isabella Hopkins Barbour (New York, 1936); Stella M. Drumm (ed.), *Down the Santa Fé Trail and Into Mexico. The Diary of Susan Shelby Magoffin, 1846–1847* (New Haven, 1926); George C. Furber, *Twelve Months Volunteer: or Journal of a Private . . . in the Campaign in Mexico . . .* (Cincinnati, 1849); James K. Holland, "Diary of a Texan Volunteer in the Mexican War," in *Southwestern Historical Quarterly* (Austin), XXX (1926–1927), 1–33; William L. Marcy, "Diary and Memoranda of William L. Marcy, 1849–1851," in *American Historical Review* (New York), XXIV (1919), 444–62; Eleanor Damon Pace (ed.), "The Diary and Letters of William P. Rogers, 1846–1862," in *Southwestern Historical Quarterly,* XXXII (1928–1929), 259–99; and Milo Milton Quaife (ed.), *The Diary of James K. Polk During His Presidency, 1845 to 1849 . . .* , 4 vols. (Chicago, 1910). Useful for the Mexican War and for earlier periods of Taylor's life is W. A. Croffut (ed.), *Fifty Years in Camp and Field. Diary of Major-General Ethan Allen Hitchcock, U.S.A.* (New York, 1909). Grant Foreman (ed.), *A Traveler in Indian Territory. The Journal of Ethan Allen Hitchcock, late Major-General in the United States Army* (Cedar Rapids, 1930), is helpful in connection with Taylor's work on the Southwestern frontier.

Autobiographies, Memoirs, and Reminiscences

Reminiscent works vary greatly in value and must always be used with care. Several works of this nature, however, proved to be helpful and contributed to this study. For Taylor's years in the Wisconsin area the following accounts were used: Robert Anderson, "Reminiscences of the Black Hawk War," in *Wisconsin Historical Collections,* X (1909 reprint), 167–76; Caleb Atwater, *Remarks Made on a Tour to Prairie du Chien; Thence to Washington City in 1829* (Columbus, 1831); James W. Biddle, "Recollections of Green Bay in 1816–17," in *Wisconsin Historical Collections,* I (1903 reprint), 49–63; Albert G. Ellis, "Fifty-Four Years' Recollections of Men and Events in Wisconsin," *ibid.,* VII (1908 reprint), 205–68; George W. Featherstonhaugh, *A Canoe Voyage up the Minnay Sotor . . .* , 2 vols. (London, 1847); C. F. Hoffman, *A Winter in the Far West,* 2 vols. (London, 1835); Charles A. Murray, *Travels in North America During the Years 1834, 1835, and 1836 . . .* (London, 1841).

Two of the best books of this nature, generally accurate and showing few prejudices, are *Two Wars: An Autobiography of Gen. Samuel G. French* (Nashville, 1901), and William Seaton Henry, *Campaign Sketches of the War with Mexico* (New York, 1847). Other accounts which also proved helpful for the Mexican War are: *A Campaign in Mexico, or a Glimpse at Life in Camp* (Philadelphia, 1847); Ulysses S. Grant, *Personal Memoirs,* 2 vols. (New York, 1885–1886); John Blount Robinson, *Reminiscences of a Campaign in Mexico, by a Member of the "Bloody First"* (Nashville, 1849); Winfield Scott, *Memoirs,* 2 vols. (New York, 1864); Lewis Wallace, *Lew Wallace: An Autobiography,* 2 vols. (New York, 1906).

Harriet A. Weed (ed.), *Life of Thurlow Weed Including His Autobiography and a Memoir,* 2 vols. (Boston, 1883–1884), contains recollections of the important New York Whig leader, which are useful for Taylor's political career. Additional light is shed on this subject by Myrta Lockett Avary (ed.), *Recollections of Alexander H. Stephens, His Diary Kept When a Prisoner at Fort Warren, Boston Harbour, 1865 . . .* (New York, 1910); Thomas H. Benton, *Thirty Years' View,* 2 vols. (New York, 1881); Fredrika Bremer, *The Homes of the New World: Impressions of America* (New York, 1853); Ben Perley Poore, *Perley's Reminiscences of Sixty Years in the National Metropolis,* 2 vols. (Philadelphia, 1886); Nathan Sargent, *Public Men and Events from the Commencement of Mr. Monroe's Administration, in 1817, to the Close of Mr. Fillmore's Administration, in 1853,* 2 vols. (Philadelphia, 1875).

Government Documents

Publications of the United States Government constitute one of the most important sources for the study of Taylor's public life and the problems connected therewith. Almost every aspect of his military career is elucidated by such documents. Indispensable for the period down to 1836 is the series, *American State Papers. Documents, legislative and executive, of the Congress of the United States . . . selected and edited under the authority of Congress . . . ,* 38 vols. (Washington, 1832–1861). The most important documents for the portion of the Mexican War in which Taylor participated are available in the following: *Message from the President of the United States, Relative to an Invasion and Commencement of Hostilities by Mexico*

(*House Executive Documents,* No. 196, 29 Cong., 1 Sess.); *Message from the President of the United States, Transmitting Despatches from General Taylor . . .* (*House Executive Documents,* No. 197, 29 Cong., 1 Sess.); *Message from the President of the United States, Transmitting Copies of all the Official Despatches Received from General Taylor . . .* (*House Executive Documents,* No. 207, 29 Cong., 1 Sess.); *Message from the President of the United States, Transmitting Official Reports from General Taylor* (*House Executive Documents,* No. 209, 29 Cong., 1 Sess.); *Message from the President of the United States, Transmitting the correspondence with General Taylor, Since the Commencement of Hostilities with Mexico, not Already Published* (*House Executive Documents,* No. 119, 29 Cong., 2 Sess.); *Message from the President of the United States . . . at the Commencement of the First Session of the Thirtieth Congress . . .* (*Senate Executive Documents,* No. 1, 30 Cong., 1 Sess.); and *Message from the President of the United States, with the Correspondence . . . Between the Secretary of War and Other Officers of the Government, on the Subject of the Mexican War* (*House Executive Documents,* No. 60, 30 Cong., 1 Sess.).

For the domestic and foreign problems of Taylor's presidency the entire set of congressional documents and reports for the first session of the Thirty-first Congress was extensively used. The *Congressional Globe, Containing the Debates and Proceedings* is equally useful for this period. It is indispensable for a study of the legislative problems of Taylor's administration and of his relationship thereto.

Other government publications which were of value are: *Agriculture of the United States in 1860, Compiled from the Original Returns of the Eighth Census . . .* (Washington, 1864); *The Cholera Epidemic of 1873* (*House Executive Documents,* No. 95, 43 Cong., 2 Sess.); Charles J. Kappler (ed.), *Indian Affairs: Laws and Treaties,* 4 vols. (Washington, 1904–1929); *The Statutes at Large of the United States of America,* 17 vols. (Boston, 1845–1873); Clarence E. Carter (ed.), *The Territorial Papers of the United States,* 11 vols. in progress (Washington, 1934–); Frederick W. Hodge, *Handbook of American Indians North of Mexico,* 2 vols. (Washington, 1912); Francis B. Heitman, *Historical Register and Dictionary of the United States Army . . .*, 2 vols. (Washington, 1903).

Newspapers and Periodicals

For the biographer of Zachary Taylor, as for almost every other student of American life in the first half of the nineteenth century, *Niles' Weekly Register,* published after August, 1837, as *Niles' National Register* (Philadelphia, 1811–1849), is of great value. It contains important documents relative to Taylor's military activities from the War of 1812 through the Mexican War and news and documents of significance for the presidential campaign of 1848.

For the general period of Taylor's political activity the following papers were consulted: Washington *Daily Union* (1848–1850); New York *Weekly Tribune* (January, 1849–July, 1850); Philadelphia *Public Ledger* (January, 1849–July, 1850); and the Washington *Republic* (June 13, 1849–July 15, 1850). This latter paper was the organ of the Taylor administration and is indispensable for a study of it.

In addition, many newspapers were consulted for specific references to Taylor's activities. These papers, with their dates, were: Baltimore *American and Commercial Daily Advertiser,* 1849; Frankfort *Daily Commonwealth,* 1849; New Orleans *Daily Delta,* 1846, 1848; Louisville *Chronicle,* 1849; Natchez *Mississippi Free Trader and Natchez Gazette,* 1848; New Orleans *Daily Picayune,* 1847; Richmond *Daily Whig,* 1850; and Louisville *Weekly Courier,* 1847, 1848, 1849.

Special Articles

Theodore C. Atchison, "David R. Atchison: A Study in American Politics," in *Missouri Historical Review* (Columbia), XXIV (1929–1930), 502–15, and George H. Haynes, "President of the United States for a Single Day," in *American Historical Review,* XXX (1924–1925), 308–10, discuss the question who was President from noon on Sunday, March 4, 1849, until Taylor was inaugurated on March 5. William C. Binkley, "The Question of Texan Jurisdiction in New Mexico under the United States, 1848–1850," in *Southwestern Historical Quarterly,* XXIV (1920–1921), 1–38, is a scholarly treatment of one phase of the Compromise of 1850. Two other important articles dealing with this Compromise are Frank H. Hodder, "The Authorship of the Compromise of 1850," in *Mississippi Valley Historical Review* (Cedar Rapids), XXII (1935–1936), 525–36, and

Joseph H. Parks, "John Bell and the Compromise of 1850," in *Journal of Southern History* (Baton Rouge), IX (1943), 328–56. William P. Brandon, "The Galphin Claim," in *Georgia Historical Quarterly* (Savannah), XV (1931), 113–41, is an unprejudiced discussion of this controversial subject. Jackson B. Davis, "The Life of Richard Taylor," in *Louisiana Historical Quarterly* (New Orleans), XXIV (1941), 49–126, is the best account of General Taylor's son. The patronage problem of Taylor's administration is elucidated by the careful study of Carl Russell Fish, "Removal of Officials by the Presidents of the United States," in American Historical Association, *Annual Report, 1899* (Washington, 1900), I, 67–86. Kate L. Gregg, "The War of 1812 on the Missouri Frontier," in *Missouri Historical Review,* XXXIII (1938–1939), 3–22, 184–202, 326–48, and Edgar B. Wesley, "James Callaway in the War of 1812," in Missouri Historical Society *Collections* (St. Louis), V (1927–1928), 38–81, shed important light on Taylor's activities on the upper Mississippi during the War of 1812. Holman Hamilton, "Zachary Taylor in Mississippi," in *Journal of Mississippi History* (Jackson), III (1941), 130–39, and William A. Love, "General Jackson's Military Road," in *Mississippi Historical Society Publications* (University), XI (1910), 401–17, are helpful in connection with the earlier part of Taylor's military career. His life at Fort Crawford and vicinity during the 1830's is clarified by numerous articles, including: Charles Bracken, "Further Strictures on Ford's Black Hawk War," in *Wisconsin Historical Collections,* II (1903 reprint), 402–14; Ella C. Brunson, "Alfred Brunson, Pioneer of Wisconsin Methodism," in *Wisconsin Magazine of History* (Menasha), II (1918–1919), 129–48; Walter L. Fleming, "Jefferson Davis' First Marriage," in *Mississippi Historical Society Publications,* XII (1912), 21–36; Lucius H. Langworthy, "Dubuque: Its History, Mines, Indian Legends, etc.," in *Iowa Journal of History and Politics* (Iowa City), VIII (1910), 366–422; Jacob Van der Zee, "Early History of Lead Mining in the Iowa Country," *ibid.,* XIII (1915), 3–52; Oliver P. Shiras, "The Mines of Spain," in *Annals of Iowa* (Des Moines), 3d Series, V (1901–1903), 321–34; Ida M. Street, "A Chapter of Indian History," *ibid.,* III (1897–1899), 601–23, VI (1903–1905), 364–75; R. G. Thwaites, "The Story of the Black Hawk War," in *Wisconsin Historical Collections,* XII (1892), 217–65. Other articles that shed light on one aspect or another of Taylor's life are: R. C. Buley, "Indiana in the Mexican

War," in *Indiana Magazine of History,* XV (1919), 261–326, XVI (1920), 46–68; Louis C. Duncan, "A Medical History of General Zachary Taylor's Army of Occupation in Texas and Mexico, 1845–1847," in the *Military Surgeon* (Washington), XLVIII (1921), 76–104; John H. Fonda, "Early Wisconsin," in *Wisconsin Historical Collections,* V (1907 reprint), 205–84; Herbert D. Foster, "Webster's Seventh of March Speech and the Secession Movement, 1850," in *American Historical Review,* XXVII (1921–1922), 245–70; J. Fair Hardin, "Four Forgotten Frontier Army Posts of Western Louisiana," in *Louisiana Historical Quarterly,* XVI (1933), 5–26, 279–92, 441–53, 670–80; J. B. S. Jacobs, Sr., "Inhabitants at Green Bay, September 14, 1818," in *Wisconsin Historical Collections,* X (1909 reprint), 136–38; Willard Rouse Jillson, "Early Western Exploration," in *Register of the Kentucky State Historical Society,* XXXIII (1935), 70–77; Louise Phelps Kellogg, "Old Fort Howard," in *Wisconsin Magazine of History* (Evansville), XVIII (1934–1935), 125–40; John W. Monette, "The Mississippi Floods," in *Mississippi Historical Society Publications* (Oxford), VII (1903), 454–72; Charles O. Paullin, "Abraham Lincoln in Congress, 1847–1849," in *Journal of the Illinois State Historical Society,* XIV (1921–1922), 85–89; "Sketch of the Life of Major Zachary Taylor of the United States' Army," in *Western Review and Miscellaneous Magazine* (Lexington), I (1819–1820), 36–46; Lota M. Spell, "The Anglo-Saxon Press in Mexico, 1846–1848," in *American Historical Review,* XXXVIII (1932–1933), 20–31; Rex Wallace Strickland, "History of Fannin County, 1836–1843," in *Southwestern Historical Quarterly,* XXXIV (1930–1931), 38–68.

Biographies

Zachary Taylor's sudden emergence on the national scene at the time of his victories in the Mexican War and his nomination for the presidency resulted in the publication of numerous biographies. All of these were hastily prepared and most of them were brief, uncritical summaries of his military career, expanded in some cases by the inclusion of his more important dispatches to the War Department. The best of these early biographies is H. Montgomery, *The Life of Major General Zachary Taylor* (Auburn, N. Y., 1847), which was enlarged and revised several times in the next few years, the twentieth edition appearing in 1851. Other biographies which proved useful were: John Frost, *Life of Major General Zachary Taylor . . .* (New York, 1847); Joseph Reese Fry, *A Life of Gen. Zachary Taylor . . .* (Philadelphia, 1847); *General Taylor and His Staff . . .* (Philadelphia, 1848); *Taylor and His Generals . . .* (Philadelphia, 1847). A somewhat more critical biography of Taylor, but confined almost entirely to his military career, is Oliver Otis Howard, *General Taylor* (New York, 1892), a volume in the Great Commanders series. Holman Hamilton, *Zachary Taylor, Soldier of the Republic* (Indianapolis, 1941), is a scholarly and readable account of Taylor's life through the Mexican War.

Biographies of Taylor's military associates are valuable at many points. Charles W. Elliott, *Winfield Scott: The Soldier and the Man* (New York, 1937), is a thorough and unbiased life of Taylor's superior officer during the Mexican War. Douglas Southall Freeman, *R. E. Lee: A Biography,* 4 vols. (New York, 1934–1935), is a masterpiece of biographical writing. George Meade, *The Life and Letters of George Gordon Meade,* 2 vols. (New York, 1913), is especially valuable because of the many letters printed therein. Robert M. McElroy, *Jefferson Davis, the Unreal and the Real,* 2 vols. (New York, 1937), is one of the most recent and one of the best biographies of Taylor's son-in-law who served under him in the Mexican War.

For Taylor's political career biographies of his contemporaries are indispensable. Frederic Bancroft, *The Life of William H. Seward,* 2 vols. (New York, 1900), is the standard life of the influential Whig senator from New York. Thurlow Weed Barnes, *Memoir of Thurlow Weed* (Boston, 1884), is an inadequate biography of the powerful New York leader of the Whig party. Mary Ann Coleman, *Life of John J. Crittenden,* 2 vols. (Philadelphia, 1871), though a family biography, contains many letters and is exceedingly valuable. Ulrich B. Phillips, *The Life of Robert Toombs* (New York, 1913), is an excellent study of this southern Whig leader. George R. Poage, *Henry Clay and the Whig Party* (Chapel Hill, 1936), is not strictly a biography, but it is a penetrating analysis of the latter part of Clay's career. Mary W. Williams, "John Middleton Clayton," in Samuel Flagg Bemis (ed.), *The American Secretaries of State and Their Diplomacy* (New York, 1927–1929), VI, 3–74, is the best account of the diplomacy of Taylor's Secretary of State.

Other biographies that shed light on some phase of Taylor's

life are: Irving Brant, *James Madison, The Virginia Revolutionist* (Indianapolis, 1941); Wilfrid H. Callcott, *Santa Anna: The Story of an Enigma Who Once Was Mexico* (Norman, 1936); Oliver P. Chitwood, *John Tyler, Champion of the Old South* (New York, 1939); Cyrenus Cole, *I am a Man. The Indian Black Hawk* (Iowa City, 1938); George Ticknor Curtis, *Life of Daniel Webster*, 2 vols. (New York, 1870); George M. Dallas, *Life and Writings of Alexander James Dallas* (Philadelphia, 1871); Charles B. Going, *David Wilmot, Free-Soiler* (New York, 1924); Charles E. Hamlin, *The Life and Times of Hannibal Hamlin* (Cambridge, 1899); Hamilton A. Hill, *Memoir of Abbott Lawrence* (Boston, 1883); Mary Mann, *Life of Horace Mann* (Boston, 1891); E. I. McCormac, *James K. Polk, A Political Biography* (Berkeley, 1922); A. C. McLaughlin, *Lewis Cass* (Boston, 1891).

Pamphlets

Pamphlets published during the campaign of 1848 and speeches and sermons presented at the time of Taylor's death and printed in pamphlet form constitute a significant source for this biography. Many of these contain no statement as to authorship or place or date of publication. Two campaign pamphlets published under authority of the National and Jackson Democratic Association Committee in support of the Democratic candidate are: *Allowances and Extra Pay. A Plain Statement of Facts from the Record, Showing Gen. Taylor to Have Received $74,864.04 of "allowances," Besides his Regular Pay, and General Cass to Have Received Not One Cent, Except for Actual Services Rendered the Government*, an answer to the Whig charge that Cass had received excessive sums of money from the government; and *General Taylor's Two Faces* (Washington, 1848). Three pamphlets urging Taylor's election are: *A Sketch of the Life and Public Services of General Zachary Taylor, The People's Candidate for the Presidency, with Considerations in Favor of his Election* (Washington, 1848); *Gen. Taylor's Moral, Intellectual, and Professional Character, as Drawn by the Hon. John J. Crittenden* [and others] . . . (Washington, 1848); *Reasons Good and True for Supporting the Nomination of General Zachary Taylor*.

Of the numerous sermons and speeches eulogizing the departed President, the following were found to be helpful: Ward

Bullard, *President Taylor and the Times. A Sermon on the Death of the Late President, Preached at Grand Isle, July 21, 1850 . . .* (Windsor, 1850); *Obituary Addresses Delivered on the Occasion of the Death of Zachary Taylor, President of the United States, in the Senate and House of Representatives, July 10, 1850 . . .* (Washington, 1850); George L. Prentiss, *Eulogy on the Life and Character of Gen. Zachary Taylor, Late President of the United States . . .* (New Bedford, 1850); W. A. Stearns, *A Discourse on the Death of the President. Preached July 14, 1850, to the First Evangelical Congregational Society, Cambridgeport* (Cambridge, 1850).

Histories and Monographs

Good secondary works on the many aspects of the nation's development with which Taylor was connected are numerous. They served not only to clarify the background of many problems but also to elucidate Taylor's own actions and policies. Works which are useful for his years in Kentucky are: *Centenary of Kentucky. Proceedings at the Celebration by the Filson Club . . . of the One Hundredth Anniversary of the Admission of Kentucky . . .* (Filson Club *Publications,* No. 7, Louisville, 1892); Thomas D. Clark, *A History of Kentucky* (New York, 1937); Reuben T. Durrett, *The Centenary of Louisville . . .* (Filson Club *Publications,* No. 8, Louisville, 1893); *Historical Sketches of Kentucky: Embracing Its History, Antiquities, and Natural Curiosities . . .* (Maysville, Ky., and Cincinnati, Ohio, 1848); Archer B. Hulbert, *The Ohio River: A Course of Empire* (New York, 1906); Willard Rouse Jillson, *The Kentucky Land Grants* (Louisville, 1925); J. Stoddard Johnston, *Memorial History of Louisville from its First Settlement to the Year 1896,* 2 vols. (Chicago and New York [1896]); Louise Phelps Kellogg (ed.), *Frontier Advance on the Upper Ohio, 1778–1779* (Madison, 1916); Robert M. McElroy, *Kentucky in the Nation's History* (New York, 1909); Alice E. Trabue, *A Corner in Celebrities* (Louisville, 1922).

Three works helpful in connection with the organization and administration of the army are: James B. Fry, *The History and Legal Effect of Brevets in the Armies of Great Britain and the United States . . .* (New York, 1877); Raphael P. Thian, *Legislative History of the General Staff of the Army of the United States* (Washington, 1901); and the same author's *Notes Illus-*

trating the Military Geography of the United States (Washington, 1881).

Two brief but scholarly works dealing with the army's work on the Western frontier are Henry P. Beers, *The Western Military Frontier, 1815–1846* (Philadelphia, 1935), and Edgar B. Wesley, *Guarding the Frontier: A Study of Frontier Defense from 1815 to 1825* (Minneapolis, 1935). Grant Foreman's numerous and informative works on the Southwestern frontier shed light on Taylor's activities in that area. These works include: *Indians and Pioneers. The Story of the American Southwest before 1830* (Norman, 1936); *Pioneer Days in the Early Southwest* (Cleveland, 1926); *Indian Removal. The Emigration of the Five Civilized Tribes of Indians* (Norman, 1932); *Advancing the Frontier, 1830–1860* (Norman, 1933); *The Five Civilized Tribes* (Norman, 1934).

Three useful volumes in connection with military events on the upper Mississippi are Marcus L. Hansen, *Old Fort Snelling, 1819–1858* (Iowa City, 1918); Bruce E. Mahan, *Old Fort Crawford and the Frontier* (Iowa City, 1926); and Frank E. Stevens, *The Black Hawk War . . .* (Chicago, 1903). The latter is one of the best accounts of that conflict.

Albert C. Ramsey (ed.), *The Other Side: or Notes for the History of the War Between Mexico and the United States* (New York, ca. 1849), is very useful for a Mexican view of that war. Samuel C. Reid, Jr., *The Scouting Expeditions of McCulloch's Texas Rangers* (Philadelphia, 1848), sheds light on Taylor's campaigns in northern Mexico. Two of the best histories of the Mexican War are George L. Rives, *The United States and Mexico, 1821–1848,* 2 vols. (New York, 1913), and Justin H. Smith, *The War with Mexico,* 2 vols. (New York, 1919). The latter work is very critical of General Taylor but is indispensable to any student of the subject. T. B. Thorpe, *Our Army at Monterey . . .* (Philadelphia, 1847), is based in part upon information furnished by participants.

For the election of 1848 and the domestic problems of Taylor's administration the following works proved helpful: Cleo Hearon, *Mississippi and the Compromise of 1850* (University, Miss., 1914); Henry R. Mueller, *The Whig Party in Pennsylvania* (New York, 1922); James S. Pike, *First Blows of the Civil War: The Ten Years of Preliminary Conflict in the United States, from 1850 to 1860* (New York, 1879); Henry T. Shanks, *The Secession Movement in Virginia, 1847–1861* (Richmond,

1934); Richard H. Shryock, *Georgia and the Union in 1850* (Durham, 1926); Theodore C. Smith, *The Liberty and Free-Soil Parties in the Northwest* (New York, 1897); Ralph E. Twitchell, *The History of the Military Occupation of the Territory of New Mexico from 1846 to 1851 by the Government of the United States . . .* (Denver, 1909).

Three works dealing with Canadian-American relations and useful for Taylor's foreign policy are: C. D. Allin and G. M. Jones, *Annexation, Preferential Trade and Reciprocity: an Outline of the Canadian Annexation Movement 1849–50 . . .* (Toronto, 1912); Donald C. Masters, *The Reciprocity Treaty of 1854 . . .* (London, 1937); C. C. Tansill, *The Canadian Reciprocity Treaty of 1854* (Baltimore, 1922).

Light is shed upon the Cuban problem during Taylor's administration by Robert G. Caldwell, *The López Expeditions to Cuba, 1848–1851* (Princeton, 1915) and Herminio Portell Vilá, *Historia de Cuba En Sus Relaciones Con Los Estados Unidos y España,* 4 vols. (La Habana, 1938–1941).

Merle E. Curti, *Austria and the United States, 1848–1852* (Northampton, 1926), and John G. Gazley, *American Opinion of German Unification, 1848–1871* (New York, 1926), are both useful for the study of Taylor's policy relative to the Hungarian revolt.

J. S. Chambers, *The Conquest of Cholera* (New York, 1938), is an authoritative study of this significant problem and was helpful in connection with the Black Hawk War. Charles S. Sydnor, *Slavery in Mississippi* (New York, 1933), is indispensable for a study of plantation life in that state.

INDEX

Abercrombie, John J., 89
Adams, Charles Francis, and election of 1848, 287
Adams, John Quincy, President, 60; and brevet commissions, 73; on use of bloodhounds in Seminole War, 117-18; on relations with Cuba, 341
Agriculture, Taylor's interest in, 12, 55-56, 255-64, 403; Taylor urges increased aid to, 394-95
Agua Nueva, Taylor concentrates troops at, 226, 229; Taylor withdraws from, 230, 231, 232; Taylor again occupies, 237
Alabama, troops in, 46; Taylor on opportunities in, 47
Albany, N. Y., 286, 403
Alexander, Milton K., in Black Hawk War, 80
Allen, Charles, at Whig convention, 283
Allen, William, 131
Allerton, Isaac, 3
Alligator, Seminole chief, 107; surrenders to Taylor, 113; on Cherokee lands, 142, 143
Allison, J. S., Taylor's brother-in-law, 128; Taylor's letters to, in election of 1848, 279-81, 287
Alvear, Don Carlos Maria de, 397
American Fur Company, 70
American Revolution, 1, 3
Ampudia, Pedro de, commands at Matamoros, 168; at Monterrey, 197, 198, 203-204, 205, 206, 207; at San Luis Potosí, 213
Anderson, W. P., 34
Andrews, Israel D., 363
Apalachicola Indians, 115-16
Apalachicola River, 100, 115, 124
Aransas Bay, 155
Arbuckle, Matthew, on Southwest frontier, 53; Taylor succeeds as commander of Second Military Department, 132-33
Argentine Federation, 397
Arista, Mariano, commands at Matamoros, 169, 170, 171, 193; at battle of Resaca de la Palma, 177; abandons Matamoros, 180
Arkansas, military road in, 91; Taylor's headquarters in, 133-46; troops from, at Buena Vista, 229, 232, 233, 239
Arkansas River, explored by Richard Taylor, 4; Fort Smith on, 53
Armistead, W. K., in Seminole War, 125
Armstrong, William, 141
Atchison, David R., 307
Atkinson, Henry, 51, 52, 132; marries, 61; commands in Northwest, 69; in Black Hawk War, 78-82; on furlough, 94; returns to duty, 95
Atwood, Jesse, paints portraits of Taylor, 185
Austria, American relations with, strained by Hungarian question, 364-67
Ayer, Elisha, schoolmaster, 11

Babcock, Samuel, 58
Bad Axe, battle of, in Black Hawk War, 80, 81, 82
Baltimore, Md., Independents of, withdraw support from Taylor, 286; and filibustering activities, 342; Taylor in, 402, 403, 404
Barbour, James, Secretary of War, 60
Barbourville, Va., 5
Barnburners, in election of 1848, 287-88
Baton Rouge, La., 48, 49, 95, 260; Taylor commands at, 54-56, 67, 130-32; Taylor on court-martial

Baton Rouge, La., *continued*
duty at, 74; Taylor's residence in 1848, 254, 275-76, 284, 297; Taylor bids farewell to citizens of, 302, 368
Bay St. Louis, Miss., Taylor's headquarters at, 49-50, 130
Bayou Sara, La., 48
Beall, Lloyd J., 148
Beargrass Creek, site of Richard Taylor's Kentucky plantation, 6, 9, 258, 407
Bedford Springs, Penna., 402
Bell, John, Secretary of War, 130-31; dines at White House, 306; proposes compromise, 378, 379; defends Taylor on Senate floor, 385
Bell, Mrs. John, dines at White House, 306
Benjamin, Judah P., accompanies Taylor to Washington, 303; dinner guest of Polk, 306
Benton, Thomas Hart, 131, 398; and Taylor's report on Missouri Volunteers at Okeechobee, 111-12; and brevet commissions, 160; and command of Vera Cruz expedition, 224, 225; and Taylor's annual message, 374; and Compromise of 1850, 379
Berry, Taylor, 38
Binney, Horace, considered by Taylor for Cabinet, 311, 316
Bissell, William H., at Buena Vista, 229
Black Hawk, driven west of the Mississippi River, 77; returns to Rock River home, 77; pursued by troops, 78; attacks Illinois settlements, 79; pursued across Wisconsin, 80; defeated at battle of Bad Axe, 80-81; captured, 82
Black Hawk War, 88, 89, 90, 100; causes of, 76-77; Taylor's account of, 78-82; final engagement of, 80-81
Bliss, William Wallace Smith, joins Taylor's staff, 134; marries Betty Taylor, 135, 303; admires Taylor, 140; reports Taylor dangerously ill, 149; and authorship of Taylor's dispatches, 172-73; carries Allison letter to Taylor, 279; accompanies Mrs. Taylor to Washington, 303; in Washington, 304; dinner guest of Polk, 306; Taylor's secretary, 400
Blue Ridge Mountains, 2, 5
Boone, Daniel, 5
Boonesboro, Ky., 6
Boston, Mass., 401
Bowles, William A., at Buena Vista, 229, 234, 240
Boyd, Daniel, Indian Agent, 115
Bradbury, James W., 323, 324
Braddock, General Edward, 5
Brady, Hugh, 132
Bragg, Braxton, at Monterrey, 200; at Buena Vista, 229, 233, 235, 238
Brazil, 364
Bremer, Fredrika, describes President Taylor, 400-401; on Senate and Taylor's death, 406
Brevet commissions, problem of, 73-74, 159-60, 393
Brewster, William, 3
Brooke, George M., 46
Brown, Jacob, with Taylor on the Rio Grande, 170-71
Brown, James, 45
Brown, John, 45
Brown, Mrs. John, 45
Brown, Orlando, Commissioner of Indian Affairs, represents Crittenden in Washington, 313-14; reports long visit with Taylor, 334; finds Taylor unhappy, 405
Brunson, Alfred, at Prairie du Chien, 85
Bryan, Joseph, 327
Buchanan, James, as Secretary of State, 151-52; Taylor corresponds with, 250-51; and Taylor's Pennsylvania tour, 402
Buel, Alexander W., 365
Buena Vista, battlefield of, 230-31; position of troops, 232; first day of battle of, 233; second day, 234-36; stories of Taylor and, 238; casualties, 239; effect of, on Taylor's presidential boom, 268
Buffalo, N. Y., 83, 402; Free-Soil Convention at, 287-88

Bullitt, A. C., and election of 1848, 285; accompanies Taylor to Washington, 303; edits *Republic,* 332, 333, 385; dines at White House, 398
Bulwer, Sir Henry Lytton, on Taylor's Cabinet, 318; negotiates treaty with Clayton, 359-61; on Taylor's characteristics, 408-409
Burnley, Albert T., and election of 1848, 276; criticizes Cabinet, 326; part owner of *Republic,* 332-33; finds Taylor haggard, 405
Butler, E. G. W., Taylor corresponds with, 205
Butler, William O., in Mexican War, 196, 219, 221, 246; vice-presidential candidate, 296

Cabinet, members of Taylor's, 310; selection of Taylor's, 310-18; gives Taylor trouble, 318-21, 325-27, 331-35
Cadwalader, T., 58
Calderón de la Barca, Angel, protests filibustering activities, 344
California, 162, 163, 392, 404; occupied by United States, 216-17; need for government in, 369-70; Taylor sends agent to, 370; drafts constitution, 372; admission of, opposed by South, 376-78, 391; and Clay's compromise, 379, 384, 387, 389-90
Call, R. K., in Seminole War, 103-104
Callaway, James, 31
Camargo, Mex., 196, 197, 198, 206, 210, 219, 220, 245; occupied by Taylor, 194-95
Canada, and the War of 1812, 20, 32; Northwest Indians influenced from, 40; and annexation, 338-39; and reciprocal trade, 362-63
Cantonment Leavenworth, 80
Cárdenas, Cuba, captured, 345
Carlisle, Penna., 402
Cass, Lewis, Secretary of War, 59; criticized by Taylor, 252; and election of 1848, 268, 287-88, 289, 292, 295-96, 299-300; dines at White House, 306; urges break with Austria, 367; and Compromise of 1850, 379, 380, 385
Catron, John, dines at White House, 306
Catron, Mrs. John, dines at White House, 306
Central America, and Anglo-American diplomacy, 354-61
Chamberlain, S. E., 238
Chambers, Talbot, 41
Chambersburg, Penna., 402
Charleston, S. C., Independents of, nominate Taylor, 286
Chase, Salmon P., and Compromise of 1850, 379
Cherokee Indians, in Indian Territory, 53, 135, 137, 138, 139, 140, 142-43
Chesapeake, frigate, 13
Chicago, Ill., 40, 83
Chickasaw Indians, in Indian Territory, 136
Chihuahua, Mex., expedition against, 217
Chippewa Indians, 68, 84
Choctaw Indians, 136, 139
Cholera, at time of Black Hawk War, 83-84
Cincinnati, Ohio, 57, 58, 265, 304
Clark, George Rogers, 10
Clarke, Charles E., 330
Clarksville, Tenn., 272
Clay, Henry, 10, 20, 60, 405; and election of 1848, 268, 269-71, 274, 275, 276, 281-83, 288; and Taylor's Cabinet, 317, 326; withholds support from Taylor, 320-21; on the national crisis, 369; his compromise proposals, 378-80; his controversy with Taylor, 381, 383-85, 389-91
Clay, Henry, Jr., killed at Buena Vista, 239
Clay, James, chargé d'affaires in Portugal, 320-21, 337, 353
Clayton, John M., 306, 338, 344, 364, 367; defends Taylor in Senate, 209; and election of 1848, 268, 271, 282, 296; selected for Secretary of State, 310, 314-15; opposed by Toombs, 315, 320; denounced by Truman Smith, 315; influences

Clayton, John M., *continued*
formation of Cabinet, 316-17; offers to resign, 318, 326, 335; and patronage, 322, 325; continued opposition to, 326-27, 331; consults Taylor on foreign affairs, 336, 349; and Cuban relations, 346-47, 348-49; and controversy with France, 350-52; pushes claims against Portugal, 353-54; negotiates canal treaty with Great Britain, 354-61; and Canadian reciprocity, 363; and Taylor's California policy, 371, 377
Clayton-Bulwer Treaty, 354-61
Cleveland, Grover, 265
Clinch, Duncan L., 75
Clingman, Thomas L., 381, 382 n., 387 n.
Collamer, Jacob, 326, 331, 335; selected for Postmaster General, 310, 317; and patronage, 322
Colman, George, Jr., 86
Columbia River, 61
Columbus, Miss., 48
Comanche Indians, 141
Compromise of 1850, problems giving rise to, 368-74; numerous proposals in Congress, 378-79; proposals debated, 379-87; adopted, 389; Taylor's opposition to, 389-91
Congress, authorizes increase in army, 13; declares war on Great Britain, 20; reduces army following War of 1812, 35; further reduces army, 50; and reorganization of militia, 58-59; and Taylor's report on Missouri troops at Okeechobee, 111-12; debates use of bloodhounds in Florida, 117-18; and annexation of Texas, 148, 151; declares war on Mexico, 170; adopts resolutions of thanks to Taylor, 179, 209; debates Taylor's patronage policy, 323-24; and Galphin claim, 327, 329-31; investigates Ewing's activities, 331-32; and trade problems, 363-64; and Hungarian revolt, 365-66; receives Taylor's annual message, 373-74, 392; and speakership contest, 374-75; and Taylor's California policy, 376-78; compromise proposals in, 378-79; debates compromise proposals, 379-87; passes compromise measures, 389; considers other domestic problems, 392-96; and Taylor's death, 406, 407
Congressional Cemetery, 407
Conner, David, in Mexican War, 163, 179-80, 185
Conrad, C. M., urges Taylor to abandon his territorial policy, 387; his eulogy on Taylor, 408, 409
Convent of the Visitation, 400
Cooper, James Fenimore, 294
Cornwallis, General Lord, 3
Corpus Christi, Texas, selected for occupation, 153; Taylor's troops occupy, 153-64
Corpus Christi Bay, 154, 155
Corwin, Thomas, and election of 1848, 271, 282, 300; dines at White House, 398
Costa Rica, and Anglo-American diplomacy, 354, 358, 359
Cotton, Taylor's interest in, 55-56, 257; low price of, in 1840's, 260
Covington, E. F., 89
Crampton, John F., and Canadian border problems, 338-39; reports Taylor friendly toward Great Britain, 354; confers with Clayton and Taylor on canal diplomacy, 356-57; seeks reciprocal trade treaty, 363
Crawford County, Wisconsin, 85
Crawford, George, selected for Secretary of War, 310, 311, 316; and relations with Seward, 320; and Galphin claim, 327-31; and Compromise of 1850, 372, 387
Creek Indians, 101, 114, 115, 135, 139, 141, 142
Creole, and Cuban filibusters, 345-46
Crittenden, John Jordan, Taylor corresponds with, 204-205, 222-23, 242, 273, 274; defends Taylor in Senate, 209; and the election of 1848, 268, 270, 271, 273, 274, 275,

279, 280, 282; Taylor consults on way to Washington, 304, 311, 314; declines Cabinet post, 311-12, 317; his influence with administration, 313-14, 318; and election of Clay to Senate, 320; and Taylor's Cabinet troubles, 326; informed by Burnley as to *Republic*, 333; informed by Brown of visit with Taylor, 334; approves Taylor's California policy, 371
Crittenden, Thomas, 270
Croghan, George, 11, 33, 36
Croghan, William, 10, 60
Cross, Trueman, 168
Cuba, and American filibustering expeditions, 341-48
Cumberland Gap, 5
Cumberland River, 7
Cummings, Alexander, in Seminole War, 118
Cutler, Enos, 95
Cypress Grove, Taylor's plantation, 255-62

Daily Delta (New Orleans), 169
Daily Union (Washington), organ of Polk administration, 252; on Taylor's patronage policy, 322; on Taylor's Cabinet, 326, 327, 332, 352; on Taylor's foreign policy, 340, 352; on influence of Bliss, 400
Dallas, A. J., 35-36, 51
Davenport, William, Taylor corresponds with, 111, 246; in Seminole War, 118, 124
Davis, Jefferson, drives trespassers from Iowa lead mines, 89; marries Sarah Knox Taylor, 96-98; at Monterrey, 201, 206; at Buena Vista, 229, 239; his plantation visited by Taylor, 259-60; and the election of 1848, 290-91, 298; calls on Polk with Taylor, 306; dines at White House, 306; and Compromise of 1850, 379, 382; introduces army retirement bill, 393; on Taylor's reading habits, 409
Davis, Mrs. Jefferson, 399-400
Davis, Joseph, Taylor visits his plantation, 260
Delaware, carried by Taylor in 1848, 299
Delony, Edward, 272
Democratic party, in election of 1848, 287-89, 295
Denmark, 339, 340
Desertion from United States Army, problem of, 57
Des Moines River, 27, 31
Detroit, Mich., 24, 32, 39
District of Columbia, and Compromise of 1850, 369, 379, 384
Dixons Ferry, on Rock River, 78
Dobbins, Stephen D., in Mexican War, 176
Dodge, Henry, in Black Hawk War, 80
Donelson, Andrew J., in Texas, 150, 151, 153
Douglas, Stephen A., and Compromise of 1850, 379, 380, 383 n., 389
Draper, Simeon, 403
Dubuque, Iowa, lead mines at, 88, 89
Duncan, James, and battle of Palo Alto, 174, 175

East Pascagoula, Miss., Taylor's family in, 250
Eighth Infantry, 46, 48, 52, 175
Elgin, Lord, 362
Encarnacion, Mex., 230
Erie, Penna., 402
Evarts, William M., 344
Evening Journal (Albany), 266
Everett, Edward, corresponds with Taylor on European affairs, 336-37
Ewing, Thomas, 300, 326, 327, 335, 363; selected for Secretary of Home Department, 310, 317; and patronage, 322; investigated by Congress, 331-32
Express (New York), publishes Taylor's letter to Gaines, 242

Fallen Timbers, battle of, 8
Falls of the Ohio, settlement at, 5, 6; affects growth of Louisville, 12, 44
Falls of St. Anthony, 40, 69

Fashion, Taylor's sugar plantation, 262
Fielding, Henry, 86
Fifth Infantry, in Black Hawk War, 80; in Mexican War, 174
Filibustering, and Mexico, 292, 338; and Canada, 338-39; and Cuba, 341-48
Fillmore, Millard, and election of 1848, 283, 286, 287; dinner guest of Polk, 306; his influence with Taylor, 320; signs Compromise of 1850, 389; Taylor visits, 402
First Dragoons, at Buena Vista, 229
First Infantry, Taylor assigned to, 51, 52-53, 55; at Fort Snelling, 67; at Fort Crawford, 84; Taylor colonel of, 84, 87; in Seminole War, 100, 104, 106, 108, 110; at Monterrey, 200
Fish, Hamilton, 335, 403
Florence, Ala., 48
Florida, 46, 100, 101; Seminole War in, 102-124; carried by Taylor in 1848, 299
Flournoy, Thomas S., and election of 1848, 270
Foote, Henry S., and Taylor's Cuban policy, 348; and Compromise of 1850, 376, 378, 379, 386-87; speaks at Washington Monument ceremony, 405
Foreign relations, Taylor's interest in, 336-38; with Canada, 338-39, 362-63; with German Confederation, 339-40; with Cuba, 341-49; with France, 350-52; with Portugal, 353-54; with Great Britain, 354-64; with Austria, 364-67
Foreman, Grant, on causes of Seminole War, 102
Fort Armstrong, 68, 82, 83-84, 87
Fort Basinger, 105 n., 107
Fort Brooke, 115, 123
Fort Crawford, 68, 80, 90, 91, 92, 93, 94, 95; Taylor takes command at, 69; life at, 69-70, 85-87; new Fort erected, 70-71, 84-85; Scott visits, 83; cholera at, 84; Ann Taylor's wedding at, 96
Fort Cumberland, 5
Fort Dearborn, 83
Fort Fraser, 105
Fort Gardiner, 105, 110
Fort Gibson, 132, 133, 135, 136, 141
Fort Harrison, 24, 25, 26, 33; defended by Taylor, 21-23, 45
Fort Howard, 68, 70, 91; Taylor stationed at, 40-44
Fort Independence, 27
Fort Jesup, 61, 146, 149; erected by Taylor, 53; Taylor removes from, 54; Taylor's headquarters in 1844, 144, 147, 148, 153
Fort Johnson, erected by Taylor, 31
Fort King, 103, 121
Fort Knox, 18-19, 26
Fort Leavenworth, 138
Fort Mackinac, 39, 40, 41, 42
Fort McKay, 29
Fort Mellon, 104
Fort Necessity, 5
Fort Pitt, 3
Fort Scott, 138
Fort Selden, 53
Fort Smith, 53, 54; Taylor's headquarters, 133-46
Fort Snelling, 40, 70, 87; Taylor at, 67-69; Robert Crooke Wood at, 95-96
Fort Stephenson, 10-11
Fort Towson, 136, 137, 138, 145, 146
Fort Washita, established by Taylor, 136-37; Taylor visits, 146
Fort Wayne, 137-38
Fort Winnebago, 68, 70, 80, 91
Fortress Monroe, 61
Fourth Artillery, in Seminole War, 106; at Buena Vista, 229, 233
Fourth Infantry, 46, 75, 95, 172; in Seminole War, 106, 108, 110; on Texas border, 149, 153; at Monterrey, 200-201
Fox Indians, 68, 72, 88, 89, 90
Fox River, 40, 79
France, American relations with, strained, 349-52
Frankfort, Ky., visited by Monroe, 45; visited by Taylor, 302, 304
Fredericksburg, Va., 404
Free-Soil party, in election of 1848, 287-88, 290, 300

French-Canadians, at Green Bay, 41

Gaines, Edmund P., commands southern departments, 46; and defense of southwest frontier, 53, 54; commands Western Department, 69; orders Taylor to Baton Rouge, 74; in Seminole War, 103; and brevet commissions, 159; rushes troops to Taylor, 160-61, 191; Taylor's letter to, causes reprimand, 242-44
Galena, Ill., 78
Galphin claim, causes scandal in Taylor's administration, 327-31, 333, 334, 405
Galphin, George, Indian Trader, 327
García y Rey, Juan Francisco, 348-49, 352
Gardiner, George Washington, 105 n.
Garland, John, at Monterrey, 200-201
Garnett, R. S., accompanies Taylor to Washington, 303
General Armstrong, Clayton seeks damages for destruction of, 353
General Taylor, river steamer, 284
Gentry, Richard, killed in battle of Okeechobee, 108
Georgetown College, 400
Georgia, 4, 299, 300
German Confederation, and relations with United States, 339-40, 352
Ghent, Treaty of, 33
Gideon, G. S., part owner of *Republic*, 332-33
Graham, Duncan, 29
Grant, Ulysses S., on the Texas border, 149; his judgment of Taylor, 247, 249
Gratiot, Charles, and brevet commissions, 73
Gray, French S., marries Sarah Bailey Taylor, 46
Great Britain, United States fears attack by, 16; war with United States, 20-33; Mexico hopes for aid from, 162; Taylor friendly toward, 354; and isthmian canal diplomacy, 354-61; and trade with United States, 362-64
Greece, 66
Greeley, Horace, and election of 1848, 282, 283-84, 289
Green Bay, Wis., 52, 68, 91; Taylor stationed at, 40-44
Greene, John, in Seminole War, 118
Guadalupe Hidalgo, Treaty of, 292, 364
Guilford Courthouse, 3

Hall, Allan A., edits *Republic*, 333
Hall, J. Prescott, 344
Hamlin, Hannibal, and Taylor's threat to hang secessionists, 381-82
Haptonstall, Abraham, 4
Hardin, John J., at Buena Vista, 229, 239
Hare Forest, 1, 3, 5
Harmar, Josiah, 8
Harrisburg, Penna., 402
Harrison, William Henry, on Taylor's appointment to command Fort Knox, 18-19; wins battle of Tippecanoe, 19; erects Fort Harrison, 20; in the War of 1812, 20, 23, 24, 25, 32; as President, 130-31, 269
Harrodsburg, Ky., 6
Havana, Cuba, 346, 349
Hawaiian Islands, 364
Henderson, J. Pinkney, in Mexican War, 193, 196, 206
Henry, James D., in Black Hawk War, 80
Henry, W. S., at Monterrey, 202
Hilliard, Henry W., 376
Hise, Elijah, 355, 358
Hitchcock, Ethan Allen, Taylor corresponds with, 113; recommended by Taylor, 130-31; corresponds with Bliss, 134; visits Indian Territory, 137; at Fort Jesup, 149, 150; at Corpus Christi, 155, 159, 160, 161; at Matamoros, 167; on authorship of Taylor's dispatches, 172; his judgment of Taylor, 409
Holy Alliance, 66
Honduras, and Anglo-American diplomacy, 358, 359

Hopkins, Samuel, in the War of 1812, 24-26
Houston, Sam, President of Texas, 147, 148; criticizes Taylor, 210
Howard, Benjamin, in the War of 1812, 27, 29; death of, 32
Howard, Tilghman A., 151
Howard, Volney E., 394
Hull, William, 20
Hülsemann, Chevalier, 366-67
Hungary, Taylor favors independence of, 364-67
Hunt, Memucan, 146
Hunton, Logan, 285, 345

Illinois, 11, 27, 32, 88; settlers in northwest portion of, 68; theater of Black Hawk War, 78-79, 81; troops from, in Black Hawk War, 78-79; troops from, in Mexican War, 185, 229, 232, 235, 236, 239
Illinois River, 24, 79
Illinois Territory, 24, 25
Indiana, 11, 32; Indians in, 8; Taylor on duty in, 18-27; War of 1812 in, 20-27; troops from, at battle of Buena Vista, 229, 232, 233, 234, 235, 240-41
Indians, threaten early Kentucky settlements, 7-8; united by Tecumseh, 19; defeated in battle of Tippecanoe, 19; allies of the British, 20; attack Fort Harrison, 21-23; elude American troops, 24-27; oppose Taylor at Rock River, 27-30; defeated at battle of the Thames, 32; controlled by frontier posts, 40-41, 53, 68; tribes of, on the upper Mississippi, 68; warned by Taylor, 72; in Black Hawk War, 76-82; Taylor drives trespassers from land of, 88-89; Taylor helps preserve peace among, 90; Taylor serves as agent for, 92-94; and the second Seminole War, 100-25; on the Southwest frontier, 135-44; delegation of, at White House, 397
Interior, Department of, established, 310; Taylor urges agricultural bureau in, 394
Iowa, Indians in, 68; Taylor drives trespassers from Indian lands in, 88-89
Ioway Indians, 68

Jackson, Andrew, 45, 73, 82, 101, 265, 293, 322
Jackson Road, Taylor supervises construction of, 48-49
Jefferson Barracks, 69, 78; Black Hawk prisoner at, 82; fugitives from cholera at, 83; Taylor's headquarters, 94-95
Jefferson County, Ky., Indians in, 7-8; plantations in, 9
Jefferson County, Miss., 255
Jefferson, Thomas, 13, 16, 368, 382
Jesup, Thomas S., friend of Taylor, 42; Taylor corresponds with, 47, 51-52, 55, 60-61, 66, 70-71, 82; opposes plan to drop Taylor from army, 50; Quartermaster General, 50; Taylor visits, 60; and Taylor's assignment to duty in 1831, 75; in Seminole War, 104-106, 110, 113-14; his controversy with Taylor over work of Quartermaster's Department, 189-91; criticized by Taylor, 251-52
Jesup, Mrs. Thomas S., 60
Johnson, Cave, 296 n.
Johnson, Reverdy, selected for Attorney General, 310, 316-17; and the Galphin claim, 328-31
Johnson, Richard M., 45
Johnston, Josiah S., Taylor corresponds with, 73-74
Johnston, William F., 402
Johnstone, Valentine, 5
Jones, Sam, 107
Julian, George W., on Taylor as President, 398
Jumper, Seminole chief, 105; surrenders to Taylor, 106

Kearny, Stephen W., 96
Kent, Edward, 325
Kentucky, 32, 47, 48, 60, 98, 345; Taylor family removes to, 4-6; early settlement of, 6-8; Indian hunting ground, 7; militia of, fights Ohio Indians, 8; boyhood

home of Taylor, 8-12; plantations in, 9; admitted to the Union, 10; congressmen from, recommend Taylor's appointment to army, 13; troops from, in War of 1812, 24-26; Taylor settles in, following resignation from army, 38; Taylor on recruiting duty in, 44-45, 56-58; President Monroe visits, 45; economic conditions in, 64-65; Taylor on furlough in, 72-74; Taylor's children at school in, 95; Taylor visits in 1840, 128; troops from, in Mexican War, 196, 211, 229, 232, 233, 235, 239; carried by Taylor in 1848, 299; visited by Taylor in 1849, 302-304; Taylor buried in, 407
Kentucky County, 7
Kickapoo Indians, 24, 141
King, Thomas Butler, Taylor's agent in California, 370, 371, 377, 378
Kissimmee River, 106-107, 110, 113
Knights of the Golden Horseshoe, 2

Lake Erie, 32
Lake Huron, 40
Lake Koshkonong, 80
Lake Michigan, 40
Lake Nicaragua, 355
Lake Pontchartrain, 48
Lake Superior, 68
Lancaster, Penna., 402
Land Ordinance of 1785, 6
Lane, James H., at Buena Vista, 229
Lane, Joseph, at Buena Vista, 229, 233, 234
Laredo, Texas, 161
Lawrence, Abbott, declines Cabinet place, 316, 317; minister to England, 337, 358
Lawson, Thomas, Taylor corresponds with, 61-62, 78-80
Leavenworth, Henry, 69
Lee, Elizabeth, 2
Lee, Light-Horse Harry, 3
Lee, Richard, 2
Lee, Robert E., 3, 249
Letcher, Robert P., urged for Cabinet post, 314, 326; represents Crittenden in Washington, 318; minister to Mexico, 337; on Clayton's note to France, 352
Lewis, William D., 325
Liberty party, 287
Linares, Mex., 213
Lincoln, Abraham, and election of 1848, 270; at Taylor's inaugural ball, 309
Linn, Lewis F., 131
Lisbon, 353
Little Rock, Ark., 133
Locust Grove, 10-11
Logan, James, Indian Agent, 141
López, Narciso, and Cuban-American relations, 342-48
Louisiana, 65, 95, 98, 345; Taylor's view of opportunities in, 47; Taylor on duty in, 53-55, 74-75, 130, 297; Taylor purchases plantation in, 55; Taylor on furlough in, 72-74; troops from, in Seminole War, 105; troops from, in Mexican War, 169; presents sword to Taylor, 179, 193, 254; Taylor purchases sugar plantation in, 262; and election of 1848, 283, 299, 300
Louisville, Ky., 6, 7, 8, 9, 10, 11, 12, 17, 38, 39, 54, 258, 265; Taylor on recruiting duty in, 44-45, 56-58; Taylor in, 60, 65, 66, 73 n., 74, 76, 78, 128, 302, 303-304

Macomb, Alexander, commands Fifth Military Department, 39, 43; criticized by Taylor, 82; praises Taylor's victory at Lake Okeechobee, 111; negotiates with Seminoles, 119-20; death of, 135
Madison, Ambrose, 2
Madison, Dolly Todd, death of, 400
Madison, James, 10, 39, 400; related to Taylor, 2; Taylor commended to, 14; urges retention of Taylor with rank of major, 35-36; criticized by Taylor, 51; and brevet commissions, 73
Madison, Ind., Taylor injured by fall at, 304, 305
Madisonville, La., 48
Mann, A. Dudley, special diplomatic agent, 365-67

Mann, Horace, on Taylor's opposition to secession, 382-83; approves Compromise of 1850, 389; dines at White House, 399
Mansfield, Joseph, at Monterrey, 199
Marcy, William L., as Secretary of War, 157, 161, 162; orders Taylor to Rio Grande, 162-63; his controversy with Scott, 181; his instructions to Taylor at outbreak of war, 187; Taylor resents treatment by, 207-209, 214, 222-23; instructs Taylor to push south, 212; contemplates Vera Cruz expedition, 215; dissatisfied with Taylor, 224; urges appointment of Scott, 225; further controversy with Taylor, 241-44; urges Taylor as successor to Scott, 246; Taylor's contempt for, 251
Marshall, Humphrey, at Buena Vista, 229, 233, 234; on Taylor's Cabinet, 326-27; urges Taylor to abandon territorial policy, 387
Maryland, 17, 299
Mason, James M., and Compromise of 1850, 385
Massachusetts, 58, 283
Matamoros, Mex., 163, 171, 173, 175, 187, 188, 189, 191, 192, 193, 194, 196, 197, 212, 219, 250, 252; Taylor establishes camp opposite, 166-67; Taylor stops supplies to, 168; captured by Taylor, 180-81
Mattapony River, 2
May, Charles A., in Mexican War, 176-77, 229
McCall, George A., on Taylor's dispatches, 172; and the organization of New Mexico, 373, 377
McClellan, George B., in Mexican War, 190
McCormick, Charles, accompanies Taylor to Washington, 303
McIntosh, Lachlan, 3
McIntosh, Roley, 141, 142
McKee, William, at Buena Vista, 229, 239
McLane, Robert W., presidential messenger to Taylor, 215, 216, 218
McLean, John, and election of 1848, 268, 271, 282
McLeod, Collin, at Fort Howard, 43-44
McNeil, John, at Fort Howard, 42-43
McRee, Mrs. Samuel, befriends Sarah Knox Taylor, 97
Meade, George Gordon, at Corpus Christi, 156; on Taylor's dispatches, 172; at Matamoros, 181; on discipline of volunteers, 192; on Taylor at Saltillo, 216; his judgment of Taylor, 247, 248
Mejía, Francisco, in command at Matamoros, 167-68
Memphis, Tenn., 284, 302, 303
Menominee Indians, 68, 72, 88, 90
Meredith, William, selected for Secretary of the Treasury, 310, 316, 317; and patronage, 325; and Galphin claim, 327-31; and tariff policy, 363, 395, 401
Mexican War, United States troops occupy Texas, 154-64; move to Rio Grande, 164-67; skirmish with Mexican troops, 168-69; war declared, 170; battle of Palo Alto, 173-75; battle of Resaca de la Palma, 176-78; fall of Matamoros, 180; Camargo occupied, 194; battle for Monterrey, 199-204; American campaign plans, 212-15; Saltillo occupied, 216; New Mexico and California occupied, 216; Vera Cruz expedition, 218-19, 224-25; battle of Buena Vista, 231-38; end of Taylor's offensive operations in, 245-46
Mexico, 53, 292, 338, 343, 364; opposes annexation of Texas, 146, 147, 151-52; refuses to negotiate with United States, 162, 163; war on, declared by United States, 169-70
Mexico City, 187, 244, 245, 246, 252
Michigan, 32
Michigan Territory, settlers in, massacred, 79; militia from, in Black Hawk War, 80-81

Miconopy, Seminole chief, 105
Mikasuki Indians, in Seminole War, 103, 107, 114
Militia, board to reorganize, 58-59; in Black Hawk War, 78-81; use of, in Florida, opposed by Taylor, 122; in Mexican War, 191-93
Miller, John, 40, 41, 42
Mills, Madison, quoted on Mexican War, 165, 171, 174, 209, 215
Minnesota, 68
Minón, Vicente, 231, 236
Mississinewa towns, 26
Mississippi, 49, 95, 98, 345; troops from, at Monterrey, 196, 201; at battle of Buena Vista, 229, 233, 235, 239, 240; Taylor's plantation in, 255-62; and Compromise of 1850, 368, 386
Mississippi River, 67, 68, 88; explored by Richard Taylor, 4; Taylor leads expedition up, 27-31; and Black Hawk War, 80-81; floods plantations, 255, 257, 260-62
Missouri, 12, 91; Taylor's view of opportunities in, 47; troops from, in Seminole War, 105, 106-108, 111-13
Missouri Compromise, 368
Missouri River, 32, 34
Missouri Territory, 27, 32
Monclova, Mex., 213, 217
Monroe Doctrine, Taylor comments on, 66; and Clayton-Bulwer Treaty, 355, 361-62
Monroe, James, 10, 51, 66; visits Kentucky, 45; and brevet commissions, 73
Montemorelos, Mex., 219, 220
Monterrey, Mex., 180, 215, 216, 217, 218, 219, 220, 221, 224, 226, 227, 229, 241, 242, 244, 245, 246, 248; Taylor instructed to operate against, 187-88; Taylor advances on, 194-97; battle for, 198-203; occupied by Taylor, 204; troops in, 209-12; Taylor's headquarters, 249
Montpelier, home of James Madison, 2, 36
Moore, Benjamin D., 136
Morehead, C. S., on Taylor's Cabinet, 327
Morgan, Willoughby, death of, 84
Morse, S. F. B., 299
Mosquito Coast, and Anglo-American diplomacy, 354, 358, 359
Mosquito Indians, 355-61
Mountfort, John, 74

Napoleon, Louis, 352
Nashville, Tenn., 48, 49, 302, 303
Nashville Convention, 386
Natchez, Miss., 49, 57, 255, 260, 261
Natchitoches, La., 53, 54
National Intelligencer (Washington, D. C.), 388
Native American Party, 295, 300
Negro slavery, in Kentucky, 9, 12; on Taylor's plantation, 55, 72-73, 256, 257, 262; as issue in election of 1848, 287-91, 300; problem of, threatens Union, 368-91
Neutrality laws, upheld by Taylor, 338-48
New Brunswick, 338
New England, Taylor plans to visit, 401; plans abandoned, 402
New Jersey, 266, 299
New Mexico, occupied by United States, 216; and Compromise of 1850, 369, 371, 372-73, 376-77, 379, 384, 386-89, 392, 404
New Orleans, La., 11, 15, 16, 48, 49, 189, 191, 207, 284; steamers to, from Louisville, 44; Taylor departs for, 46; Taylor in, 67, 75, 128, 130, 150, 153, 154; cholera in, 84; welcomes Taylor home from Mexico, 253-54; and filibustering activities, 342, 344, 345, 349
New York, N. Y., and filibustering activities, 342, 344, 345; Taylor visits, 403
New York State, and election of 1848, 286-88, 299, 300; Taylor and patronage in, 320, 321; Taylor plans to visit, 401; plans abandoned, 402
Newport, Ky., 14, 57
Niagara Falls, N. Y., 402

Nicaragua, and Anglo-American diplomacy, 354-59
Niles' Register, 23
North Carolina, 58, 179, 299
Northwest Ordinance, 6
Nova Scotia, 338
Nueces River, 153, 155, 158, 163, 168

O'Brien, John Paul Jones, at Buena Vista, 233, 234
O'Hara, Kean, 11
Ohio, Indian battles in, 8; troops from, in Mexican War, 196; delegates from, at Whig convention, 283; Taylor fails to carry, in 1848, 300
Ohio River, 4, 5; navigation of, 11-12
Ohio Valley, 3, 23
Okeechobee, battle of, 107-11; effect of battle on Taylor, 126-27
"Omnibus Bill," 384-85, 389
Orange County, Va., 1, 3, 4, 5
Oregon, 61, 368, 369, 370
Ormsby, Stephen, 33-34
Osage Indians, 53; delegation of, at White House, 397
Osceola, Indian chief, in the Seminole War, 103
O'Sullivan, John L., favors acquisition of Cuba, 342, 343
Oulatoochee, Seminole chief, 105
Owings, Thomas D., 35

Palmerston, Lord, and Clayton-Bulwer negotiations, 357, 358, 360
Palo Alto, battle of, 173-75, 182
Panama, isthmus of, 356
Panic of 1819, effect of, on army, 50; effect of, in Kentucky, 56, 64-65; effect of, on Taylor's interests, 64-65
Parker, F. A., 339, 344
Parras, Mex., 217, 220
Patronage, problem of, in Taylor's administration, 321-25
Patterson, Robert, in command of Taylor's reserves, 196; and Tampico expedition, 212, 214, 215; and Vera Cruz expedition, 218, 219, 220, 221
Payne's Landing, Treaty of, 101-102, 114
Pearl River, 48
Pendleton, John S., and election of 1848, 270
Pennsylvania, 58; carried by Taylor in 1848, 299, 300; Taylor and patronage in, 321, 325; Taylor visits, 401-403, 404
Peoria, Ill., 24
Perry, Matthew C., 219
Perry, Oliver H., 32
Peyton, Balie, 303, 398; and election of 1848, 285; minister to Chile, 337
Philadelphia, Penna., 95; Whig convention at, 281-83
Picayune (New Orleans), 303, 332
Pillow, Gideon J., on Taylor's appearance, 184; on health of army at Camargo, 195; his letters to Polk undermine Taylor, 208, 224
Pittsburgh, Penna., 4, 5, 12, 44, 189, 401, 402
Pleasanton, Alfred, on Taylor's New Mexico policy, 387-88
Plymouth Colony, 3
Poindexter, George, Taylor corresponds with, 73-74
Poinsett, Joel R., Secretary of War, defends Taylor, 112; favors use of Florida militia, 116; approves use of bloodhounds, 116-17; instructs Taylor, 120; commends Taylor, 122-23; relieves Taylor, 125
Point Isabel, 161, 176, 178, 179, 185, 193, 248, 250; Taylor establishes base of supplies at, 166; threatened by Mexican troops, 170-71
Polk, James K., 267, 292, 298, 322, 323, 369, 398; and annexation of Texas, 152; and brevet commissions, 160; negotiates with Mexico on eve of war, 162; recommends declaration of war, 169-70; appoints Taylor to command army in Mexico, 181-82; criticizes Jesup, 190; disapproves Taylor's terms at Monterrey, 207; Taylor resents treatment by, 208, 222-23; decides on Vera Cruz expedition, 215; dissatisfied with Taylor, 224; aids

Santa Anna, 227; blames Taylor for Buena Vista, 241; further controversy of, with Taylor, 241-44; opposes Taylor as successor to Scott, 246-47; criticized by Taylor, 252; gives dinner at White House, 306; at Taylor's inauguration, 307, 309; and aid to German Confederation, 339-40; and Cuba, 341-42, 348; and Central America, 355; and trade with Canada, 363; discusses California with Taylor, 370
Poore, Ben Perley, and Taylor's annual message, 374 n.
Portell Vilá, Herminio, and Taylor's Cuban policy, 348
Portugal, American claims against, 353-54
Posey, Alexander, in Black Hawk War, 80
Potomac River, 5
Poussin, William Tell, French minister to United States, 350-52
Prairie du Chien, Wis., 69, 70, 85; fort established at, 40, 41; and cholera epidemic, 84. *See also* Fort Crawford
Preston, William Ballard, and election of 1848, 270; selected for Secretary of the Navy, 310, 311, 316; and Compromise of 1850, 369, 370, 388
Prophet, the, 19, 20
Prophets Town, 19, 25
Pyne, the Reverend Smith, and Taylor's funeral, 407

Quartermaster's Department, criticized by Taylor, 188-91
Quitman, John A., on march to Victoria, 219, 220, 221

Rapidan River, 1, 2
Read, Thomas Buchanan, 365
Reciprocal trade, between Canada and United States, 362-63
Recruiting service, of United States Army, 16, 26, 44-45, 46, 57-58
Rector, Nelson, 28, 30
Red River, 53, 54, 136-37, 145, 149
Republic (Washington), 385, 405; organ of Taylor administration, 332-33, 334; on Taylor's Pennsylvania trip, 401
Republican (Richmond), 281
Resaca de la Palma, battle of, 176-78, 182
Reynosa, Mex., occupied by Taylor, 194
Rhode Island, 179
Richmond, Va., Taylor visits, 403-404
Ridgely, Randolph, in Mexican War, 176
Riley, Bennet, 372
Rio Grande, 158, 161, 164, 166; Mexican forces on, 151, 152; position on, occupied by Taylor's troops, 162-63, 166-67; mouth of, blockaded by Taylor, 168; fleeing Mexicans drown in, 177; blocks Taylor's pursuit, 178; Taylor's line of communication, 187, 188-89, 194-95; as a defensive line, 213, 214
Ringgold, Samuel, in Mexican War, 164, 174-75
Ringgold, Thomas W., manager of Cypress Grove, 256-57
Ritchie, Thomas, criticized by Taylor, 252; attacks Taylor's administration, 322, 332, 340, 352
Rives, William C., minister to France, 337, 351-52
Rock Island, Joseph M. Street, Indian Agent at, 92, 94
Rock River, 82; Taylor leads expedition against Indians at mouth of, 27-30; valley of, home of Sacs and Foxes, 68; valley of, reoccupied by Black Hawk's party, 77-78
Roenne, Baron von, 340
Round Island, and filibustering expedition, 343-44, 347, 352
Russell, William, 26-27, 32, 34
Russia, 365

Sabine River, 53, 54
Sac Indians, 68, 89, 90; in War of 1812, 27-31; in Black Hawk War, 76-82

Saltillo, Mex., 199, 204, 217, 218, 219, 220, 226, 227, 228, 234, 236, 237, 246; Taylor decides to occupy, 213; Taylor occupies, 216; Taylor strengthens defenses of, 231, 233
San Antonio, 153, 156, 217
San Juan River (Mexico), Taylor's route follows, 187, 188, 194, 196, 197
San Juan River (Nicaragua), 355, 357, 360
San Luis Potosí, Mex., 219, 221, 245, 248; Taylor instructed to move on, 212; Taylor opposes move on, 213; Taylor advances toward, 226; Mexican forces at, 227-28, 229
Santa Anna, Antonio López de, 197, 198, 220, 391; at San Luis Potosí, 213, 228; returns to Mexico, 227; advances to attack Taylor, 228-29, 230, 232; demands surrender, 232-33; defeated by Taylor, 233-36; retreats, 237
Santa Fé, New Mex., 386, 387
Sargent, John O., edits *Republic*, 332, 333
Saunders, John, in Mexican War, 189
Saunders, Judge, and nomination of Taylor by Whigs, 283, 285-86
Scott, Winfield, 148, 190, 230, 244, 245, 246, 249, 252; appointed to United States Army, 15; rises rapidly, 33; and militia board, 58; on Taylor's integrity, 64-65; and Black Hawk War, 83; and Seminole War, 103; appointed commanding general of the army, 135; and brevet commissions, 159-60; and command of the army on the Rio Grande, 181-82; and transfer of troops from Taylor, 220-23; given command of Vera Cruz expedition, 225; his instructions disregarded by Taylor, 226, 227; his letter to Taylor intercepted, 228; criticized by Taylor, 241-42, 251; and election of 1848, 267, 268, 271, 282; his judgment of Taylor, 409
Second Artillery, 74
Second Dragoons, on the Texas border, 146, 148, 149, 153; at Buena Vista, 229
Second Infantry, 52
Seddon, James A., and Taylor's California policy, 378
Seminole Indians, 88; origin of, 100; cede lands, 101; refuse to migrate, 102; commence war, 102-103; early successes of, 103-104; defeated by Taylor at Lake Okeechobee, 107-11; many removed, 114; make "peace," 120; continue the war, 121-24; in Indian Territory, 135, 142-43
Seminole War, causes of, 100-102; commences, 102-103; failure of early army campaigns in, 103-104; Jesup prematurely announces end of, 104; additional troops ordered to, 104; battle of Lake Okeechobee, 107-11; Taylor in command, 113-14; use of bloodhounds in, 116-18; Macomb negotiates peace "treaty," 119-20; "treaty" broken, 121; continues, 121-24
Seventh Infantry, 13, 16, 32, 33, 51, 53, 55, 170
Sevier, A. H., 133
Seward, William H., and election of 1848, 282, 300; and Taylor's patronage policy, 319-20; represents Taylor, 369; his influence with Taylor alienates Southern Whigs, 375; and Compromise of 1850, 379, 383
Shaw, John, 30
Shelby, Isaac, governor of Kentucky, 24
Shenandoah Valley, 2, 5
Sherman, Thomas W., at Buena Vista, 229, 235
Signal (Cincinnati), and election of 1848, 271
Sims, John, 255
Sioux Indians, 68, 72, 81, 84, 92
Sixth Infantry, in Black Hawk War, 80; in Seminole War, 106, 108, 110; at Fort Towson, 138
Slidell, John, 162, 163
Sloat, John D., 163

Smith, E. Kirby, in Mexican War, 177
Smith, Justin H., criticizes Taylor, 248, 249
Smith, Peter Sken, in election of 1848, 278
Smith, P. F., in Seminole War, 105
Smith, Truman, and election of 1848, 270, 296-97, 338; opposes Clayton for Secretary of State, 315; declines Cabinet place, 317; and Taylor's patronage policy, 323-24, 337
Smith, Walter, 17
South America, Taylor seeks friendly relations with, 364
South Carolina, and election of 1848, 299; opposes Northern aggression, 368; and Nashville Convention, 386
Spain, 53; and Cuban-American relations, 341-48
Spotswood, Alexander, 2
Squire, Ephraim George, and canal diplomacy, 358-59
St. Augustine, Fla., 104, 118, 123, 124, 125
St. Charles Parish, Louisiana, 262
St. Clair, Arthur, 8
St. Joseph's Island, Texas, 154, 155
St. Lawrence River, 363
St. Louis, 27, 31, 32, 38, 69, 83, 95; recruiting rendezvous at, 57; cholera at, 84
Stanton, Richard H., visits Taylor at White House, 398
Steen, Enoch, at Buena Vista, 229, 232
Stephens, Alexander H., and election of 1848, 270-71, 279, 280, 296; urges Crittenden take Cabinet post, 312; defends Taylor administration on Galphin claim, 330; and Compromise of 1850, 369, 375, 381, 388
Stevens, Thaddeus, 402
Stillman, Isaiah, in Black Hawk War, 78-79, 81
Stinking Lake, 40
Street, Mary, friend of Sarah Knox Taylor, 97
Street, Joseph M., Indian Agent, 82, 92, 93, 94
Strother, Sarah Dabney, marries Richard Taylor, 1-2; mother of Zachary Taylor, 4-5; education of, 11; death of, 72
Strother, Sarah Bailey, 1
Strother, William, 1
Stuart, Alexander, 34
Suwanee River, 100, 115, 124

Tamaulipas, 207, 212
Tampa Bay, 100, 101, 103, 104, 105, 106, 115, 118, 121, 123
Tampico, Mex., 163, 207, 221; expedition against, 212-13, 218; evacuated by Mexicans, 219
Tallahassee, Fla., 115, 118, 120, 121, 124, 125
Tallahassee Indians, 114
Taney, Roger B., administers oath of office to Taylor, 308
Tariff, Taylor's views on, 272-73, 395, 401
Taylor, Ann Mackall, daughter of Taylor, 38, 47-48, 62, 98; marries Robert Crooke Wood, 96
Taylor, Elizabeth, sister of Taylor, 98, 128
Taylor, Emily, 128
Taylor, Frances, 2
Taylor, George, 72
Taylor, Hancock, uncle of Taylor, 1, 4
Taylor, Hancock, brother of Taylor, 1, 128; at wedding of Sarah Knox, 98; advised by Taylor on plantation management, 258-59
Taylor, James, great-grandfather of Taylor, 2
Taylor, James, cousin of Taylor, commends Taylor to President Madison, 14, 39
Taylor, John, 250
Taylor, Joseph Pannel, 128; appointed to United States Army, 14; honorably discharged, 37; reappointed, 38-39; in Seminole War, 109; in Mexican War, 250; Taylor informs of plantation losses, 261; his relations with

Taylor, Joseph Pannel, *continued*
Weed, 266; his relations with Seward, 320
Taylor, Margaret, daughter of Taylor, 47
Taylor, Margaret Mackall Smith, marries Taylor, 17; at army posts, 18; children of, 18, 38, 47, 62; remains at Louisville, 39; accompanies Taylor south, 46; illness of, 47-48; joins Taylor at Bay St. Louis, 49; in Louisiana, 56; health of, 62, 95, 399; and marriage of Sarah Knox, 98; in Florida, 123; travels east with Taylor, 128-29; at Fort Jesup, 153; at Baton Rouge, 250; reunited with Taylor, 253; Taylor's concern over Dick expressed to, 259; and Taylor's presidential candidacy, 275, 284; goes to Washington, 303, 304; in the White House, 399-400, 402
Taylor, Mary Elizabeth (Betty), daughter of Taylor, birth of, 62; education of, 128; marries William Wallace Smith Bliss, 135, 303; at Fort Jesup, 153; at Baton Rouge, 250; in Washington, 304, 306; hostess of White House, 399-400
Taylor, Octavia, 47
Taylor, Richard, father of Taylor, 33, 38, 60; in the Revolutionary War, 1, 3; marries, 1; receives western land, 3; explores the Mississippi Valley, 4; migrates to Kentucky, 4-6; Indian fighter, 8; develops Kentucky plantation, 9; justice of the peace, 9; collector of the port, 10; member of state constitutional conventions, 10; member of state legislature, 10; presidential elector, 10; education of, 11; death of, 72
Taylor, Richard (Dick), son of Taylor, birth of, 62; education of, 125, 409-10; at Matamoros, 250; takes charge of Cypress Grove, 259; with Taylor purchases sugar plantation, 262; becomes sole owner, 263
Taylor, Robert, 250
Taylor, Sarah Bailey, 46, 128
Taylor, Sarah Knox, 38, 47-48; birth of, 18; education of, 62; marries Jefferson Davis, 96-98; death of, 98-99
Taylor, William, 65
Taylor, William Dabney Strother, 3, 14
Taylor, Zachary, *Chronology:* ancestry, 1-3; birth, 5; taken to Kentucky, 5-6; boyhood, 8-12; education, 11; on father's plantation, 12; appointed first lieutenant in United States Army, 13; commended to Madison, 14; army pay of, 15; on duty in Kentucky, 16; joins forces at New Orleans, 16; on sick leave, 17; promoted to captain, 17; marries, 17; at Fort Knox, 18; at General Wilkinson's trial, 20; at Fort Harrison, 20-23; brevetted major, 23; marches against Indians, 24-27; on recruiting duty, 26; leads expedition up Mississippi River, 27-31; erects Fort Johnson, 31; joins expedition up Missouri River, 32; ordered to Vincennes, 32; on furlough in Kentucky, 32; promoted to major, 33; thinks of resigning, 33; reduced to captain, 35; protests to Madison, 35; resigns, 36; turns to agriculture, 38; returns to army as major, 38; at Fort Howard, 40-44; returns to Louisville, 44; assigned to recruiting, 44; and Monroe's tour of Kentucky, 45; promoted to lieutenant colonel, 46; builds military road in Mississippi, 48-49; at Bay St. Louis, 49-50; denounces army reorganization, 51-52; transferred to Louisiana, 53; erects Fort Jesup, 53-54; at Baton Rouge, 54-55; purchases plantation, 55; superintends recruiting service at Louisville, 56-58; serves on court-martial, 58; serves on militia board, 58-59; hard hit by economic conditions, 64-65; comments on Holy Alliance and

Monroe Doctrine, 66; in Louisiana, 67; at Fort Snelling, 67-69; at Fort Crawford, 69-72; on furlough, 72-74; his plantation problems, 72-73, 75; protests Jackson's policy on brevet commissions, 73-74; on duty in Louisiana, 74-75; returns to Northwest, 76; in Black Hawk War, 76-82; resumes command at Fort Crawford, 84; promoted to colonel, 84; his duties at Fort Crawford, 87-88; drives trespassers from Dubuque lead mines, 88-89; helps preserve peace among Indians, 90; builds military road, 91; serves as Indian Agent at Prairie du Chien, 92-94; at Jefferson Barracks, 94; seeks exchange with Cutler, 95; returns to Fort Crawford, 95; opposes marriage of daughter to Jefferson Davis, 96-98; ordered to Florida, 100; arrives in Florida, 102; marches against Indians, 105-107; and battle of Lake Okeechobee, 107-11; brevetted brigadier general, 111; and controversy over Missouri Volunteers, 111-13; succeeds Jesup in command, 113-14; his campaign in northern Florida, 115-19; uses bloodhounds to track Indians, 116-18; asks to be relieved, 121; continues campaign, 122; praised by Secretary Poinsett, 122-23; ill with fever, 123; his final campaign in Florida, 124; again asks to be relieved, 124; his request granted, 125; effect of Seminole War on, 126-27; visits in Kentucky, 128; goes to Washington, 128; his educational views, 129-30; takes interest in Harrison's administration, 130-31; in command of Second Military Department, 132; at Fort Smith, 133; and the Indians of the Southwest, 135-44; and Texas border troubles, 144-46; moves headquarters to Fort Jesup, 147; and annexation of Texas, 147-53; dangerously ill, 149; ordered to Texas, 152-53; occupies Corpus Christi, 154-64; and problem of brevet commissions, 159-60; ordered to Rio Grande, 162-63; advances, 164-67; blockades mouth of Rio Grande, 168; and commencement of hostilities, 169; defends Point Isabel, 170-71; his dispatches, 172-73; wins battle of Palo Alto, 173-75; and Resaca de la Palma, 176-78; hailed as hero, 178-79; occupies Matamoros, 180; appointed major general and given command of campaign against Mexico, 182; instructed to operate against Monterrey, 187; his transportation problems, 188-91, 194-95; his discipline and health problems, 192-93, 195, 209-12; occupies Camargo, 194; advances on Monterrey, 195-96; and the battle for Monterrey, 199-204; defends capitulation terms, 205-206; resents treatment by Polk and Marcy, 208, 214, 222-23; disapproves new instructions, 213-15; occupies Saltillo, 216; joined by Wool's column, 217; and Victoria expedition, 219-21; and transfer of troops to Scott, 220-23; Polk dissatisfied with, 224; advances to Agua Nueva, 226-27, 229; withdraws to La Angostura, 230; refuses to surrender, 232-33; wins battle of Buena Vista, 233-39; and controversy over Indiana troops, 240-41; further controversy with Polk and Marcy, 241-44; indisposed, 244; end of offensive operations, 245-46; his appointment to succeed Scott blocked by Polk, 246; estimate of his war services, 247-50; his correspondence, 250-52; returns to United States, 253; his reception in New Orleans, 253-54; acquires plantation in Mississippi, 255-56; his views on plantation management, 257-58, 263; places Dick in charge of plantation, 259; his plantation suffers from floods, 260-63; buys Louisiana sugar plan-

Taylor, Zachary, *continued*
tation, 262-63, his relations with Maunsel White, 263-64; early presidential boom for, 266-69; develops interest in candidacy, 267-68; Whig leaders support, 270-71; his letters in election of 1848, 271-73, 278-81; fears patronage problem, 274; remains at Baton Rouge, 275-76; seeks to be nonpartisan candidate, 277-79; his first Allison letter, 279-80; nominated by Whigs, 282-84; his letter of acceptance, 284-85; accepts nomination by independents, 286; his second Allison letter, 287; and campaign issues, 289-95; remains at Baton Rouge, 297; elected President, 299-301; resigns from army, 302; travels to Washington, 302-304; enthusiastically welcomed, 304-305; dines at White House, 306; inaugurated President, 307; his inaugural address, 308-309; and formation of his Cabinet, 309-18; experiences constant Cabinet troubles, 318-21, 325-27, 331-35; and patronage problems, 321-25; and Galphin claim, 327-31; and *Republic* (Washington), 332-33; deeply hurt by criticisms, 334-35; and conduct of foreign affairs, 336-38, 346-47, 350, 354, 356-57, 360-61; and Canadian border, 338-39; and steamer *United States,* 339-40; and relations with Cuba, 341-49; and dismissal of French Minister, 350-52; and claims against Portugal, 353-54; and Clayton-Bulwer Treaty, 354-62; leaves trade problems to Congress, 362-64; favors Hungarian independence, 364-67; urges organization of California, 370-72; urges organization of New Mexico, 373; discusses sectional issues in annual message, 373-74; loses support of Toombs and Stephens, 375; his California policy attacked, 376-78; denounces secession, 381-82, 387-88; opposes Clay's compromise, 383-85, 389-91; opposes territorial claims of Texas, 386-89; his annual message on other domestic issues, 392-96; his life in the White House, 397-401; visits Pennsylvania, 401-402; seriously ill, 402-403; returns to Washington, 403; visits Baltimore, 403; visits Richmond, 403-404; his last illness and death, 405-406; appraisal of, 407-10. *Characteristics:* as revealed in Mexican War, 247-50; as noted at his death, 407-409; physical, 184, 397, 398; dress, 184-85, 397, 401; portraits of, 185-86; firm, 14, 235, 338, 383, 391, 408; courageous, 23, 26, 36, 45, 235, 237-38, 407; honest, 65, 132, 408; sociable, 85, 306, 397-99, 404; rough and ready, 126; economical with public funds, 134, 140, 248; humane, 143, 235, 247; democratic, 186, 404; informal, 193; peace-loving, 247; thrifty and prudent, 257-58; proud, 390, 391, 404; prejudiced, 391, 409; uniformed, 398, 409; kind and friendly, 401, 408; simple, 399, 404, 408; ambitious, 409. *Letters:* to William H. Harrison, 21-22; to Benjamin Howard, 28, 30; to Taylor Berry, 38; to Thomas S. Jesup, 42-43, 47, 51-52, 55, 60-61, 66, 70-71, 82; to Thomas Lawson, 61-63, 78-80; to William Taylor, 65; to Josiah S. Johnston, 73-74; to George Poindexter, 73-74; to E. A. Hitchcock, 113, 130-31, 132, 134; to Robert Crooke Wood, 129-30, 183, 193, 196, 204-205, 208, 217, 222-23, 227, 252, 259, 267, 273, 310-11; to Joseph P. Taylor, 151, 261; to John Jordan Crittenden, 204-205, 222-23, 270, 273, 274; to Maunsel White, 205; to E. G. W. Butler, 205; to William Davenport, 246; to Thomas W. Ringgold, 257; to Hancock Taylor, 258-59; to Mrs. Zachary Taylor, 259; to Richard (Dick) Taylor, 262, 263; to Nathaniel Young, 267; to Cincinnati *Signal,*

271-72; to Peter Sken Smith, 278; to J. S. Allison, 279-80, 287; to Richmond *Republican,* 281; to Jefferson Davis, 290-91, 293; to Edward Everett, 337
Taylor Democrats, withdraw support following Whig nomination, 285-86; alienated by patronage policy, 321
Tecumseh, 19-23, 32
Tehuantepec, isthmus of, 356
Tennessee, 7, 299; troops from, in Mexican War, 195, 196, 201
Tennessee River, 48
Texas, 54; and border raids, 136, 137, 138, 145-46; and annexation, 145-53; Taylor's troops occupy, 154-64; Taylor's troops on the Rio Grande, 164-67; troops from, in Mexican War, 169, 193, 196, 199, 200, 209-10, 229; early battles of Mexican War in, 170-78; and Compromise of 1850, 368, 369, 379, 384, 386-89
Third Artillery, at Buena Vista, 229
Third Infantry, 38, 39, 41-42, 44, 46, 52, 175; on Texas border, 149, 153; sail for Corpus Christi, 154; at Monterrey, 200
Thomas, Turbey F., at Fort Howard, 44
Thompson, A. R., killed in Battle of Okeechobee, 108
Thornton, James, 258
Tigre Island, and canal diplomacy, 359
Times (London), and election of 1848, 293, 295
Tippecanoe, battle of, 19, 20, 25
Tobacco, product of Kentucky, 11-12, 38
Tocqueville, Alexis de, French Foreign Minister, 350-52
Toombs, Robert, and election of 1848, 270, 279, 296; opposes Clayton for Secretary of State, 315, 320; alienated by Taylor, 319; defends Taylor administration on Galphin claim, 330; and Compromise of 1850, 369, 374-75, 381, 387, 388
Towson, Nathan, 52
Tribune (New York), 227, 282; and election of 1848, 289; on Clay's speech attacking Taylor, 384
Twenty-sixth Infantry, 33
Twiggs, David E., Taylor seeks exchange of assignments with, 75; in Seminole War, 118, 125; in Mexican War, 159, 160, 180, 195, 219
Tyler, John, and annexation of Texas, 147-48, 150

United States, steamer purchased by German agent, 339-40
United States Army, in the Revolutionary War, 1; increase of, 13; poorly officered, 15; pay of officers in, 15, 39, 46; uniforms of, 16; suffers from disease, 16-17; reduced to peace footing, 35-36; rations of, 43; recruiting service of, 44-45, 57-58; use of, for construction work denounced by Taylor, 49-50, 71; reduction and reorganization of, ordered by Congress, 50; reorganization of, denounced by Taylor, 51-52; problem of desertion from, 57; system of compensation for officers of, criticized by Taylor, 62-63; problem of brevet commissions in, 73-74, 159-60, 393; General Regulations for, 243; recommendations on, in Taylor's annual message, 392-94. *See also* Black Hawk War, Mexican War, Seminole War
Upshur, Abel P., 147
Utah, 384

Van Buren, Martin, and election of 1848, 287-88, 289, 290, 299, 300
Vega, Diaz de la, 177
Vera Cruz, Mex., 163, 229, 230, 242, 244; expedition to, 214-15, 218-19, 220, 224-25, 228
Veto power, Taylor's views on, 293-94
Vicksburg, Miss., 255, 260
Victoria, Mex., 213; Taylor plans to occupy, 219; march to, 220-21
Vincennes, Ind., 18, 20, 22, 24, 26, 32

Virginia, 60; Taylor family in, 1-5; opposes Wilmot Proviso, 368; Taylor visits, 403-404
Virginians, westward migration of, 3, 5-6, 7

Wabash River, 18, 20, 24, 25, 26
Wabash Valley, 19, 24
Walker, Robert J., 131, 363, 395
Walker, Samuel H., 171
Wall, Henry H., 255
War of 1812, 20-33
"War-Hawks," 20
Warsaw, Ill., 31
Washington, D. C., 35, 36, 39, 87, 400, 402, 403, 404; captured by British, 32; Taylor visits, 58-60; welcomes Taylor, 304-305
Washington, George, 3, 5, 10, 297
Washington, John M., at Buena Vista, 229, 232, 234
Washington Monument, 405
Washington Seminary, 400
Wayne, Anthony, 8
Webster, Daniel, 398, 405; as Secretary of State, 131, 147; defends Taylor in Senate, 209; and election of 1848, 271, 282, 288-89; calls on Taylor, 306; and Taylor's Cabinet, 317-18, 326; withholds support from Taylor, 320; defends Taylor's Hungarian policy, 367; and Compromise of 1850, 379, 380, 383, 390; and Taylor's last illness, 406; his eulogy on Taylor, 408
Weed, Thurlow, sends political advice to Taylor, 266, 271, 282; and the second Allison letter, 286-87; and Taylor's administration, 320, 324-25, 334-35; and Taylor's threat to hang secessionists, 382
Welles, Gideon, 297; describes White House dinner party, 398-99
West Feliciana Parish, Taylor purchases plantation in, 55
West Indies, 12
Wheeling, Va., 60, 304
Whig party, and the nomination of Taylor, 265, 269-83; splits, 283; and campaign of 1848, 286-90, 296-97; lack of unity in, weakens Taylor, 319-21, 326-27, 375, 404-405
Whistler, William, 159
White House, 59, 60; President and Mrs. Polk entertain at, 306; life in, during Taylor's presidency, 397-401; Taylor's funeral service in, 407
White, Maunsel, Taylor corresponds with, 205; his relations with Taylor, 263-64
Whiteside, Samuel, 28, 30, 78
Whitlock, Ambrose, 19
Wilcox, de Lafayette, in Seminole War, 118
Wilderness Trail, 5
Wilkinson County, Mississippi, 255
Wilkinson, James, commanding general, 15; at New Orleans, 16; court-martial trial of, 20
Willard's Hotel, 304-305
William and Mary College, 11
Williams, W. G., at Monterrey, 199
Wilmot Proviso, 375, 390; as issue in election of 1848, 289-90; alarms Virginia, 368; viewed by Taylor as source of sectional conflict, 372
Winnebago Indians, 40-41, 68, 69, 82, 90, 92, 93
Winthrop, Robert C., presents Taylor to Whig leaders, 306; candidate for Speaker, 375
Wisconsin, 32, 85, 95; early settlers in, 68; final phase of Black Hawk War in, 80-82
Wisconsin Heights, battle at, in Black Hawk War, 80, 81
Wisconsin River, 29, 82
Withlacoochee River, 119, 123
Wood, John, 410
Wood, Robert Crooke, marries Ann Mackall Taylor, 96; at wedding of Sarah Knox Taylor, 98; in Florida, 123; Taylor gives views on education to, 129-30; in Mexican War, 193; Taylor corresponds with, during Mexican War, 204-205, 217, 222-23; at New Orleans, 250; Taylor gives politi-

cal views to, 267, 273, 310-11; accompanies Taylor on Pennsylvania trip, 402-403
Wood, Robert Crooke, Jr., 96
Wool, John E., 132; and Chihuahua expedition, 217, 218; at Parras, 219; at Buena Vista, 232, 235, 237, 239; succeeds Taylor, 253
Worth, William J., 166, 248; at Corpus Christi, 159, 160; at Monterrey, 195, 199-200, 202-203, 206, 209; at Saltillo, 216, 219, 220

Yell, Archibald, Governor of Arkansas, 146; at Buena Vista, 229, 239
York, Penna., 402
Young, Nathaniel, 267
Yucatan, 346
Yulee, David L., denounces Taylor's Cuban policy, 347